RACISM IN CALIFORNIA

A Reader in the History of Oppression

ROGER DANIELS

State University of New York, Fredonia

SPENCER C. OLIN, Jr.

University of California, Irvine

The Macmillan Company · New York

PREFACE

UNTIL not so long ago, historians were mainly interested in describing the actions of dominant elites and concerned themselves largely with political and military leaders. The vogue of this so-called "drum and trumpet" history is happily now past; since the 1930s social and economic history has tended to prevail. But even with the increasingly broader scope of our analysis of the past, significant areas have been virtually ignored: one of the most important of these is the systematic oppression that has been the lot of racial minorities.

By collecting some of the more perceptive accounts of how racism has operated in one state, California, we hope to help correct this deficiency. While it is now possible to give a generalized picture of the oppressions suffered by racial groups in the past, not nearly enough is known about this vital subject. We hope that some of those who read this book as students will be stimulated to do research of their own about what happened in their particular localities.

It is sometimes argued that California and Californians are more prejudiced than most of the rest of the nation. Perhaps. What is more certain is that in California there have always been greater numbers and varieties of people against whom to discriminate, or against whom to be prejudiced. Had Swedes been red, yellow, brown, or black, Minnesota might also have been a racial battleground.

We are informed by social psychologists that racial discrimination is learned behavior. Californians certainly learned that lesson thoroughly, and not only white Californians. Group hostility among the dispossessed, although not examined in this book, has existed side by side with the more common form of prejudice. Furthermore, because of the variety of pigments encountered in California, all white men were "promoted"; for example, Roman Catholics and Jews encountered significantly less prejudice than they did in the supposedly more enlightened East.

Although racism can be affected by circumstances of geography, propinquity, and population and can be practiced by any race (the treatment of East Asians in contemporary black Africa is a case in point), most of the racism in California stems from and is related to the whole American racist tradition that begins almost, but not quite, with our history. The

v

Elizabethans who colonized America brought with them no settled notions of white supremacy. John Rolfe was quite willing to marry Pocahontas—even though she had cavorted naked before almost all the English—and to take her back home under the deluded notion that he was marrying into nobility and thus improving himself. But most white colonists in North America soon learned to despise tawny Indian women—except for intercourse and work—as they learned to despise, shortly after 1619, the blacks whom they originally treated as indentured servants but quickly enslaved. Having enslaved the blacks, the whites proceeded to construct a new cosmography of racial separateness, superiority, and inferiority that eventually included yellow and brown men and then branched off into whole solar systems of ethnic acceptability.

The California variants of this racism are easy to sketch. It was a tradition based, first of all, on the conquest of a "civilized" as opposed to an "uncivilized" people, a tradition that nearly exterminated the real native sons, the Indians, and made the *Californios* (native Californians born of Spanish-speaking parents) second-class citizens in a land they had considered their own. Woven into the fabric of the California tradition was mob violence, disguised as a passion for law and order, plus the typical inferiority-superiority complex of the developing but still tributary area: blatant braggadocio coupled with constant whining about being misunderstood and mistreated by the powers back East.

The truly special feature of California racism was anti-Orientalism, although it was clearly related to the mainstream. California, and to a lesser degree the rest of the Far West, both demanded and deplored Oriental labor in the decades of primary growth. The Chinese did much of the basic construction of the early western railroads; in the heavily masculine western cities they did laundry, cooking, and other "women's work." No one will ever know how many Chinese were killed in the West from the 1850s to the 1890s—the biggest massacres were in Los Angeles and Rock Springs, Wyoming. By the middle 1870s anti-Orientalism was as firmly engraved on California politics as was white supremacy on the politics of the South. Almost automatically animosity transferred itself from group to group. Koreans, East Indians, and Filipinos all felt California's special brand of discrimination, but the real enemy for most Californians from about 1905 until shortly after World War II was of course the Japanese—man, woman, or child, alien or citizen.

To the Californian—and here we are speaking of the majority; there was always an articulate minority that felt otherwise—the Japanese was a special devil, inferior but also superior, distinctly an *untermensch* but with frightening *übermenschlich* characteristics. Sly, treacherous, hardworking, the Japanese could thrive where a white man would starve. And breed! One fanatic Japanophobe—V. S. McClatchy, who was the publisher of the Sacramento *Bee* and a director of the Associated Press—

predicted that, if unchecked, Japanese population would climb to 500,000 in the 1930s, 900,000 in the 1940s, 2,000,000 in 1963, 10,000,000 in 2003, and, for a real population explosion, 100,000,000 in 2063!

Added to these fears about immigrants, there was that phenomenon known as the "yellow peril"—the fear of invasion by armed Oriental hordes. Starting out with China as the possible invader, the scare literature quickly switched to Japan as the villain after her 1905 victory over Czarist Russia. (We should note in passing that an administration, headed by a Californian, that commits much of its treasure to building an ABM system against a *Chinese* nuclear threat is at least adhering to an old tradition.) This special "yellow peril" literature, which permeated all media, along with the racist tradition, both general and special, helps explain if not excuse our "worst wartime mistake": uprooting 110,000 innocent West Coast Japanese Americans and dumping them into ten God-forsaken interior concentration camps during World War II.

The gap left in the California labor force was partially filled by Mexicans coming north from Mexico and southern Blacks coming up from semislavery. The former had begun to come to California in large numbers after 1910, pushed by chaotic conditions in their homeland, like so many other kinds of immigrants before them, and pulled by the apparent economic opportunity in California and other parts of the United States. Outside of New Mexico, which is a special case, very few of the contemporary Mexican Americans are descended from those who were conquered by the United States of James K. Polk. The numerous Spanish-speaking people of California and the Southwest, by whatever names one calls them—Mexican American or Chicano, Spanish American or Hispano—were for decades the sleeping giant of western ethnic groups, far more quiescent than either their number or their wretched condition would in themselves indicate. They are, of course, quiet no more.

Everywhere else in the United States the black man has been the "man farthest down." This was not true, until very recently, in the Far West in general and in California in particular. As cowboy, soldier, laborer, and entrepreneur, the black man historically enjoyed higher status in the West than anywhere else in America. This was a result of both his relatively small number and the presence of groups even farther down—the Indian, the Oriental, and sometimes the Mexican American. Only when the Negro came West in large numbers during and after World War II did black men begin to be pushed toward the bottom rung in society that had traditionally been theirs. And that is perhaps why the revolt that became the symbol for a whole decade—the Watts riots—occurred in Los Angeles rather than in Chicago, New York, or Detroit where, it can be argued rationally, objective conditions were worse.

Despite all its problems, with all its sorry history of bigotry and murder and mass degradation, the West has been for most of its oppressed people a symbol of hope, a promise of a better life for their children, even for those of the dispossessed it treated the worst. It is both ironic and proper that the first striking symbolic act of what may prove to be a renaissance of the American Indian—the occupation of Alcatraz—should have occurred just a few score miles from the place where Ishi, the last of his kind, stumbled into the protective yet deadly arms of white civilization.

Although, through our selections, we tell a ghastly tale of man's inhumanity to man, we do not do so in total despair. Perhaps a better knowledge of the darker side of our history will foster among the white majority some understanding of the dire possibilities of the future, some understanding of why so many members of minority groups distrust and even hate white people. For the evidence of enduring oppression—and the material presented here is only the tip of the iceberg—should be proof enough of the Kerner Commission's major conclusion: the roots of America's racial malaise are to be found not in the habits of the oppressed but in the hearts and minds of white, middle-class Americans—those who are called today the silent majority.

R. D.
S. C. O.

CONTENTS

PART I
The First Victims: California's Indians

PART II
California's Special Race Problem: The Asians

PART III
Mexican Americans: From "Greasers" to *Chicanos*

Contents

PART I
The First Victims:
California's Indians

> Seven years ago, Humboldt county and Bay . . .
> were innocent of any knowledge of the Anglo-
> Saxon race. The Indian roamed over its wilds . . .
> until the bold and enterprising hand of the white
> man came. Now the scene is changed . . . Another
> cycle of seven years, and the last vestiges of [the
> Indian] race will be well nigh obliterated, in this
> vicinity, crushed out, like other imbecilities, under
> the iron heel of progress and the steady and re-
> sistless march of civilization, and places they once
> occupied will resound with the busy hum of in-
> dustrious whites, and the loom, the plough, and
> the anvil, will supercede the Indian arrow and
> hunting knife.
>
> The Humboldt *Times* (May 2, 1857)

THE plight of the California Indian is perhaps nowhere better expressed than in the photograph of an emaciated, tattered Ishi, taken
after he had stumbled into the town of Oroville in northern California
on August 29, 1911. Although his eyes reflected both fear and hatred
of the white men who had exterminated his tribe, Ishi was compelled
by exhaustion and starvation to seek refuge among white strangers.
Theodora Kroeber's remarkable biography, *Ishi in Two Worlds* (see
Selection 4), provides an excellent account of the demise of Ishi's
tribe, the Yahi, one significant example of the process by which
Indian civilization in California was destroyed by the Anglo-American settlers.

The Anglo-American system of Indian exploitation is best understood when compared with the Spanish-American colonial system
that preceded it. As Sherburne Cook points out (in Selections 1, 2),
the basic difference between the two systems is found in the method
of colonization. The Spanish mission system required that Indians
be removed from their original habitats and then be converted from
"heathen barbarians" to "good Christians." Spanish policy encouraged

close association and racial mixture between Spaniards and Indians. Completely absent from the Anglo-American program, on the other hand, was any religious focus or encouragement of integration. Instead, Anglo-American settlers rejected intermarriage and miscegenation in favor of total exclusion: Indians were to be exterminated, segregated in reservations, or driven into remote areas where they would pose no threat to the white settlements.

Public awareness of the inhumane and perfidious treatment of California Indians was greatly heightened in the early 1880's by the publication of Helen Hunt Jackson's *A Century of Dishonor*. The furor caused by the first edition of that work in 1881 prompted President Chester Alan Arthur to appoint Mrs. Jackson a Commissioner of Indian Affairs. It was in that capacity that she prepared the scathing report on the condition of California's Mission Indians that was appended to the second edition of her famous work, a portion of which appears in this section (see Selection 3). Whereas *A Century of Dishonor*, and her subsequent novel, *Ramona*, aroused public sentiment on behalf of the California Indian, abuses continued.

From the time of the Dawes Act (1887) until the present day, a number of "new deals" have been made for Indians, both in California and the nation, including President Richard Nixon's act of July, 1970. But conditions still are often as bad (or worse) as when Mrs. Jackson first shocked the national conscience. California Indians today remain the state's most destitute minority, having an average life span of only forty-two years. They experience fully all the classic ill-effects of poverty. Despite a few limited gains—such as a ruling in 1944 by a Federal Court of Claims that provided small financial compensation for land taken from the Indians (see Selection 5)—the rights and possessions of this California minority have been under constant seige for generations.

In the late 1960s a new assertiveness and militancy began to characterize the Indians' reactions to a white-dominated world, which is perhaps best illustrated in California by the invasion and occupancy of Alcatraz Island in late 1969—abandoned federal land to which the Indians had a symbolic, if not a legal, right. (See Selections 6 and 7.) With a new slogan—"Red Power"—Indians have begun to demand complete control of their own affairs, without white interference. If the paramount goals of the "Indian Revolution" of the 1970s are to be achieved, there must be a dramatic reversal of the policy of greed and double-cross that for so long has dominated relations between white government and exploited tribes.

I

Conflict Between the California Indian and White Civilization

SHERBURNE F. COOK

> *Sherburne F. Cook is professor emeritus of physiology at the University of California, Berkeley, and author of* Conflict Between the Indian and White Civilization. *In the following two selections he explains why California Indians were much less successful against Anglos than against Spaniards, and describes how those Indians were gradually converted from a race of peaceful seed-gatherers to aggressive cavalrymen. The peak of their resistance was achieved in 1845, after which increasing penetration by Anglo-Americans overwhelmed the natives. In the final analysis, according to Cook, the California Indian was defeated by superior numbers, not superior intelligence.*

The American Invasion, 1848–1870

WHEN the California Indian was confronted with the problem of contact and competition with the white race, his success was much less marked with the Anglo-American than with the Ibero-American branch. To be sure, his success against the latter had been far from noteworthy; both in the missions and in the native habitat the aboriginal population had declined, and the Indian had been forced to give ground politically and racially before the advance of Spanish colonization. However, the nonmission Indian had demonstrated a certain power of resilience and, in the realm of physical activity, had been able to evolve a new behavior pattern which, if he had been left alone, might have permitted him to cope on fairly even terms with the invading race. The valley and northern tribes were evincing a fair capacity for adaptation, in the strictly material sense, to the new environment imposed by the entrance of a new biological group. Furthermore, the native culture had by no means utterly collapsed. To a certain extent in the missions and predominantly in the aboriginal habitat the Indian had retained his primitive social and religious character and, indeed, had appropriated a few features of the

SOURCE: R. F. Heizer and M. A. Whipple, eds., *The California Indians* (Berkeley and Los Angeles: University of California Press, 1951), pp. 465–474. Originally published by the University of California Press; reprinted by permission of the author and The Regents of the University of California.

white civilization, modifying them and incorporating them into his own system.

When the Indian was forced to withstand the shock and impact of the Anglo-Saxon invasion, his failure in all these respects was virtually complete. In the physical and demographic spheres his competitive inferiority was such as to come very close to bringing about his literal extermination. His social structure was not only utterly disorganized, but almost completely wiped out. Culturally, he has been forced to make a slow, painful adjustment, ending with the adoption of the alien system, and he has now lost all but fragments of the aboriginal pattern. The present study undertakes to describe some of the processes involved in this racial failure and some of the factors determining its extent.

Without embarking upon any attempt to analyze the differences between the Anglo-American and Ibero-American personality, social order, or culture, certain points of divergence between the two groups may be mentioned briefly in so far as they affected Indian relations in California. Perhaps these points may be allocated to two prime categories: differences in mode of colonization and differences in economic and social attitude toward the aborigine.

The divergent Indian reaction to Spanish clerical authority, as demonstrated by the mission neophytes, and to Spanish civil authority, as shown by the unconverted interior tribes, is clear evidence that the two modes of interracial contact were fundamentally different. The opinion may be advanced that the determining factor was aggregation versus dissemination. The fatal effects of the altruistic mission lay, first, in the removal of the native from his original habitat and, second, in his subjection to continuous close association with the foreign environment and race. The relative preservation of the gentile element was due to the failure of the Spanish actually to occupy the territory of the Indian. This same distinction in the type of interracial contact appears when the Spanish system as a whole is contrasted with the American.

The great interior of the State was penetrated many times by the Spaniards. Repeatedly they entered the lands of the Indians, but they did not settle and stay on these lands. Between the frequent but still temporary foreign incursions the natives were able to maintain their life and social order more or less unaltered. At least they were not called upon to make any continuous and permanent adjustment to a change in their own environment. When the Americans arrived, they took over the Indian habitat and made it their own. The aborigines were forced, therefore, to adapt themselves, on their own ground, to a new environment. The final effect was precisely the same as if they had been bodily removed and set down in a strange region. They were subjected not to invasion but to inundation.

Another factor of significance here is that of numbers. Other things being equal, the intensity of conflict and the weight thrown against the primitive group will roughly follow the numerical strength of the new or invading species. This general principle has been demonstrated repeatedly with the lower organisms in their parasite-host or predator-prey relationships, and it holds similarly for human beings. The Spanish type of colonization was such that the invading and ruling caste or race was always small in numbers. In California, for example, the whole coastal strip was taken and held by little more than one hundred persons. By 1845 the entire population of the *gente de razon* did not exceed 4,000. Against this may be set the native population of over 100,000. The Americans, on the other hand, entered the region in great numbers. Undoubtedly they would have continued to do so, for by 1848 they were already coming in by the hundreds. Owing to the fortuitous discovery of gold in that year, however, they poured in by thousands to flood the country. Furthermore, because of the nature of mining, they swarmed in hordes into those hill and mountain retreats which the Spaniards had never even penetrated. The Indians, therefore, were overwhelmed by tremendous numbers of aliens at all points and at much the same time. The conversion of their past primitive range and habitat into a group of civilized communities was thus accomplished in an incredibly short period.

Both branches of the white race arrived on the Pacific Coast with a heritage of long experience with the Indian; both had developed a well-formulated mental attitude and a definite policy with respect to the natives. But these attitudes and policies were conditioned by the widely differing pioneering and colonial experience of the two branches in the preceding centuries. Both Anglo-Saxons and Spanish had pursued an avowed course of exploitation of New World resources. The Spanish, however, had systematically availed themselves of human resources, whereas the English had tapped only material wealth. Whatever the causes of the divergence, by the nineteenth century the Ibero-Americans consistently followed the procedure of utilizing the natives and incorporating them in their social and economic structure, whereas the Anglo-Americans rigidly excluded them from their own social order. It followed, therefore, that in opening up California the Spanish system undertook as far as possible to employ the Indians, even by force, in useful pursuits. This in turn meant that the aboriginal race was an economic asset and as such was to be conserved. Destruction of individual life occurred only when and if the Indian actively resisted the process of amalgamation or definitely failed to conform to the conqueror's scheme of existence. Wholesale slaughter or annihilation was definitely undesirable.

The Anglo-American system, on the other hand, had no place for the Indian. If the latter could of his own initiative find subsistence within its framework, there was a priori nothing to prevent such adjustment. But if there was any conflict whatsoever with the system, the native was to be eliminated ruthlessly, either by outright extermination or the slower method of segregation in ghetto-like reservations. Accompanying this economic difference was another divergence of great social significance. The Spanish colonial system always envisaged the retention of the native as the basis of the population and simultaneously encouraged racial mixture. The result was naturally widespread hybridization, especially among the lower classes. Thorough and complete mestization, as in some parts of Spanish America, would have resulted in the disappearance of the California Indian as a pure line strain but would not have destroyed his race or eliminated it as a factor in the body politic. Nor would it necessarily have involved long and bloody physical conflict during the period of racial reorganization. The American civilization, on the contrary, viewed miscegenation with the greatest antipathy and relegated the mestizo, or half-breed, to the same status as his Indian parent. Consequently, no blood bond could ever become established which would mitigate the indifference and contempt with which the Indians were regarded.

These, and other differences, were reinforced by a powerful tradition relating to the Indian. Among the Ibero-Americans, the Indian was regarded, if not with definite attachment, at least with tolerance and sympathy, as perhaps not yet an equal but as a human being entitled to the rights and privileges of his class. His life was almost as sacred as that of a white man; his soul was entitled to salvation. He was permitted to testify in court. Theoretically, his property was inviolate. At best, he could participate in civic and political activity; at worst, he was deemed a child before the law. This fundamentally friendly attitude was seldom manifested by the Anglo-Americans. The latter, coming fresh from two centuries of bitter border warfare and intolerant aggression, brought with them an implacable hatred of the red race, which made no discrimination between tribes or individuals. All Indians were vermin, to be treated as such. It is therefore not surprising that physical violence was the rule rather than the exception. The native's life was worthless, for no American could even be brought to trial for killing an Indian. What little property the Indian possessed could be taken or destroyed at the slightest provocation. He had no civil or legal rights whatever. Finally, since the quickest and easiest way to get rid of his troublesome presence was to kill him off, this procedure was adopted as standard for some years. Thus was carried on the policy which had wiped out *en masse* tribe after tribe across the continent.

In comparing the objective effects wrought by the Ibero-American and Anglo-Saxon civilizations on the native population, it must not be supposed that the differences just mentioned were absolute, for human nature is much the same everywhere, despite policies and tradition. The

Spanish at times certainly resorted to barbaric physical violence, and the Americans frequently treated their Indians with humanity and justice. Nevertheless, the broad tendencies were apparent and were reflected in the details of the two types of racial contact.

The Indian Response

We have dwelt at some length upon the shock to the native welfare which followed contact with Ibero-American civilization. . . . From this discussion one might gain the impression that the physical collapse of the interior tribes was complete, that the wild Indian was utterly unable to compete with the invading race and was doomed to early extinction. Such an impression would not be wholly justified.

In the first place, the actual numerical decline in population, although severe, was not as great as that suffered by the same or similar Indians either in the missions or under American domination. In a previous paper (*Population Trends*, 1940) I have shown that the total number of gentile baptisms in the missions was nearly 53,600. The neophytes living in the establishments at the close of the era were either these same gentiles or their descendants, and numbered, 14,900. The difference, 38,700, denotes, therefore, the decline suffered by this group or segment of California aborigines. Using relative values, we may calculate the decline, or ratio of reduction to original population, as 72 per cent. During the American period the decline was even greater. It may be calculated . . . that the estimated population of all California Indians north of the Tehachapi was 72,050 in 1848 and 12,500 in 1880. Hence the decline was about 82 per cent. For the six tribes affected by Spanish colonization from 1800 to 1848, the corresponding figures are 58,900 and 35,950, or a decline of only 31 per cent. Thus from the standpoint of population alone these tribes made a showing which, although in the absolute rather poor, was relatively better against the Spanish civil colonial system than against the mission system or the American settlement.

Not only in population changes do group reactions and group adaptation to new environmental factors become evident. Usually there may be observed physical activities carried on in unison by a sufficient number of individuals to warrant their being regarded as group responses. The direction of such an activity may be negative or positive, that is, tending to remove the affected group from the environment or, conversely, to remove certain components of the environment from the group. It has been pointed out with reference to the mission Indians that this type of response usually took the negative form. The Indians generally attempted to escape, thus generating the widespread phenomenon of fugitivism. Seldom was the activity positively directed, toward active physical resistance or insurrection. The wild Indians evinced a different type of behavior. With them the positive reaction predominated over the negative. With the exception of temporary flight to escape the ravages of an invading party, the interior natives held their ground and resisted the onslaught. Moreover, not only did they stand their ground over a large territory, but they actually, and with some success, took the offensive. Together with this active response they underwent considerable physical and military adaptation.

The evolution of the response of resistance or adaptation is quite clear cut. On their first appearances among new tribes and subtribes, the exploring expeditions found the natives peaceful and inclined to be friendly. The customary hospitality was shown, presents were exchanged, and the gospel was heard from the priests with sympathy. As party followed party, however, and the natives saw their people drawn off to the missions or heard more and more tales of mission life, their first favorable attitude changed to one of hostility and fear. At this stage, the explorers and convert hunters began to find the villages empty, or were greeted with showers of arrows as they approached. Retaliation and "chastisement" were then in order. Gentiles were carried off by force rather than persuasion, and atrocities began to occur. By the decade 1820–1830, the people of the interior valleys and hills had definitely embarked upon a policy of physical resistance, not through any political or cultural unification, but through a common response to a uniform style of treatment.

The general effect of these events was to bring about a shift in the entire social horizon of the natives, particularly that of the Yokuts, Miwok, and Wappo. The disruptive forces . . . had also the effect of generating an entirely new kind of civilization. To put it in essence: a peaceful, sedentary, highly localized group underwent conversion into a semiwarlike, seminomadic group. Obviously this process was by no means complete by 1848, nor did it affect all component parts of the native masses equally. But its beginnings had become very apparent.

We notice the inception of the change in a few rather sensational events, events which are indicative of the more fundamental, although much less obvious, changes going on underneath. In 1797 occurred the so-called "Raymundo affair." This individual, "Raymundo el Californio," took some forty neophytes on a fugitive hunt in Contra Costa County. They were set upon by gentiles and virtually destroyed, much to the horror and alarm of the local authorities. In 1807 over one hundred neophytes escaped from the missions to the rancherias of Carquinez Strait, where they were cut to pieces by gentiles, only thirty getting back to the mission. In 1813 Soto with twelve soldiers and one hundred auxiliaries was fought to a standstill in the marshes of the Delta by the consolidated rancherias of the region. At about this period, the Indians began to find leaders. Pomponio and Joscolo did excellently, and Estanislao, the Miwok, was a real genius. Expedition after expedition was broken up by this brave people, until Vallejo invaded their territory in 1829 with cavalry, artillery, and all the panoply of war. Even the final campaign, which took a heavy toll of life and did the Miwok great damage, utterly failed to subjugate them.

Meanwhile the Indians were learning new methods of defense. Their acquisition of firearms was slow. Indeed, it is doubtful whether they had secured any appreciable stock of firearms prior to 1848. Their failure in this respect is not to be ascribed to lack of knowledge or aggressiveness, but rather to the fact that there were no guns to be had. The Spanish themselves were very poorly outfitted. There were no large stocks which could be stolen, and powder was such a rarity that at one time the governor had to commandeer all private supplies in order to fit out an expedition. On the other hand, the natives very quickly learned the tactics of defense. Their original method was to stand up in masses and try to overwhelm the enemy with the fire power of swarms of arrows. But experience soon taught them that this weapon was relatively useless against Spanish leather armor, and the range was too short to enable them to hold up against gunfire. They soon resorted to hit-and-run tactics—a heavy assault from ambush followed by a retreat into the impenetrable tule swamps or the chapparal, or else systematic sniping from cover. The Miwok under Estanislao developed a defense almost European in character. Against Sánchez and also Vallejo in 1829, Estanislao fortified a hill with brush breastworks and, if the word "fossas" can be so interpreted, an actual system of trenches. Against these defenses Sánchez failed completely, and Vallejo, even with a cannon, was not able to penetrate them until he resorted to a flank attack and covered his front by setting the chapparal on fire.

Considering that all available accounts of this early fighting come from Spanish-Mexican officialdom and from prejudiced survivors, it is clear that throughout the early decades of the nineteenth century the valley tribes put up a pretty good fight. Despite repeated small-scale incursions and full-dress campaigns by the military, in which they were often beaten, they held the Spanish settlement to the coast. This, after all, is the critical point, for the successful defense of an area demands that any permanent lodgement be prevented, rather than that every stabbing invasion be annihilated. Such relative success indicates that the Yokuts and Miwok were able, with sufficient rapidity, to make a drastic reorientation of their ideas of physical conflict.

But this reorientation did not stop with an improved defensive. By the time of secularization, the natives had begun to pass actually to the offensive. One reads in every general history of the times a great deal about the activity of the valley Indians, and to a lesser extent of those north of the Bay, in raiding and stealing domestic livestock, in particular cattle and horses. This phenomenon is one of great biological and cultural significance. It is mentioned here, however, only as it bears on offensive warfare.

Very early in mission history, outlying heathen began to slip in and run off stock. As the years went on, they learned two things, perhaps subconsciously. They learned that with the correct technique such raids were very easy to carry out, and that they were highly irritating to the white men. Furthermore, the acquisition of horses enabled the Indians to improve their methods by providing fast transportation. As the great herds of cattle and horses spread out from the coastal ranches, the opportunities increased, until by 1835 stock raiding was universal.

The acquisition of horses and the practice derived from years of experience wrought a further extension of their warfare, for it is but a short step from the quick dash to cut away stock to the serious armed cavalry assault on a fixed point, such as a ranch house or settlement. These developments follow rather naturally. The essential point in this discussion is that the valley people possessed sufficient mental agility and racial adaptive power to utilize their opportunity. Thus, from a race of slow, unwarlike, sedentary seed gatherers, these tribes were evolving rapidly into a group of fast, shifty, quite clever cavalrymen. This was a physical response, an adaptation to new conditions of the first order of magnitude.

As a result of this process, by 1845 the valley Indians had made inland expeditions and invasions very costly and dangerous, but, more important, they had also actually begun to drive in the Spanish frontier. The change of status becomes apparent from the official records after the Estanislao campaigns of 1829. During 1830 and 1831 there was a period of quiescence, but in 1833 complaints began to arise that the valley Indians were committing serious depredations. They seem in this to have been aided and perhaps organized by outside adventurers—American trappers and, particularly, New Mexicans who penetrated by way of the Colorado River. The following years saw an intensification of the same process. In 1834 M. G. Vallejo proposed an expedition to subjugate the Indians raiding San José and "lay a formal siege to the place where the natives are fortified." In 1836 conditions in San José had become so bad that the citizens had to petition the governor for help. In 1838 several rancheros were killed in raids in the Monterey district, and in 1839 the Indians attacked the grain storehouse at Santa Clara. In 1841, Mission San Juan was attacked, and hardly a ranch was spared from Santa Barbara to the Strait of Carquinez. The most spectacular raid occurred in 1840, when a band of heathen penetrated as far west as San Luis Obispo and ran off a thousand head of stock.

Meanwhile the government adhered to the old policy of counterattack-ng by expeditions. Dozens of these were sent out, but with very poor success. It is true that many Indians were killed and many villages destroyed, but the raiding continued. Finally a change of policy was contemplated, although not carried out. In 1840, the governor by decree established a force of twenty men to remain permanently on the border to act as military police and prevent the Indians from entering the passes of the coast range. Micheltorena, in 1843, proposed to build a stockade in Pacheco Pass, but the plan fell through. This shift in basic procedure from offensive to defensive is the best evidence we have that the Indian assault was really effective.

What would have happened if external conditions had not changed we can only conjecture. The Indian offensive reached its peak about 1845, or perhaps earlier, and then rapidly diminished. The reason for the diminution does not lie in any efforts put forth by the California government or its people (with the exception of the energetic action of Vallejo in the north). Indeed, the Spanish regime was showing no ability whatever to cope with the situation. Rather, the reason lies in the penetration of Americans and other foreigners into the valley itself on a basis of settlement, not mere expeditionary raiding. These men were able to attack the Indians from the rear, so to speak, and were present in numbers adequate to reduce the Indians' effectiveness. We see, therefore, that the adaption of the natives to the Spanish type of colonization was not only sharp and clear in the qualitative sense, but was also of considerable magnitude. In fact, had the status of, say, 1840 remained unaltered, it is entirely possible that the response of the wild natives would have enabled them to establish a permanent physical equilibrium with Ibero-American civilization.

To sum up the foregoing discussion, it appears that the first effect of white impact on the native California Indian was to reduce his numbers through warfare, disease, and forced removal. The native racial response, however, was subsequently sufficiently powerful to minimize these influences and permit the evolution of a type of behavior calculated to insure his ultimate survival.

When we survey the racial conflict between the Ibero-American and the Indian, we cannot but be impressed by the far better showing made by the Indian in the wild than by the Indian in the mission. From the demographic standpoint there is no doubt that the Indian in his native environment withstood the shock of the new invasion better than he did when transported to the surroundings characteristic of mission life. He did so in spite of the fact that his numbers in the missions were not depleted by homicide and warfare, and that indeed he was protected quite effectively from physical competition. But perhaps this statement gives the wrong impression. Perhaps he survived better in the field because he was not protected, because he was forced to utilize his best adaptive power. Subjection to severe hardship and social disruption may well have been more potent agents in bringing out his full capacity than the easy existence and stable social order of the missions.

Other factors, however, may have been preponderant. It has been set forth at some length in a previous essay (*The Indian versus the Spanish Mission*, Ibero-Americana, No. 21 [1943]) how the racial fiber of the native decayed morally and culturally in the missions, how confinement, labor, punishment, inadequate diet, homesickness, sex anomalies, and other social or cultural forces, sapped his collective strength and his will to resistance and survival. Any detailed consideration of such matters cannot be undertaken here, but the suggestion may be advanced, at least tentatively, that the cultural aspects of mission existence largely account for the difference in behavior between the two similar groups of Indians. If this line of reasoning be granted, then the extremely important bearing of the cultural on the strictly biological becomes apparent. Indeed, one may go so far as to maintain that it is impossible to secure an adequate picture of the mechanism whereby primitive human races react physically and demographically without taking account of the social and psychological factors concerned. For analytical purposes, some distinction must be made; for synthetic purposes no separation is possible.

2

The Destruction of the California Indian

SHERBURNE F. COOK

ON January 7, 1858, the San Francisco *Bulletin* quoted the Red Bluffs *Beacon* concerning the recent demise of one Bill Farr: ". . . Bill was a terror to the Indians, having killed a great many in his time; some of whom, as he said himself, he shot to see them fall."

On August 28, 1855, Captain H. M. Judah, at Fort Jones, reported to his commanding general: "Since the recent disturbances on the Klamath, it appears to be the unanimous decision of the miners in this section of the state that no male Indian will hereafter be permitted to reside among them or frequent their vicinity under the penalty of being shot down. . . ."

D. N. Cooley, agent at the Tule River Farm, wrote in his annual report, August 17, 1866: "A cruel, cowardly vagabond, given to thieving, gambling, drunkenness, and all that is vicious, without one redeeming trait, is a true picture of the California Digger. . . ."

There must be some explanation for these statements, which may be regarded as commonplace for their time. As a starting point it is worthwhile to consider the philosophy of the people who migrated from the United States to California after the acquisition of the territory and the discovery of gold. Prior to their advent, Upper California had been under the control of Ibero-Americans who brought the tradition of the missions and a racial tolerance sufficiently broad to encompass free intermarriage. It is true that they based their material culture upon the ruthless economic exploitation of the native, but they never even remotely contemplated his physical destruction.

The Anglo-Americans, in contrast to those of Spanish and Mexican derivation, had been engaged for 200 years in a murderous struggle with the indigenous peoples of North America, first for survival, then for occupation and conquest. Armed hostility rapidly crystallized a fundamental cultural disparity so as to produce an implacable hatred of the red race. This hatred was inflamed by the prolonged and competent resistance offered by the warlike tribes who inhabited the Mississippi

SOURCE: Sherburne F. Cook, "The Destruction of the California Indian," *California Monthly*, LXXIX (December 1968), 15-19. Reprinted by permission of the author and *California Monthly*.

basin. To those who crossed the plains in covered wagons, every Indian was a deadly enemy. When these pioneers reached the Pacific, they did not recognize the generally peaceable nature of the aboriginal Californians, but carried over against them the fury generated by decades of bitter warfare on the frontier. This hostility was quite misdirected.

We need only consider that scarcely 100 men in the Portola-Serra expedition of 1789 had occupied and consolidated an area held by 50 to 100,000 natives, and had brought the latter into a religious system operated by only a few score priests and soldiers. Indeed, by 1845 there were still less than 10,000 white people in the entire state. Hence we may imagine the impact of the 100,000 gold seekers and adventurers who swarmed through the Golden Gate within the interval of a year or two. This horde was reinforced by other immigrants, and so by the early fifties close to a quarter of a million persons, mostly Americans, had settled in California.

Some idea of what happened to the natives may be obtained merely by following their number through the mid-nineteenth century. A reasonable estimate of the Indian population within the state in 1769 would be a quarter of a million. During the Spanish and Mexican period up to 1845 there was steady attrition among the inhabitants of the central coast, the San Joaquin Valley, and southern California. Most of the casualties were referable to disturbance of native society, minor warfare in the interior, and a high mortality caused by disease both among the wild tribes of the Central Valley, and within the mission establishments. Just prior to the Gold Rush there probably were fully 175,000 Indians left, 40 to 50,000 of whom lived in the coastal regions south from San Francisco Bay to the Mexican border. Of the remainder, some lived in the San Joaquin basin, but most still existed relatively undisturbed in the northern Coast Ranges, across the mountains to the Shasta area, and down the Sierra foothills all the way to the Tehachapi. In 1849 it was precisely these regions which were overrun by gold seekers. Population estimates for the next few years are unsatisfactory, but the best evidence indicates that there were 75 to 100,000 Indians still to be found in 1850–51. By 1880 conditions had sufficiently stabilized to permit a fairly good count, and at that time there can have been no more than 20,000.

The period since 1880 has seen a trend toward an increase, and there may now be 30 or 40,000 persons who possess Indian blood. However, the augmentation has occurred primarily through mixture with other races, so there are extremely few individuals alive who are of pure California Indian stock.

Apart from a probable fall in birth rate, concerning which we have very little factual knowledge, the immediate causes of decline in numbers were disease, homicide, and starvation.

As far back as the 1830s, withering epidemics of smallpox and malaria swept through the Central Valley and the Coast Ranges, killing several thousand. Moreover, even at the missions, where living conditions otherwise were quite good, the extremely high mortality rate can be attributed in large part to such infections as measles, typhoid, and tuberculosis, and to venereal disease. Among the non-missionized tribes these maladies quickly became endemic, particularly after the massive immigration of 1849 distributed all the pathogens known to man amid a scene of universal bad sanitation, water pollution, and complete lack of social control.

Actual physical conflict between the races accounted directly for much mortality. It must be understood that an Indian's life counted as nothing. No non-Indian, of whatever ethnic origin, could be held responsible for the death of a native, nor could any legal action be taken against him. Specifically, we ought to distinguish between two types of killing, military and social homicide.

Military activity began in conjunction with the occupation of California during the Mexican War of 1845–48. It followed entirely conventional lines. Small bodies of troops established "forts" throughout the territory, the primary purpose of which was to hold in check and pacify the Indians, who, according to all previous experience, would soon initiate strong physical resistance. As one might expect, the least sign of armed hostility was countered by a crushing military expedition, in the course of which it was standard practice to burn the native villages and destroy all stored food. Occasionally these operations went so far as to offend the conscience of even the contemporary society. Here might be mentioned the infamous Clear Lake Massacre of 1850 and the Humboldt Bay Massacre of 1860, on both of which occasions armed white men, military and civilian alike, slaughtered dozens of helpless women and children.

Social homicide was the result of the ordinary, day-to-day quarrelling, fighting, and shooting, with or without benefit of liquor, which characterized the culture of the 1850s in California. That many Indians should be the victims is easily appreciated, particularly since no retribution whatever could be visited upon the guilty parties. I once made a count of the deaths incurred by Indians from 1852 to 1865 which were reported in four prominent newspapers, two in San Francisco, one each in Sacramento and Marysville. My total was 289, of which 73 were executions or lynchings during or after the commission of a crime or misdemeanor. The number is not very great, but it is indicative of the brutal atmosphere in which the native population carried on its existence. In this context it might be appropriate to quote an item from the *Alta California* (San Francisco) for August 8, 1854: "Two Indians were found murdered in our streets the past week, by persons unknown, and dumped into the common receptacle made and provided for such cases."

The third factor in the destruction of the red man in our state was economic. Everyone must eat. When the aboriginal sources of subsistence were denied to the Indian, and when no substitute means of support were permitted him, he had no recourse but to fight and be killed quickly, or to starve and die slowly.

The native food supply was copious, but there were two commodities which surpassed all others in importance: fish from the rivers and acorns from the oak forests. The placering of every water course in the Sierra foothills and the northern Coast Ranges so muddied the water as to damage seriously the runs of salmon and steelhead. Farming operations in the flat country destroyed much of the acorn reserve. But the most destructive effect was produced by the simple occupation of the land. Since the Indian had no property rights, he was dispossessed and driven out wherever a farmer wished to settle, or a miner wanted to pan gold. The situation is epitomized in a single brief sign, two words: "No trespassing." If, at the present day, I violate such an order, and enter private property, I may perhaps be arrested, got to court, and be fined a few dollars. The Indian did not go to court; he was shot.

The effects of this mass eviction were manifold. On the one hand, the Indian might resort to stealing cattle for food, and precipitate a local "war." On the other hand, he might move into a settlement or town and try to exist by scavenging and beggary. Living thus in utter squalor and poverty, he became a serious social problem.

One might properly ask why this horde of mendicants were not absorbed by the labor market, which, in a pioneer community always finds room for workers. The answer is complex. One fundamental difference between the Hispanic and the Anglo-American cultures has always been the fact that the former utilized the native as its primary source of labor whereas the latter never did. There simply was no place in the American cosmos for the Indian. Such a condition is remarkable in view of the extensive reliance placed upon the Negro, both slave and free. Certain psychological factors are also involved, among them the bitter animosity previously mentioned. In addition, there was a deep-rooted feeling among settlers and pioneers that the Indian was mentally and morally incapable of productive effort. He was lazy, shiftless, dirty, and incompetent.

It is true that the American native had never encountered labor of the type favored by white men; long, tedious, exhausting hours and days spent at physical tasks on the farm and in the factory. From the standpoint of his own experience there was no reason for such effort, and, at least in California, he found adaptive transition too difficult to accomplish in the face of an intolerant, hostile, social environment.

The personal violence and economic suffering to which the California Indian was subjected was accompanied by a moral degradation such as has been the lot of few minority groups in the New World. Civil liberty as we understand the term, and as, even in 1850, it was embodied in the

Constitution, simply did not apply to the aborigine. He did not vote; he did not hold office; he had no police protection; he was not permitted to testify in court; he could not accuse a white man of any legal infraction, nor could he bring suit for any damages. He could be picked up without a warrant and could be held in jail without bail and upon no charge. If he were arrested, the then prevailing indenture system permitted any white man to secure his services for a period of days or weeks without pay. In theory the white man furnished food and lodging. If the Indian absconded he could be brought back by force.

One of the worst manifestations of oppression was in the area of sex. Particularly in the gold mining regions there existed thousands of unattached white men, frequently of the lowest character. It was quite customary for these individuals to make such use as they wished of the native women. If the latter, or their men-folk objected, force was applied without hesitation. These relationships were often more than casual. Many whites took Indian women as concubines and lived with them for extended periods, thus earning for themselves as a class the name of "squaw men." Furthermore, prostitution was common, and the local press gives accounts of Indian women selling themselves for a mouthful of food.

Of all the indignities to which the California natives were exposed, probably the most vicious was the kidnapping of small children in the mountains for sale to white citizens in the towns. The practice began before the American occupation of California, when the Spanish-speaking ranchers raided local tribes to capture transient labor. But by 1860 the kidnapping of children had reached the dimensions of an industry. In an editorial on July 19, 1862, the *Sacramento Union* stated that a class of "pestilent" whites were actually killing adults to get the children to sell. The latter brought from $30 to $200 apiece, and might be seen in every fourth white man's house. It may be estimated that fully 3,000 children were thus stolen during the fifteen years from 1852 to 1867. Several attempts were made to prosecute known operators in this business, but legal technicalities and outright acquittals prevented any from being brought to punishment.

After 1849, as California began to fill up with sober and responsible immigrants from the East, who came to establish homes, not to mine gold, the atrocities which were being inflicted upon the native population began to arouse public indignation. At first, efforts to bring relief were sporadic and ineffective. A few important landowners in the Central Valley "treated their Indians well." Groups of ladies in San Francisco and elsewhere made collections of food and clothing for the benefit of small numbers of indigents. It was very clear that private good will and charity could not touch the problem. But the Federal Government was at the time beginning to develop the Reservation System.

There is an opinion current that the Reservations were nothing more than concentration camps, and it must be admitted that at their worst there was a certain degree of resemblance. However, the theory on which they were based was relatively altruistic, even though the practice often fell far short of the theory.

In the middle of the nineteenth century, especially in the eastern part of the United States, where no one had seen a wild Indian for decades, there grew up a fairly strong humanitarian sentiment directed against the white people in the West who were seeing wild Indians all the time. This feeling undoubtedly went hand in hand with the rising abolition movement. It was argued quite cogently that if the Negroes were to be liberated from slavery, at least some of the Indians should be liberated from conditions which could be regarded as worse than slavery.

Out of this sentiment, and out of the many hit-or-miss, helter-skelter schemes for "doing something," emerged the Reservations. Moreover, behind their inception, lay an official, legalistic theory not unlike what we see today in urban redevelopment. The argument ran with the Indians, as it runs today with owners of condemned property, that society had dispossessed them of valuable lands and homes which, in all equity, should be replaced by something just as good.

It is true that, a century or more ago, there were great areas of vacant land in the plains and Great Basin regions to which the remnants of the eastern and middle western tribes could be moved. The fact was recognized that these forced migrants would have to be given help in order to get established and make a living under the American economic system. Hence they were to be supplied with tools, with seed, and with building materials, as well as with land itself. On the whole, the system probably was as good as could have been devised at the time, and under the existing circumstances.

Nevertheless, as applied to California, and as there administered, it was a failure. The reason lay basically in the peculiar political organization of the local natives and the complete disregard by white society of the ancient habitats and cultural values. California was unique in the United States in that instead of a few large tribes such as the Iroquois, Sioux or Apache, it contained dozens of little ones. Each one had its own clearly defined home with surrounding territory for foraging not more than a few miles. Each one had lived in that home for generations. To uproot such a tribe forcibly and transport it to a far place under strange conditions inflicted a profound emotional and psychic injury.

The dislocations to which the California native groups were subjected were carried out in a most callous and brutal manner. People from the upper Sacramento Valley were thrown together with others from the coast in localities which neither one had ever seen before. Some of these were in heavily forested northern areas where little natural food existed, and where cultivation was difficult for experienced white farmers, to say nothing of utterly unsophisticated aborigines. Moreover, the Reservation Indians for many years were systematically attacked and plundered by neighboring whites and their most desirable land was preempted without ceremony.

It was anticipated that such abuses would be abated by the resident agents, who, under federal law, were vested with broad discretionary powers over both the Reservation inhabitants and the surrounding white community. However, these functionaries, as a class, have always enjoyed a very low reputation for both integrity and competence. A sweeping indictment may contain some element of injustice, because a perusal of their annual reports leaves the impression that many agents honestly tried to make the system succeed. On the other hand, there unquestionably were many who were corrupt, or at least indifferent, and who shared the universal public antipathy toward their charges. Under such conditions of chaotic administration, and in the face of solid local hostility, the entire Reservation organization fell into a state of collapse, and had to be completely renovated in the late 1860s.

By that time the Indian population had shrunk to insignificance. This alone brought some relief. When California civil society finally settled down after the confusion and uproar of the Mexican War, the gold stampede, and the Civil War, it was found that there really were not enough Indians left to cause much trouble, perhaps 20,000 in all. Of these, many were uneasily established on Reservations such as Hupa, Round Valley, and Palm Springs, where the government took care of them as a rule by outright subventions. The others had retreated into the obscurity of the remote valleys of the Coast Ranges, the Sierra Nevada, or little oases in the southern desert, supporting themselves by subsistence farming reinforced by frequent federal aid. Here they have slowly gathered themselves together and are now beginning to ask why they may not be regarded as full American citizens.

3

Report on the Condition and Needs of the Mission Indians of California
HELEN HUNT JACKSON

> *In the early 1880s, New England author Helen Hunt Jackson sent copies of her reformist tract,* A Century of Dishonor, *to each member of Congress. Her concern for the American Indian led to her appointment to a special commission to investigate the condition of Indians in southern California. During a five-week tour she visited numerous missions, ranches, and pueblos. Her findings formed the basis of a report to the Commissioner of Indian Affairs on the needs of the Mission Indians, later appended to a new edition of her book. Her experiences in California also provided material for a novel,* Ramona.

XV. Report on the Condition and Needs of the Mission Indians of California, Made by Special Agents Helen Jackson and Abbot Kinney, to the Commissioner of Indian Affairs

SIR,—In compliance with our instructions bearing dates November 28th, 1882, and January 12th, 1883, we have the honor to submit to you the following report on the subject of the Mission Indians in Southern California.

The term "Mission Indians" dates back over one hundred years, to the time of the Franciscan missions in California. It then included all Indians who lived in the mission establishments, or were under the care of the Franciscan Fathers. Very naturally the term has continued to be applied to the descendants of those Indians. In the classification of the Indian Bureau, however, it is now used in a somewhat restricted sense, embracing only those Indians living in the three southernmost counties

SOURCE: Helen Hunt Jackson, *A Century of Dishonor: A Sketch of the United States Government's Dealings With Some of the Indian Tribes* (Boston: Roberts Brothers, 1885), pp. 458-474. [NOTE: This was a new edition enlarged by the addition of a report on the needs of the Mission Indians of California.]

of California, and known as Serranos, Cahuillas, San Luisenos, and Dieguinos; the last two names having evidently come from the names of the southernmost two missions, San Luis Rey and San Diego. A census taken in 1880, of these bands, gives their number as follows:

Serranos	381
Cahuillas	675
San Luisenos	1,120
Dieguinos	731
Total	2,907

This estimate probably falls considerably short of the real numbers, as there are no doubt in hiding, so to speak, in remote and inaccessible spots, many individuals, families, or even villages, that have never been counted. These Indians are living for the most part in small and isolated villages; some on reservations set apart for them by Executive order; some on Government land not reserved, and some upon lands included within the boundaries of confirmed Mexican grants.

Considerable numbers of these Indians are also to be found on the outskirts of white settlements, as at Riverside, San Bernardino, or in the colonies in the San Gabriel Valley, where they live like gypsies in brush huts, here to-day, gone to-morrow, eking out a miserable existence by days' works, the wages of which are too often spent for whiskey in the village saloons. Travellers in Southern California, who have formed their impressions of the Mission Indians from these wretched wayside creatures, would be greatly surprised at the sight of some of the Indian villages in the mountain valleys, where, freer from the contaminating influence of the white race, are industrious, peaceable communities, cultivating ground, keeping stock, carrying on their own simple manufactures of pottery, mats, baskets, &c., and making their living,—a very poor living, it is true; but they are independent and self-respecting in it, and ask nothing at the hands of the United States Government now, except that it will protect them in the ownership of their lands,—lands which, in many instances, have been in continuous occupation and cultivation by their ancestors for over one hundred years.

From tract after tract of such lands they have been driven out, year by year, by the white settlers of the country, until they can retreat no farther; some of their villages being literally in the last tillable spot on the desert's edge or in mountain fastnesses. Yet there are in Southern California to-day many fertile valleys, which only thirty years ago were like garden spots with these same Indians' wheat-fields, orchards, and vineyards. Now, there is left in these valleys no trace of the Indians' occupation, except the ruins of their adobe houses; in some instances these houses, still standing, are occupied by the robber whites who drove them out. The responsibility for this wrong rests, perhaps, equally divided between the United States Government, which permitted lands thus occupied by peaceful agricultural communities to be put "in market," and the white men who were not restrained either by humanity or by a sense of justice, from "filing" homestead claims on lands which had been fenced, irrigated, tilled, and lived on by Indians for many generations. The Government cannot justify this neglect on the plea of ignorance. Repeatedly, in the course of the last thirty years, both the regular agents in charge of the Mission Indians and special agents sent out to investigate their condition have made to the Indian Bureau full reports setting forth these facts.

In 1873 one of these special agents, giving an account of the San Pasquale Indians, mentioned the fact that a white man had just pre-empted the land on which the greater part of the village was situated. He had paid the price of the land to the register of the district land office, and was daily expecting his patent from Washington. "He owned," the agent says, "that it was hard to wrest from these well-disposed and industrious creatures the homes they had built up; but," said he, "if I had not done it, somebody else would; for all agree that the Indian has no right to public lands." This San Pasquale village was a regularly organized Indian pueblo, formed by about one hundred neophytes of the San Luis Rey Mission, under and in accordance with the provisions of the Secularization Act in 1834. The record of its founding is preserved in the Mexican archives at San Francisco. These Indians had herds of cattle, horses, and sheep; they raised grains, and had orchards and vineyards. The whole valley in which this village lay was at one time set off by Executive order as a reservation, but by the efforts of designing men the order was speedily revoked; and no sooner has this been done than the process of dispossessing the Indians began. There is now, on the site of that old Indian pueblo, a white settlement numbering 35 voters. The Indians are all gone,—some to other villages; some living near by in cañons and nooks in the hills, from which, on the occasional visits of the priest, they gather and hold services in the half-ruined adobe chapel built by them in the days of their prosperity.

This story of the San Pasquale Indians is only a fair showing of the experiences of the Mission Indians during the past fifty years. Almost without exception they have been submissive and peaceable through it all, and have retreated again and again to new refuges. In a few instances there have been slight insurrections among them, and threatenings of retaliation; but in the main their history has been one of almost incredible long suffering and patience under wrongs.

In 1851 one of the San Luiseno bands, the Aqua Caliente Indians, in the north part of San Diego County, made an attack on the house of a white settler, and there was for a time great fear of a general uprising of all the Indians in the country. It is probable that this was instigated by the Mexicans, and that there was a concerted plan for driving the Americans out of the country. The outbreak was easily quelled, however; four of the chiefs were tried by court-martial and shot by order of General Heintzelman, and in January of the following year a treaty was made with the San Luiseno and Dieguino Indians, setting off for them large tracts of land. This treaty was made by a United States commissioner, Dr. Wozencraft, and Lieutenant Hamilton, representing the Army, and Col. J. J. Warner, the settler whose house had been attacked. The greater part of the lands which were by this treaty assigned to the Indians are now within the boundaries of grants confirmed and patented since that time; but there are many Indian villages still remaining on them, and all Indians living on such lands are supposed to be there solely on the tolerance and at the mercy of the owners of said ranches, and to be liable to ejectment by law. Whether this be so or not is a point which it would seem to be wise to test before the courts. It is certain that in the case of all these Mission Indians the rights involved are quite different from and superior to the mere "occupancy" right of the wild and uncivilized Indian.

At the time of the surrender of California to the United States these Mission Indians had been for over seventy years the subjects, first of the Spanish Government, secondly of the Mexican. They came under the jurisdiction of the United States by treaty provisions,—the treaty of Guadalupe Hidalgo, between the United States and Mexico, in 1848. At this time they were so far civilized that they had become the chief dependence of the Mexican and white settlers for all service indoors and out. In the admirable report upon these Indians made to the Interior Department in 1853, by the Hon. B. D. Wilson, of Los Angeles, are the following statements:—

These same Indians had built all the houses in the country, planted all the fields and vineyards. Under the Missions there were masons, carpenters, plasterers, soap-makers, tanners, shoe-makers, blacksmiths, millers, bakers, cooks, brick-makers, carters and cart-makers, weavers and spinners, saddlers, shepherds, agriculturalists, horticulturalists, vineros, vaqueros; in a word, they filled all the laborious occupations known to civilized society.

The intentions of the Mexican Government toward these Indians were wise and humane. At this distance of time, and in face of the melancholy facts of the Indians' subsequent history, it is painful to go over the details of the plans devised one short half-century ago for their benefit. In 1830 there were in the twenty-one missions in California some 20,000 or 30,000 Indians, living comfortable and industrious lives under the control of the

Franciscan Fathers. The Spanish colonization plan had, from the outset, contemplated the turning of these mission establishments into pueblos as soon as the Indians should have become sufficiently civilized to make this feasible. The Mexican Government, carrying out the same general plan, issued in 1833 an act, called the Secularization Act, decreeing that this change should be made. This act provided that the Indians should have assigned to them cattle, horses, and sheep from the mission herds; also, lands for cultivation. One article of Governor Figueroa's regulations for the carrying out of the Secularization Act provided that there should be given to every head of a family, and to all above twenty-one years of age, though they had no family, a lot of land not exceeding 400 varas square, nor less than 100. There was also to be given to them in common, enough land for pasturing and watering their cattle. Another article provided that one-half the cattle of each mission school should be divided among the Indians of that mission in a proportionable and equitable manner; also one-half of the chattels, instruments, seeds, &c. Restrictions were to be placed on the disposition of this property. The Indians were forbidden "to sell, burden, or alienate under any pretext the lands given them. Neither can they sell the cattle." The commissioners charged with the carrying out of these provisions were ordered to "explain all the arrangements to the Indians with suavity and patience;" to tell them that the lands and property will be divided among them so that each one may "work, maintain, and govern himself without dependence on any one." It was also provided that the rancherias (villages) situated at a distance from the missions, and containing over twenty-five families, might, if they chose, form separate pueblos, and the distribution of lands and property to them should take place in the same manner provided for those living near the missions.

These provisions were in no case faithfully carried out. The administration of the Missions' vast estates and property was too great a temptation for human nature, especially in a time of revolution and misrule. The history of the thirteen years between the passing of the Secularization Act and the conquest of California is a record of shameful fraud and pillage, of which the Indians were the most hapless victims. Instead of being permitted each one to work, maintain, and govern himself without dependence on any one, as they had been promised, their rights to their plats of land were in the majority of cases ignored; they were forced to labor on the mission lands like slaves; in many instances they were hired out in gangs to cruel masters. From these cruelties and oppressions they fled by hundreds, returning to their old wilderness homes. Those who remained in the neighborhood of the pueblos became constantly more and more demoralized, and were subjected to every form of outrage. By a decree of the Los Angeles aqumiento, about the time of our taking possession of California, all Indians found without passes, either from the alcalde of the pueblos in which they lived, or from their "masters [significant phrase], were to be treated as horse-thieves and enemies." At this time there were, according to Mr. Wilson's report, whole streets in Los Angeles where every other house was a grog-shop for Indians; and every Saturday night the town was filled with Indians in every stage of intoxication. Those who were helpless and insensible were carried to the jail, locked up, and on Monday morning bound out to the highest bidders at the jail gates. "The Indian has a quick sense of justice," says Mr. Wilson; "he can never see why he is sold out to service for an indefinite period for intemperance, while the white man goes unpunished for the same thing, and the very richest and best men, to his eye, are such as tempt him to drink, and sometimes will pay him for his labor in no other way." Even the sober and industrious and best skilled among them could earn but little; it having become a custom to pay an Indian only half the wages of a white man.

From this brief and necessarily fragmentary sketch of the position and state of the Mission Indians under the Mexican Government, at the time of the surrender of California to the United States, it will be seen that our Government received by the treaty of Guadalupe Hidalgo a legacy of a singularly helpless race in a singularly anomalous position. It would have been very difficult, even at the outset, to devise practicable methods of dealing justly with these people, and preserving to them their rights. But with every year of our neglect the difficulties have increased and the wrongs have been multiplied, until now it is, humanly speaking, impossible to render to them full measure of justice. All that is left in our power is to make them some atonement. Fortunately for them, their numbers have greatly diminished. Suffering, hunger, disease, and vice have cut down more than half of their numbers in the last thirty years; but the remnant is worth saving. Setting aside all question of their claim as a matter of atonement for injustice done, they are deserving of help on their own merits. No one can visit their settlements, such as Aqua Caliente, Saboba, Cahuilla Valley, Santa Ysabel, without having a sentiment of respect and profound sympathy for men who, friendless, poor, without protection from the law, have still continued to work, planting, fencing, irrigating, building houses on lands from which long experience has taught them that the white man can drive them off any day he chooses. That drunkenness, gambling, and other immoralities are sadly prevalent among them, cannot be denied; but the only wonder is that so many remain honest and virtuous under conditions which make practically null and void for them most of the motives which keep white men honest and virtuous.

4

Episodes in Extermination
THEODORA KROEBER

> *In the years that followed the publication of Helen Hunt Jackson's* A Century of Dishonor, *conditions for California Indians improved very little, if any. Without a doubt, during the late nineteenth century the Indian suffered more from prejudice and discrimination in California than did any other minority. Perhaps the most vivid and compelling account of the extermination of this minority is Theodora Kroeber's* Ishi in Two Worlds. *Ishi was the last survivor of the Yana tribe of northern California. After being discovered in a state of complete exhaustion near Oroville in August, 1911, Ishi was brought to the University of California's museum of anthropology by Professors Alfred L. Kroeber and Thomas T. Waterman. There he lived for several years as the "last wild Indian in North America."*

WITH the signing of the Treaty of Guadalupe Hidalgo by Mexico and the United States in 1848, the Spanish-Mexican phase of the invasion of California ended, to be followed immediately by the Anglo-Saxon, represented as yet in the upper Sacramento Valley by only a few white grantees, their families and households, none of them in Yana country proper. Jim Payne, to be sure, moved from the valley into the hills, settling on Antelope Creek close to a cave which came to be known as Paynes Cave. But this was not before 1875, nor were there many other permanent settlers on Ishi's ancestral land before the late 'seventies and 'eighties.

But with the discovery that the gravel of creek and riverbeds in the red foothill country of California carried gold, what had been a trickle of new immigration became a stream pouring down the western face of the Sierra, a never ending stream as it would seem now, a hundred and more years after its beginnings. The so-called historical or documented period of Yana history began when old and discontinuous trails to oak flats, along creeks, or over low divides, became united into prospectors' trails, and were later widened to allow covered wagons to travel them.

SOURCE: Theodora Kroeber, *Ishi in Two Worlds: A Biography of the Last Wild Indian in North America* (Berkeley and Los Angeles: University of California Press, 1962), pp. 42–51, 62–64. Originally published by the University of California Press; reprinted by permission of The Regents of the University of California.

One such trail skirts Lassen Peak to the south, passes through Deer Creek Meadows, follows the watershed between Deer Creek and Mill Creek, and continues down Mill Creek to the Sacramento River at Los Molinos, cutting through the rugged but beautiful southern heartland of the Yahi country. It came to be known as the Old Lassen Trail, named, as was the peak it skirted, for Peter Lassen, whose rancho near the mouth of Deer Creek was the end of the long, long trek for those emigrants who came west by this route.

In 1850, ten or more years before Ishi's birth, the Yana occupied some 2,000 to 2,400 square miles of land recognized as their own; they and their Indian neighbors distinguished four linguistic, territorial, and cultural groups in the little nation of two or three thousand people—life was as it always had been. By 1872, twenty-two years later, and when Ishi was perhaps ten years old, there were *no* Southern Yana left; and only some twenty or thirty scattered *individuals* of the Northern and Central Yana remained alive. As for the fourth group, the Yahi, they were believed to have been entirely exterminated also, and so they were except for a handful, Ishi among them.

This death of a whole people came after the fiercest and most uncompromising resistance that the intruders were to meet anywhere on the west coast. And, at the bloody heart of this last stand of the Yana, were Ishi's people, the Yahi, a tribelet of probably no more than three or four hundred souls, counting the women, the very young, and the old. How so small, and to the newcomers so unimportant, a fragment of humanity succeeded in involving the United States Army as well as citizen vigilante groups is a tale soon told, a tale which satisfies the Greek ideal of starkness of tragedy and unity of time.

Disastrous to the Indians as had been the Ibero-American invasion of California, it was, all in all, less destructive of human life and values than was the Anglo-American. The earlier invasion remained small in numbers, being in the hundreds to the Indians' thousands. However cruel or culture-bound were many of those who peopled the land, they were nonetheless responsible officers of church or state or military; or they were vaqueros or farmers—answerable to authority, every one. Also, they were Mediterranean in their racial outlook. This meant that intermarriage with indigenes and the emergence of the *mestizo* were regarded as natural results of conquest.

The Anglo-Saxons, by contrast, reversed the ratio of whites to Indians, coming in inundating numbers—there were as many as a hundred thousand of them in a single year. They lacked any formal church control and, during all the fateful years for Indian survival, were without adequate state or military restraints, so that both the excesses and cruelties and crimes, and the efforts to bring them under some sort of surveillance and control, were pretty much up to the frontiersmen themselves. Anglo-

Saxons tended to racism then as now. A person with a skin color different from their own was thought to be intellectually and morally inferior; marriage with him was an antisocial act, sometimes legally forbidden; whatever the source for a sense of wonder and sacredness, if non-Christian, it was considered to be superstition and to be reprehensible. The early Anglo-Saxon emigrants were of two sorts: one, moral, ethical, and law-abiding, even if the laws were of local manufacture; the other, made up of the floaters, the irregulars, the failures at home, in revolt against the old customary home behavior patterns, and contemptuous of restrictions attempted on the spot by their soberer companions. Among the second group were also the outrightly criminal. Both sorts were in agreement, however, that the Indian was an inferior, and both used him as indentured laborer, slave, or concubine, and deprived him of life as well as freedom if he threatened to be in any way troublesome. White men who married Indian women were regarded with contempt. Half-breeds, especially the unhappy spawn of concubinage and rape, were classed as "natives," with all the disadvantages implicit in that special and by white definition second-class category.

It is with reluctance that the statistics which follow are offered at all, for the nature of the available source material can but rarely yield exact figures. Since all information is from white sources, and since an account of an Indian murder of a white was more acceptable copy than the reverse event, any inaccuracy in ratio will minimize the extent of the disproportion. The author finds a total of not more than twenty authenticated murders of whites by Indians who were or who were thought to have been Yana; six or eight of these killings, however, occurred out of presumable Yana range. This figure agrees closely with Professor Waterman's, who reports a total of twelve. This is not to say that there were no more than twelve or twenty murders of whites by Yana Indians. We have only hearsay and fragmentary record of much that went on in those remote hills and cañons on either side of Lassen Trail. During the years of the destruction of the Yana only some six hundred Yana deaths by violence from white settlers are of record—otherwise, the accounts say "several," "many," "a few"—not exact numbers which yield exact totals, not to mention those deaths of which no formal record survives. The ratios suggested by the meager Yana data, of one white person murdered for every thirty to fifty Indians, understates but indicates the drift of the vital statistics for the bloody years of Yana history: 1850–1872.

It was in the early 'sixties that the whole white population of the Sacramento Valley was in an uproar of rage and fear over the murder of five white children by hill Indians—probably Yahi. But the soberly estimated numbers of kidnappings of Indian children by whites in California to be sold as slaves or kept as cheap help was, between the years 1852 and

1867, from three to four *thousand;* every Indian woman, girl, and girl-child was potentially and in thousands of cases actually subject to repeated rape, to kidnapping, and to prostitution. Prostitution was unknown to aboriginal California, as were the venereal diseases which accounted for from forty to as high as eighty per cent of Indian deaths during the first twenty years following the gold rush. Professor S. F. Cook's series of monographs on Indian-Caucasian relations in California are the principal source for the estimated totals given in this paragraph, his ordering of all known pertinent data being an exhaustive and informed study of population statistics on both the Ibero- and the Anglo-American invasions.

The Caucasians brought with them also the "common" diseases, which included measles, chicken pox, smallpox, tuberculosis, malaria, typhoid, dysentery, influenza, pneumonia, and others, seeding them all willy-nilly through a population wholly without immunity. The mission Indians who had received these same diseases from the Spaniards were already, in 1848, extinct or much reduced; in any case, they had never been in the hill and mining country of Lassen nor mingled with its people. One or another of the introduced infections continued through several generations to kill numbers of Indians. The worst of the decimation—according to Cook an average of sixty per cent for the population of the state as a whole—was, naturally, in the first ten years. In no case did disease alone exterminate a whole people, and exposure to infection fell most heavily upon those valley Indians who bowed before the new order, and whose land was "settled."

Forced migrations account for some hundreds of Yana deaths; but death by shooting and particularly by mass-murder shooting interspersed with hangings were the usual and popular techniques of extermination. The Yahi opposed to this mass murder a courageous and spirited opposition, raiding when they could, killing when they could, and killing where it hurt as they were being hurt. But the taking of a horse, a mule, a cow, or a sheep; a bag of barley; even the firing of a barn now and then and the occasional murder of an innocent child or woman appear in the totals a puny revenge. The story is not a pretty one. It seems proper, at this distance, to confront the facts and the judgments which flow from the facts.

Many of us in California number among our ancestors a grandparent or a great-grandparent who came from somewhere in the "east," either with the Forty-niners or in the later waves of immigration following close upon them, family units these later ones, burdened with wagons and horses and cattle and oxen: men and women moving out from their country's earlier centers, homeless, but looking for a home. We have been taught to regard with pride the courage and ingenuity of these ancestors, their stubbornness in carving out a good life for their children. It is neither meet nor needful to withdraw such affectionate respect and admiration; it is perhaps well to remind ourselves that the best and gentlest of them did not question their right to appropriate land belonging to someone else, if Indian—the legal phrase was "justifiable conquest." However broad and real governmental and popular approval was, this invasion was like the classic barbarian invasions—a forced intrusion upon a settled population, and its replacement by the intruders. Such invasions have occurred many times, and continue to occur in the history of mankind, but also as well in the history of all forms of life; they are a part of the biological urge of each plant and animal to make or to take a place for itself and its descendants. Invasion, then, is a necessitous act in the Darwinian sense of struggle and survival; it is instinctive, primitive, and in itself inhumane.

That the invasion we are examining aroused a maximum of mutual fear and hate, was probably due in the first instance to the opening of a trail through a country before inviolate, and to the habit and psychology of some small part of the Forty-niners who did the opening. The first prospectors, miners, hunters, and trappers to travel Lassen and the other trails were a hard and hardy company. They came unencumbered with women or children; or with baggage beyond what a mule could carry. And they had their guns, by which they lived. They had been further hardened by a rough trip over a wide country not easy or friendly to cross, and their trek had been slowed and bloodied, and ended for some of their companions by Indians who contested their crossing and harried them; these were mounted and armed Indians, seemingly fearless.

In the company of these first comers were the inevitable trigger-happy few whose habit had become to shoot an Indian, any Indian, on sight; who counted *coup* under the slogan, "The only good Indian is a dead Indian," and who were possessed of the special skill of scalping, something previously unknown to California's aborigines. There was one such of whom Waterman writes: "On good authority I can report the case of an old prospector-pioneer-miner-trapper of this region [Butte County], who had on his bed even in recent years a blanket lined with Indian scalps. These had been taken years before. He had never been a government scout, soldier, or officer of the law. The Indians he had killed purely on his own account. No reckoning was at any time demanded of him."

By the time there was a resident and sober and responsible citizenry living in townships in the valley, that is, by the early 'sixties, the Yana— those who were still alive—had learned to distrust every white person as a possible killer out for gratuitous murder. So far as they could, they paid back in kind. Very few of the newcomers settled in actual Yana country before the 'eighties. The rub was that their oxen and cattle and sheep and pigs ranged the hills in such numbers that the native food sources such as the seeds of various grasses and the small varieties of oaks bearing acorns within reach of a woman's gathering (and equally of a pig's rooting) were depleted or destroyed. At the same time, the once free and open streams for fishing were appropriated or polluted or both, thus increasingly restricting Ishi's people, who were ordered off at the point of a gun if need be, and pushed back more and more into the inaccessible cañons of their streams. Hydraulic mining poured thousands of cubic yards of silt into the Sacramento River. This ruined many hundreds of acres of farming land in the valley, and diminished the size of the salmon runs up the tributaries where the Yana lived. The rich, open meadows on which these foothill Indians depended for varietal seasonal foods were tramped out, and the sometimes widely placed stands of large acorn oaks were increasingly denied them.

Always close to hunger, they became hungrier. They had raided beyond their borders and fought when they had to during all their history, if reciprocal land use between neighbors broke down. They raided and fought back now with every skill and device they could muster, having learned some new techniques from those who were responsible for the wholesale killings, scalpings, kidnappings, and rapings which were visited upon them and their near neighbors during the first years of emigrant travel over "Old Lassen Trail"—not so old then. The Yana image of the white man became fixed during those days when it was a careless boast that "You can't tell one Indian from another." The Yana found themselves, too, indifferent to making distinctions between one white person and another.

In actual fact, both the Yana and the new settlers did make distinctions. Indians were blamed, with or without evidence, for every out-of-the-way killing, for every cabin burning, for every stealing of stock or tools or clothes. But never the close-by Indians, "our" Indians: it was Indians at a distance, "wild" Indians who had done the deed. The Mill Creeks, as Ishi's people, the Yahi, were by then called, came in for maximum blame. They were actually responsible for more depredation than were other Indians; the valley Indians had feared them in the old days, and passed along their fear to their white neighbors; in any case, the Yahi were "wild," refusing to be "our" Indians to anyone. There seems to have been a discernible pattern among the stealings and murders committed by the Yahi: time after time they returned to the same ranch or cabin or stock pen or range; some they never troubled. Beyond this, they stole when they were hungry and cold; they murdered after murder had been done among them, so nearly as one can read the evidence. Of this, Richard Gernon, a surveyor in Red Bluff, who spent many years working in and about the Mill Creek country, says in a letter to Professor Waterman, November 3, 1914: "You have been misinformed about them [the Mill

Creeks] robbing my camp. . . . It is a remarkable thing, that the white men who hunted the Mill Creek Indians, between the years 1854 and 1865, have always had their camps robbed in after years. And those who never hunted those Indians never had anything stolen from them by the Indians." It is to be noted that the same names appear and reappear in the stories of reprisals and counterreprisals. Some people showed a predilection for Indian scouting and vigilante service, others did not, and were involved only when fear following upon women and children being made the victims of Yahi revenge roused a whole countryside.

Of the twenty-two years, 1850–1872, the first ten after the gold rush might be said to have been the years of preparation. In those years, between disease and murderings and loss of free movement, the Yana became a desperate people. And the new settlers, their stereotype of the Yana as fixed and inaccurate as the Yana's of them, were exasperated by raids on their stock and destruction of their property, and fearful for their lives. Along Deer Creek and Mill Creek it was as elsewhere in California: the years of the Civil War were also the years when the clash between the Indians and whites reached its climax, breaking out more and more often into open hostility and violence after ten years of increasing tension. The outcome at this distance is seen never to have been in doubt. The Indians were doomed. But to those embroiled or close at hand, Indian and white, the inequality of the struggle was not apparent.

.   .   .   .

The years 1857, 1858, and 1859 were those of the greatest belligerency and success of the Yahi and their fellow Yana who were not too exposed. This was before Ishi was born. Like good guerrillas, they struck unexpectedly and swiftly, and for the rest, kept out of sight. Their depredations were credited to the accessible, exposed border Yana, or even more absurdly, to remote groups of valley Indians who had never put up any resistance and had long since been without means or spirit for it.

Yana Indians were indentured in numbers—this was legal in California until 1861—and they were kidnapped and murdered, yet none of these measures stopped their continuing depredations. By 1859, the cry in the settlements was for the physical removal of all Indians. The word went out from Sacramento to Washington that something must be done to appease the white hysteria and to protect the hundreds of peaceable and innocent valley Indians who might become its first victims, for by this time *no* live Indian was a good Indian, or immune from violence. Hastily, but with good intent, a reservation of sorts called Nome Lackee was made ready some twenty miles west of Tehama. Small and not-so-small groups of Indians were rounded up at gun point and herded there, a hundred and eighty-one Southern Yana being the largest number in a single forced migration of which there is record. Nome Lackee was abandoned in

1861, and seemingly with good reason, since all the Indians who had been taken there were either dead or had escaped. The Southern Yana, much depleted even before the removals of 1859, did not survive after that time as a people. Most of them died from disease, exposure, or the shock of displacement, A few must have lived on, attached to a small band or household of Indians of another tribe. Sam Batwi, for example, was half Maidu, half Southern Yana by ancestry, although he spoke Northern Yana. When the linguist Edward Sapir worked with Batwi, it was to record the Northern dialect to which Batwi was able a few times to add a recollected Southern variant of word or sound. But he had not spoken Southern Yana nor heard it since he was a young child; nor were Sapir or other linguists then or later able to learn of anyone living who knew the dialect.

In 1859 the white settlers were not relying on reservations and the military. From their own number they collected three thousand dollars as a beginning fund to be used to fight the Mill Creeks. The sum was deposited with the storekeeper at the Mayhew stage station on Deer Creek. And it was in the same year—a fateful year for Ishi's people—that the names of two civilian leaders, Robert A. Anderson and his friend and companion Hiram Good occur and recur whenever there was trouble afoot in Yana country. Anderson and Good were natural trackers and scouts who came to know the back country almost as well as did the Indians; and who were, before long, making forays into Yahi strongholds. In 1909 Anderson wrote his memoirs of those years; they were published in Chico under the title *Fighting the Mill Creeks*. Today they are an invaluable source for precisely the subject matter of their title. To read them is to realize that Anderson saw himself in no such rarefied and noble role as did the men he led. His fighting days began when he was not yet twenty years old. He was sheriff of Butte County at twenty-five. There is more than a touch of Twainian humor in his accounts of his own many unsuccessful expeditions into the hills when the Yahi outwitted and eluded him; of the (to him) hilarious spectacle of a frustrated company, officers and men, returning after weeks of the most arduous chasing up and down lava cliffs, without having so much as glimpsed a fresh spoor of Indian, much less an Indian; of the times when he and his pal Hiram were distracted from their game of trying for Indian scalps by a chance encounter with one or sometimes several grizzly bears. He matched wits and physical prowess with Indians and grizzlies alike: both, in his opinion, "infested" the region and should be cleared out. He and Good, Anderson says, used to argue at length about how the clearing out was to be done. Good was for leaving the women and children alone; Anderson believed that immolation was the only effective way to be rid of Indians, and grizzlies, too, no doubt. Older and presumably wiser men than Anderson subscribed, literally, to his philosophy—they supported him and his "guards" from their own pockets—and it should be said that Anderson writes retrospectively in his memoirs, "It is but just that I should mention the circumstances which raised the hand of the Mill Creeks against the whites. As in almost every similar instance in American History, the first act of injustice, the first spilling of blood, must be laid at the white man's door."

5

K-344—Legal Redress?

KENNETH M. JOHNSON

For seventy-five years after the United States Senate refused to ratify the reservation treaties of the early 1850's (by which California Indians were to be compensated for land taken from them during the American occupation), the rights of these Indians to their lands remained unresolved. Finally, in 1928, under prodding from the California delegation, Congress acknowledged that a grave injustice had been done. It authorized the Attorney General of California to bring suit against the United States on behalf of the California Indians. A special census in 1928 determined that there were approximately 23,540 living descendants of California Indians who would be entitled to receive financial compensation. The final decision in the case of the Indians of the State of California vs. The United States (or K-344, which is the court file number of the case) was not rendered until 1944. The Federal Court of Claims awarded the Indians approximately $5 million, or a mere $200 per person. This money was not given directly to the Indians, however, but was held "for their benefit" in the Treasury of the United States (with an interest of 4 per cent), to be appropriated by Congress for "health, industrial and other purposes for the benefit of said Indians, including the purchase of lands and building of homes." No per capita payments were ever made to the Indians.

THE disclosure of the treaties [of the early 1850's] created quite an amount of comment and a new interest in Indian affairs. However most of the activity at this time was devoted to improving conditions in the reservations and rancherias and not to consideration of compensation for lost lands. As time passed several organizations made studies of the various aspects of the problems of the California Indian. Chief among these organizations was the Commonwealth Club of San Francisco. This group, composed principally of business and professional men, has long been interested in the workings of government at every level and in social problems in general. It was and is an active, potent group; its Friday

SOURCE: Kenneth M. Johnson, *K-344, or the Indians of California vs. The United States* (Los Angeles: Dawson's Book Shop, 1966), pp. 61–65, 69–71, 73–80. Reprinted by permission of the author and Dawson's Book Shop.

luncheons, addressed by a prominent speaker, are a feature of life in downtown San Francisco. The Club prides itself in the fact that it will always be willing to hear from both sides where controversial issues are concerned. As early as 1909 the Club had looked into the Indian questions, and in 1924 a special Section on Indian Affairs was formed for the purpose of making a complete study of the rights, wrongs, and present condition of the California Indians.

Another group that was active in this area was the Native Sons of the Golden West. Study committees were formed, and publicity as to the needs of the California Indians appeared in its magazine, *The Grizzly Bear*. In 1922 and again in 1925 there were articles of real importance in arousing public opinion. There were many other groups active in the cause of the California Indian; among these were the Indian Welfare Committee of the Federated Women's Clubs, the California Indian Rights Association, Inc., the Northern California Indian Association, the Mission Indian Federation, and the Women's Christian Temperance Union. At the time here considered this latter organization had a surprising amount of political power. All of this activity led to two conclusions: first, the Indians had rights in land for which they had not received adequate compensation, and second, the only remedy was in the Congress of the United States. The first major effort in Congress was in 1920, when Representative John E. Raker introduced a bill (H.R. 12788, 66th Congress, Second Session) providing for relief for the California Indians. It was proposed that any tribe or band, through the use of private attorneys, could bring a suit against the United States. The measure did not refer to the treaties, but did provide "for determination of the amount, if any, due said tribes or bands from the United States for lands formerly occupied and claimed by them in the said State, which lands are alleged to have been taken from them without compensation. . . ." This bill did not pass, and other bills introduced during the next seven years suffered the same fate.

In 1926 the section of the Commonwealth Club on Indian Affairs made its formal report on various aspects of the problems of California Indians, and made suggestions as to remedial legislation. Two members, in retrospect, appear to have had the most to do in formulating policy as to legislation; these were a San Francisco attorney, Charles de Y. Elkus, and Mrs. Julius Kahn, who succeeded her husband upon his death as a Representative in Congress. Elkus had a lifelong interest in Indian welfare, not only in California, but also in the Southwest. The Commonwealth Club report recognized the land rights of the Indians and proposed to sponsor a Federal law providing for a forum to determine and evaluate claims based on such rights. Active planning was begun in 1927, not only by the Commonwealth Club, but also by others. The general thought was to have an action brought by the Attorney General of California based on the rejected treaties. As a start the California Legislature in 1927 enacted a law entitled "An Act to authorize the attorney general to bring suit against the United States in the court of claims in behalf of the Indians of the State of California in the event that the Congress of the United States authorizes the same."

Various meetings were held with the California delegation in Congress and a bill was drafted to permit an action in the Court of Claims. This was introduced in Congress in the early part of 1928 by Representative Clarence Lea from Lake County. Lea was a good choice; he had been born in Lake County, which had been a center of Indian population. He had a personal knowledge of Indian difficulties and was sympathetic to what was trying to be accomplished. In addition he was well liked and influential in Washington. After some amendments, which were later to provide difficulties, the bill was passed, bearing the title of "The California Indians' Jurisdictional Act of 1928"; it was also commonly known as the "Lea Act."

The law started out by defining California Indians as those who were resident in the State on June 1, 1852 and their descendants now living in the State. The next section was very broad and tied the legislation to the treaties.

SEC. 2. All claims of whatsoever nature the Indians as defined in Section 1 of this Act may have against the United States by reason of lands taken from them in the State of California by the United States without compensation, or for the failure or refusal of the United States to compensate them for their interest in lands in said state which the United States appropriated to its own purposes without the consent of said Indians, may be submitted to the Court of Claims by the Attorney General of the State of California acting for and on behalf of said Indians for determination of the equitable amount due said Indians from the United States; and jurisdiction is hereby conferred upon the Court of Claims of the United States, with the right of either party to appeal to the Supreme Court of the United States, to hear and determine all such equitable claims of said Indians against the United States and to render final decree thereon.

It is hereby declared that the loss to said Indians on account of their failure to secure the lands and compensation provided for in the eighteen unratified treaties is sufficient ground for equitable relief.

The above satisfactory beginning (which was in Lea's bill as introduced) was obviously the result of very careful draftsmanship; the treaties were recognized as forming the basis for claims, and the use of the word "equitable" was to suggest to the court that it could do justice and achieve a fair result in the broadest sense of these terms and not be limited to strict legal rules. However, this broad declaration of policy was hamstrung by two amendments which were illogical, to say the least. The first was that any awards under the act would be limited to the value of what had been granted in the treaties of 1851, and that the value of any lands so granted could not be in excess of $1.25 per acre. The second was that from the amount so determined there should be deducted all monies paid or expenditures made for the benefit of *all* of the California Indians from the beginning to the date of the award under an action commenced under the act. Thus the act gave with one hand and took away with the other. There were provisions providing that if judgment should go against the United States, the State of California could be compensated for its necessary expenses, but that no reimbursement shall be made to the State for the services rendered by its attorney general. Finally the act provided:

SEC. 6. The amount of any judgment shall be placed in the Treasury of the United States to the credit of the Indians of California and shall draw interest at the rate of 4 per centum per annum and shall thereafter be subject to appropriation by Congress for educational health, industrial, and other purposes for the benefit of said Indians, including the purchase of lands and building of homes, and no part of said judgment shall be paid out in per capita payments to said Indians. . . .

While the Lea Act had, as indicated, some undesirable features, it was a step forward, as it was the first act of Congress of this nature after twenty years of effort. As a result of this those interested felt optimistic and requested the attorney general not to proceed until after the next session of Congress in order to have the act improved by amendment; however at the close of the next session nothing had been accomplished.

. . . .

The accumulation of facts continued slowly, and some rather significant statistics became apparent. The Indians originally had loosely possessed and under the quitclaim provisions of the treaties had relinquished to the United States approximately 75,000,000 acres of land in California; the lands promised in the treaties totalled 8,619,000 acres; lands actually made available in the reservations and rancherias amounted to 624,000 acres. In graph form the first figure would be a column two and one-quarter inches high, the second three-eights of an inch, and the last less than one-sixteenth of an inch. To put it another way, a basket ball, a golf ball, and a BB shot.

The first important figure arrived at was the value of the lands, articles, and services promised by the treaties. Land was, of course, uniformly valued at $1.25 per acre; as to the cattle, shovels, coarse pants, and linsey cloth the economists were called in and values as of 1852 determined. Even here, in one of the simple calculations, controversy was to later develop; what prices were to be used, Eastern or Western, wholesale or retail, and what is the value of a teacher who never taught? It had been agreed that the first estimate of the value of the treaty properties would be made by the Attorney General and that of the setoff by the United States. The initial conclusion of the Attorney General was that the value of the treaty properties was between sixteen and nineteen million dollars. This tentative finding was reached in 1932.

The case was purposely allowed to drag in the hope that the act could be amended so as to be of greater benefit to the Indians. In every session of Congress beginning with 1930 and including 1943 various bills were introduced to lessen the unfairness of the Jurisdictional Act. Except for one bill all failed to pass; the exception (S. 1793, 74th Congress, 1st Session, 1935) was introduced by Representative Lea, who had introduced the original measure; however it was vetoed by President Roosevelt. In the thirties Lea was a perennial author of Indian legislation, and later Senator Sheridan Downey was to do the same. After Senator Downey had retired I was associated with him in a case, and there were two things about which he loved to reminisce: the 160 acre limitation as to water in California, and his efforts on behalf of the California Indians. He termed the latter most disheartening, but pointed out that the early efforts were made during the period of the great depression and the latter while World War II was in full swing; neither period presented a favorable climate for additional Federal expenditures. The curious and unhappy formula of deducting all Indian benefits from those promised the treaty Indians was year after year discussed before House and Senate committees on Indian affairs, but the results were nil.

.   .   .   .

In November, 1938, the up and coming District Attorney of Alameda County, Earl Warren, was elected Attorney General of the State of California and succeeded U. S. Webb as of January 2, 1939. From this point K-344 was under the control of the man that was later to be Governor of the State and Chief Justice of the United States. Warren decided to reactivate the case, and most of the important briefs bear his name. From a procedural standpoint, under the rules of the Court of Claims, there would be two steps. First the Court would determine if there was any liability, and then the amount of such liability. Finally the case came on for hearing as to liability on May 7, 1941, and the position of the plaintiffs was presented by Earl Warren and Hartwell H. Linney, Assistant Attorney General. Warren presented the factual background, and Linney argued the law. Certain of the organizations representing the Indians requested the Court to delay its decision, and Chief Justice Whaley stated that he would for a "reasonable time." The request was by those who had developed a most unusual maneuver. While Congress could hardly be expected to change the law as to a matter then on trial, it was pointed out that in effect there were two trials, the first as to liability, and the second as to amount, and that Congress could change the ground rules as to amounts as this was still to be considered. It was an ingenious plan, but it failed to move Congress.

The Court did indeed delay; however on October 5, 1942, its opinion was announced by Chief Justice Richard H. Whaley.

The Court is of the opinion that the plaintiffs are entitled to recover the value of the land set out and described in the eighteen unratified treaties at the price per acre named in the jurisdictional act, and the value of the other articles, chattels, and services as of the date of the failure of the Senate to ratify the treaties. As this claim does not involve a taking of land by the Government for which just compensation shall be made, but only compensation for an equitable claim, no allowance of interest is permitted or allowable.

The case will be referred to a Commissioner of the Court to ascertain the values and report to the Court. If a stipulation cannot be entered into, both parties may take testimony on these issues.

The decision was both sweet and bitter. The question of liability had finally been successfully determined after ninety years, but interest which was of such great importance was denied. The opinion appeared to contain an inherent conflict; first was the conclusion that a recovery could be had on the basis of land lost; next there could be no interest because there had been no taking. Based on this and other matters Warren moved for a new trial on November 30, 1942. The motion was denied on January 4, 1943. This time the Court moved quickly.

In the election in the fall of 1942 Warren was elected Governor, and Robert W. Kenny Attorney General. Kenny recalls that when he took over from Warren K-344 was one of the pending cases particularly discussed. Warren was strong in his belief that the motion for a new trial should have been granted and urged Kenny to appeal to the United States Supreme Court. On March 29, 1943 Kenny did file in the Supreme Court a petition for a writ of certiorari to review the decision of the Court of Claims, particularly on the question of interest and the denial of the motion for a new trial. On June 7, 1943, without opinion, the Supreme Court denied the petition.

The first step in K-344 had now reached a final conclusion: the next was to work with the Commissioner on values. The major work in this area had already been accomplished, and what remained was for each side to evaluate the accuracy and completeness of the figures dug out over a period of years. In one area Kenny was successful in saving a good many dollars. It will be recalled that the lands promised in the treaties were to be valued at $1.25 per acre. As to the lands which had been granted by the United States to the Indians the Government proposed that an appraisal value be used. Kenny was successful in insisting that these lands were also to have a value of $1.25 per acre. The Commissioner proceeded with his studies and finally produced a set of valuations that appeared fair to him, proceeding under limitations previously set. Kenny reached the opinion that the computations were basically correct and little or nothing would be gained by a court trial on these issues, and that pursuant to the suggestion of the Court, there should be a settlement of the case by stipulation.

In the latter part of 1943 Kenny had several meetings with the United States Attorney General, and it was agreed that the attorney for the Indians would draft a stipulation based on the Commissioner's findings and that in the absence of unforeseen problems it would be agreed to. This meant that the Indians would get about five million dollars, and this was very disappointing to the Indians and their supporters. Considerable pressure was put on Kenny to go to trial. It was to combat this pressure that caused Kenny to issue his booklet on the case. [See Robert W. Kenny, *History and Proposed Settlement, Claims of California Indians* (Sacramento, 1944).] The book was an explanation of the case, a popular analysis of the deficiencies of the Jurisdictional Act which could not be escaped, and a plea for and justification of the proposed compromise settlement. Kenny pointed out that liability had been established, and the case laid a foundation for a future easy solution of overall claims. The value of the rights of the treaty Indians had been found to be about $17,500,000; this was for about one-half of the then Indian population. Congress thus by a simple appropriation of about $35,000,000 could grant full compensation without further trials or expensive investigations. Also the publicity attendant to a settlement at the relatively low figure that seemed inevitable, should prod Congress into the action desired. Kenny closed his report and plea as follows:

Thus the proposed settlement in which both sides have endeavored to proceed with fairness and consideration of the best interests of the Indians of California and of the United States not only provides a maximum recovery under the existing law, but provides a suggested yardstick for possible future Congressional action without the necessity for any future litigation.

It is realized that the amount of the proposed settlement or award herein provided for will no doubt be deemed inadequate both by the Indians of California and by their friends and advisors. However, I feel it my duty to point out that, regardless of the adequacy or inadequacy of the proposed settlement, there are urgent reasons, in our opinion why it should be accepted.

(a) First, it is my carefully considered opinion that if forced to trial in the Court of Claims under the present Jurisdictional Act we could not secure an award for the plaintiffs as favorable as this settlement. The reasons for that conclusion should by now be obvious to all persons familiar with this case and cognizant of the difficulties, if not the impossibilities of establishing by competent and admissable evidence the proof that would be required to justify the court in making an award.

(b) There now seems to be no room for doubt that the Congress will not amend the Jurisdictional Act so as to broaden the base of the award as proposed in numerous bills in both the Senate and the House. Over a period of at least ten years consistent efforts have been made to have the Jurisdictional Act amended but all the proposed bills have failed of passage except S. 1793, 74th Congress, 1st Session, which was vetoed by the President. . . .

(c) If the proposed settlement is accepted by the Indians and is consummated these results will have been achieved:

1. The sum of $5,165,863.46 will be placed in the Treasury of the United States, with interest at four per cent, and will be available for the use and benefit of the Indians of California in accordance with such appropriations therefrom as the Congress may make.

2. The Jurisdictional Act will have served its purpose to the limited extent possible thereunder.

3. Through the establishment of a formula for the computing of an award based upon the promises made to the treaty Indians, a further award may be computed based upon assumed promises of like character to the non-treaty Indians.

Kenny, of course, had full authority to settle the litigation without reference to the Indians themselves; however as a matter of policy he desired that the Indians should know what was going on and that there be at least tacit approval. Each organization of Indians was invited to Sacramento and there were many meetings where the stipulation proposal was explained. Kenny has stated that the Indians were very difficult to deal with and were ultra suspicious. The limitations of the Jurisdictional Act had not been very well or generally understood, and there had been an earlier feeling that much more would be secured. To the Indians this was just another case where the white man was letting them down. Kenny was very patient and finally convinced the leaders that what he proposed was the best course of action possible.

Kenny then informed United States Attorney General Biddle that he was ready to enter into a stipulation based on the report of the Commissioner on values. As agreed earlier Kenny prepared the stipulation and with a few minor changes it was signed by both parties and submitted to the Court. The total amount of the benefits promised by the treaties, less the value of Government lands granted later, was found to be $17,053,-941.98. The setoff amount, largely based on the totals of Congressional appropriations directly or indirectly for the benefit of the California Indians, was $12,029,099.64. The stipulation was accepted by the Court, and on December 4, 1944, it issued its judgment, and the following are the closing paragraphs:

VIII

That the aforesaid offsets in the total sum of $12,029,099.64, as set out in paragraph VII, shall be deducted from the total amount which the plaintiff is entitled to recover, as stated in paragraph VI above, namely, $17,053,941.98, making the net amount for which judgment may be entered by the Court the sum of $5,024,842.34.

Whereupon, following the filing of a report by the Commissioner stating that "net recovery in favor of the plaintiffs is recommended in the sum of $5,024,842.34," it was ordered December 4, 1944, that judgment for the plaintiffs be entered in the net sum of $5,024,842.24.

Thus after fifteen years and four months K-344 had come to an end. However a few related matters remained to be settled; California was entitled to costs, other than the salary of the Attorney General, and reference to these were omitted in the judgment. The majority of cost items had already been paid, but California was still asking for about $27,000. There was some dispute, but the claim was finally paid. The following are the first and last entires in the docket for K-344 maintained in the office of the Attorney General:

8-14-29   Petition filed.
. . . .
4-26-46   Rec'd. check for $27,842
           expense per decree of 5-7-45;
           ck. fwd. to Controller.
           — Closed —

6

The Language of Stereotype, Distortion, Inaccuracy

LOWELL JOHN BEAN

In an attempt to counter the stereotype of the Indian as lazy, shiftless, and immoral, Rupert Costo, a Cahuilla Indian and President of the American Indian Historical Society, launched a campaign in the mid-1960s to improve the teaching of the history of American Indians in California schools. In numerous appearances before the State Curriculum Commission, Costo and other Indian representatives presented specific criteria to eliminate inaccuracies and misconceptions that were prevalent in State-adopted textbooks. The concerns and allegations expressed by Costo and his supporters are represented in this article by Lowell John Bean, a faculty member at California State College, Hayward. Bean's article, which originally appeared in the Fall, 1969, issue of The Indian Historian, *examines the "distortion of reality" in Helen Bauer's widely used fourth-grade text,* California Indian Days. *The State Curriculum Commission, after reading and discussing the Bean article, and after listening to extensive testimony, rejected the Bauer book for readoption. In 1970, the American Indian Historical Society published* The American Indians in California History, *which is intended to provide a more accurate account of the role of the Indian in this state.*

THIS text contains frequent errors in data, as well as omissions of significant fact, despite the easily accessible data on the native peoples of the region. Since the author provides no indication of her sources of information, it is assumed from the nature of the data presented, that several have been used, some ethnographical and others from governmental agencies.

Most of the data presented are generally in error. A statement suggest-

SOURCE: Lowell John Bean, "The Case of the Fourth Grade Textbook 'California Indian Days,' by Helen Bauer," reprinted in *Textbooks and the American Indian,* (San Francisco: The Indian Historian Press, Inc., 1970), pp. 220–226. Rupert Costo, ed. and Jeannettee Henry, writer. Reprinted by the permission of The Indian Historian Press, Inc.

ing that the planting of crops was unknown, is incorrect, (Forbes, 1963). Another gross error is the statement that there are only "about seventy sites where pictographs have been found" in California. There are more than that many sites recorded in the Cahuilla area of southern California alone. The Chumash area is even more dramatic with its representations of aboriginal art, (Grant, 1966). Numerous errors of fact occur in the recording of plant names and plant uses. The rendering of Indian words into English is upon occasion incorrect. Words from a single language are used as representative of all; thus by implication the word is construed as having been used by all California language groups.

Some notable examples of omission are: while yucca species are discussed, the most important of this species in California aboriginal subsistence—the yucca whipplei—is not mentioned at all, although its use is described but without indicating the species itself (Barrows, 1900; Kroeber, 1924). When yucca Schidigera is discussed as a food source, the blossom, which was a prime source of food, is entirely overlooked. It is as though it were explained that the Greek people utilized the leaf of the grape in cooking, but failed to mention that the grape itself was used as food, for wine, and many other purposes. When game animals are mentioned, it is significant that antelope, elk, and mountain sheep, three big-game animals commonly hunted in the California region, are not mentioned; nor is the list of other animals, insects and birds at all representative of the vast variety of fauna used by the people of this region for food. Other omissions occur when house types are discussed. The significant ceremonial-community house, for example, is not discussed at all, nor is the variation of housing adequately treated.

A particular image of the Indian of California emerges when the choice of words selected to describe the cultures is examined. In "California Indian Days," homes and houses become "huts"; culture is always "custom"; and homes are always "simple." When native California's finest aboriginal pottery is described, it is classified as being "rather well made" (page 32). A sacred, beautifully-choreographed dance is performed "wildly" (page 126). Throughout Mrs. Bauer's book, the Indian receives somewhat less than equal comparison with the currently dominant culture. The Indian "roams" in his territory. Consequently his relation to land would seem to be physical rather than social.

This type of insidious prejudice, implicit stereotyping and patronizing racial self-importance continues throughout the book. Such phrases as "they took food from places" (page 11), rather than that they collected and gathered, with utmost care, and the most sophisticated knowledge of their environment, exemplifies an insistence that aboriginal culture was "simple" in the "primitive" connotation. In "California Indian Days" the author says "they lived their simple way of life . . ." (page 3).

Referring to archaeological data, "what they left behind were things that told of their simple but useful way of life . . ." (page 23). The use of the word "simple" in these contexts does not suggest an attempt at legiti-mate cross-cultural comparison, but rather indicates a categorical denial that anything complex or sophisticated could have existed in native California. This constant reference to a diminutive, diminished status of Indian culture is carried through to other aspects of the California aboriginal cultures; their homes are little, their stories are characterized as a "sort of sing-song story" (page 68). "Each tribe," says Bauer, "had some kind of music. Music to them was not a tune, but more a humming or low, slow chanting in time to the stomping of feet or the clapping of hands" (page 90). The fact that musicologists and mythographers have addressed many scholarly articles to the California Indians' oral literature and music; and that these aesthetic expressions are ranked as complex, unique, and highly important cultural contributions, is totally ignored. (See Dockstadter, 1957.)

Rather than seek answers to questions in the available scholarly litera-ture, the author indulges in conjecture, often gratuitous, and frequently imputing doubt upon the ability of the Indians to reason effectively. Upon the arrival of the Spanish the California Indian "perhaps thought of them as gods from the 'spirit world' " (page 20). Regarding their land the Indians knew so well, and with which they identified so very intensely, Bauer says "they must have loved their beautiful California home." If it is argued that this type of language exemplifies the "discovery" method of the learning process, then the argument is a specious excuse for lan-guage that is actually patronizing and inept—the semantics of the self-important dominant culture.

In art and literature, the unnecessary conjecture reaches another level of gratuity. Body paintings are "perhaps there to frighten bad spirits . . ." (page 35). Pictographs and petrographs of the area "appear to be a kind of Indian art . . ." (page 94). And the rich oral literature of the California Indian was developed "because they could not understand all these things, they made up stories about them" (page 128). In this vein the author continues, and the implication to most readers will be that European culture doesn't make things up, and European culture DOES understand "these things." The false-face image is further enlarged when Bauer says, "these stories were told from father to son and from one tribe to another, until they seemed to be true . . ." (page 128). The rationality and intelligence of the Indian is further denied because of a series of "lucky" circumstances. And so the reader is told that Indians were "lucky" to find so many oak trees in California, and some were "lucky" to have strong soapstone jars (page 61). More, "when they were lucky every family in the village had a feast" (page 61). The fact that acorns were useful because of skillful and demanding processing techniques, one of the greatest inventions of early man, and that the soapstone jars were quarried, shaped, polished and decorated, and that feasts were the consequence of careful planning and arduous hunting, gathering and storage techniques, is not brought to the attention of the reader.

In addition to the unnecessary conjectures already mentioned, invidious comparisons as well contribute to the distorted Indian "image," comparisons which place the Indian in a negative position. For example, California Indians are said to have "left behind no famous ruins of cities, no temple, or great works of art as some other people" (page 23), and "The Indians of the Colorado River make the poorest (!) examples of baskets in California." Any positive purpose of these statements escapes this reader. A positive statement regarding the densely populated coastal villages of the Gabrieleno Indians and the Chumash Indians might be appropriate, but at the very least a rational cause might be offered to the reader for the comparison of California Indians with those of other traditions and circumstances. Nor is it acknowledged that the Colorado River Indians did not need to emphasize basketry as an aesthetic or utilitarian form because they had a well developed pottery industry. In fact, the opportunity for pointing out to the student reader the relationship between developments of material culture and ecological need and potential, might have been taken successfully with these same examples.

Oversimplification can produce distortion and a negative view of a cultural situation as effectively as incorrect data. Bauer's book manages this in several areas of Indian life: child training and care, division of labor, marriage, ritual and religion are some examples. It is said that "in cold weather, a rabbit skin was thrown over the cradle," to protect the infant (page 119); boys were "given many harmless tests to prove their bravery" (page 68); dancing is characterized as being done for fun, or "wild" in character. The purpose of dancing in one instance is because "they wanted luck in hunting or to find something that would make them rich or to be cured of an illness" (page 49). Marriage arrangements are also seen as rather simple affairs "the young man who gave the most gifts (to the bride's parents) was almost always able to get the girl he wanted for his wife" (page 124).

The author's characterization of the division of labor denies what is a particularly obvious factor of aboriginal California life; that the sexual dichotomization of roles was not as rigidly defined as it was with some other American Indian groups. Thus, to Bauer, "women were the gatherers and men the hunters." This oversimplification prevents the reader from appreciating the orderly and well integrated nature of social organization involved in subsistence, which included the young and the old, men and women, in cooperative units, the goal of which was an efficient exploitation of complex environments. Furthermore, the social organizational aspects of the labor process is attributed to a wish to make work a happy occasion rather than a desire for efficient exploitation. The reader is told, "in the fall, when the oaks had ripe acorns, women left their homes in the village, usually in a group to make the harvest task happier" (page 49). This is analogous to saying that workers in an automobile factory go to a factory to work together because it makes the work a happier occasion.

The art and religion of California's Indian culture receive interpretative distortion when the artistically innovative Colorado River pottery industry is ignored and their pottery is reduced to that which "was good enough for their daily needs: cooking and family baskets and pots and water and storage jars . . ." (page 88). The elaborate effigies and painted ware which museums and private collectors are so anxious to acquire today, is ignored. In religion too, the Indian is not allowed total humanness. They do not "exactly pray for what they wanted . . . they danced and sang about their needs . . ." nor did anyone "teach the Indians about religion . . ." (page 115). The style absurdly enough continues: "No one taught Indians about religion . . . where they came from or where they were going. Even though it was a mystery, Indians had their own ideas about things . . ." (page 115). One has the right to conclude that Indians had no religion, but merely "ideas about things." A total ignorance regarding the sophistication and pervasiveness of religion among California Indians is demonstrated here. But more to the point is that it is not permitted the Indian to have a systematic and recognized religion in this book! Would it be incorrect to read in such a passage, the meaning that "they did not have a CHRISTIAN religion, therefore they did not have one at all?"

Other distortions appear with regularity. The personality characteristics of the California Indians are reduced to an absurd stereotype. The technique of stereotyping by categorical adjectives which we see applied to various ethnic groups is present here too. The Indian becomes "easygoing," "free," and "happy," "patient," "never worrying." Such behavioral characteristics would have guaranteed starvation and death to California aboriginal populations. Quite the contrary is true, however. Rigidly structured social relationships, technological innovations, trade systems, rituals and philosophy, which aided in the management of Indian resources, were usual in California cultures; but explanations given in this book reflect the very opposite. The data in "California Indian Days" then, appears to be contorted to support definite prejudices. Bauer sees food gathering times as "vacations," and the use of steatite for bowls and jars and arrows as "factors of luck." She says, "a supply of acorns can be found with little work . . ." (page 48), and the Indians are a patient people, who "never hurried or worried very much . . . what they couldn't find one day they found at another time and another place . . ." (page 49).

Life at the mission is described as "secure . . ." (page 136). The author asks "Is this what the Indian really wanted? They had been used to a free life. How hard it must have been for them to stay in one place when they had been so used to roaming, to be farmers instead of food gatherers and hunters. So many kinds of work and living had to be learned . . ." (page 136). While the intention of the author may quite possibly have been to describe the Indian plight in the missions with some sympathy, it is hardly a true statement.

The discovery of gold is correlated with America's interest in California, whereas gold had been discovered long before this time. We are told that the Indian at this time had difficulty understanding a European economic system. They could not understand "the mad scramble for the shiny gold . . ." (page 139). This, despite the fact that a large number of Indians were well integrated into the economy of Mexican California and some were even important rancho owners and officials, in Spanish and Mexican California. The American period is inaccurately credited with protecting Indians. Bauer says that nothing was done to protect the Indians until the 1850's (page 140). A study of the history with the opening of the American period in the 1850's will adequately disprove this statement.

The increasing loss of Indian lands is noted in this way: "Year after year the Indians lost more and more of their land . . ." (page 141). This is a rather passive explanation. It might more accurately have read "more and more land was taken until . . ."

Following several generations of contact with European cultures, Bauer says the Indian is "in a condition of bewilderment . . . Everything is strange to him, life is very different and very fast . . ." (page 143). While this may very well be true in certain instances, it fails to account for the successful adaptation of thousands of California Indians into every phase of contemporary American culture; or for the many educated Indian people in the arts, education, social science and welfare, and the hundreds of college students who are Indian.

Finally, there is addenda to the book, including a chart indicating the locations and main differences among tribes. This, instead of providing additional data, provides instead increased confusion. The charts are set up to compare several aspects of Indian culture: tribal names and languages, territories, clothing and ornaments, houses, foods, baskets, boats, customs, and other information. The categories themselves preclude the possibility of placing emphasis on many significant factors of aboriginal culture. The charts, by omission, would appear to indicate many facets of culture are nonexistent; for example, under the category "houses," they are described for the Yahi but not for the Karok. Is the reader to conclude that the Karok did not have houses? The tribes are not compared, nor are they contrasted, although the format would lend itself to that task. More to the point, is the fact that the selected data is often trivial in nature, adding little understanding or appreciation of the cultures. Sometimes, in fact, the information is incorrect.

In conclusion, we must judge this book as being condescending and patronizing to people of another culture. It is stereotypic in its conception of the people it strives to describe, and inaccurate historically and ethnographically. Furthermore, it deliberately obscures facts of historic importance, such as occur in the omission of the facts of brutality and exploitation occurring throughout the European occupation.

7

The Alcatraz Proclamation: To the Great White Father and All His People
INDIANS OF ALL TRIBES

In November, 1969, a group of 300 Indians occupied the deserted prison-island of Alcatraz in San Francisco Bay, offering to buy the island from the federal government for "$24 in glass beads and cloth." The Indians immediately announced their intention to develop an Indian Cultural Center on Alcatraz Island, including an institute of native American studies, an Indian medical center, an ecological-research center, and an Indian museum. The Alcatraz Proclamation, issued by the Indians of All Tribes, illustrates a new militancy and unity among American Indians.

PROCLAMATION:

TO THE GREAT WHITE FATHER AND ALL HIS PEOPLE

WE, the native Americans, re-claim the land known as Alcatraz Island in the name of all American Indians by right of discovery.

We wish to be fair and honorable in our dealings with the Caucasian inhabitants of this land, and hereby offer the following treaty:

We will purchase said Alcatraz Island for twenty-four dollars (24) in glass beads and red cloth, a precedent set by the white man's purchase of a similar island about 300 years ago. We know that $24 in trade goods for these 16 acres is more than was paid when Manhattan Island was sold, but we know that land values have risen over the years. Our offer of $1.24 per acre is greater than the 47 cents per acre the white men are now paying the California Indians for their land.

We will give to the inhabitants of this island a portion of the land for their own to be held in trust by the American Indian Affairs and by the bureau of Caucasian Affairs to hold in perpetuity—for as long as the sun shall rise and the rivers go down to the sea. We will further guide the inhabitants in the proper way of living. We will offer them our religion,

SOURCE: *Indians of All Tribes News*, I (January 1970), pp. 2–3. Reprinted by permission of the Council of the Alcatraz Indians.

our education, our life-ways, in order to help them achieve our level of civilization and thus raise them and all their white brothers up from their savage and unhappy state. We offer this treaty in good faith and wish to be fair and honorable in our dealings with all white men.

We feel that this so-called Alcatraz is more th[a]n suitable for an Indian reservation, as determined by the white man's own standards. By this we mean that this place resembles most Indian reservations in that:

1. It is isolated from modern facilities, and without adequate means of transportation.
2. It has no fresh running water.
3. It has inadequate sanitation facilities.
4. There are no oil or mineral rights.
5. There is no industry and so unemployment is very great.
6. There are no health care facilities.
7. The soil is rocky and non-productive; and the land does not support game.
8. There are no educational facilities.
9. The population has always exceeded the land base.
10. The population has always been held as prisoners and kept dependent upon others.

Further, it would be fitting and symbolic that ships from all over the world, entering the Golden Gate, would first see Indian land, and thus be reminded of the true history of this nation. This tiny island would be a symbol of the great lands once ruled by free and noble Indians.

What use will we make of this land?

Since the San Francisco Indian Center burned down, there is no place for Indians to assemble and carry on tribal life here in the white man's city. Therefore, we plan to develop on this island several Indian institutions:

1. A CENTER FOR NATIVE AMERICAN STUDIES will be developed which will educate them to the skills and knowledge relevant to improve the lives and spirits of all Indian peoples. Attached to this center will be traveling universities, managed by Indians, which will go to the Indian Reservations, learning those necessary and relevant materials now about.
2. AN AMERICAN INDIAN SPIRITUAL CENTER which will practice our ancient tribal religious and sacred healing ceremonies. Our cultural arts will be featured and our young people trained in music, dance, and healing rituals.
3. AN INDIAN CENTER OF ECOLOGY which will train and sup-

port our young people in scientific research and practice to restore our lands and waters to their pure and natural state. We will work to de-pollute the air and waters of the Bay Area. We will seek to restore fish and animal life to the area and to revitalize sea life which has been threatened by the white man's way. We will set up facilities to desalt sea water for human benefit.

4. A GREAT INDIAN TRAINING SCHOOL will be developed to teach our people how to make a living in the world, improve our standard of living, and to end hunger and unemployment among all our people. This training school will include a center for Indian arts and crafts, and an Indian restaurant serving native foods, which will restore Indian culinary arts. This center will display Indian arts and offer Indian foods to the public, so that all may know of the beauty and spirit of the traditional INDIAN ways.

Some of the present buildings will be taken over to develop an AMERICAN INDIAN MUSEUM, which will depict our native food & other cultural contributions we have given to the world. Another part of the museum will present some of the things the white man has given to the Indians in return for the land and life he took: disease, alcohol, poverty and cultural decimation (As symbolized by old tin cans, barbed wire, rubber tires, plastic containers, etc). Part of the museum will remain a dungeon to symbolize both those Indian captives who were incarcerated for challenging white authority, and those who were imprisoned on reservations. The museum will show the noble and the tragic events of Indian history, including the broken treaties, the documentary of the Trail of Tears, the Massacre of Wounded Knee, as well as the victory over Yellow Hair Custer and his army.

In the name of all Indians, therefore, we re-claim this island for our Indian nations, for all these reasons. We feel this claim is just and proper, and that this land should rightfully be granted to us for as long as the rivers shall run and the sun shall shine.

Signed,

Indians Of All Tribes
November 1969
San Francisco, California

PART II
California's Special Race Problem: The Asians

A Jap is a Jap.
Lieutenant General John L. De Witt (1942)

[The evacuation of the Japanese Americans gave] constitutional sanctity for a policy of mass incarceration under military auspices . . . That process betrayed all Americans.
Morton Grodzins, *Americans Betrayed* (1949)

THE presence of large numbers of Asians is *the* factor that has made the California ethnic experience unique. Although Asians, immigrant and native born, have also contributed to the growth of other western states, only in the Golden State did the Asian presence become a major issue in state politics, an issue that had national and international ramifications. (See the census data in Selection 9.) The Chinese began coming to California during the Gold Rush—the Chinese characters for California can also be translated "Golden Mountain"—and were at first welcomed by almost all as needed adjuncts to the labor force. Within a few years, however, they became hated and feared by their fellow Californians, including many of the dispossessed Californios who were perhaps pleased to find a group even more despised than themselves. Although much has been written about the uniqueness of the Asian migrants, their experience had much in common with other late nineteenth-century newcomers to America. (See Selection 8.) The anti-Chinese movement began in the mining districts and the metropolis of San Francisco, but soon spread throughout the state. (See Selections 10 and 11.) California's anti-Oriental crusade won its first great national victory in 1882 when Congress passed the Chinese Exclusion Act, which is also significant as the first ethnically discriminatory immigration legislation in our history. Although this international insult caused bitter feelings in China, the impotence of that nation gave our diplomats little cause for concern about the Chinese reactions.

Beginning in the 1890s a new Asian "menace" appeared as significant numbers of Japanese began to arrive in California. (See Selection 12.) By the first decade of the twentieth century a formidable anti-Japanese movement had developed and soon spread the length and breadth of the state. (See Selections 13 and 14.) The culmination of the movement came in 1924 when Congress gave organized California racism its second great triumph with the insertion of language that resulted in Japanese exclusion under the Immigration Act of 1924. The following decade saw the anti-Oriental crusade focus on yet a third group, the Filipinos. (See Selection 15.)

But the real triumph of the anti-Japanese movement occurred in 1942 with the evacuation of all the Japanese—citizen and alien alike—from California and the rest of the Pacific slope. Among those clamoring in favor of this atrocity was the man who later became the greatest Chief Justice of this century, Earl Warren. (See Selection 16.) Justified as a "military necessity," we now know that even from a strictly military point of view the Japanese incarceration inhibited rather than strengthened the war effort. (See Selection 17.) From the standpoint of the Constitution of the United States, it was a disaster.

Since the war, most of California's resident Asians have become progressively middle class; one eminent sociologist has styled the Japanese Americans "our model minority." Yet, as income and education data reveal, despite their impressive educational achievement, Asians in California are still economically disadvantaged. (See Selections 8 and 9.) Whereas most voices in the contemporary Asian American community call for moderation and deplore ethnic militancy, some of the younger members of the community have become radicalized and see most of their elders as "bananas," or "yellow on the outside but white on the inside."

The Asian American success story is not universal. Some of the worst slums in California are in San Francisco's Chinatown, where thousands—largely recent immigrants from Hong Kong and Taiwan —are inadequately housed, clothed, and fed. Most Filipinos are still largely restricted to employment in California's "factories in the fields"; many of them are important and often overlooked allies of the Mexican Americans who dominate Cesar Chavez's farm workers movement.

The Asian American has played a significant role in California's past; the role that he will play in her future is not as clear. Many community leaders would have him ally with the white establishment forces; others, primarily among the young, see him as an important part of what some call a "Third World" movement composed of all non-Anglos. The majority of Asian Americans seem to lean closer to the first position; when blacks move into an Oriental neighborhood, the tendency is for the latter to flee to the suburbs, a reaction identical to that of most whites. But Asians, because of their history and their color, are not exactly like whites, and the ways in which they come to grips with their ambiguous status is for them and the future to decide.

8

Westerners from the East:
Oriental Immigrants Reappraised
ROGER DANIELS

In this retrospective essay, first delivered to the Western History Association in 1963, the general outlines of Asian immigration to the United States are sketched and brought into a national and a regional perspective.

DESPITE their generally democratic outlook, western historians have done something less than justice to a group that found much injustice in the West—the Chinese and Japanese immigrants of the last hundred and sixteen years. Although in respect to some immigrant groups sheer neglect is the major failing, that charge does not apply here. From Hubert Howe Bancroft to the present day, historians of the American West have paid a good deal of attention to Asian migrants, although the treatment of contemporary scholars is a far cry from the San Franciscan's fulminations against "Mongolians." For all this improvement, however, the coverage in western (Pacific coast and California) histories is deficient and still reminiscent of the prejudice which disgraced the first century of Oriental migration to these parts. But rather than detail the historiography of this mistreatment, this essay will assay an interpretation of the major features of Asian immigrant life in western society to the present day.

The first thing to do, of course, is to get the basic demographic facts straight. Despite all sorts of loose writing about "hordes" and "waves" of immigrants, the numerical incidence of Orientals was very small when compared to the influx of other new immigrants. First came the Chinese, who began arriving just after the forty-niners; by the sixties they were considered a distinct social problem, and by the seventies most white Californians were convinced that Chinese immigration must stop, with some holding Dennis Kearney's extremist position. Chinese population continued to grow, however, despite the sandlotter and more respectable

SOURCE: Roger Daniels, "Westerners from the East: Oriental Immigrants Reappraised," *Pacific Historical Review*, 35 (November, 1966), pp. 373–383. Copyright © 1966 by the Pacific Coast Branch, American Historical Association. Reprinted by permission of the author and the Branch.

proponents of exclusion, and almost certainly reached its peak in the mid-seventies when there were 110,000 to 115,000 Chinese in the nation, all but a few of these in the Far West and more than 70 per cent of the total in California. In the early seventies, perhaps one Californian in ten was a Chinese. The opposition of their fellow Californians was essentially economic, but had distinct social overtones. As one contemporary put it, John Chinaman "worked cheap and smelled bad." The Chinese, as every one knows, were subjected to constant indignities, harassment, and murder, both legal and extralegal. In 1882, when the Chinese Exclusion Act was signed by President Arthur, the Chinese issue ceased to be central to California politics, and Chinese population in the state began what was to be a steep four-decade decline. By the time exclusion was made "permanent," in 1902, Chinese were less than 3 per cent of California's population.

At about this time, however, Japanese began to come in significant numbers to California and the rest of the west. A partial reenactment of the Chinese episode ensued, with certain differences. Japanese tended to achieve higher economic status, became landowners in significant numbers, and, perhaps even more important, had a modern and aggressive nation ready to speak for them. Although the international consequences of the anti-Japanese movement were much more serious than those of the anti-Chinese, the domestic result was essentially the same. By 1924 the golden door was slammed shut by Congress, and for almost twenty years there was no legal immigration of Orientals to this country. Japanese have never amounted to as much as three per cent of the California population, while on the national scale the figure is miniscule: Oriental population, Japanese and Chinese combined, never constituted as much as four-tenths of one per cent of the total. Yet the national political parties and the national legislature were willing for more than three-quarters of a century to have our laws explicitly discriminate against Asian immigrants and their native-born children. From this point of view, then, the Oriental immigrant has been in a special category: his was the first ethnic group against whom our immigration laws discriminated, and the only group ever totally barred.

Apart from this, however, apart from mere race and underprivileged legal position, was there anything different about these people? Was there something that set them apart from the tens of millions of other immigrants who came here? Historians have thought so and still think so. One survey of American immigration specifically excluded Orientals from its pages because "the study of European immigration should not be complicated for the student by confusing it with the very different problems of Chinese and Japanese immigration." Another treated the Asians at some length, but insisted that their history was but "a brief and strange interlude in the general account of the great migrations to America." In general, historians of the last few decades have shown little sympathy with the excluders, but have combined this with very little understanding of the excluded, insisting or implying that Asians were somehow outside the canon of immigrant history. Other immigrant groups were celebrated for what they had accomplished; Orientals were important for what was done to them.

This concentration on the excluders rather than the excluded is not a mere eccentricity. Part of the problem is the great paucity of immigrant materials, America letters and the like, and the unfortunate fact that if they did come to hand, few, if any, western historians would be able to read them. This has resulted, even for the most recent scholarship, in works that treat the Oriental immigrants as faceless, nameless groups, mere economic pawns in the hands of others, or of the blind forces of the economy.

But even more important, perhaps, is the facile, not always voiced assumption that Orientals were, somehow, different. It seems much more reasonable to make the opposite assumption: that immigrants from Asia were, first of all, immigrants, and that, until uncontrovertible evidence to the contrary is offered, the generalizations which apply to most immigrants also apply to Asians. None of this is to deny that there were cultural differences between immigrants from Asia and immigrants from Europe, but of course there were and are differences between immigrants from different geographical and social strata of Europe and between Asian immigrants, as will be pointed out later. Let us assume, then, that both the Chinese and Japanese were essentially "new" rather than "old" immigrants. Most of them came to this country during the great industrial and agricultural expansion which took place between the end of the Civil War and the outbreak of World War I. Most of them did not have initially the capital necessary to set up their own business or to buy a farm; most of them did not have the education or training to practice a learned profession or to enter one of the skilled trades. So far the parallel between the Asians and those from eastern and southern Europe is almost perfect. There was one major difference; most of the European immigrants stayed East and became unskilled industrial labor. The Chinese and Japanese were westerners, and largely Californians at that. Although some of the Chinese were employed as cheap unskilled and semi-skilled labor, the real need was for agricultural rather than industrial toil. From a labor force point of view then, the chief difference between immigrants was that one group became industrial proletarians while the other became agricultural proletarians. And we must remember that this difference was dictated by the nature of the region to which they came rather than by their own choice.

Immigration, however, is more than a matter of economics. Many of the most virulent opponents of Chinese and Japanese immigrants grudgingly admitted their economic worth; however, they argued, since Orientals were unassimilable, were hostile to American institutions, and particularly since they did not intend to stay in the United States and become real Americans, that Asians should be excluded. Not all nineteenth-century American historians accepted the western judgment that any white man was superior to any Oriental. Woodrow Wilson, for example, in his *History of the American People,* insisted that the Chinese

were more to be desired, as workmen if not as citizens, than most of the coarse crew that came crowding in every year at the eastern ports. They had, no doubt, many an unsavory habit, bred unwholesome squalor in the crowded quarters in which they most abounded in the western seaports, and seemed separated by their very nature from the people among whom they had come to live; but it was their skill, their intelligence, their hardy power of labor, their knack at succeeding and driving duller rivals out, rather than their alien habits, that made them feared and hated. . . . The unlikely fellows who came in at the eastern ports were tolerated because they usurped no place but the very lowest in the scale of labor.

Archetypical perhaps of far western opinion were the views of Chester Rowell, Fresno editor and brain truster to Hiram Johnson, who feared, in 1907, that the Japanese might annex California—that "by peacefully overrunning the land they could . . . Orientalize" our culture. It is not accidental that the two writers I have quoted each belonged, in his own way, to the persuasion generally known as "progressive." As a rule it was the liberal rather than the conservative, the labor organizer rather than the employer, the proponent of change rather than the defender of the status quo who sparked and organized the first half-century of anti-Oriental agitation. Although there are a number of instances of Orientals being used as strike-breakers, these incidents in no wise justify one socialist characterization of the immigrants as "an inflowing horde of alien scabs." In fact, in the few recorded cases where they were admitted to membership, Orientals seem to have been creditable trade unionists. "New immigrant" conflicts with organized labor were nationwide, as Europeans too were viewed by labor leaders as unorganizable and thus largely excluded from the labor movement until the CIO organizing drives of the thirties and forties. This conflict is reflected in labor's demand for immigration restriction which the middle class progressives were eager to satisfy. In this, western labor led the way, as the problem of seemingly unorganizable new immigrant competition first became acute in San Francisco during the winter of 1869–1870. This struggle against what seemed to be unfair competition—a view shared by men as diverse as Dennis Kearney, Samuel Gompers, E. A. Ross and Morris Hillquit—became an important part of the program of organized labor. One can be repelled by the racist, anti-immigrant views expressed in the course of the struggle and still realize, however sadly, that within the context of the times they could hardly be otherwise. Since, with the close of the frontier, continued immigration appeared to many to be primarily a source of cheap labor, some kind of restriction became almost a foregone conclusion. The West's successful struggle against Orientals served as a persuasive example to labor and the nation.

How did Oriental immigrants react to this long campaign of harassment? In part by retreating into areas of the economy where their conflicts with organized labor would be minimal. By the early twentieth century practically none were found in the growing western industrial sector, and the statistical incidence of small agricultural and commercial proprietors among them becomes striking. In 1929, for example, Orientals in the United States operated 50 per cent more commercial establishments per capita than did the general population. While this has been interpreted as indicating a great success in pursuing the American Dream, my view is that this mostly represented a retreat from competition, a way of not assimilating rather than successful assimilation. These small businesses tended to follow Oriental rather than American operational patterns. That is, there usually was a high level of employment vis-à-vis gross, with maximum use being made of family members of all ages. Even when employees were not family members, as in the larger Chinese laundries, patriarchial rather than managerial practices prevailed, along with longer hours and lower wages than in the industry as a whole. In New York City, in 1963, the typical laundry owner provided two hot meals, usually ate with his workers, and in general served as elder brother as well as employer.

Although much of their earliest employment was non-urban—in mines, railroad construction, and even more important, agriculture—Chinese quickly abandoned rural areas and headed for the cities. The Japanese, conversely, continue in agriculture where today in California one Japanese in four is employed, as opposed to fewer than 5 per cent of the whites. No other aspect of Oriental immigrant life has been so well investigated. It was Oriental labor that made much of California's agriculture possible in the nineteenth century; in the twentieth, Japanese innovators helped to reshape it. The Japanese tradition of intensive cultivation made them unmatchable competitors, and deeply resented when pitted against those who followed the resource-intensive practices typical of American agriculture. By 1920, Japanese controlled about one per cent of California's farm land; they marketed 10 per cent of the dollar volume of California's crops. They brought new crops as well as new techniques. George Shima (1863–1926), the millionaire "potato king," not only introduced successful commercial potato farming to the Pacific coast, but also pioneered corporative managerial methods within the agricultural empire he ran on reclaimed islands in the San Joaquin Valley.

The differences between Chinese and Japanese in this country are noticeable in more than occupation and abode. One recent study has attempted to explain this by pointing to the fact that, in the Nippon from which the Japanese came, a "modern" kinship structure had already evolved, while this was not the case in China. Without entering into the problems of determinism, familial or otherwise, it seems to me that there is a much simpler answer. When the exclusion law stopped immigration, the sex ratio of the Chinese population was about fifteen males for every female. This caused a steadily declining Chinese population until 1930 and gave the Chinese community, which had all sorts of anti-assimilationist forces working within and without it, the additional handicap of having more greybeards than young men. This double demographic imbalance, sex and age, was exacerbated by legal and cultural phenomena. From 1882 to 1943 not even a citizen Chinese could bring an alien Chinese wife into the United States; because of the extreme woman shortage many went to China to get married. The children of these unions were citizens and could be brought here with the proper papers and a little bit of luck. This migration, which helps to explain why so many citizen Chinese have not mastered English, was dominated by male rather than female offspring. However, one should not assume that the Chinese took no active assimilatory steps. In 1895 a group of native-born Chinese formed the Native Sons of the Golden State, which was a typically second generation organization, reminiscent more of the Sons of Italy or the American Hellenic Educational Progressive Association than the notorious and somewhat maligned tongs.

In the Japanese community, this sexual imbalance, although quite extreme in the early days of immigration, as it was with all new immigrants, was largely mitigated by more than a decade of "picture bride" immigration, a phenomenon not unknown among the Europeans. The irony of the Japanese situation was that, just as the clash between the young men and the greybeards should have been most acute, it was declared no contest by Uncle Sam, who indiscriminately herded enemy-alien father and citizen son into concentration camps. This hastened the Nisei or second generation take over, which was coming anyway. For those interested in these communities, there are two charming memoirs which illuminate, in a thousand ways, their difference. Monica Sone, *Nisei Daughter*, tells of a Seattle girlhood, while Jade Snow Wong, *Fifth Chinese Daughter*, deals with life in San Francisco's Chinatown (this is as sensitive a book about an American foreign language community as any I know).

The war years brought changes for both groups. Chinese changed from

culture villains—Fu Manchu and the Hatchet Man—to culture heroes—
Terry and the Pirates and Mme. Chiang Kai-Shek, while Japanese became
first subhuman—low enough to drop an A-bomb on—and then almost
superhuman. This latter quick change is nicely shown in two Gallup
polls: in 1942 Americans found Japanese "treacherous, sly, cruel and warlike" while in 1961 they were "hard-working, artistic, intelligent and
progressive." It should be noted that our new sophistication in foreign
affairs—there are "good" and "bad" Chinese both on Taiwan and the
mainland—has prevented Mao's unpopularity from rubbing off on American Chinese.

The war years also brought the first legal crack in exclusion: Congress,
a little embarrassed by domestic racism in the war against the Axis,
repealed Chinese exclusion in 1943. Nine years later the otherwise discriminatory McCarran-Walter Act token-integrated Japanese and other
Asians into the National Origins quota system. Other events which tended
to ameliorate feelings about Orientals were the admission of Hawaii—
which sends Chinese and Japanese to Congress—and the growing inter-
nationalism of American life.

Despite all these pluses, however, statistics demonstrate conclusively
that Chinese and Japanese are still discriminated against. In the nation
today they number 700,000, almost two-thirds of them Japanese. Since
the largest single concentration is in California where one-third of all
Japanese and two-fifths of all Chinese live, California census data can
be used to document the charge. The discrimination shows most clearly
in the education and income data—it is a good rule of thumb that they
go hand-in-hand in our technological society. For Orientals this is a
half-truth. Although California's Chinese and Japanese are better educated than California's white population, they don't get the money which
traditionally goes with the sheepskin. Although college graduates are
11 per cent more likely to be found among Japanese males than among
white males, and 24 per cent more frequent among Chinese males, white
men make considerably more money. For every $51.00 received by a
white Californian, Japanese get $43.00 and Chinese $38.00. If we look
only at the very well off, the imbalance is even greater. A white man's
chances of achieving an annual income of $10,000 or more are 78 per
cent better than for a Chinese and 57 per cent better than for a Japanese.

To summarize the history and the data, the Orientals in general and
the Japanese in particular have come a long way in their pursuit of the
American Dream. Nothing is said here about social behavior, assuming
that the relative nonoccurrence of things like juvenile delinquency and
venereal disease among what westerners used to regard as "unclean Orientals" is proverbial. But it should be crystal clear that despite behavior,
despite achievement, once you've been number 2, you have to try much
harder than number 1, just to catch up.

But in the final analysis the categories and constructs dealt with in the foregoing are but the bones of history: for real insight into the past, flesh and blood is needed—the flesh and blood of human experience. This essay will offer two examples of this kind of substance. Since there is a large-scale research project now at work on a history of the Japanese in the United States, Chinese examples will be furnished. Unless we come across a memoir account or a batch of letters, how can we tell what it was like to be a Chinese shopkeeper in Sacramento in 1890? Probably some insight into this can be gained by looking at the accounts of Oriental immigration into other "Anglo-Saxon" commonwealth, where the first immigrants came somewhat later and thus survived to fall into the clutches of inquiring sociologists. The following account, by an immigrant to Wellington, New Zealand, in the early 1920's, who worked in his "uncle's" fruitshop, might have some relevance:

My generation . . . really worked for a living, [the pioneer told Ng Bickleen Fong of the University at Otago,] not like the young Chinese of today. We had to open the shop at 7 a.m. . . . we closed between midnight and 1. Then we had to clean the shop and get ready for reopening a few hours later. . . . Except for two meals we had no time off during the day. On Sundays we slept in, cleaned the shop, washed the vegetables, helped to cook a big dinner, then went to church or for a stroll outside—that was our only recreation. . . . Saturday nights were a nightmare that we all dreaded . . . drunkards would come into the shop for some fun. Shelves of fruit were pulled down . . . tomatoes . . . were thrown at us . . . the police didn't do much. . . . In those days, instead of delivering in a truck, we had to carry the case or sack on our shoulder. . . . Not infrequently we were pushed over by people who wanted "some fun," our goods scattered in the street amidst a chorus of "Ching Chong Chinaman." It made our blood boil, but we kept our poker face. We were Chinese.

A little bit closer to home, there is a great deal that western historians could do to bring these lost pioneers back to literary life. Not at all typical is the second example, a Chinese immigrant who became a Montana farmer, married a Swedish girl, raised a family, and won the respect of his neighbors.

He was born Sing On somewhere in China about the year of Lincoln's first election. In 1873, somehow, he arrived in Montana Territory, living first in Helena, where he supported himself and attended public school. He then moved, first to Chouteau and then to Teton county where he farmed 480 acres. In 1879 the Montana Territorial Assembly passed an act changing his name to George Taylor, and on some later patriotic date he, himself, embellished it to George Washington Taylor. In 1890 he married Lena Bloom, their union being blessed by four boys and three girls. In early 1917, his eldest son, Albert Henry Taylor, was a sergeant of Company D, 2nd Montana Regiment, serving on the Mexican border. The Taylors can be found, like flies in amber, embedded in a petition of the Montana Legislature which asked Congress to grant citizenship to the father who was certified as an "honorable . . . and upright man . . . opposed to anarchy and polygamy." The 65th Congress did not act on that petition, and the legislative record contains nothing more of the Taylor family.

Neither Miss Fong's shopkeeper, nor George Washington Taylor, nor anyone like them is now in the history books; this condition should not be a permanent one.

9

A Demographic and Socioeconomic Perspective

CALIFORNIA FAIR EMPLOYMENT PRACTICES COMMISSION

This data, extrapolated from the 1960 census, puts into demographic and socioeconomic focus the status of Californians of Asian ancestry. Note comments regarding this data in Selection 8, p. 64.

Population

CALIFORNIANS of Japanese, Chinese, and Filipino descent totaled 318,376 in 1960. Among the 50 states, California was second only to Hawaii in residents of Japanese and Filipino extraction; its Chinese population was double that of any other state (table A). More than one-third of all United States residents of Japanese, Chinese, and Filipino ancestry lived in California in 1960.

POPULATION, 1960

Ancestry	United States	California	California as Percent of United States
Japanese	464,332	157,317	33.9
Chinese	237,292	95,600	40.3
Filipino	176,310	65,459	37.1
Total	877,934	318,376	36.3

Although less numerous than Californians of Spanish surname (1,426,-538) and Negroes (883,861), California's Japanese, Chinese, and Filipino population is growing rapidly. High rates of natural increase and sub-

SOURCE: California Fair Employment Practices Commission, State of California, Department of Industrial Relations, Division of Fair Employment Practices, *Californians of Japanese, Chinese, Filipino Ancestry: Population, Employment, Income, Education* (San Francisco, 1965), 52 pp.

JAPANESE, CHINESE, AND FILIPINO POPULATION
UNITED STATES AND SELECTED STATES, 1960

Japanese	Japanese Population	Percent of Total Japanese Population in the United States
United States, total	464,332	100.0
Hawaii	203,455	43.8
California	157,317	33.9
Washington	16,652	3.6
Illinois	14,074	3.0
New York	8,702	1.9
Colorado	6,846	1.5
Oregon	5,016	1.1
Utah	4,371	0.9
Texas	4,053	0.9
Other states	43,846	9.4

Chinese	Chinese Population	Percent of Total Chinese Population in the United States
United States, total	237,292	100.0
California	95,600	40.3
Hawaii	38,197	16.1
New York	37,573	15.8
Illinois	7,047	3.0
Massachusetts	6,745	2.8
Washington	5,491	2.3
Texas	4,172	1.8
Oregon	2,995	1.3
Arizona	2,936	1.2
Other states	36,536	15.4

Filipino	Filipino Population	Percent of Total Filipino Population in the United States
United States, total	176,310	100.0
Hawaii	69,070	39.2
California	65,459	37.1
Washington	7,110	4.0
New York	5,403	3.1
Illinois	3,587	2.0
Other states	25,681	14.6

SOURCE: U. S. Bureau of the Census. Based on a complete count of the population.

CALIFORNIANS OF CHINESE, JAPANESE, AND FILIPINO ANCESTRY, BY SEX
1850–1960

Year	Total Population			Chinese			Japanese			Filipino		
	Both sexes	Men	Women	Both sexes	Men	Women	Both sexes	Men	Women	Both sexes	Men	Women
1850	92,597	85,580	7,017	[a]791	[a]789	[a]2	—	—	—	—	—	—
1860	379,994	273,337	106,657	34,933	33,149	1,784	—	—	—	—	—	—
1870	560,247	349,479	210,768	49,277	45,404	3,873	33	25	8	—	—	—
1880	864,694	518,176	346,518	75,132	71,244	3,888	86	81	5	—	—	—
1890	1,213,398	702,779	510,619	72,472	69,382	3,090	1,147	1,036	111	—	—	—
1900	1,485,053	820,531	664,522	45,753	42,297	3,456	10,151	9,598	553	—	—	—
1910	2,377,549	1,322,978	1,054,571	36,248	33,003	3,245	41,356	35,116	6,240	5	[b]	[b]
1920	3,426,861	1,813,591	1,613,270	28,812	24,230	4,582	71,952	45,414	26,538	2,674	[b]	[b]
1930	5,677,251	2,942,595	2,734,656	37,361	27,988	9,373	97,456	56,440	41,016	30,470	28,625	1,845
1940	6,907,387	3,515,730	3,391,657	39,556	27,331	12,225	93,717	52,550	41,167	31,408	[b]	[b]
1950	10,586,223	5,295,629	5,290,594	58,324	36,051	22,273	84,956	45,633	39,323	40,424	30,819	9,605
1960	15,717,204	7,836,707	7,880,497	95,600	53,627	41,973	157,317	78,453	78,864	65,459	42,422	23,037

[a] Source: Estimated by G. B. Densmore in *The Chinese in California* published in 1880.
[b] Not available.
SOURCE: U. S. Bureau of the Census.

69

stantial immigration between 1950 and 1960 gave rise to a 73 percent increase in the State's combined population of the three racial groups. The Japanese showed the highest growth rate—85 per cent—during the decade. This compares with a 64 percent increase for Chinese and a 62 percent gain for Filipinos. The white population grew by 46 percent during the decade.

California's Japanese population in 1960 was almost equally divided between men and women. Chinese men outnumbered women by a ratio of 56 to 44. Among Filipinos, the sex ratio was even more unequal—men outnumbered women by almost 2 to 1.

Men in all three groups were older, on the whole, than the women. The difference was greatest among Filipinos: 48 percent of the men were 45 years of age or older, compared with 10 percent of the women. The age disparity between Filipino men and women, as well as the larger number of men than women, reflects the immigration of large numbers of single Filipino men following World War I to work in California *agriculture*.

Japanese, Chinese, and Filipino women were comparatively young. The under 35 year age group accounted for 78 percent of the Filipino women, 70 percent of the Chinese women, and 65 percent of the Japanese women. Fifty-five percent of the white women were under 35.

AGE DISTRIBUTION OF POPULATION, BY SEX, CALIFORNIA, 1960

Age	Japanese Male	Female	Chinese Male	Female	Filipino Male	Female	White Male	Female
Under 35	61.7	65.0	58.8	69.7	46.0	78.0	57.9	55.0
35–44	18.2	17.7	14.6	13.6	6.4	11.9	14.4	14.6
45 and over	20.1	17.3	26.6	16.7	47.6	10.1	27.7	30.4
Total	100.0	100.0	100.0	100.0	100.0	100.0	100.0	100.0

Place of Birth and In-migration

Of all Japanese Americans in 13 western states in 1960, 82 percent were native-born (born in the United States, its territories, or possessions).[1] The proportion of native-born Chinese Americans in the 13 states was

[1] Data not available for California alone. States included were: California, Alaska, Arizona, Colorado, Hawaii, Idaho, Montana, Nevada, New Mexico, Oregon, Utah, Washington, and Wyoming.

considerably lower—69 percent. Among Filipinos, 52 percent were American-born.

One-fifth of all Japanese and Filipino Californians had migrated here from other states or countries since 1955. In-migration among the Japanese was equally divided between other countries and other states—10 percent from each. More Filipinos had migrated from other countries (14 percent) than from other states (7 percent). Californians of Chinese descent had the lowest in-migration rates during the past five years both from other countries (7 percent) and from other states (5 percent).

Area of Residence

Between 1950 and 1960, the three racial groups participated in the general movement of the State's population from rural to urban areas. The proportion of Japanese living in urban areas rose from 70 percent to 87 percent. The Chinese, already overwhelmingly concentrated in cities and towns in 1950 (94 percent in urban areas) made a further shift (to 96 percent) in 1960. The shift from rural to urban areas was greatest, however, among Filipinos—from 60 percent in 1950 to 80 percent in 1960.

The majority of California's Japanese population, 52 percent, resided in the Los Angeles-Long Beach Metropolitan Area in 1960. Sixteen percent were in the San Francisco-Oakland Metropolitan Area. The largest group of Chinese residents, 55 percent, were in the San Francisco-Oakland Metropolitan Area. Twenty-one percent were in the Los Angeles-Long Beach Metropolitan Area.

The Filipino population was more widely dispersed throughout the State than were the Japanese and Chinese. One-third were in the San Francisco-Oakland Metropolitan Area; 20 percent were in Los Angeles-Long Beach. Thirty-two percent of all Filipinos lived outside the State's major metropolitan areas.

Educational Attainment

There were striking differences in the educational attainments of the three racial groups in 1960. Both Japanese men and women were ahead of the white population in the level of education achieved. Eighty percent of both Japanese men and women had completed one or more years of high school, compared with 73 percent of white men and 76 percent of white women. The same relationship held at the college level: 29 and 21 percent of Japanese men and women had completed at least one year of college, compared with 24 and 20 percent of white men and women.

The educational picture for the Chinese was one of extremes; a relatively high proportion of both men and women had completed at least one year of college, but approximately 40 percent of both Chinese men and women had not gone beyond eighth grade. Many of these (16 percent of the men and 19 percent of the women) were reported as having had no schooling at all.

More than half of all Filipino men and almost one-third of the women had not gone beyond the eighth grade. Filipino women achieved a higher education at all levels than Filipino men. Filipino women had the highest proportion among all racial groups, including whites, with at least one year of college.

EDUCATIONAL ATTAINMENT	PERCENT OF POPULATION 14 YEARS OLD AND OVER	
Not having gone beyond 8th grade	Male	Female
Filipino	53.1	30.6
Spanish surname	51.5	48.0
Chinese	40.8	38.7
Negro	37.9	34.0
White (including Spanish surname)	27.2	24.4
Japanese	19.5	20.1
Having completed one or more years of high school		
Filipino	46.9	69.4
Spanish surname	48.5	52.0
Chinese	59.2	61.3
Negro	62.1	66.0
White (including Spanish surname)	72.8	75.6
Japanese	80.5	79.9
Having completed one or more years of college		
Spanish surname	8.8	6.2
Negro	12.7	13.6
Filipino	13.4	24.3
White (including Spanish surname)	24.1	19.6
Japanese	28.8	20.6
Chinese	29.2	23.2

Industry Distribution

In 1960, the largest proportion of Japanese, 25 percent, and of Filipinos, 29 percent, were employed in *agriculture*. Although Japanese and Filipinos together comprised only 1.7 percent of the State's total employment, they accounted for 9.3 percent of all those employed in *agriculture, forestry, and fisheries*.

The largest proportion of Chinese, 39 percent, worked in *wholesale and retail trade*. *Manufacturing* industries accounted for the second largest group—16 percent.

The industry pattern of employed workers varied by metropolitan area. In Los Angeles-Long Beach, a larger proportion of Japanese were employed in *manufacturing and trade*, 22 percent in each, than in *agriculture*, 19 percent. Of the Filipinos in this area, 27 percent were in *manufacturing* and 26 percent in *trade*, with only 5 percent in *agriculture*.

In the San Francisco-Oakland Metropolitan Area, the largest proportion of Japanese, 20 percent, worked in *personal service* industries. Seventeen percent were in *trade;* 15 percent in *professional and related services*. Of the Filipinos employed in the Bay Area, *trade* accounted for 17 percent and *manufacturing* for 14 percent.

There was less variation in the industry distribution of Chinese workers by metropolitan area. *Trade* accounted for the largest proportion in all metropolitan areas for which figures were available: 38 percent in Los Angeles-Long Beach, 35 percent in San Francisco-Oakland, and 41 percent in Sacramento.

Occupation

The agricultural background of Japanese and Filipino workers in California was evident in their 1960 occupational structure. Among Japanese men, 21 percent were *farmers and farm managers;* another 9 percent were *farm laborers and foremen*. Of the Filipino men, 3 percent were *farmers and farm managers;* 28 percent were *farm laborers and foremen*.

The concentration of Chinese workers in urban centers was reflected in their occupations. Twenty-one percent of the Chinese men worked in *service occupations*, except private household; 14 percent were in *managerial and proprietorship* positions.

Professional and technical occupations accounted for a sizable proportion of both Chinese and Japanese men, 17 percent and 15 percent, respectively. Only 4 percent of Filipino men were in these occupations. More than half of all Filipino men were either *farm laborers or service workers*.

A shift toward more highly skilled occupations during the last decade is evident among men in all three racial groups, as shown below.

PERCENT OF EMPLOYED MEN 14 YEARS OF
AGE OR OLDER

Industry	Filipino 1950	Filipino 1960	Japanese 1950	Japanese 1960	Chinese 1950	Chinese 1960
Total, California	100.0	100.0	100.0	100.0	100.0	100.0
Farm laborers and foremen	48.9	27.5	19.4	9.2	2.3	0.8
Service workers, except private household	23.1	26.2	5.4	3.5	26.4	20.6
Operatives and kindred workers	6.4	10.8	6.5	9.1	13.3	12.1
Farmers and farm managers	5.8	2.9	17.1	21.4	2.2	1.2
Laborers, except farm and mine	4.0	5.0	17.9	5.9	2.2	1.9
Craftsmen, foremen, and kindred workers	3.4	6.7	5.2	10.4	5.1	6.6
Clerical, sales, and kindred workers	2.5	5.5	8.8	12.7	17.2	18.2
Managers, officials, and proprietors, except farm	2.0	2.0	8.6	7.9	20.9	14.3
Private household workers	1.8	1.0	3.2	1.1	3.0	1.4
Professional, technical, and kindred workers	0.8	3.6	4.4	15.0	6.3	16.9
Other and not reported	1.3	8.8	3.5	3.8	1.1	6.0

Chinese and Japanese women were employed outside the home more extensively than either Filipino or white women. Of every 100 women 14 years of age or older, the number in the civilian labor force was: Chinese, 47; Japanese, 46; Filipino, 35; white, 35.

Approximately one-third of all employed Japanese, Chinese, and Filipino women were *clerical workers*. The second largest occupational group for Japanese and Chinese women was *operatives and kindred workers;* for Filipino women, *service, except private household.*

Unemployment

Unemployment rates in 1960 for both Japanese and Chinese men and women were lower than for white men and women. Among Japanese men 14 years old and over, 2.6 percent were unemployed, compared with

5.5 percent for white men. For Japanese women, the rate was 3.1 percent, compared with 6.3 percent for white women. Chinese men had an unemployment rate of 4.9 percent; women, 5.1 percent. Unemployment rates were highest among Filipinos: 7.8 percent for men and 13.6 percent for women. The Census count, taken during April, does not coincide with the peak seasonal employment period for farm workers, which is a sizable occupational group for Filipino men.

Income

The median annual income in 1959 of persons 14 years old and over was $4,388 for Japanese men, $3,803 for Chinese men, and $2,925 for Filipino men.[2] Men in all three racial groups had median incomes below that of men in the white population, $5,109. The median income for Filipino men was also considerably below that of men of other minority racial groups, as shown below.

MEDIAN ANNUAL INCOME IN 1959,
PERSONS 14 YEARS OF AGE AND
OVER, CALIFORNIA

Population group	Male	Female
Filipino	$2,925	$1,591
Negro	3,553	1,596
Chinese	3,803	1,997
Spanish surname	3,849	1,534
Japanese	4,388	2,144
White (including Spanish surname)	5,109	1,812

Among women, the median annual income in 1959 of both Japanese and Chinese women exceeded that of women in the white population. Filipino women earned less than Japanese, Chinese, white, and Negro women, but more than women of Spanish surname.

The median income figures given above include persons 14 years old and over. In order to exclude students and inexperienced workers, separate figures were compiled for men 25 years old and over. Almost half (48 percent) of the Filipino men in this age group earned less than $3,000 during 1959; 28 percent earned less than $2,000. One-third of the Chinese

2 The "median" is the middle value of the income distribution: half of the group has an income equal to or below the median income figure; the other half has an income equal to or above the median amount.

men and one-fourth of the Japanese men earned less than $3,000 during 1959. One-fifth of the men in the white population earned less than $3,000 in 1959.

ANNUAL INCOME OF MEN 25 YEARS OLD AND OVER
CALIFORNIA, 1959

Population group	Under $2,000	Under $3,000	Under $5,000
Filipino	27.6 percent	48.0 percent	79.2 percent
Negro	22.0 "	34.2 "	70.9 "
Chinese	21.2 "	33.6 "	61.6 "
Spanish surname	20.8 "	30.9 "	59.9 "
Japanese	16.5 "	26.1 "	52.9 "
White (including Spanish surname)	14.1 "	21.1 "	40.4 "

Size of Family

Filipino families tended to be larger, on the whole, than either Japanese or Chinese families in 13 western states. Thirty percent of the Filipino families were comprised of six or more persons. Among Chinese families, 21 percent had six or more members; among Japanese, 18 percent. Size-of-family data are shown below for various racial groups in the western states.

PERCENT OF FAMILIES IN 13 WESTERN STATES, 1960 [a]

Size of family	Spanish surname [b]	Filipino	Chinese	Negro	Japanese	White, incl. Spanish surname
2 persons	17.9	21.2	19.1	32.1	20.5	34.6
3 "	17.4	17.2	20.1	21.0	20.5	20.6
4 "	18.4	17.5	22.1	16.2	23.1	20.2
5 "	15.5	14.6	17.8	11.6	17.6	13.1
6 or more	30.8	29.5	20.9	19.1	18.3	11.5
Total	100.0	100.0	100.0	100.0	100.0	100.0

[a] Data not available for California alone. States included were: California, Alaska, Arizona, Colorado, Hawaii, Idaho, Montana, Nevada, New Mexico, Oregon, Utah, Washington, and Wyoming.

[b] Based on five southwestern states: California, Arizona, Colorado, New Mexico, and Texas.

10

The Bases of Anti-Chinese Sentiment

ELMER SANDMEYER

> *Published in 1939, Sandmeyer's intensive study of the anti-Chinese movement is still the standard work on the subject. It has been supplemented, but not superseded, by Gunther Barth,* Bitter Strength: A History of the Chinese in the United States, *1850–1870 (Cambridge: Harvard University Press, 1964) and Alexander Saxton,* The Indispensable Enemy *(Berkeley and Los Angeles: University of California Press, 1971).*

NO single cause furnished the motivation of the anti-Chinese movement in California. It was only through the combination of a variety of motives, appealing to diversified groups, together with an auspicious political situation, that the movement for the exclusion of the Chinese was able to succeed.

The range of the motives which served as the bases of the anti-Chinese sentiment in California may be seen in two statements made in 1876. According to the first of these, Californians were convinced,

That he is a slave, reduced to the lowest terms of beggarly economy, and is no fit competitor for an American freeman.

That he herds in scores, in small dens, where a white man and wife could hardly breathe, and has none of the wants of a civilized white man.

That he has neither wife nor child, nor expects to have any.

That his sister is a prostitute from instinct, religion, education, and interest, and degrading to all around her.

That American men, women and children cannot be what free people should be, and compete with such degraded creatures in the labor market.

That wherever they are numerous, as in San Francisco, by a secret machinery of their own, they defy the law, keep up the manners and customs of China, and utterly disregard all the laws of health, decency and morality.

That they are driving the white population from the state, reducing laboring men to despair, laboring women to prostitution, and boys and girls to hoodlums and convicts.

That the health, wealth, prosperity and happiness of our State demand their explusion from our shores.

SOURCE: Elmer Sandmeyer, *The Anti-Chinese Movement in California* (Urbana: University of Illinois Press, 1939), pp. 25–39. Reprinted by permission of the University of Illinois Press.

The official spokesman of San Francisco before the Joint Special Committee of Congress expressed a similar view:

The burden of our accusation against them is that they come in conflict with our labor interests; that they can never assimilate with us; that they are a perpetual, unchanging, and unchangeable alien element that can never become homogeneous; that their civilization is demoralizing and degrading to our people; that they degrade and dishonor labor; that they can never become citizens, and that an alien, degraded labor class, without desire of citizenship, without education, and without interest in the country it inhabits, is an element both demoralizing and dangerous to the community within which it exists.

These charges were repeated in so many speeches, editorials, and other forms of expression that one can hardly escape the conviction that they represented widely prevalent belief.

The contents of these charges may be considered under three heads: the economic, the moral and religious, and the social and political. Of the charges which may be designated as economic none was more frequently nor more persistently used than that of coolieism. While the evidence thus far presented indicates that the motivating influences of Chinese immigration were essentially like those operating among Europeans, Californians were convinced that Chinese laborers came to this country under servile or "coolie" contracts. Senator Sargent had the support of widespread public opinion when he insisted that, in spite of laws forbidding the importation of coolies, the Chinese coming to California were not free, but were bound to service for a term of years, the faithful performance of their contracts being secured by their families at home, and that while these contracts were void under our laws, they were made effective by the superstitions of the coolies.

These charges were not new to Californians. The attempt to pass the Tingley Bill in 1852 for the enforcement of contracts made in China had been defeated only after bitter debate. The following year members of the Chinese Companies admitted that they had imported men under contract but, finding it unprofitable, had discontinued the practice. Californians were inclined to accept this evidence, and the statements of Frederick F. Low to the effect that Chinese laborers were too poor to finance their passage, and of Thomas H. King that practically all Chinese men came under contract for a definite period of years, rather than the report of a special committee of the legislature in 1862 or the later statement of the attorney of the Six Companies denying the existence of coolie contracts among the Chinese in California. Public opinion, as represented in the press, tended to identify Chinese labor with Negro slavery in the south, a slavery not of law, but of condition and custom.

Coolies are such pauper Chinese as are hired in bulk and by contract at Chinese ports, to be hired out by the contracting party in this or any other foreign country to which by the terms of the contract they are to be shipped. The contracting parties for California are the Six Companies, and they have imported more than nine-tenths of all the Chinese who have come to this state . . . When the coolie arrives here he is as rigidly under the control of the contractor who brought him as ever an African slave was under his master in South Carolina or Louisiana. There is no escape from the contractor or the contract.

This conviction of Californians was buttressed by the knowledge that traffic in Chinese "coolie" or contract labor was being carried on to the West Indies and South America. The term "coolie" had been applied to the Chinese by foreigners, and in the sense in which it generally was used it meant simply common laborers, with no implication whatever of involuntary servitude. But the term came to be applied to the system of transporting contract laborers to the mines and plantations of the Spanish and British, and was soon current in connection with the Chinese in California. The "coolie traffic" to the West Indies and South America had begun before the middle of the century, and by 1871 more than one hundred thousand had been sent to Cuba alone.

Most of this traffic centered at Macao, Amoy, and Hong Kong. The recruiting, which was handled either by "coolie brokers" on a commission basis or by merchants as a speculative proposition, was permeated with fraud and graft, kidnapping, and inveigling into gambling debts. The Chinese spoke of the traffic as "the buying and selling of pigs." Conditions in transit can be compared only with the horrors of the "middle passage" of the African slave trade. Little provision was made for the comfort of the coolies, and instances were not infrequent of revolts among them, resulting often in death and destruction. The risks involved in the traffic made it difficult to procure ships.

The reprehensible methods of many of those engaged in the traffic furnished many perplexing problems for the consuls in China. The Chinese government was opposed to the traffic, but did little about it, largely because of the lack of consuls in foreign countries. In 1862 Americans were prohibited from participating in it. Within the British Empire the government had exercised a certain amount of supervision over the trade from the beginning, and by 1874 had assumed full control so far as its own subjects and territories were concerned. The worst elements came to center at Macao, and the supervision of the Portuguese government was very lax. Finally, through the efforts of the British and Chinese governments and by action of Portugal, the Macao traffic was terminated, leaving only Hong Kong and the treaty ports. The Chinese government, however, barred the traffic from the treaty ports after the report of an investigating committee sent to Cuba in 1876. There is evidence, however, that the trade continued illegally for some years longer.

What connection, if any, existed between this traffic and the immigration of Chinese to California? As we have seen, American ships had been rather extensively engaged in the traffic. Reports of consular officials, admissions by members of the Chinese Companies, and the attempt to pass the Tingley "Coolie Bill" are evidence that in the early years Chinese came to California under such contracts. Californians were convinced that the traffic was being continued long after it had been prohibited. As proof they pointed to the apparent control exercised by the Chinese Six Companies over the immigrants, to the fact that Chinese laborers were brought into the country in large numbers for the railroads and other corporations, and to the plausible statements of men who were presumed to know the facts. On the other hand, the Chinese Six Companies earnestly denied that they controlled these laborers, and the men who knew them best insisted that they were not imported under the notorious coolie system. The difference, however, seems to have been chiefly one of degree rather than of kind. The evidence is conclusive that by far the majority of the Chinese who came to California had their transportation provided by others and bound themselves to make repayment. In the words of one of the most thorough students of this problem,

There is no doubt that the greater part of the Chinese emigration to California was financed and controlled by merchant brokers, acting either independently or through Trading Guilds. . . . Under the credit-ticket system Chinese brokers paid the expenses of the coolie emigration. Until the debt so incurred by the coolie was paid off the broker had a lien on his services—a lien that might or might not be sold to a bona fide employer of labor. . . . By the credit-ticket system . . . was made possible the large emigration of Southern Chinese to U. S. A., Canada and Australia which commenced during the fifties of last century and continued until it was gradually restricted or prohibited by the legislatures of these English-speaking states.

Foreigners in China differed in their statements regarding this traffic. Peter Parker, S. Wells Williams, and Sir Arthur Edward Kennedy, colonial governor at Hong Kong, declared that the shipments to California were not of the notorious contract coolie order, and that they were so recognized by the Chinese. United States Consuls Denny and Bailey, however, insisted that there was no difference between those going to California and those bound for Cuba and other places in the West Indies and South America. The most evident difference was that, while the contracts of the "coolie traffic" were sold and the coolie had nothing to say as to whom he should serve, the broker retained the "credit ticket" of the California immigrant. In other words, the laborer's obligation was direct to the broker, and while the latter exercised a close supervision over him, the laborer was free to choose his employer so long as he made his monthly payments.

Californians, in constantly increasing numbers, either doubted that t difference existed or discounted its significance, holding that the living and working conditions of the Chinese were those of slavery, even if legal evidence were lacking. The absence of tangible evidence was accounted for on the ground that the agreements were never brought into American courts but were enforced by Chinese methods. Substantial proof of this was found in the control exercised by the Companies through an agreement with the shipping concerns, that no ticket should be sold to a Chinese unless he presented a certificate from his Company to the effect that all of his obligations had been met. When notice was posted that the legislature had prohibited this practice the Six Companies posted a counterblast:

If anyone does not pay what has been expended, the companies will get out a warrant and arrest him and deliver him over to the American courts, and then if the Chinaman loses his baggage and passage ticket it will not be any concern of the companies.

Whatever the actual conditions may have been, appearances convinced the average Californian that in the Chinese laborer he was meeting competition that had many of the earmarks of slavery. And the Civil War was altogether too recent to make those earmarks attractive.

No charge against the Chinese was made more frequently nor with more sympathetic hearing than that relating to their low standard of living. Practically all of the Chinese laborers in California were single men and lived in very restricted quarters. In most cases they came, not to settle permanently, but to accumulate an amount sufficient to enable them to return to China and live in comparative comfort. Accustomed to living on a few cents a day, with the higher wage scale in California the laborer hoped to be able to attain his goal in a relatively short time, even with the increased cost of supplies. Hence, ". . . . they work on patiently for years, saving every cent, living cheaply and working cheaply."

Those who opposed Chinese cheap labor urged that the American laborer, with his ideal of a home and family, could not compete with the Chinese because he could not live on the Chinese level of wages. Hence, American immigrants, so greatly desired in California, would not come, or if they came, would not stay. Comparisons were made with Gresham's Law of money, and with conditions in the south, where free labor was unable and unwilling to compete with slave labor. As a sample of outside opinion concerning California labor conditions the *Denver News* was quoted, "Give California a wide berth, for the laborer is not worthy of his hire in that state, even when there is work for him to do." The presence of Chinese laborers was held responsible for an increasing number of "hoodlums" among the young men of California, because the Chinese preempted the opportunities for finding work, and their wage scale degraded labor to a level so low that white boys would not engage in it. At the same time commodity prices to the consumer were not lowered.

Many employers welcomed the Chinese laborer because his low wage scale enabled them to inaugurate undertakings which otherwise might not have been able to compete with the older establishments in the east. Others claimed that white labor was not available, while some insisted that the Chinese created additional labor for the whites, of a higher grade than that done by the Chinese. This was one phase of the question on which California disagreed with the east. Postmaster General Key, after a visit to California, spoke very highly of Chinese laborers. "It is wonderful to see how little a Chinaman can live on." What was, perhaps, a common view in the east was:

> If the people of California were capable of viewing their own interest without passion or prejudice, they would perceive they have a great advantage over the rest of the country in the cheapness of Chinese labor. It favors a rapid development of the resources of that wonderful state. It enables them to undersell in all markets every exportable article which their soil, climate and mineral wealth enable them to produce.

Especially irritating to opponents of the Chinese were the statements of easterners, on the basis of very meagre information, belittling the problem of Chinese labor. When President Anderson of Chicago University and Henry Ward Beecher, after short visits to California, gave lectures and interviews deriding the opposition to the Chinese and accusing Californians of gross exaggeration regarding the danger from Chinese immigration, the press answered with bitter denunciation. The *Post*, which was probably the most radical anti-Chinese newspaper in the state, said,

> It is difficult to preserve good temper in the face of such balderdash from such a source. This sensational word monger (Beecher) taunts us with the theory of evolution, and twittingly declares that if least fitted to survive, then we should go to the wall. . . . But only let the general government release our people from federal obligations, and with our own state laws and local enactments we will free ourselves from the leprous evil, or, failing in that, with the same right arms that founded this western empire, will prove to the world that the imperial Saxon race, though but a million strong, can maintain its claim even against four hundred million serfs to possess and forever hold untrammeled the fair continent of America. . . . The silence of the grave would be all that would tell of the Chinaman's existence here.

, Many Californians opposed Chinese labor because it represented a standard upon which no European could live. As one writer insisted, the Chinese were denounced, not because they sold their labor cheaply, but because their civilization was such that they *could* sell cheaply. In other words, Californians objected to the Chinese because they were willing to be the mudsills of society. And it was considered a turn in the tide when an eastern writer pointed out that the reason why the white laborers could not compete with the Chinese was that the standard of living of the whites made larger and more diverse requirements than the narrow range of wants of the Chinese, and that "the survival of the fittest" was not a valid argument; one might just as well argue the superiority of the Canadian thistle because it overcomes useful grasses.

This phase of the working of a low standard of living was not appreciated by all Californians. Some of those who favored their employment claimed that Chinese cheap labor had an effect very much like that of machinery, apparently depriving men of work but actually providing more jobs. This argument was opposed by Henry George. He insisted that "the essential thing about Chinese laborers is that they are cheap laborers." While the principal effect of labor-saving machinery is on production, increasing and cheapening it, the effect of cheap labor is chiefly on distribution. With cheap labor production remains practically the same, but the laborer has less purchasing power. Actually, the higher labor is, the more efficient it is likely to be. Thus cheap labor may even raise the cost of production, since there may be less units produced, due both to the lower efficiency and to the lower purchasing power of cheap labor. George's argument was too involved to become a popular one, but even the ordinary citizen could see the force of his statement that the cheap laborer compels other laborers to work cheaply.

This cheap labor made an insidious appeal to Californians because it offered comforts at small cost and relief from the unusually high prices of white labor. Many even of those opposed to the Chinese patronized them. William Wellock, one of Denis Kearney's lieutenants, charged that the product of the more than ten thousand Chinese cigarmakers in San Francisco was being consumed, not by Stanford, Crocker, Flood and other wealthy men, but by the workingmen. Asserting that the Chinese came and remained because Californians were profiting by their presence, editors complained:

> The Chinaman is here because his presence pays, and he will remain and continue to increase so long as there is money in him. When the time comes that he is no longer profitable *that* generation will take care of him and will send him back. We will not do it so long as the pockets into which the profit of his labor flows continue to be those appertaining to our pantaloons.

They do not go because the people of California, while protesting against their presence, continue to utilize their labor in a hundred ways. In this matter private interest dominates public interest.

The decades of most intensive anti-Chinese agitation were burdened with problems of railroad, land, and other monopolies, and anything smacking of monopoly was certain to arouse instant antagonism. Californians saw in the Chinese a developing monopoly of sinister mien. As they entered one field of activity after another it was claimed that they not only drove out American laborers but also tended to monopolize the industry. This was charged particularly in regard to cigar and shoe making and certain types of garment manufacture. They were credited with great imitative skill, and it was claimed that the only industry into which the Chinese had gone without monopolizing it was that of woolen manufacture, and that this was due to the large amount of capital required. "Where little capital is required, there the Mongol is sure to triumph."

When eastern interests objected to the anti-Chinese agitation on the ground that it would injure our trade opportunities in China, Californians replied that this trade was very one-sided. Figures were quoted showing that our exports to China in 1878 totaled more than $23,000,000 and our imports over $18,000,000, but that some $16,000,000 of our exports were in gold and silver bullion, very largely remittances by Chinese in California, covering not only about five millions in savings, but also purchases of Chinese goods. It was charged that the Chinese purchased most of their food and clothing in China, and that factories for the duplication of American goods were being set up in China.

We may sell them samples of goods, but in a short period they will make goods as good as the sample. . . . It is not at all improbable that within twenty years we shall find the East demanding protection from Chinese cheap labor in China as loudly as California now demands protection from the same kind of labor within her own limits. The fundamental fact of this question is that at home or abroad the Chinese can produce cheaper than any other people in existence.

The Chinese were charged with contributing to monopoly in connection with the great landholders and the railroads. The latter had received large grants from the government, while the former had acquired the Spanish and Mexican holdings, and were included in the general anti-monopoly agitation. Since these landed interests were among the most ardent advocates of continued Chinese immigration the charge was frequently voiced that California was in danger of having a "caste system of lords and serfs" foisted upon it, the great holders of land and the railroads being represented as "Chinese emigration bureaus" and the largest

"Chinese employment offices" on the coast. The anti-Chinese element in California looked upon these "monopolists" as among the chief mainstays of the Chinese. The claim of eastern newspapers that the "better class" of Californians favored the Chinese was answered with,

> Nobody is in favor of anything of the kind but the cormorants, desert-grabbers and other Judas Iscariots of their race, who would sell the whole land—people, liberties, institutions and all—for their own private aggrandizement. . . .

These great landowners were regarded as worse than the plantation owners of slave days. The only way to solve the situation was to break up the large holdings into small farms. "The Mongolian will be ground out with the growth of genuine American circumstances." When J. C. G. Kennedy appeared in Washington on behalf of the Chinese Six Companies and of the "agricultural interests" of California, it was alleged that he had been connected with the slave interest before the Civil War and that President Lincoln had removed him from office because of his activities in this cause. His actions were denounced.

It is the nearest to an open declaration upon the part of the Mexican grantholders of California of a deliberate purpose to make a struggle for "Chinese cheap labor" that has yet come to our notice. The great landowners are evidently on the warpath.

From an economic viewpoint employers and those seeking employment differed widely concerning the effect of the Chinese in the state. With few exceptions employers considered them beneficial as a flexible supply of labor, cheap, submissive, and efficient; but those whose only capital was their ability to work were almost unanimous in the opinion that the Chinese were highly detrimental to the best interests of the state. Each group saw the problem through the spectacles of its own economic interests.

Of scarcely less frequent mention in the opposition to the Chinese were charges concerning their morals. Like all frontier societies, California was not distinguished for its devotion to religious and moral ideals, but this did not prevent the most severe strictures upon immoral practices of a different sort. One of the leaders against the Chinese declared,

> their moral condition is as bad and degraded as four thousand years of heathenism can make it, and . . . their physical condition is as low as the practice of all the crimes that have been known since history was written can make it.

In some cases the charge against the Chinese was simply that they were dishonest and unreliable, and that the entire business life of China was permeated by the idea that every person who handled a transaction should take his share of graft. More specifically, they were accused of having no regard for the sanctity of an oath. As early as 1854 legislation was proposed forbidding Chinese testimony against whites, and while it did not pass, a decision of the state supreme court during the year accomplished the same purpose. Several later attempts to admit Chinese testimony were defeated, and this attitude was urged by Pacific coast senators with such force in 1870 as to prevent their admission to naturalization. Of like character was the charge of falsifying tax records. Numerous instances were cited to show the smuggling of Chinese immigrants and the violation or evasion of internal revenue and poll tax laws.

Of the other vices charged to the Chinese those of opium smoking and gambling were outstanding. Opium dens were numerous in San Francisco, but since the effect of smoking was quieting, the addicts did not come in conflict with the police as did inebriated whites. However, when white people began to frequent the opium resorts more notice was taken of them. Games of chance seem to have been the chief means of excitement and recreation for the Chinese. At one time it was claimed that there were in San Francisco Chinatown more than one hundred fan-tan games and nine organized lottery companies with three hundred agencies and two drawings daily, patronized by thousands of both whites and Chinese. This situation had been in existence for years, and the police were accused of conniving with the gambling element. The police, however, declared that since gambling was a natural passion with the Chinese, they would evade any legal restriction; that gambling was being carried on behind barred doors, and that it was almost impossible for a white man to enter.

No phase of the Chinese question attracted more attention than that of prostitution. It was charged that there was not a single home, in the American sense, among all of the Chinese on the coast, and that of the four thousand Chinese women in the state all were either prostitutes or concubines. It was generally charged, also, that these women were purchased, kidnapped, or lured by panderers in China, brought to America under contract, and sold to Chinese men, either as concubines or for professional prostitution. "They are bought and sold like slaves at the will of their masters." Apparently this traffic began quite early. Frequent protests were made against the practice and against the conditions attending it, and on one occasion the heads of the Chinese Companies offered their assistance in curbing the traffic. The Page Act of 1875 was thought to have stopped it, but within a few years an extensive system of smuggling was unearthed.

On first consideration one might regard the moral and religious phase of this question as insignificant, since it is hardly true that Chinese practices were "worse" than those of Californians. But the methods of the Chinese were different, and this fact alone was enough to make them an object of attack. To Californians the immoralities of the Chinese seemed to be an integral part of their way of living, ingrained through many centuries of practice, rather than an occasional excursion into a by-path. As a contemporary writer expressed it,

They live in close quarters, not coarsely filthy like ignorant and besotted Irish, but bearing a savor of inherent and refined uncleanliness that is almost more disgusting. Their whole civilization impresses me as a low, disciplined, perfected, sensuous sensualism. Everything in their life and their habits seems cut and dried like their food. There is no sign of that abandonment to an emotion, to a passion, good or bad, that marks the western races. . . . The whole matter of the Chinese religion seems very negative and inconclusive; and apparently it has little hold upon them. There is no fanaticism in it,—no appreciable degree of earnestness about it.

Opposition on the basis of religion, however, was not directed primarily against the religious beliefs of the Chinese. The religious question was raised chiefly as a reaction to the attitude of the Protestant churches, toward restrictive legislation. The movement against the Chinese came during a period of great missionary activity on the part of most of the American churches, and several denominations had undertaken work among the Chinese, both on the coast and in China. The church leaders feared that the anti-Chinese agitation would have an adverse effect upon this work. Their utterances, resolutions, and memorials to Congress opposing measures for the restriction of Chinese immigration elicited bitter criticism from the California press, both for their utterances and for their missionary endeavors. When eastern Methodists sent memorials against the Fifteen Passenger Bill to President Hayes, the *Post*

. . . [protested] most emphatically against the criminal recklessness of religious fanaticism in the East in its bearing upon the Chinese question. . . . The Chinese, whether they profess Christianity or not, remain at heart worshipers of their ancestors. This is their religion, and none other. . . . Our opinion is that the time, money and effort wasted on Chinese missions could be turned to very much better account among our own people.

The religious forces on the coast, however, were not unanimous in favoring unrestricted immigration. The first voices of dissent were those of Roman Catholic priests. Gradually disaffection made its appearance among the Protestants. A representative of one of the more liberal groups criticised an eastern religious paper for calling the agitation against the Chinese "a crazy labor reform movement, headed by Kearney and the hoodlums of San Francisco," because the evil effects of the Chinese made it a much larger question than this. However, "we must strike while the iron is hot even if Denis Kearney is blowing the bellows." Even the Methodists, who were generally regarded as the chief opponents of restriction, displayed tendencies toward a change of attitude. Some of the most prominent leaders took a decided stand against the further immigration of the Chinese. The most notable religious declaration against the Chinese, however, was that of S. V. Blakeslee before the State Association of Congregational Churches in 1877, in which he compared the conditions in California with those under slavery in the south. Thus, while eastern religious defenders of the Chinese were irritating California restrictions, religious leaders on the coast tended more and more to oppose unrestricted immigration.

No one source furnished such unfailing inspiration for criticism of the Chinese, especially from the social and political viewpoint, as the evils of Chinatown. No matter when nor how often the need might arise, a short tour of Chinatown would supply ample material for any amount or degree of condemnation. Within four years of statehood a committee reported this district overcrowded, the houses filthy beyond imagination, pervaded by a "stench almost insupportable," numerous sick in every dwelling, excessive fire hazards due to inadequate cooking facilities, the women all prostitutes and the men inveterate gamblers. Later reports on Chinatown were elaborations of this one, as may be seen from that of the health inspectors in 1870:

> All though the dark and dingy garrets and cellars, steaming with air breathed over and over, and filled with the fumes of opium, they groped their way with candle in hand and hanging on to their official noses until they found a door or window where they could procure a fresh breath of air. Rooms, which would be considered close quarters for a single white man, were occupied by shelves a foot and a half wide, placed one above another on all sides of the room, and on these from twenty to forty Chinamen are stowed away to sleep. In many of these places there is scarcely a chance for even a breath of fresh air to creep in, and the occupants are obliged to breathe over and over again the limited allowance. How life can exist in such a place is a mystery. Besides being crowded in the manner above stated, in many of the lodging-houses filth has been allowed to accumulate to the depth of several inches, and in a number of instances the moisture, leach-like, was found dripping from rooms above. In the cellars and underground coops, which frequently extend back half a block, there is no way to obtain a circulation of air—all that does creep in being by the narrow door of the street. Here they burn oil lamps and cook their food, the smoke which fills the air, and curls lazily up out of the door when it chances to be open.

Sporadic attempts were made to remedy or remove the evil, but instead Chinatown expanded and similar conditions were reported in other cities, until it was said, "The overcrowding of Chinatown is productive of more evils than any other habit of these semi-barbarians."

In addition to the stench, filth, crowding, and general dilapidation with which Chinatown was accused of afflicting the community, another serious charge was made that the Chinese were introducing foreign diseases among the whites. For instance, it was claimed by both civil and medical authorities that Chinese men and women were afflicted with venereal disease to an uncommon degree. The Chinese prostitutes were accused of luring young boys into their houses and of infecting them with the disease. A medical journal charged that the blood stream of the Anglo-Saxon population was being poisoned through the American men who, "by thousands nightly," visited these resorts. A cause of rather frequent concern to the officials were outbreaks of smallpox. The Chinese were suspected as the source of the disease, since cases appeared among them while they were still on shipboard. They were condemned especially for not reporting their cases of the disease. "It (Chinatown) is almost invariably the seed-bed of smallpox, whence the scourge is sent abroad into the city."

The most exciting charge under this head, however, was that the Chinese were introducing leprosy into California. The very strangeness of the disease made this charge all the more ominous. It was claimed that wherever Chinese coolies had gone leprosy had developed, and that purchasers of Chinese goods were likely to contract the disease. Dr. Charles C. O'Donnell, a politically minded physician, discovered a case in a Chinese washhouse, placed him in an express wagon and drove through the streets, haranguing the crowds on the street corners concerning the dangers to which the community was being exposed. The contention of some physicians that it was not real leprosy but rather a "sporadic case of elephantiasis" did not help matters a great deal. During a period of less than ten years the Board of Supervisors of San Francisco arranged for the deportation of forty-eight cases.

What many considered the most fundamental objection to the Chinese was their difference from Americans in racial characteristics and their unwillingness to adopt American customs and ideals. Some felt that the difficulty was merely superficial, and that if the Chinese would adopt western garb and mingle with Americans the most bitter prejudices against them would disappear. Others, however, were convinced that the difference was much deeper, holding that the Chinese civilization had crystallized and that they could not assimilate with the American people. Even if no natural barrier existed, the Chinese were so devoted to their native land that, in case of death in this country, their bones were to be returned to China. It was claimed that they showed no inclination to make this country their permanent home nor to become citizens; indeed,

it was felt that they were not fitted to become citizens, for they were
imbued with monarchistic ideals and would become the tools of bosses.

Considering all of these factors it is not surprising that the leaders
of the movement against the Chinese should claim to see in the situation a
great struggle between Asiatic and American ideals and civilizations. It
may be called race prejudice, but race prejudice is not instinctive. It
generally has an economic or social basis, a fear due to a lower standard
of living or to a higher standard of effort. One editor expressed it during
the heat of the agitation:

We have won this glorious land inch by inch from the red man in vain; we
have beaten back the legions of George the Third for nothing; we have sup-
pressed rebellion and maintained the integrity of our country for no good
purpose whatsoever, if we are now to surrender it to a horde of Chinese, simply
because they are so degraded that they can live on almost nothing, and underbid our own flesh and blood in the labor market. The people of California
cannot endure it.

It is of interest here to note that the Chinese were not the first, as
they were not the last, against whom such statements were directed.
Just as the American frontier has had a tendency to repeat itself across
the country, so agitation against the influx of new racial groups has
recurred in our history. A generation before the agitation against the
Chinese it was said of the Irish that "they do more work for less money
than the native workingman, and live on a lower standard, thereby de-
creasing wages."

The foreigners in general retained their pride for the fatherland and associated together in clannish exclusiveness, forming their own secret societies, which
were sometimes political, and even their own military companies. In addition,
they constituted a source of political evil with citizenship often illegally conferred upon them and as the ignorant tools of corrupt politicians in innumerable election frauds.

If we place beside this California's official declaration concerning the
Chinese the comparison is obvious:

During their entire settlement in California they have never adapted themselves to our habits, modes of dress, or our educational system, have never
learned the sanctity of an oath, never desired to become citizens, or to perform
the duties of citizenship, never discovered the difference between right and
wrong, never ceased the worship of their idol gods, or advanced a step beyond
the musty traditions of their native hive. Impregnable to all the influences of
our Anglo-Saxon life, they remain the same stolid Asiatics that have floated
on the rivers and slaved in the fields of China for thirty centuries of time.

These, then, constituted California's indictment against the Chinese. Most important was economic competition, with its threat of the degradation of labor and the intrenchment of monopoly. Chinese moral and religious practices differed from those of Americans and seemed ingrained and unchangeable. Racial differences, the apparent unconcern for American political and social institutions, and clannishness which produced the inevitable "Chinatown" served as constant and never-failing sources of complaint. By the frequent reiteration of these charges Californians convinced themselves and their neighbors, and finally the United States, that an effective remedy must be found.

₁ₙₑ Anti-Chinese Movement in Los Angeles

WILLIAM R. LOCKLEAR

Anti-Chinese sentiment eventually embraced all of California. This study microscopically examines its operation in the then sleepy town of Los Angeles. Similar studies could be made for almost every part of California.

THE Anti-Chinese movement in California which led to the Chinese exclusion act of 1882 was essentially a product of agitation in San Francisco and Northern California. It was here that the population of the state, both Chinese and non-Chinese, was concentrated, and it was here that agitation against the Chinese originated and developed. Yet, one event in Southern California history—the massacre of nineteen Chinese at Los Angeles in 1871—brought nation-wide attention to the California movement, and this event has come to represent, or rather to misrepresent, the character of Los Angeles' role in the campaign to restrict Chinese immigration. The facts are, however, that agitation in Los Angeles developed far later than it did in San Francisco, was more difficult to arouse and sustain, and was, on the whole less passionate and less violent.

California's resentment to the "Celestials" was first manifested among the miners of Northern California when the Chinese became numerically ominous in 1852. As large Chinese populations congregated in northern cities agitation spread among the urban laborers, who feared the results of competing with them. Over the years, sympathetic and ambitious officeholders produced a mass of state and local legislation designed to stem the tide of immigration and to drive the Chinese away, but the courts declared most of the acts unconstitutional. The pulse of this agitation seems to have quickened during depression years or years in which immigration was particularly high, and it subsided to dormancy only when some relief from either "evil" was obtained.

In justification of the agitation a series of objections to the Chinese was voiced, of which the validity of several is still open to debate. But

SOURCE: William R. Locklear, "The Celestials and the Angels: A Study of the Anti-Chinese Movement in Los Angeles to 1882," *Southern California Quarterly,* 42 (September, 1960), pp. 239–250, 253–254. Reprinted by permission of The Historical Society of Southern California.

whether factually true or not the Californians responded to them as if they were, and, thus, they became semi-conscious part of almost every citizen's perspective. The Chinese immigrant was characterized as merely a slave of another color—an intolerable situation after 1865. Moreover, because his needs were few, he could work at a very low rate of pay, thereby underselling white labor, throwing Americans out of jobs and causing their destitute families to turn to crime and prostitution. He was further described as a heathen and inveterate liar who had no respect for American social, religious or political institutions. He lived in "herds" amid squalor, gambled, smoked opium and forced chinese women into prostitution, thus endangering the health and morality of the community. An ironic complaint was added that he—this "immoral, filthy heathen"—refused to assimilate with the white population!

Underlying these objections, many of which were applicable to the white community as well, was a deep-seated racial prejudice among the Caucasians which had previously been vented against the Indian, the Negro and the dark-skinned Frenchman and Latin-American. The refusal of the Chinese to adopt American dress and customs tended to intensify this basic animosity. But the critical element seems to have been the great numbers of Chinese who immigrated. To many Californians there was a very real threat of a Mongolian invasion that would extend the frontiers of the Chinese empire into California. As late as 1882 there was published "A Short and Truthful History of the Taking of California and Oregon by the Chinese, in the year A.D. 1899," written by a "survivor." At one time or another all of these elements found expression in Los Angeles, but usually on a very reduced scale.

Popular sentiment against the Chinese did not appear in Los Angeles until 1876, the massacre of 1871 notwithstanding. This was almost two full decades after organized, labor opposition expressed itself in San Francisco. Of the several factors which account for this delay the lack of a sizeable Chinese population is paramount. In 1850 only two Chinese resided among 1,610 Angelenos. Ten years later, while the city's population had risen to 4,385, there were just nine Chinese present. The Chinese community grew considerably during the sixties totaling 172 in 1870, but this was still only three per cent of the city's population. In contrast, San Francisco housed over 2,700 Chinese in 1860 and more than 12,000 in 1870. Railroad construction around Los Angeles after 1875 drew "carloads" of Chinese into the area and set the stage for local agitation.

A second factor in Los Angeles' delayed reaction derives from the local economy. Southern California was "cow country" in the fifties and sixties. Most of the town's business enterprise was devoted only to meeting the more immediate of local needs and was conducted by self-employed craftsmen. It was only after severe droughts decimated the herds in the sixties that agriculture and horticulture became serious endeavors. When they took hold in the seventies and gave Los Angeles new life, the population then increased rapidly and introduced a laboring force that could identify itself with state-wide labor opposition to the Chinese.

The lack of economic opportunity partially explains the slow growth of a Chinese community as well. More significant however, was the surplus of opportunity which existed, in spite of racial antagonism, in and around San Francisco, the port-of-entry for Chinese immigrants. Then, too, the early reputation of Los Angeles did little to attract visitors. A primitive and undeveloped town, it had a "larger percentage of bad characters than any other city" in the country.

Estimates of killings in the early fifties ran close to thirty a month, and as late as 1870 the *Los Angeles Star* had reason to announce, "All Quiet—No murders or suicides occurred in Los Angeles yesterday."

Except for an occasional dedicated sheriff the police force was of little value to the citizens, and could not always be clearly identified from the lawless element. In 1870 the city marshal and one of his officers shot it out with each other in front of the court house, arguing over which one deserved a particular reward for the return of a Chinese prostitute. The marshal died of his wounds.

In the absence of effective law enforcement vigilante activities substituted the law of the noose for the law of the courts. On one occasion in 1855 the city mayor temporarily resigned his office to lead a lynch mob. By the mid-sixties a deep-seated tradition of lawlessness and mob action was well-established which was not checked until a shocked public-conscience reacted to the slaughter of 1871.

Under such circumstances it is easy to understand why Joseph Newmark had to pay a Chinese servant $100 per month to come to Los Angeles from San Francisco. (At that same time he was paying an Indian and his wife only 50 cents a day for their combined services.) Even by 1867 Benjamin D. Wilson, for whom Mount Wilson is named, was having to import Chinese laborers from San Francisco instead of being able to find them on the local labor market. When Chinese finally did begin coming to Los Angeles it was more likely due to pressures and prejudices in the north than to any irresistible attraction in Los Angeles.

If there was ever any direct competition between Chinese labor and white labor in early Los Angeles it must have been brief and of no serious proportion. By the seventies the Chinese were concentrated in a few occupational fields which, for all intents and purposes, had become their particular fortes. As domestic help they were well regarded and came to replace the Indians and Negroes who had formerly monopolized such endeavors. In 1872 eleven Chinese laundries employed nearly half of the city's "Celestial" population while only two "white" laundries were operating. During the seventies Chinese gardeners undertook to supply Los Angeles homes with vegetables, and they came to dominate that field, too. Though individual Chinese appeared in other occupations their total number was never significant.

During the sixties the clannish "Celestials" congregated in one area—along a short street which in the Mexican period had been known as *Calle de los Negros*, but since then called "Nigger Alley" by the race-conscious whites. Long before the arrival of the Chinese this vicinity had deteriorated into a slum and was the established center of gambling, drinking and prostitution in Los Angeles. The selection of this site seems to have been voluntary on the part of the Chinese rather than as a result of any restrictions against their lodging in other parts of town. It is likely that low rents were a major consideration in the selection. Negro Alley (as the name appeared most often in print) was about forty feet wide and 500 feet long and was bordered on either side by veranda-fronted adobes. Most of the Chinese living and business activities were stuffed into its narrow, multi-roomed apartments. (In the main only washhouses were located in other parts of town.) This became the nucleus of a gradually expanding Chinatown, and it was here that the Chinese set up their opium dens and houses of prostitution.

With the introduction of the first Chinese woman in 1859 Angelenos became acutely aware of one facet of the objections to Chinese immigration. Within six weeks of her arrival this first "Celestial" lady tried to commit suicide. And though the chivalry of the *Star's* editor allowed, "Family squabbles seem to have driven her to the rash undertaking," it is more likely that her after-hours assignment was the motivation. In mid-1861 over a dozen other females arrived, and the Chinese community was immediately taken to task for its "unblushing conduct." Strangely enough, the Chinese merchants, who were also the owners of the prosti-tutes, enjoyed favorable reputations among the citizens of Los Angeles.

There was, to be sure, a local awareness of the agitation being conducted in the north during this period, and in time the insulation of distance and difficult communication gave way before the mounting cries of the anti-Chinese. With the gradual influx of disappointed gold-seekers and "busted" businessmen from up-state first-hand Chinese prejudices were introduced, for it was common practice among the northerners to attribute all their misfortunes to the "yellow-skinned" scapegoat. And though it took considerable time for these seeds to blossom, they had been planted in a fertile soil where racial animosity was currently being directed toward the Indian, Negro and a sizeable Mexican population.

As early as 1857 the topic discussed at a meeting of the local Mechanics'

Institute was: "Is the importation of Chinamen into this State advantageous to the people thereof in its present and future results?" At that time there were only three Chinese living in the city. The word "importation" is indicative of the attitude most often expressed in Los Angeles throughout the next decade. There seems to have been real moral indignation which grew out of the belief that Chinese laborers were actually slaves. An 1867 editorial in the *Semi-Weekly News* analyzed Chinese "coolieism" and concluded that it possessed "more than all the evils of African slavery, without any one of its redeeming virtues."

In the late sixties there is occasional evidence of changing attitudes. When Benjamin D. Wilson was campaigning for state senator in 1869 he was "slanderously" accused of employing Chinese while posing as a friend of labor, and in 1870 real concern arose over the possibility of Chinese being given the right of naturalization. Two new laundries began business in 1870, basing their advertising appeal on not employing Chinese. And in April 1871 a warning was posted in the Mexican section of town that no Chinese should try to settle there. However, these were isolated cases and did not reflect wholesale public resentment to the Chinese. There had been no local reaction to the signing of the Burlingame Treaty in 1868 in which the United States and China recognized "the inalienable right of man to change his home . . . and the mutual advantage of the free migration and emigration of their citizens . . . for purposes of curiosity, of trade or as permanent residents." Nor did Los Angeles send any representatives to the anti-Chinese convention held in San Francisco during August, 1870.

Even from the vantage point of history, nothing occurred in the months immediately preceding the 1871 massacre that would have permitted its prediction. Nonetheless, on the evening of October 24 a mob of 500 "Angels," enraged over the killing of a white by some "Celestials," stormed through Negro Alley leaving eighteen dead Chinese in its wake —fifteen of them suspended from make-shift gallows. A nineteenth victim died from bullet wounds three days later. In addition to the slaughter the Chinese quarters were looted of over $30,000 in money and personal property.

One cannot contest that this was a very real expression of anti-Chinese sentiment among a portion of the population. The mob did not seek out the guilty parties, but gave way to blind racism in taking revenge against the entire Chinese community. However, no evidence exists to suggest that this attitude was representative of Los Angeles as a whole. There is no way of knowing how many people swelled the ranks of the mob merely out of curiosity or from a compelling sense of horror. A heroic few actively opposed the onslaught, and through their efforts reduced the number of victims by perhaps as many as ten. Others tried less successfully to temper the crowd with words. Elsewhere in town whites were hiding Chinese in their homes in case the mob should enlarge its hunting ground. The following day, the newspapers agreed in blaming the "scum and dregs of the city" for the outrage, and though this smacks of civic white-wash, judging from Los Angeles' reputation, the figure of 500 may not have been large enough to embrace even the "bad" element in town. Moreover, the extensive pillage that took place and the fact that the Chinese settlement was located in the center of the local slum lessens much of the skepticism such a statement arouses. On October 26 a City Council member stated that some of the police, apparently seeking to share in hidden Chinese savings, offered bribes to incite the mob.

Within the context of this study a most important point regarding the massacre of 1871 is that it was not a part of any anti-Chinese movement. It was not an attempt to drive the Chinese from town nor to discourage others from coming. At this time there was no anti-Chinese movement afoot in the city. The Chinese population was still quite small and was engaged in occupations which did not directly complete with any significant number of whites. And though 1869–71 were depression years economic pressures were easing by mid-1871, and just two weeks before the massacre the *Star* observed, "There are fewer idlers and men out of employment in Los Angeles than in any other city of its size on the Pacific Coast." The murdering and looting of October 24 seems to have been more the dying breath of a period of general lawlessness than an expression of any city-wide sentiment against the Chinese.

Except for a single, insignificant meeting in 1873 the anti-Chinese movement did not gain expression in Los Angeles until 1876. Anti-coolie clubs in northern California revived agitation in 1873 when a new influx of immigrants intensified an already unfavorable employment situation, and Los Angeles responded in June with its own anti-Chinese meeting. But no enthusiasm could be generated among the Angelenos, and the agitation died out immediately. Actually Los Angeles took a critical view of the northern agitation. Of the anti-Chinese legislation being considered in San Francisco the *Star* editorialized, "To cut off the queues ('pigtails') of those who are here, and to awe away from us those who are in our midst by refusing to let them remove the bones of their dead to the sacred soil of their fathers, is a recourse unworthy of intelligent men." It also pointed out that "this kind of persecution will weaken the cause of the anti-Chinese, and make friends for the Mongolians," and suggested that the energy of the agitators be directed toward obtaining Congressional action.

State-wide agitation reached new heights in 1876. Recent immigration had been greater than any time since 1852, while economic conditions had deteriorated measurably. By this time every political party in the state and nation included anti-Chinese planks in their platforms, and sufficient pressure was finally brought to bear in Congress that a Joint Special Committee was sent to San Francisco in late 1876 to investigate Chinese immigration.

Even Los Angeles entered into the agitation and organized an Anti-Coolie Club in May. The club was favorably endorsed and initially grew rapidly. But though the meetings it sponsored during the summer were well attended, club membership never exceeded 300. In its platform the club sought abrogation of the Burlingame Treaty and Congressional action to restrict Chinese immigration. It denounced the use of illegal or violent measures and circulated anti-Chinese petitions which were forwarded to representatives in Congress with 2,500 signatures. The only concrete achievement of the club, however, was inducing the City Council to award no public works contracts to persons who employed Chinese. The insignificance of Los Angeles in the over-all movement is effectively implied in the *Report* of the Joint Special Committee—of over 1,200 pages of testimony recorded only two referred to the local situation.

Despite the meager immediate results of this agitation in Los Angeles, the short-lived Anti-Coolie Club left a legacy of some consequence. Local laborers now identified themselves closely with state-wide labor opposition to the Chinese. Furthermore, membership in the club had transcended class lines by enlisting some of the "wealthiest and most prominent men" of the community, and some of these influential sympathizers were later to lead the workingmen in their political attempts at correcting various social and economic evils.

Local agitation in 1876 and subsequent years resulted from several factors. Construction of the Southern Pacific and other railroads brought large numbers of Chinese into the area after 1875, and the unemployed of Los Angeles saw in them the cause of all their misfortunes. In anticipation of the rail connection with San Francisco local business men overextended themselves. This was forcibly brought home when, instead of ushering in an era of prosperity, completion of the railroad in 1876 introduced an after effect to the Panic of 1873. Coupled with a serious drought in 1876–77 this brought on a depression which lasted to the end of the decade.

For these ills the Chinese, the railroads and "big business" were variously blamed, but the larger part of the Los Angeles populace remained aloof from anti-Chinese activities. A visitor to the city in 1876 noted that while anti-Chinese sentiment was "highly developed" there was still a great demand for Oriental labor and domestic help. In this regard, annual attempts by workingmen after 1876 to organize boycotts against Chinese and Chinese-employing businesses, though heavily pledged to, failed miserably.

On the heels of destructive riots in San Francisco, some of which were markedly anti-Chinese, a meeting of Los Angeles laborers was called for August 3, 1877. Rumors that San Francisco "toughs" were drifting into the city to attend the meeting led to the hurried organization of a Committee of Safety to aid police in maintaining order. So imminent was violence believed to be that the *Star* even reprinted an editorial from the Los Angeles *Evening Express* rather than take the time to write one of its own. This editorial reflected the current situation and attitude of Los Angeles and anticipated in its hopes the course that local agitation would take in the future.

The workingmen have no grievances that can be remedied by a demonstration. Public opinion in Los Angeles is a unit of the Chinese problem. Both political parties have declared against the policy of the unrestricted immigration, and the men who favor their introduction are very few. The Chinese who are here now, are here lawfully, and if we are to get rid of them it will have to be done lawfully. To fan the flame of prejudice against these people by tumultuous meetings can only lead to violence, and the people of this city will not tolerate violence. We cannot forget that scenes were witnessed in this city six years ago which were disgraceful and inhuman in the extreme, and which called forth the condemnation of the civilized world. These must not be reenacted, and if any movement is on the tapis which may render it possible that Chinamen will again be seen hanging to our gate-posts, it must be nipped in the bud. We shall go as far as any newspaper in a rational and lawful effort to remedy the Chinese evil, but we shall discountenance with all our power and influence any movement that may lead to violence. The Chinese problem is now in the hands of Congress, the only constitutional power which can deal with it. Whatever influence we can bring to bear upon that body to remedy the evil will do good; but violence at the present time would only react upon the question and set it back for years.

As things turned out, the laborers showed no more inclination toward violence than they had the previous year. During August the new Labor Organization of Los Angeles declared for "peaceful and legal" eradication of the Chinese "evil" and gave over the bulk of its constitution to setting forth a host of grievances against the city and county governments. When Denis Kearney, the incendiary agitator of San Francisco, delivered a tirade in Los Angeles during December he was described as "most violent and abusive" and local workingmen continued in their peaceful attack upon the problems of the day.

Through changing leadership the Labor Organization of Los Angeles evolved into Workingmen's Club No. 1, which in turn became the nucleus of the local Workingmen's Party, the name of which was a considerable misnomer. The Workingmen's objectives were sufficiently broad to appeal to almost every male citizen, regardless of occupation or economic status. Concentrating on reforms of social inequality, corruption in government, and malpractices of the railroads and business monopolies as well as the Chinese issue, the platform attracted a membership of laborers, farmers and small business men. By advocating peaceful and legal measures for the achievement of its goals the Workingmen's Party won enough public endorsement that in February, 1878, its representatives got an article inserted into the city charter providing that, "The Mayor and Council are prohibited from entering into any contract for public works or improvements, unless a proviso be inserted in the said contract to the effect that Chinese labor shall not be employed on such works or improvements."

The conservative leadership of the local Workingmen guided them along a course independent of the Kearney-influenced party in the north. Their platform and ticket for the municipal elections of 1878 revealed the continued heterogeneity of their ranks. To enhance its chances for success the party nominated several non-Workingmen for leading offices. Certain party elements opposed this, of course, but the voices they raised were nothing in comparison to the ruckus that followed the later discovery that some of these men, including the candidate for mayor, employed Chinese! Party demands that they discharge such employees proved fruitless and frustrating. Despite the obvious inconsistency between the aims of the Workingmen and the practices of some of their candidates, a reform-conscious electorate gave them an overwhelming vote of confidence, seating Workingmen in twelve of fifteen City Council chairs and giving them a majority of the others offices. The Workingmen's candidate for mayor and at least one other Chinese-employing ticket member were among the office winners.

The only anti-Chinese campaign pledge of the Workingmen's Party had been to tax the Chinese so heavily as to force them beyond the city limits. Among the city councilmen the Workingmen's anti-Chinese element was well represented, and they set out immediately to fulfill at least this one promise. As their weapon they selected the business license tax and aimed it directly at launderers and vegetable peddlers.

The Chinese had dominated the laundry business since the sixties, and in 1879 Chinese laundries probably outnumbered the non-Chinese by nearly ten to one, while employing close to 300 of their countrymen. As for the vegetable peddlers, 200 Chinese truckmen employed at least fifty wagons in carrying out their door-to-door trade. In 1876 Chinese vegetable peddlers had outnumbered non-Chinese forty-seven to two. To maintain their monopoly they gathered in Negro Alley each morning at dawn and exchanged particular items of produce to insure that each peddler had a full selection to offer his patrons. It was reported in 1879 that nine out of ten families relied upon the Chinese for their vegetable supplies.

Under the tax ordinance proposed in January, 1879, "regular" laundries (as differentiated from "poor women who do washing") were to be taxed $25.00 per month, instead of $5.00 as formerly. The vegetable peddlers, who had been paying $3.00 per month per wagon since 1877, were now to pay $20.00 each month. For vegetable peddlers who walked, a monthly tax of $10.00 was to be levied. And so as not to miss the rest of the Chinese community, a tax of $5.00 per month was proposed for "all aliens ineligible to the privilege of becoming citizens of the United States, who were employed in any capacity in the city of Los Angeles."

The simple economics of this tactic and the public conscience of the Council proved to be stumbling blocks, however. In order to meet municipal expenses and to liquidate a part of the large city debt it would be necessary to recoup the revenue losses that would result from a Chinese exodus. To accomplish this no tax reduction was given to other businesses (one of the other Workingmen's campaign promises); it was, in fact, increased five-fold on some, and for the first time in Los Angeles a tax was to be made on professional pursuits.

Thus, the ordinance drew criticism from many quarters. And an editorial in the *Herald* suggests that there was not unanimous agreement even over the Chinese provisions:

. . . The question as to whether a man of whatever color, race or previous condition of servitude, can be legislated out of his means of earning a livelihood, is a grave one, and it is by no means concluded when a City Council has announced its sovereign pleasure. The Chinese should go, but the place to secure this going is the National Capital.

Under such an economic threat the myth of "docile John Chinaman" was quickly exploded. The Chinese vegetable peddlers taxed themselves $2.00 each to obtain legal aid in testing the constitutionality of the law. And to enlist public sympathy they gave two-days' notice and then went on strike, intending to remain out three weeks. However, some doubts apparently arose about the wisdom of this tactic, and they returned to their wagons after four days. The laundrymen, on the other hand, chose to adopt a wait-and-see attitude, but rumor soon had it that the "wily Mongolians" were plotting to establish an enormous laundry under one roof, thereby having to pay only one tax.

With the very real possibility of expensive litigation facing the city, the Council reduced the fees to $6.00 and $12.00 per month on laundries and vegetable wagons, respectively, and withdrew the tax on employed persons not eligible for citizenship. Although the laundrymen quietly accepted the new tax, which was merely a 20 per cent increase over the former, the vegetable vendors pushed a test case before the courts and won. A county court justice found the tax "oppressive, partial, unfair and in restraint of trade and therefore void." Encouraged by this success the vendors refused to pay even the revised fee of $5.00 and went on strike again in May. Available sources did not reveal the success or failure of this particular effort, but the vendors were soon back at work. In August they petitioned the Council for a reduction to $2.00 and enlisted enough sympathy among customers that several petitions from local housewives asked that the license tax on vegetable peddlers be completely abolished. These efforts, however, gained no further concessions.

In conjunction with trying to tax the Chinese out of town the Workingmen had simultaneously organized a boycott against Chinese goods and labor. There was even established an "Anti-Chinese Vegetable and Produce Market." Though subscription to the boycott was heavy the pledges were most often observed in their neglect. The only pledge reported honored by the *Star* was the replacement of all Chinese help with whites by the United States Hotel in March.

If there was any one aspect of the Chinese issue upon which public opinion was united it was the blight of Chinatown. Though a number of non-Chinese still lived along Negro Alley, the health menace caused by accumulated filth was attributed solely to the "Celestials." The Chinese themselves owned no real estate in Los Angeles, and their landlords had regularly refused to cooperate with earlier efforts to eliminate the eye-sore. In 1877 a frustrated City Council had to settle for merely changing the official name of Negro Alley by incorporating it into Los Angeles Street. When the Workingmen took office public hopes were high that at last some progress would be made, but the best the Workingmen could do was to prorate among the owners the cost of fumigating the area. Later attempts to improve the situation were equally unsuccessful, until 1888 when Los Angeles Street was physically extended, and the adobe apartments of Negro Alley were demolished.

The Workingmen suffered one defeat after another in their campaign against the Chinese. The state "Lodging House Law of 1876," better remembered as the "Cubic Air" law, required that 500 cubic feet of air exist for each tenant of a building. That no effort was made to apply the law in Los Angeles before 1879 reflects the general lack of active resentment to the Chinese, and the conditions under which it failed in that year certainly suggest a continuation of public apathy. In January of 1879 the City Health Officer caused ten Chinese to be arrested for violation of the law. But the city was unable to get a conviction. With absolute evidence on the side of the prosecution, the jury disagreed nine to three for acquittal. Instead of ordering a retrial the judge dismissed the case, explaining that the city could lose a fortune in pursuing such a hopeless cause. Thereafter the law became a dead-letter in Los Angeles.

Anti-Chinese sentiment in Los Angeles decreased rapidly during late

1879 and 1880. The failures of the Workingmen and their defeat in the next election, the improvement of economic conditions, and the departure of large numbers of Chinese for railroad construction in Arizona, all were factors. At the height of the Workingmen's agitation in 1879 the Chinese population may have exceeded 1,000, but the 1880 census recorded only 605 Orientals among more than 11,000 inhabitants. And by the end of the year that figure had been "substantially reduced." The temporary blossoming of agitation in early 1879 can best be attributed to the political advantage labor interests held during the year, although the size of the Chinese community should not be disregarded. That the campaign lasted as long as it did illustrates the determination of the Workingmen, rather than prolonged public endorsement.

In November, 1880, a new treaty was negotiated with China in which the United States was permitted to "regulate, limit or suspend" the immigration of Chinese laborers. This was a major step toward achievement of the anti-Chinese movement's goal, but Los Angeles gave it no particular attention. Jobs were plentiful enough and sentiment against the Chinese was so reduced by July, 1881, that the Los Angeles Woolen Mills began replacing white laborers who refused to work a 15-hour day with Chinese, and no issue was made of the action.

In the early months of 1882, when statewide agitation over the impending passage of a Chinese restriction bill was high, the *Los Angeles Times* put forth a distasteful and unsuccessful campaign to arouse the citizenry. A series of articles attributed the majority of major crimes in California to the Chinese, representing American hoodlums as "tame and insignificant" in comparison. Other articles purported that a "prominent physician" held Chinese wash-houses responsible for the appearance of cases of mysterious "syphilitic sores" among "moral persons." The *Times* supported these accusations with the "well known fact that so impure has become the Chinese nation as a whole that the custom of handshaking is unknown among them."

Seated amid the snowballing excitement in Northern California, the governor set aside March 4, 1882, as a legal holiday for the purpose of each locality helping to demonstrate state-wide opposition to further immigration. The Los Angeles rally was well attended. The city band played, a cannon was fired which "smashed every window in the neighborhood," and a resolution was drawn up and sent on to Washington to encourage Congress. This jubilant holiday may have occasioned the half-hearted attempt in April to exclude the Chinese from the city, relying upon the 1879 state constitution and subsequent laws for the authority to do so. However, the matter was immediately dropped when the city attorney pointed out the obvious conflict of such an ordinance with the federal constitution.

In 1882 local newspapers showed mixed reaction to President Arthur's veto of a twenty year restriction bill. The *Evening Express* called it an abuse of the veto power while the *Times* agreed with the president that such a long period of restriction amounted to exclusion and thereby constituted a spiritual breach of the new treaty with China. In other parts of the state the President was being hanged in effigy. Some localities organized anti-Chinese leagues with the express purpose of expelling the Chinese forcibly. However, no such reaction found expression among Angelenos. On May 6, 1882, President Arthur signed a bill which provided for suspension of the immigration of Chinese laborers for ten years.[4] While most of California celebrated Los Angeles accepted the news without any demonstration. The rabidly anti-Chinese *Times* extended a soft note of thanks to Pacific Coast congressmen without further comment. At the next meeting of the City Council the achievement was not even mentioned.

Anti-Chinese agitation in Los Angeles did not die with the passage of this act in 1882. In a very real sense it had died in 1879 with the demise of the Workingmen. The indifference exhibited by Angelenos when restriction finally was achieved was representative of the local attitude throughout most of the pre-1882 campaign. The slaughter that occurred in 1871 is misleading when regarded as an episode of the anti-Chinese movement. The only relation that might be drawn is that the massacre tended to retard such a movement in Los Angeles and perhaps exerted a sobering influence on the character of the local campaign. Over most of the period covered here there were too few Chinese in the city to warrant concerted agitation. Nor was the laboring element of Los Angeles either large enough or well enough organized in these years to arouse and sustain popular sympathy for their cause, especially among a population that obviously found Chinese services and prices irresistible.

An enlarged laboring class resurrected anti-Chinese agitation from its grave in 1885–1886, but with results similar to those of 1879. The futility of the anti-Chinese movement in Los Angeles is well illustrated by the "death-bed" appeal of the 1886 campaign—that the City Council should at least compel Chinese launderers to write their tickets in English!

12

Anti-Japanese Agitation

YAMATO ICHIHASHI

> *One of the pioneers of California ethnic history, the late Professor Yamato Ichihashi, taught for many years at Stanford University. Often characterized as an apologist for Japan and the Japanese—a characterization that contains some truth—his work remains valuable to the student of racial prejudice and discrimination.*

HAVING presented and discussed the more salient facts relating to Japanese immigrants, we are now ready to tell the story of anti-Japanese movements in America. These movements, though arising out of the presence of a limited number of Japanese in the Pacific Coast states, have often involved the foreign policies of the United States and Japan and have, at times, even threatened amicable relations between the two countries.

To repeat what the writer has stated earlier, the only sore spot still unhealed in relations between America and Japan is the discriminatory exclusion of Japanese from the United States. The deep resentment of the Japanese against this treatment is not fully appreciated in this country. This may sound rather extravagant to those who are not familiar with the peculiar character of some of the factors underlying the movements. What follows, it is hoped, will clarify the situation.

Speaking of the origin of anti-Japanese movements an American writer gives the following observation under the heading, "The Japanese Inherited the Prejudice against the Chinese":

the immigration of the Japanese followed that of the Chinese. The whole history of the Japanese has been colored by that fact. The Chinese came to the West under such circumstances that they stood in striking contrast to all other elements in the population. With a different language, with queue and different dress, with no family life, with different customs, and steeled against change as they were, the reaction against them was strong and immediate

SOURCE: Yamato Ichihashi, *Japanese in the United States: A Critical Study of the Problems of the Japanese Immigrants and Their Children* (Palo Alto: Stanford University Press, 1932), pp. 228–242. Reprinted by permission of the publishers, Stanford University Press. Copyright 1932 by the Board of Trustees of the Leland Stanford Junior University.

when they ceased to be objects of curiosity. That they underbid others when seeking employment merely added strength to the reaction and fury to the opposition with which they would have met under any circumstances. As a result of the struggle that ensued they were assigned the inferior place they unprotestingly accepted. The Chinaman was a good loser. Then came the Japanese. They came from the same "quarter of the earth," were of related color, had a similar language, accepted the same economic rank as the Chinese, frequently occupied their bunkhouses, and underbid for work as did the Chinaman. What wonder, though they were vastly different peoples, that the Japanese should be set down as being in the same category as the Chinese? In men's minds they were assigned the same place to begin with. Moreover, it was assumed that they should continue to occupy it. Not to do so was to be regarded as undesirable.

Although we may not agree with this statement in its every detail, there is no denying that the Japanese have inherited the prejudice against the Chinese. The first cry, "Japs must go," was heard as early as 1887, or five years after the enactment of the Chinese exclusion law. Its author was Dr. O'Donnell of San Francisco, whose political and professional reputation was of doubtful character. He was unable to make it even a municipal political issue, for the following reasons: There were no more than 400 Japanese in the entire state, most of them engaged in domestic service and a very few as farm hands. They were not competing in any field with whites. The Japanese wore American dress and wore no queue. The general public was still unconscious of their presence and the working classes were indifferent. Thus O'Donnell failed to capitalize the Japanese in order to attain his political end as he had done successfully with the Chinese.

Three years later (1890), however, Japanese cobblers numbering fifteen, employed by one Chase, the owner of a shoe factory in San Francisco, were violently attacked by members of the shoemakers' union. The attack was launched against the factory owner for employing Japanese in a manner offensive to the union; these Japanese worked in a separate shop, the existence of which was kept secret from the white employees. At any rate, the Japanese, finding it impossible to remain in the factory because Chase failed to provide necessary protection for them, left it and sought work in families and on ranches.

In 1892 a Japanese restaurant in San Francisco was attacked by members of the local cooks' and waiters' union, but without causing much material damage to the proprietor. The same year agitation was started for the exclusion of Japanese children from public schools and for the establishment of a separate school for them. The writer cannot state how many Japanese children were then attending the public schools of San Francisco. According to the census of 1890 there were in the United

States 2,039 Japanese, of whom 1,532 were living in the Pacific Coast states. According to various estimates made by old Japanese residents to the writer, it is not far wrong to put the total number of Japanese in the city at about 600. But how many of these attended schools cannot be stated. It is interesting to note that that year saw the first Japanese graduate from a grammar school; apparently there could not have been many Japanese in public schools, and therefore the agitation must be considered entirely political, owing to the influence of interested individuals. Nothing came out of this attempt. Moreover, no manifestation of hostility occurred until 1900.

The year 1900 saw two events in San Francisco that counted much against Japanese. A Chinese afflicted with bubonic plague was discovered in the Chinatown of the city, and the municipal officers concerned became panic-stricken, held all the Orientals residing in the city responsible for possible spread of the dreaded plague, and adopted extreme measures. For instance, a violent form of injecting Asiatics, both men and women, against the disease was practiced in public; the resident Japanese vainly protested against this, and then resorted to diplomatic representations. An injunction was obtained and the injecting was discontinued. The Japanese naturally felt that their rough handling by the municipal officers in this connection was an unwarranted act of hostility toward them; in fact, many medical men considered the municipal practice contrary to both medical science and moral decency.

The other event of the year was a mass meeting called to consider the re-enactment of the Chinese exclusion law, soon to expire. Among the speakers were Mayor James Phelan, Professor Edward Alsworth Ross of Stanford University, and several labor leaders and politicians. These men sounded a strong note of opposition to the immigration of Japanese laborers; not only was a resolution adopted urging Congress to re-enact the Chinese exclusion law, but it was further resolved to urge the adoption of an Act of Congress or such other measures as might be necessary for the total exclusion of all classes of Japanese other than members of the diplomatic staff. It added, "such a law has become a necessity not only on the grounds set forth in the policy of Chinese exclusion but because of additional reasons resting in the fact that the assumed virtue of the Japanese—i.e., their partial adoption of American customs—makes them the more dangerous as competitors." Thus we see the first crystallization of the hitherto sporadic acts and sentiments of hostility against Japanese.

In a message (1901) of Governor Henry T. Gage to the state legislature of California we find the following passage:

The peril from Chinese labor finds a similar danger in the unrestricted immigration of Japanese laborers. The cheapness of that labor is likewise a menace to American labor, and a new treaty with Japan for such restriction, as well as the passage of laws by Congress, is desired for the protection of Americans.

I therefore most earnestly appeal to your honorable bodies for the passage as a matter of urgency of appropriate resolutions instructing our Senators and requesting our Representatives in Congress for the immediate institution of all proper measures leading to the revision of the existing treaties with China and Japan, and the passage of all necessary laws and resolutions for the protection of American labor against the immigration of oriental laborers.

Accordingly, the legislature adopted a joint resolution, and a memorial was addressed to Congress asking for the restriction of Japanese immigration. The governor's message and the subsequent appeal to Congress by the state legislature were the first move against Japanese on the part of the government of California. It may be noted, in passing, that the legislature of Nevada adopted similar resolutions.

Turning to another source of information, we discover that hostile feelings against Japanese immigration were by no means confined to California. In the *Report of the United States Industrial Commission* (1900), Volume XV, many pages are devoted to a discussion of Chinese and Japanese. The current characterization of Japanese immigrants may be learned from this official report:

The official records of the immigration office do not show any startling increase in the number of Japanese immigrants to the United States. For the last 5 years they show an average of about 2,000 Japanese arrivals each year. The total number of Japanese immigrants for the fiscal year ending June 1, 1898, was 2,230, about 1,500 of whom were classified as farm hands and gave as their destination California. The total arrivals of Japanese in San Francisco for the fiscal year ending June 30, 1899, were 1,667, of whom 120 were females.

The records of the immigration office fail to account for the great hordes of Japanese coolies who have already secured a monopoly of the labor in the agricultural industries of the Pacific States. In the State of California alone there is to-day a great army of Japanese coolies, numbering upwards of 20,000. They do not colonize as do the Chinese: they are scattered about the State, doing work in the orchards, vineyards, gardens, and hop and sugar-beet fields.

They are more servile than the Chinese, but less obedient and far less desirable. They have most of the vices of the Chinese, with none of their virtues. They underbid the Chinese in everything, and are as a class tricky, unreliable, and dishonest.

The number of Japanese coolie laborers in California to-day is greater than the total number of Japanese arrivals shown by the immigration records at all of the United States ports for the last 10 years. How, then, came they among us? This is another Asiatic mystery. The movement, the motives, the coming and going of these stoical, strange Mongolians are as a closed book to the white races. As with the birds of passage, to-day there may not be one in sight, to-morrow they may be with us in countless thousands.

So continues this official statement. Obviously the above is not to be accepted as a statement of facts, for such it is decidedly not, but it does unmistakably show the lines which anti-Japanese movements were to follow. In fact, the statement may be justly interpreted as an official epitome of anti-Japanese ideas and feelings thus far expressed sporadically by those who were interested in agitation against Japanese immigration.

These movements remained ineffective as far as Congress was concerned, but they affected the emigration policy of the Japanese government. As we have already stated, the Japanese government took measures to discourage emigration of laborers to the United States; consequently, until 1898, the number of annual arrivals here never exceeded 2,000, but 17,700 reached here between 1898 and 1900, and of this number 12,626 came in 1900. What occasioned this concentration of arrivals the writer cannot explain. However, this fact and the discovery of the hostility manifested in California once more led the Japanese government to restrict emigration to this country, a restriction clearly reflected in the number reaching here during 1901–1910, although it is true that during the same decade many Japanese migrated here from Hawaii. The Japanese government, of course, had no control over these migrants.

In California, too, anti-Japanese activities subsided, and we hear nothing of these until 1904. The Immigration Commission observes:

> Though the American Federation of Labor, at its annual convention held in San Francisco in November, 1904, resolved, in response to a local demand, that the terms of the Chinese exclusion act should be extended so as to exclude Japanese and Koreans as well as Chinese laborers, there was little discussion of Japanese immigration until 1905.

Thus far leaders in the campaign against Japanese immigration had been labor leaders and politicians who catered to the labor vote; but in 1905 there appeared a new type of champion, a newspaper. Of course, the press had not ignored the agitation, but it had not shown interest to the extent of capitalizing the Japanese question for its own ends. When in the spring of 1905 the "Japanese and Korean League" was organized by labor interests, with one Tveitmoe, the secretary of the Building Trades Council, as its president, the *San Francisco Chronicle*, little patronized by the working classes, took up the campaign by publishing a series of sensational articles, the first of which appeared on February 23, 1905. These articles called attention to the number of Japanese already here, discussed the supposed evils connected with their immigration, and emphasized the dangers of future immigration of this kind. This press campaign proved effective with the state legislature, and on March 1 the latter passed a resolution demanding of Congress that action be taken immediately, by treaty or otherwise, to restrict the further immigration of Japanese laborers.

Perhaps it is superfluous to inform American readers that at this time the Union Labor party was in control of the municipal affairs of San Francisco. On May 6, 1905, the Board of Education passed a resolution to establish separate schools for Chinese and Japanese children, although no action was taken on the resolution for more than a year. On April 18, 1906, the city was visited by a calamitous earthquake accompanied by devastating fires, leaving municipal affairs in a chaotic state, and this state of affairs was not checked by the men who controlled the government. Safety was not maintained. Secretary Metcalf, who was dispatched to the city to investigate the school question which we shall presently discuss, stated in his report to the President:

The police records of San Francisco show that between May 6, 1906, and November 5, 1906, 290 cases of assaults, ranging from simple assaults to assaults with deadly weapons and assaults with murderous intent, were reported to the police.

Strikes made the bad situation in the city worse, and the same report says, "assaults have from time to time been made upon Japanese residents in the city of San Francisco." The Japanese Consul addressed a letter to the Chief of Police dated August 17, 1906, which in part reads:

In this connection I would like to state that one of the secretaries of the Consulate was also menaced by young toughs in the same vicinity about the same time. As unprovoked assaults of this kind upon my countrymen have been quite frequent of late, I have to earnestly ask that steps be taken by your honorable department to afford them protection to which they are entitled.

Nor did the Japanese business establishments escape attacks. As to these the Metcalf report says:

I personally interviewed the restaurant-keepers and took down their statements. George Sugihara, a restaurant-keeper, at 177 Third Street, stated that the boycott commenced on October 3 and continued until October 24; that on the first day the boycotters distributed match boxes on which was written: "White men and women, patronize your own race"; that at about noon of the second day a large number of men came to his place of business and asked the people who were about to enter his restaurant not to patronize the Japanese restaurants; that customers attempting to enter his place of business were sometimes restrained by force, and that blows were also struck; that on or about the 10th or 11th of the month the boycotters came three times a day—morning, noon and evening; that sometimes they threw bricks and stones into his place; that one of the waiters asked them the reason why they did these things and they replied, "Ask the policemen"; that it was very seldom that a policeman was to be seen on the scene; that he complained to the policeman on the beat; that sometimes the policeman spoke to the boycotters and appeared to be friendly with them; that whenever a policeman appeared who was unfriendly to the boycotters, the boycotters left; that on one occasion when he asked the boycotters how long they intended to keep up the boycott, they replied, "Until the end—until the Japanese give up their business, pack up their goods, and return to the place whence they came."

Mr. Sugihara also said that there was an agreement to pay the boycotters for the purpose of declaring the boycott off; that all the facts were known to Mr. Imura, president of the Japanese Union, and that the proposition to pay cash to the Cooks and Waiters' Union was made by Mr. Imura representing the Japanese Union and that the amount to be paid was $350; that he, Sugihara, did not know the name of the person to whom the money was to be paid by Imura; that he was present on October 25 or 26, when $100 of the $350 was paid. . . .

This case is typical of attacks suffered by Japanese business establishments; the boycotters appealed to race prejudice, a very common practice; the individual policemen were not interested in restraining the boycott; but the most surprising aspect of the boycott was extortion. Readers may be interested to know that the balance of $250 was also paid to a man named W. S. Stevenson, and that when this was done the boycott was called off. The municipal officers of the time were notorious grafters, and perhaps the trade unionists saw no wrong in extortion. The Japanese were willing to bribe their attackers because they saw no other method of protecting their own interests. In spite of these abuses, the Japanese remained patient because they realized the circumstances under which the city was then struggling. Probably nothing of international import would have resulted from the violent attacks and the damages caused. But in the midst of these hardships and sufferings on the part of Japanese residents, the San Francisco Board of Education adopted a long-threatened act prompted by the public resentment of Japanese. On October 11, 1906, the Board passed the following resolution:

> Resolved that in accordance with Article 10, Section 1662 of the School Law of California, principals are hereby directed to send all Chinese, Japanese and Korean children to the Oriental School, situated on the south side of Clay Street, between Powell and Mason Streets, on and after Monday, October 15, 1906.

When the resolution was made public, Japanese and Americans, except the anti-Japanese group, were shocked; they did not expect the municipal government would participate to that extent in the anti-Japanese campaign, primarily a movement of local organized labor. Perhaps the fact that the Labor Party controlled the government is the explanation of the Board's action. At any rate, the press of America and Japan took up the question and discussed it widely. The local Japanese residents appealed to the Board to rescind its action, but in vain. The Interdenominational Missionary Conference did the same, with similar result. The press in

Japan criticized the action as "unfair" and "discriminatory"; the press in America was divided in opinion; those who were engaged in teaching condemned the action, but without accomplishing any result. When October 15 arrived the principals, in compliance with resolution, refused to admit to their schools the Japanese pupils who had heretofore attended them and instructed them to attend the Oriental School. Whereupon the local Japanese appealed to the Japanese government to solve this vexed question, which in turn protested to the federal government on the basis of the American-Japanese treaty of 1894. President Roosevelt appointed Secretary Metcalf to investigate the whole issue.

At this juncture it is well to digress for a moment to say a few words concerning the resentment of Americans against "interference" of the Japanese government relating to happenings on American soil. The American attitude on this point is clearly expressed in the following statement:

> Not the least factor in begetting opposition to the Japanese is to be found in the attitude of the Japanese government towards its immigrants, and the solicitude of their semipublic organizations for the welfare of the members of their race on American soil. Without implying that it is objectionable or the contrary, it is true that the Japanese government has evinced an unusual interest in the whereabouts and activities of its subjects.

There is no doubt that paternalism is a characteristic of the Japanese government, a government which emerged from feudalism only half a century ago, for the present constitutional government came into being in 1889. It is also true that no government is free from solicitude concerning the welfare of its subjects residing abroad; we all know how various governments look after their nationals residing, for example, in China. In this country immigrants are expected to become ultimately genuine American citizens; European governments, on the whole, had no occasion to interfere on behalf of their subjects residing in America. Chinese, the first among those ineligible to citizenship to come to America, were subjected to many indignities, but their government either did not function well or was not respected by foreign governments. Japanese, too, are not allowed to naturalize, but their government is well organized and is apparently respected. In 1905 Japan emerged victorious over Russia; she was being recognized as a great power at the time when the school incident occurred. Regardless of the wisdom of solicitude on the part of the Japanese government, it is not difficult to understand why that government could not have remained indifferent when its subjects were being maltreated in a country where they were not able to seek protection as citizens. In this respect the Japanese government appears conspicuous in contrast to the Chinese government only because the latter proved helpless.

Returning to our story, according to the report submitted to the President by Secretary Metcalf, there were in all 93 Japanese attending the public schools of San Francisco; these were distributed among twenty-three schools. Of these, 68 were born in Japan and 25 in the United States; boys numbered 65 and girls, 28. Below are given two tables showing the distribution of these Japanese pupils by age and grade:

AGE DISTRIBUTION OF JAPANESE PUPILS

Age	Number	Age	Number
6 years	2	14 years	4
7 years	5	15 years	10
8 years	9	16 years	9
9 years	3	17 years	12
10 years	7	18 years	6
11 years	5	19 years	4
12 years	8	20 years	2
13 years	7		

DISTRIBUTION OF JAPANESE PUPILS IN GRADE SCHOOLS

	Number		Number
1st grade	7	5th grade	11
2d grade	10	6th grade	13
3d grade	12	7th grade	7
4th grade	16	8th grade	17

These are the essential facts relating to the Japanese pupils then attending the public schools who were involved in the segregation act of the San Francisco Board. Its proponents indulged in the customary method of vilification. Readers may be interested in a sample of the charges brought against the Japanese. Here is a part of a speech made in the House of Representatives on March 13, 1906, by a California member, E. A. Hayes:

A close acquaintance shows one that unblushing lying is so universal among the Japanese as to be one of the leading national traits; that commercial honor, even among her commercial classes, is so rare as to be only the exception that proves the reverse rule, and that the vast majority of the Japanese people do not understand the meaning of the word "morality," but are given up to practice of licentiousness more generally than any nation in the world justly making any pretenses to civilization. I am told by those who have lived in Japan and understand its language that there is no word in Japanese corresponding to "sin," because there is in the ordinary Japanese mind no conception of its meaning. There is no word corresponding to the word "home," because there is nothing the Japanese domestic life corresponding to the home as we know it. The Japanese language has no term for "privacy." They lack the term and the clear idea because they lack the practice.

Many other charges were made, such as that the presence of young Japanese boys in school would inevitably result in imparting immorality to young American girls. It appears that proponents of the action, finding it necessary to vilify the Japanese in this manner in order to justify their stand before the public, must have been conscious of something wrong in that stand. Perhaps the Japanese ought to abide by a good advice given by an American writer on this point. He says:

In connection with the anti-Japanese agitation many things have been said highly insulting to the Japanese and intended to be so. But the Japanese should not take these utterances too much to heart, for they do not represent, I feel confident, the thought of the real majority, even of California.

In fact, we find in the report of Secretary Metcalf the following observation:

Many of the foremost educators in the State, on the other hand, are strongly opposed to the action of the San Francisco Board of Education. Japanese are admitted to the University of California, an institution maintained and supported by the State. They are also admitted to, and gladly welcomed at, Stanford University. San Francisco, so far as known, is the only city which has discriminated against Japanese children. I talked with a number of prominent labor men, and they all said that they had no objection to Japanese children attending the primary grades; that they wanted the Japanese children now in the United States to have the same school privileges as children of other nations. . . .

Thus local sympathizers were not lacking at the time, but their effort proved ineffective. Its solution had to be sought through the federal government. On the basis of Secretary Metcalf's report President Roosevelt started to seek a solution of the issue. In his message to Congress December 3, 1907, we find the following passage:

I am prompted to say this by the attitude of hostility here and there assumed toward the Japanese in this country. This hostility is sporadic and is limited to a very few places. Nevertheless, it is most discreditable to us as a people and may be fraught with the gravest consequences to the nation. . . . Through the Red Cross, the Japanese people sent over $100,000 to the sufferers of San Francisco, and the gift was accepted with gratitude by our people. The courtesy of the Japanese, nationally and individually, has become proverbial. . . . They are welcome, socially and intellectually, in all our colleges and institutions of higher learning, in all our professional and social bodies. . . . Here and there a most unworthy feeling has manifested itself toward the Japanese—the feeling that has been shown in shutting them out from the common schools of San Francisco and in mutterings against them in one or two other places because of their efficiency as workers. To shut them out from the public schools is a wicked absurdity when there are no first-class colleges in the land, including the universities and colleges of California, which do not gladly welcome Japanese students, and on which the Japanese students do not reflect credit.

I ask fair treatment for the Japanese as I would ask fair treatment for Germans or Englishmen, Frenchmen, Russians, or Italians. . . . In the matter now before me affecting the Japanese, everything that is in my power to do will be done, and all the forces, military and civil, of the United States which I may lawfully employ will be so employed.

This attack on San Francisco and this vindication of the Japanese did not in the end help the cause of the Japanese. At any rate, in response to the protest of the Japanese government based on the treaty, the federal government, on January 17, 1907, instituted two suits, one in the Federal Circuit Court and the other in the State Supreme Court, "for the purpose of enforcing the provisions of the treaty with Japanese giving the Japanese equal school advantages." The following summary of the suits was reported by a local newspaper:

It is alleged that the United States Government partly supports the schools of the State, having made a grant of public lands for this purpose, with the understanding that all the schools and institutions benefited thereby should be conducted in conformity with the Constitution of the United States, and all treaties made by the authority of the United States. It is denied that the Japanese are in any sense Mongolians, but are a separate and distinct race, and can not be properly included among those affected by the provisions of the State code requiring the segregation of all pupils of Indian or Mongolian descent. It is alleged that the segregation of the Japanese children is in violation of the existing treaty rights of Japan, who, it is alleged, are entitled to the same treatment as the most favored nations. It is contended that the law of California does not justify any such action as the Board of Education has taken in respect to the Japanese school children, and that, if it does, then it is null and void.

It would have been interesting to learn decisions of the courts, but the suits were dismissed, as President Roosevelt had found another method of settling the issue. Almost simultaneously with the institution of the suits, the President invited Mayor Schmitz and the members of the School Board to Washington to talk over the school matter. This conference between the President and the San Francisco municipal officers resulted in compromise measures settling the whole question, it was thought, of Japanese immigration. The measures proved to be the first important step culminating in the exclusion of Japanese. . . .

13

The Progressives Draw the Color Line
ROGER DANIELS

> *This detailed analysis of the anti-Japanese movement, originally a doctoral dissertation at the University of California, Los Angeles, highlights the relationships between regional racism, national politics, and international relations.*

> The fear-laden anti-Japanese emotion of the people [of California] is a sleeping lion.
> —Japanese Consul General Nagai,
> November 29, 1912
> Ill fares the land,
> to hastening ills a prey,
> Where Japs accumulate,
> day by day.
> Elk Grove *Citizen*,
> January 18, 1913

BEFORE Theodore Roosevelt's intervention during the winter of 1906–1907, the Japanese question had not been a campaign issue, but from that time until 1914 the crusade to "keep California white" can be understood only in partisan political terms. This is not to say that there was no genuine anti-Japanese feeling; it was ever present and, from all the evidence, constantly increasing. The "California position" was still nationally unpopular, however, and most California politicians were very susceptible to advice from their national party leaders. Had California been an independent republic, or had there been no contrary pressures from Washington, most of the anti-Japanese bills introduced in its legislature would have passed without difficulty. In reality, no significant anti-Japanese legislation was passed until 1913. The Alien Land Law of that year must be viewed against the background of the three election campaigns and the convolutions of the two fruitless legislative sessions which came before.

SOURCE: Roger Daniels, *The Politics of Prejudice: The Anti-Japanese Movement in California and the Struggle for Japanese Exclusion* (Berkeley and Los Angeles: University of California Press, 1962), pp. 46–64. Originally published by the University of California Press; reprinted by permission of The Regents of the University of California.

The Democratic party—which did not elect a governor in California between 1894 and 1938—began in 1908 to make the Japanese issue its own. In that year it adopted a plank deprecating "the recommendation of the republican president in his message to Congress in December, 1906, wherein he recommended . . . that 'an act be passed specifically providing for the naturalization of Japanese' " and adding that "we are unalterably opposed to the naturalization of any Asiatics."

Similarly, during the presidential campaign, some Democrats argued that "Labor's choice [is] Bryan—Japs' choice [is] Taft." One important Democratic campaigner made this argument a key point: to James D. Phelan must go whatever honor there is in having originated this tactic. Little realizing that it would be a major issue in California politics for almost two decades, the few editors who noticed Phelan's last-minute effort were amused. One writer felt that a "novelty in the way of campaign argument" had been furnished when Phelan gave as a "reason why people should vote for Bryan" the warning that only the Great Commoner could prevent "the Pacific slope [from] being overrun by Hordes of Japanese." Despite this effort, the Democrats lost California by a large margin.

As soon as the next legislature assembled, in January, 1909, it became clear that the anti-Japanese issue was no laughing matter. On the first day for submitting bills, five discriminatory measures were introduced and seemed to have broad support from the legislators. The most important were: an alien land act which would allow aliens five years to become citizens or forfeit their lands and also would limit leases to aliens to one year's duration; a school segregation bill which specifically mentioned Japanese; and a municipal segregation ordinance which would give cities the power to confine Japanese and other Orientals in ghettos. Roosevelt and Root, when they learned of the renewal of the agitation, called upon Governor Gillett to prevent the passage of any invidious legislation and pointed out that under the Gentlemen's Agreement more Japanese were leaving the country than were coming in. Once the coöperation of the governor and his lieutenants had been achieved, there was no likelihood of passage of any important anti-Oriental legislation. By February 13 Roosevelt was able to notify President-elect Taft that "the Republican machine finally came to my help" and to assure him that everything was under control.

As a face-saving measure, the legislature passed a resolution asking that Congress extend the Chinese Exclusion Act to "include all Asiatics" and also, at the governor's suggestion, passed a bill ordering the State Labor Commissioner to investigate and report on "the Japanese of the State." Despite its negative statutory results, the sitting produced its share of anti-Japanese oratory. Most attention was centered on school segregation;

the bill providing this was actually passed by the assembly, but, under the administration's pressure, it was reconsidered by that body and defeated. The leading anti-Japanese orator of 1909 was Grove Johnson, the father and political opponent of the rising reformer, Hiram Johnson. In a typical passage he denounced executive interference:

> I know more about the Japanese than Governor Gillett and President Roosevelt put together. I am not responsible to either of them. I am responsible to the mothers and fathers of Sacramento County who have their little daughters sitting side by side in the school rooms with matured Japs, with their base minds, their lascivious thoughts, multiplied by their race and strengthened by their mode of life. . . . I have seen Japanese twenty-five years old sitting in the seats next to the pure maids of California. . . . I shudder . . . to think of such a condition.

In the upper house Senator Marc Anthony was equally indignant about the "invasion . . . of coolie laborers from the empire of Japan," the encroachments of "the executive branch of the Federal Government," and the "commercialism of New England." He asserted that "in twenty years Japanese in the United States have shipped $200,000,000 in gold from the United States to Japan, accentuating the late financial stringency."

Neither the assemblyman's shuddering nor the senator's indignation touched upon what was to be the real issue. School segregation was never again the paramount issue, although it remained a talking point, and Anthony's self-contradictory arguments (if they controlled that much money, the Japanese certainly were not coolies) were soon forgotten. After 1909 the main issue became the successive attempts to check the acquisition of agricultural land by the Issei.

Reactions to the legislature's failure to act on the Japanese question in 1909 were varied. As might have been expected, some Democrats and the Asiatic Exclusion League were outraged. League president Tvietmoe berated Roosevelt, Gillett, and the assemblymen who had "betrayed California and voted for the Japs." On the other hand, there were, for the first time, influential California voices calling for moderation. Added to the protests of a few religious groups were the authoritative tones of the spokesmen for the business community. The Chambers of Commerce of both San Francisco and Los Angeles petitioned the legislature not to pass anti-Japanese legislation, because the "Oriental trade passing through the ports of this State has assumed large proportions and is likely to be seriously crippled by such . . . action." The San Francisco *Chronicle*, the chief instigator of anti-Japanese agitation in 1905, now felt that further action was unnecessary, because the immigration had "virtually ceased" and the Japanese government would "in good faith . . . prevent" additional immigration. Also in opposition were a few large-scale farmers like Lee A. Phillips, whose California Delta Farms, Inc., controlled 65,000 acres and had profitable relations with Japanese laborers and tenants. As Chester Rowell noted, the holders of such views were a "minority . . . in California, but those who hold [them] own a great deal of California." Business and labor were now again in their usual polar positions. Their attitudes were dictated by what they believed to be enlightened self-interest. But California, like much of the country during what is called the Progressive Era, was entering into a period of essentially middle-class political leadership. The 1909 legislature was the last to be dominated by the conservative Republicans and the Southern Pacific Railroad. In the next election, the California Progressives, still nominally Republicans, captured the state and made Hiram Johnson chief executive. The historian of California progressivism has pointed out that, while one of their cardinal objectives was to restore competition, the progressives felt that there were limits to competition. "To the progressive mind, one of these limits should be the color line." The middle-class progressive liked to think of himself as enlightened and free of prejudice; yet at the same time he insisted that separate races could not mix. As one of the chief progressive spokesmen put it:

"[Racial discrimination] is blind and uncontrollable prejudice . . . yet social separateness seems to be imposed by the very law of nature." "Race . . . counts more than anything else in the world. It is the mark God placed on those whom he put asunder. It is grounded in the instincts of man, and is not amenable to reason." "[An educated Japanese] would not be a welcomed suitor for the hand of any American's daughter [but] an Italian of the commonest standing and qualities would be a more welcomed suitor than the finest gentleman of Japan. So the line is biological, and we draw it at the biological point—at the propagation of the species." "[Intermarriage between a Japanese and a White would be] a sort of international adultery. . . . The instinct of self-preservation of our race demands that its future members shall be members of our race. . . . Personally, I think this instinct is wise and beneficial." "If we deal with this race question now, our descendants will have no race questions to deal with. If Californians do not deal with it now, they, like ante-bellum South Carolinians, will leave a race question which their descendants will have to deal with, and against which they will be helpless." "The only time to solve a race problem is before it begins." "It is for the white peoples to resolve and the brown peoples to accept the permanent physical separation of their races. But as to those who are already over the border, it is for Californians to treat them justly, and for Easterners to be sympathetic and Japanese forebearing if occasionally they fail to do so."

Such were the assumptions which motivated most of the progressives. As a rule, the progressives did not initiate anti-Japanese agitation, and were scornful of those who made it their chief stock-in-trade. Most progressives would have been satisfied to leave the matter in the hands of the federal government. After the Japanese question had been used successfully by their opponents, however, the progressives were determined to break the Democratic monopoly. During the 1910 campaign, in which the governorship was at stake, the Democrats and their allies continued to monopolize the anti-Oriental issue. Theodore Bell, Hiram Johnson's Democratic opponent, frankly courted the Asiatic Exclusion League, while Johnson did everything but openly insult it. State Senator J. B. Sanford, the "Grey Eagle of Ukiah," promised his constituents that "if reëlected" he would "use every legitimate effort in his power to secure passage" of an anti-Asiatic land bill: "The Democratic platform endorses [this] bill, and Theodore A. Bell says, that if elected Governor, he will sign such a measure."The Republicans, progressive and conservative, generally ignored this issue. Hiram Johnson's early political success was in no wise owing, as has been alleged, to manipulation of the Japanese question. If anything, his failure to use it cost him votes. As long as a friend was in the White House and that friend urged moderation, Johnson and his supporters "sat upon the lid" and prevented any legislation. This, in essence, is what happened in the 1911 legislature.

In his inaugural address, Governor Johnson pointedly ignored the Japanese problem, but from the first working day of the session it was evident that the legislators would not follow his lead. Altogether, twenty-seven anti-Japanese measures were introduced. The campaign to defeat them, however, had been started a month before the legislature met. In early December, 1910, Secretary of State Philander C. Knox informed the Japanese ambassador, Uchida, that Governor-elect Johnson had given Theodore Roosevelt assurances that he would do everything he could to prevent anti-Japanese legislation. When the first bills were introduced Johnson sent copies to Knox and added, "I think I can assure you that the committees of both Houses that will have in charge measures of this character, are wholly sane and trustworthy, and that, doubtless, they will be guided by the wishes of the Federal Administration". As the session wore on, two things soon became apparent: the senate was more insistent upon anti-Japanese legislation than the assembly, and strong efforts were being made to pass some sort of alien land act. The two most important bills were introduced by Senators Larkins and Sanford (senate bills 2 and 24). The first applied sanctions equally to all aliens, while the second only inhibited the rights of "aliens ineligible to citizenship."

This phrase, "aliens ineligible to citizenship," was vital to most anti-Japanese legislative proposals (which rarely specifically mention Japanese) and it merits explanation. In a series of decisions dating from the 1870's, the courts had ruled that since the original naturalization statute had limited naturalization to "free white persons" (this had been broadened to include Africans after the Civil War), Chinese and other Orientals were aliens ineligible to citizenship until Congress should legislate to the contrary. The Supreme Court had not yet ruled on a case involving a Japanese (and would not do so until 1922), but it was correctly assumed that Japanese fell under the same ban. Californians therefore had a convenient excuse for arguing that the laws of the United States discriminated against Orientals, not the laws of California. Any law which restricted land tenure to citizens in California would operate against Japanese, but it was felt by all moderates that a general alien land bill would be less insulting to Japan than one which applied only to aliens ineligible to citizenship. There were alien land bills on the books of several non-Pacific Coast states and the District of Columbia; most of these had been inspired by the general nativist feelings that tinged so much of the Populist revolt, and had been in no way directed against Orientals.

Another argument used to justify action by California was the fact that in Japan no alien could hold land. We have seen that Theodore Roosevelt used this hypothetical justification as early as 1905. It was specious on three counts. First, the Japanese law applied to all foreigners alike and the Japanese naturalization laws were nondiscriminatory; second, in Japan a foreigner could get a nine-hundred-and-ninety-nine-year lease (such leaseholders paid all the taxes on the property), and, third, American legal treatment of resident aliens had almost always been identical, without regard to their national origin, and any invidious departure from that precedent could rightly be regarded as discrimination. But there was nothing in law or treaty to prevent Californians from deliberately discriminating against resident aliens in the matter of agricultural land tenure.

While various anti-Japanese measures were being debated in Sacramento, two different sets of negotiations were under way in Washington. The diplomatic representatives of Japan and the United States were ironing out the details of a new treaty, and delegations from San Francisco and New Orleans were vying for the honor and profit of being host to what became the Panama-Pacific International Exposition of 1915, celebrating the opening of the Panama Canal. Among the leading California lobbyists for the exposition was Patrick Henry McCarthy, whom we met earlier as the chief patron of the Asiatic Exclusion League. He had since fallen heir to the mantle of the convicted Schmitz and Ruef, taken over the Union Labor machine, and was now mayor of San Francisco. In exchange for the support of the national administration for San Francisco's ultimately successful bid, McCarthy agreed to use his influence to halt the anti-Japanese agitation, at least temporarily. The mayor was as good as his word, and on February 13, 1911, the following startling communication was read into the record of the legislature:

the Asiatic Exclusion League regrets that regardless of the previous communication on the subject we have not been afforded an opportunity to examine the anti-alien Asiatic bills [now pending]. It is the sense of the board that such bills as these at the present time are not conducive to the final enactment of effective and permanent Asiatic exclusion legislation. . . . We respectfully request that you proceed cautiously in this manner, as pressing measures of this kind would mean irreparable injury to the exclusion cause.

O. A. Tvietmoe, President

This remarkable *volte-face*, whose motivation was not then understood, had little influence on the legislature. The incident is noteworthy on two counts: it marks the end of the effective influence of the labor-dominated Asiatic Exclusion League, which completely disintegrated within two years, and marks the beginning of the influence of the Panama-Pacific International Exposition. The businessmen who ran the exposition tried to check anti-Japanese legislation because they feared that it might prove detrimental to the success of their venture, in which the people of California had a ten-million-dollar stake.

By the end of January, although the anti-Japanese bills were still in committee, Johnson informed the State Department as follows:

a very strong sentiment exists in California in favor of . . . an act which will prevent Japanese from acquiring and holding land. . . . We believe, therefore, that before the session is closed the legislature will take up and finally adopt some measure upon the subject; and if this becomes apparent, the Lieutenant Governor, the Speaker and myself believe that [the Larkins Bill], general in character, specifically preserving rights under treaties, might be presented to the exclusion of more radical measures. If . . . legislation upon the subject is inevitable . . . would such a course . . . be acceptable to you?

Secretary Knox wired in reply that both he and the President would "strongly deprecate any legislation aimed directly or indirectly at Japanese subjects," but agreed that as a last resort a general bill would be preferred. Knox expressed the "sincere hope that any such situation may be avoided or at least postponed through your good offices."

In late February a garbled report of the contents of the newly signed but as yet unratified treaty with Japan created the belief that the Gentlemen's Agreement had been abandoned. An exchange of telegrams between the President and the governor was sent to the legislature, giving assurance that the exclusion arrangements were being maintained. In addition, Johnson issued a vigorous statement: "I know nothing of the contents of the treaty. The matter in which the people of the State are interested is exclusion. The question therefore is 'Do we get exclusion?' The President of the United States says we do and that ends the matter so far as I am concerned."

After an extremely long delay—more than two months—California's "sane and trustworthy" Senate Judiciary Committee reported out unfavorably a substitute anti-Japanese land bill on March 15. The bill reported was of the "aliens ineligible to citizenship" variety. After six days of delay and parliamentary maneuvering, the bill was passed by a vote of 29 to 3.

Johnson informed Washington of the senate's action and received in reply a long telegram from Acting Secretary of State F. M. Huntington Wilson expressing the hope that passage of the bill might be avoided. Huntington Wilson, in a very undiplomatic manner, went on to "point out how unfortunate it would be if action in the California Legislature should be such as to require [the President] to hesitate to extend . . . invitations to participate in the Panama-Pacific International Exposition, an occasion which requires that atmosphere of a settled spirit of good will and considerateness to all nations."

Johnson, who was as jealous of his prerogatives as any Balkan potentate, felt, with some justification, that the tone of this message was "particularly offensive." "Extraordinary care and pains have been taken," he wired Huntington Wilson, "to follow the suggestions and advice of the Federal Government. . . . The Governor of California has a veto. . . . There shall be no legislation discriminatory in character." He added, however, that

the State of California reserves the right to legislate as it may see fit in reference to its lands. [In addition] the statutes of the United States contain an alien land bill. . . . Do you deny to California the right to pass or the propriety of the passage of such an alien land bill? [Nevertheless] no discriminatory measure shall become a law at this time, and I repeat that this is said to you, not because of your telegram or its threat, but because the only design of this administration is to be just and do that which will redound to the peace, the dignity, the advantage and best interests of the state and nation.

The next day Johnson requested permission to publish Huntington Wilson's telegram of March 23. By this time the more tactful Knox had returned to Washington; he suavely denied that there had been any threat, smoothed Johnson's ruffled feathers, and requested no publicity, a wish Johnson respected.

The anti-Japanese land bill was sent to the assembly on March 23 and was quickly referred to its Judiciary Committee, which had been holding several similar assembly measures since the beginning of the session. None of these was reported out until the day of adjournment, March 27. Under the constitution of California, a bill must have three readings, on three separate days, before passage. The anti-Japanese bills had had only one reading. The approval of two thirds of the assemblymen could have suspended this constitutional provision, but, with the administration and the floor leaders opposed, that was patently impossible, so no attempt to force passage was made. The anti-Japanese forces had been frustrated again.

Senator Sanford wrote bitterly to Phelan that "the manner in which the [anti-Japanese] bill was defeated in the Assembly was most cowardly. . . . I am going after this alien land bill [in 1913] in a red hot way. I shall be pleased to receive any suggestions from you that you may see fit to give." But Phelan had his attention focused on an event closer at hand: the presidential election of 1912. By early October, 1911, he had thrown his support behind the reform governor of New Jersey, Woodrow Wilson, as did State Senator Anthony Caminetti. Most California Democrats, however, along with William Randolph Hearst, supported the candidacy of Champ Clark of Missouri.

As soon as it became clear that Wilson was the candidate to beat, his opponents began scouring his published works to find ammunition for the "stop Wilson" movement. The five-volume *A History of the American People* (1901–1902) furnished a goodly supply. As his biographer points out, it was history from a "conservative point of view" which Wilson "would not have written if he had known he was some day to become a presidential candidate." Various passages in the work insulted most of the non-Southern voters to whom a liberal Democratic candidate traditionally appeals. In the East it was Wilson's denunciation of the new immigrants which most embarrassed his supporters. In California the Hearst papers seized upon his statements about Orientals. Professor Wilson had written of the Chinese that they

were more to be desired, as workmen if not as citizens, than most of the coarse crew that came crowding in every year at the eastern ports. They had, no doubt, many an unsavory habit, bred unwholesome squalor in the crowded quarters where they most abounded in the western seaports, and seemed separated by their very nature from the people among whom they had come to live; but it was their skill, their intelligence, their hardy power of labor, their knack at succeeding and driving duller rivals out, rather than their alien habits, that made them feared and hated. . . . The unlikely fellows who came in at the eastern ports were tolerated because they usurped no place but the very lowest in scale of labor.

Soon after the Hearst campaign against Wilson began, Phelan wired to William F. McCombs, chairman of the Democratic National Committee:

Has governor spoken against oriental coolie immigration? Charged here volume five history he favors same. Should declare against coolies as unassimilable and destructive to republican government and white labor. Answer.

Phelan continued to press McCombs, who finally suggested that Phelan write to Wilson directly. In mid-April Phelan put the whole California case to Wilson in a lengthy letter.

We on the Pacific Coast [Phelan informed the candidate] will be pleased to know your views at this time on the subject of Oriental immigration. Permit me to briefly state the situation. . . . The Japanese have invaded the Central valleys of California. Take, for example, one highly productive fruit growing valley known as the Vaca Valley. There, the Japanese, refusing to work for wages after the first year or so, bargained for a share of the crop, and finally ousted in many instances the tenant farmers by offering the land owner larger returns, and in some instances acquired . . . the property by purchase. The white man is thus driven off the land to move farther away. The village stores, churches and homes suffer and in many instances are left without patronage or occupants. In other words, the Japanese are a blight on our civilization, destructive of the home life of the people, driving the natives to the city for employment. . . . The Hawaiian Islands are now practically a possession of Japan, as California will be unless the Japanese question is solved. . . .

President Taft last spring surrendered a clause in the Japanese treaty giving us the right to regulate immigration. No protest was raised by our legislature, because Governor Johnson and others were in Washington seeking the President's support for the Panama-Pacific Exposition. I wrote a protest, however, in the *National Monthly*, Buffalo, New York, of April, 1911, to which I beg to refer you. It is vital, I believe, for our civilization [and] for the preservation of our domestic institutions . . . that Oriental coolies be excluded from these shores.

In the campaign, this question will be raised and I would like to be able to answer such charges as have been made against your History. . . . Even where coolies are capable of doing a day's work, as they admittedly are, the question is, should they be allowed, in a fierce competition, to lower the standards of living . . . of members of the white race, who stand for home life, Republican Government and Western civilization? [If Japanese immigration continues] California would be a plantation and the white population would for a period of time, possibly, remain as overseers, but, indeed, with my knowledge of the Japanese, that would be for a very short time. The end would soon supervene.

To this last appeal Wilson replied with a telegram tailored to Phelan's specifications; he merely put his name to a statement Phelan had drafted:

In the matter of Chinese and Japanese coolie immigration [the candidate's message read] I stand for the national policy of exclusion. We cannot make a homogeneous population out of a people who do not blend with the Caucasian race. Their lower standard of living as laborers will crowd out the white agriculturalist and is, in other fields, a most serious industrial menace. The success of free democratic institutions demands of our people education, intelligence and patriotism and the state should protect them against unjust and impossible competition. Remunerative labor is the basis of contentment. Democracy rests on the equality of the citizen. Oriental coolieism will give us another race problem to solve and surely we have had our lesson.

Phelan wired McCombs: "I received Governor Wilson's wire on Oriental question and put it out at once. It made a good impression and answered Hearst just as he printed his last letter." The impression seems not to have been deep enough, for Wilson lost the California primary decisively six days later. But, after Wilson's nomination and throughout the campaign (which in California was purely Wilson versus Theodore Roosevelt, since Hiram Johnson's Progressives had taken over the Republican party and the national Republican nominee, Taft, was not even on the ballot), Wilson's message was used to telling effect. His statement was printed on a small card with Roosevelt's 1906 statement in favor of naturalizing the Japanese on the reverse. This card was distributed in large numbers. The state Democratic plank called for an alien land act to "prevent any alien not eligible to citizenship from owning land in the State of California." With Roosevelt as their candidate, the Progressives had to bear this in silence.

In the November election in California the Progressives nosed out the Democrats by 174 votes in a canvass of almost 700,000. The significant fact, however, was that the Democrats captured 44 per cent of the vote, by far their best showing since Grover Cleveland carried the state in 1892. In a postelection analysis Phelan reported to McCombs: "The Japanese question gave us in part the farmer's support. We used [Wilson's] views to good advantage by wide spread publicity in the labor districts, more particularly, and also in the rural communities." Hiram Johnson, who was Roosevelt's running mate, later told Roosevelt that the cards on the Japanese question, "distributed literally by the hundreds of thousands," had cost the Bull Moosers "at least ten thousand votes." The Japanese consul general in San Francisco did not need prophetic powers to realize that the "sleeping lion" of anti-Japanese feeling might roar into action in the coming legislature.

The directors of the Panama-Pacific International Exposition were also aware of the danger and acted accordingly. As early as January, 1912, they learned from semiofficial sources that any discriminatory legislation might result in Japan's taking "little, if any interest in the exposition." Since it was generally felt that the Japanese exhibit would be one of the most important features of the fair, the directors were prepared to go to great lengths to prevent anti-Japanese legislation.

At the end of December, 1912, A. C. Baker was assigned by his fellow directors of the Panama-Pacific International Exposition to make contact with Robert J. Hudspeth of Jersey City, a Wilson appointee to the Democratic National Committee. Baker wired Hudspeth that "If [Wilson] would send a confidential telegram to his representative in California suggesting that he prefers no anti-Japanese legislation be enacted . . . it would be desirable both [to] the Wilson administration [and] the Exposition. . . . Could you use your good offices in bringing this to the attention of President-elect Wilson immediately?" If Wilson ever received this message, he chose not to act on it. In fact, at no time between his election in November, 1912, and his inauguration in March, 1913, did the President-elect give any indication that he had the slightest inkling that his California campaigning had helped create a situation that would embarrass his administration from its very outset.

The outgoing administration also refused to take effective action. The Japanese ambassador, Chinda, called on both Taft and Knox in January, 1913, and asked them to try to prevent passage of anti-Japanese measures. Two years earlier, before the breach between the conservative and progressive wings of the Republican party had become serious, the President and his Secretary of State, with Johnson's coöperation, had been able to take effective preventive measures. In 1913, however, discouraged by their own rejection at the polls and by the party split, which Hiram Johnson had abetted, Taft and Knox made no direct attempt to forestall legislation, nor, it would seem, did they alert the President-elect to the imminent danger. Knox did tell Chinda that he had written to influential members of the California Legislature, but probably these were not members of the controlling Progressive faction.

Throughout the 1913 legislative session, the Panama-Pacific International Exposition again made extensive efforts, both direct and indirect, to prevent anti-Japanese legislation. On January 6, at a special meeting of the Exposition board of directors, who were drawn from the financial and commercial leadership of San Francisco, lists of legislators who might introduce such legislation were distributed to the directors, and it was ordered that "any member of the Board having knowledge as to how any of these Legislators could be influenced" should inform the Exposition president, Charles Caldwell Moore.

On the same day a nine-man Exposition delegation visited the state capitol, where the new legislature was organizing itself. They first had a "conference of several hours with the Governor," in which a "plan of campaign was outlined to head off any agitation" for an alien land act. Governor Johnson "displayed warm interest in the entire matter and assured President Moore of his heartiest cooperation." Members of the delegation saw individually almost every senator and assemblyman and tried to get everyone to agree not to introduce any anti-Japanese bills during that session. The Exposition spokesmen agreed that the question of Japanese landownership had to be met sometime, but felt that "there was no pressing need for it [now]." Johnson and most of the legislators indicated to the delegation that so long as no anti-Japanese bills were introduced they themselves would not introduce any, but they refused to commit themselves to oppose anti-Japanese bills actually introduced.

On January 13, the first day for the introduction of bills, anti-Japanese measures were proposed by Democratic and Progressives in both houses. As in 1911, two different kinds of alien land bills were introduced: one set barred all aliens from the ownership of land; the other barred only those aliens who were "ineligible to citizenship." As we have seen, Johnson and his forces had adroitly opposed anti-Japanese legislation in 1911. For the first two and a half months of 1913 there is no evidence that the Johnson forces, as such, threw their weight on one side or the other. Both sets of bills slowly proceeded through the legislative process. Under a new procedure the legislature met for a month, adjourned for a month, and in early March returned to complete the session.

While the legislature took its recess, Woodrow Wilson became President of the United States. On the second day of his administration Japanese Ambassador Chinda called to discuss the pending legislation in California. "The President commented that the constitution did not allow the Federal Government to intervene in matters relating to the rights of the individual states," Chinda informed his chief, Baron Makino. He understood, however, that the administration would "exercise its influence as far as possible in compliance with the desires of the Japanese Government." On March 13 Secretary of State Bryan gave Chinda similar assurances. Between March 15 and April 1 both Wilson and Bryan informed the ambassador that they were writing Californians to drop anti-Japanese measures.

While the ambassador's main concern was with legislation in California, there was also an anti-Japanese measure pending in the state of Washington, where a Democrat, Eugene Lister, was governor. It is instructive to observe the different way in which Wilson handled each situation. Wilson suggested to Bryan that he write to Governor Lister "urging him to use his influence with the state legislature 'to prevent *discrimination*— that is urge that the bill [pending] be so drawn as to make ownership depend upon something other than race.' " With Hiram Johnson, the Progressive governor of California, a different method was used. Wilson told Chinda that "in view of Johnson's emotional character" it would be useless to appeal to him directly. But Wilson was willing to make indirect appeals.

On March 17, Johnson wrote to Chester H. Rowell, one of his closest advisors, that

the situation [relating to the proposed alien land bills] is unique and interesting now, and not only interesting, but one out of which we can get a good deal of satisfaction. [Democratic State Senator Anthony] Caminetti apparently comes authoritatively to ask that we go slow with Japanese legislation. This is confidential. I think before the session adjourns the present administration at Washington may be asking us in exactly the same fashion as previous administrations have asked us, to take no position.

If Wilson hoped to get results from such tactics, he had completely mis-judged Johnson's "emotional character."

Although he had not yet taken any public position on the legislation, it is now quite clear that from about the middle of March Johnson was the behind-the-scenes manager of the alien land bill. At the governor's suggestion, the directors of the Panama-Pacific International Exposition came to Sacramento early in April to attempt to stem the anti-Japanese tide. This second Exposition delegation, which went before a joint meet-ing of the legislature on April 2, served to intensify rather than lessen anti-Japanese feeling. Johnson himself later described the affair:

I arranged for a public hearing in the Assembly Chamber, when publicly the Exposition people could present their case to the legislators. At that hearing the farmers appeared, and the debate between the very plain rugged, untutored and uncultured men from the fields and our astute and educated, plug-hatted brigade who represented the Exposition was most interesting and memorable. When it had ceased the Exposition people retired crestfallen; the audience roared its approval of the farmers and the Committee in charge of the bill immediately and unanimously reported that it "do pass."

It is hard to believe that a man as politically astute as Hiram Johnson could not have foreseen the result; the "spontaneous" demonstration by the "rugged farmers" has all the earmarks of a well-rehearsed perfor-mance. The most impressive "farmer" seems to have been one Ralph Newman, a former Congregational minister.

Near my home [Newman declaimed] is an eighty-acre tract of as fine land as there is in California. On that tract lives a Japanese. With that Japanese lives a white woman. In that woman's arms is a baby.

What is that baby? It isn't a Japanese. It isn't white. It is a germ of the mightiest problem that ever faced this state; a problem that will make the black problem of the South look white.

James D. Phelan and Paul Scharrenberg, who represented the California State Federation of Labor, also appeared in favor of the anti-Japanese bill and contributed to what one writer called "the Exposition's Last Stand." Phelan later remembered that he had said:

Gentlemen, the exposition will be in California only a year, while the white race, I hope, will be here forever. . . . Japan may not exhibit at our fair, but we cannot sell our birth-right for a tea barden. She is impudent and audacious in her position. If she does not exhibit we shall survive.

While the Assembly was still considering the bill, Johnson received two telegrams from Washington, both sent by William Kent, a Pro-gressive California congressman friendly to President Wilson. The first message advised that "Legislation against alien land tenure in order to be void of unnecessary offense should exclude all aliens but should exempt from excluding . . . those who have been permitted to file satisfactory first papers for naturalization." The second informed the governor: "Message sent is based on highest authority. This is confidential."

Johnson replied by pointing out to Kent that previous administrations had communicated directly with the governor of the state and insisted that Wilson communicate directly with him if he had anything to say. Rowell, who was shown the exchange of messages, scored Wilson's "petty and cowardly attitude" and expressed the hope that Johnson's telegram would "smoke [Wilson] out into saying . . . officially the things" he has said privately.

Wilson did not "smoke out" easily. The next communication came from Secretary of State Bryan, who requested only the full text of measures pending and asked that Johnson refrain from signing any bill passed until the federal government could present arguments for a possible veto. Johnson replied: ". . . it is necessary if any feature of the bill is obnoxious to the views of the state department that the legislature be advised at once." Ineffectual telegraphic sparring continued for more than a week. Up until April 17 the Progressive majority in both houses of the legislature was pressing for an antialien bill general in terms, which, despite its obvious intent, would have been less offensive to Japan. Johnson had assured Bryan that the final bill would be couched in those terms. Then there was a change of policy. As Johnson explained to Rowell:

> The Senate Bill was carefully prepared, as you know, but since the agitation commenced the pressure has been tremendous upon the members of the legislature from those interested in foreign corporations, to exclude [from the bill] all foreign corporations, except those in which the holders of the majority of the stock were ineligible to citizenship.

Johnson then made an admission he would never make in public statements on the matter: "Of course, this points the bill."

Meanwhile, California discrimination against Japanese had again created an international crisis. Jingoes and extremists in Japan were screaming for war with the United States. On April 17 "a crowd of some 20,000 Japanese in Tokyo cheered wildly as a member of the Diet demanded the sending of the Imperial fleet to California to protect Japanese subjects and maintain the nation's dignity." Wilson and Bryan, despite their obvious reluctance, had to take some sort of positive action. Yet Bryan, probably unwittingly, had already fumbled the only likely chance for an amicable settlement. On April 12 Ambassador Chinda voluntarily offered a concession which might have served to allay the California agitation: he suggested that Japan might be willing to curb the coming of the "picture brides." Bryan ignored this offer. Had he accepted it, he would have had, like Roosevelt in 1907, something to offer California in exchange for coöperation. As it turned out, he came to California empty-handed; he returned without results.

Wilson was finally "smoked out" on April 22. In identical telegrams to Johnson and the legislature the President appealed "with the utmost confidence to the people, the government, and the Legislature of California" and asserted that if they deemed it necessary "to exclude all aliens who have not declared their intention to become citizens from the privileges of landownership" there could be no complaint. He went on to imply, speciously, that the bill under consideration would violate treaty rights of the Japanese, and ended his request with a high-flown reference to "national policy and national honor." Johnson's answer insisted that the bill did not violate the treaty—a position the State Department itself later took in answering the Japanese protests.

Wilson then requested that Johnson receive Secretary of State Bryan "for the purpose of consulting . . . and cooperating with you and [the members of the legislature] in the framing of a law which would meet the views of the people of the State and yet leave untouched the international obligations of the United States." Johnson agreed, and Bryan started the four-day train ride to California.

While Bryan was traveling all formal legislative proceedings on the land bills ceased; but during that time Johnson, together with Ulysses S. Webb, the state attorney general, and Francis J. Heney, a leading Progressive, drafted a substitute bill that explicitly protected all rights under the 1911 treaty with Japan and eliminated the phrase "aliens ineligible to citizenship" by the substitution of the equally offensive phrases "all aliens eligible to citizenship" and "all aliens other than . . ." Johnson commented soon afterward that

we all thought, of course, that [Bryan] was coming here with something of great importance to impart, and the gravity of the situation was during this period of waiting, more keenly felt than at any other time. When Mr. Bryan arrived, immediately we arranged for his consultation with the legislature, and that consultation, at his suggestion, was made *executive*. The very suggestion aroused to the highest pitch the interest of the legislators, and the first meeting with Mr. Bryan was held with the idea prevalent that he would make such disclosures as would render imparative postponement of our measure.

If Johnson and the legislators entertained such expectations, they were soon disabused. The transcript of Bryan's two executive meetings with the California legislature runs to 113 typewritten pages and demonstrates clearly that the onetime "Boy Orator of the Platte" had lost none of his vocal staying power in middle age. Johnson's acid comment that "Mr.

Bryan presented nothing that could not have been transmitted within the limits of a night letter, without using all of the allotted words," is reasonably accurate. Bryan himself stated: "I came here with no program. I came simply to confer." Bryan's hands were tied by the President, who had instructed him not "to sanction particular statutes or forms of legislation." Bryan's unprecedented trip seems mostly to have been a matter of window dressing; since the proceedings were secret, the Japanese must have surmised that the administration was making Herculean, if belated, efforts to avert invidious legislation. Most of the outnumbered Democrats in the legislature, including Sanford and Caminetti, heretofore ardent proponents of all anti-Japanese legislation, did indeed vote to postpone consideration of the bill to the next legislature, but this was a hopeless effort. The Johnson administration's bill was pushed through both houses in less than four days, passing the senate by 35 to 2 and the assembly by 72 to 3. At Wilson's request, Johnson held the measure for a time; he then signed it on May 19.

Johnson wrote a long letter to Bryan justifying his action. Organizing his arguments like the trained lawyer he was, the governor, in terms reminiscent of his tart telegram to Huntington Wilson two years before, insisted that:

> By the law adopted we offer no offense; we make no discrimination. The offense and discrimination are contained, it is claimed, in the use of the words "eligible to citizenship." . . . We do not mention the Japanese or any other race. . . . If invidious discriminations ever were made in this regard, the United States made [them] when the United States declared who were and who were not eligible for citizenship. . . . If discrimination it is discrimination against California. We insist that justly no offense can be taken by any nation to this law. . . . We of California . . . have violated absolutely no treaty rights; we have shown no shadow of discrimination; we have given no nation the right to be justified in taking offense.

Was Johnson the mover or the moved? Was the long-deferred anti-Japanese legislation inevitable, or could it have been avoided in 1913? Johnson himself claimed credit for the passage of the bill. He wrote to his political mentor, Theodore Roosevelt, that he regarded the passage of the bill as a political triumph:

> It was perfectly obvious to me that when we had started upon our course, there was nothing to do but to go through with it and pass our bill. Of course, all of our timid legislators would have liked to recede, and at times I had extraordinary difficulty in making them understand that having started we must finish and I really believe that many of them went through with the matter more in personal loyalty than because they had any stomach for the particular kind of legislation . . . you can pardon, perhaps a little malicious

pleasure, that I took out of the attitude of our democratic brethren and the democrats of the national administration. I think we have laid the ghost. I know that never again in California can the Japanese question be a political question, except as we shall want it to be.

Under Johnson's leadership the California legislature committed a wanton action—wanton because Johnson, at least, knew well that Japanese land tenure in California would not be seriously affected by it. In effect, the Alien Land Law limited leases of agricultural land to Japanese to maximum terms of three years and barred further land purchases by Japanese aliens. It was quite simple for the attorneys who represented Japanese interests in California to evade the intent of this law, as Californians were soon to discover. One of Johnson's chief advisers pointed this out to him before the bill had been drafted. "It will be perfectly easy," wrote Chester Rowell, "to evade the law by transferring to . . . local representatives enough stock to make fifty-one per cent of it ostensibly held by American citizens." For the growing number of Issei who had American-born children, it was even simpler: they merely had the stock or title vested in their citizen children, whose legal guardianship they naturally assumed.

The passage of the Alien Land Law was regarded as a severe affront by the Japanese government, which protested to Washington vigorously. A long exchange of notes came to nothing. Both governments took rather absurd positions: the Japanese claimed that their treaty rights had been violated, while the American contended that there was, in fact, no discrimination intended by California.

The greater part of the nation's press, particularly in the East, opposed the California law. The controversy became a national issue lasting for several months. Between April 4 and the end of May there were stories on the California land law in the New York *Times* on every day but three; twenty-seven times during that period it was deemed front-page news.

Within California there was a certain amount of dissatisfaction with the Alien Land Law of 1913. The Anti-Jap Laundry League insisted later that "the law as it stands means little or nothing." Theodore Bell, leader of the anti-Wilson Democratic faction in the state, argued that the "Johnson machine has made a bad mess"; the law did not, in his opinion, restrict the Japanese enough, and he threatened to invoke the newly enacted initiative to get a stronger law. Harry Chandler, of the Los Angeles *Times*, a prominent conservative spokesman, attacked the law as an "unwise and uncalled for measure." A leading Protestant periodical in the state felt that it was "unfortunate" and inspired by the "rudimentary race hatred and race prejudice" that was "deeply imbedded in the social life of California."

These, however, were minority views; most Californians seemed to believe, as their governor professed to, that they had "laid the ghost of the Japanese question." For a few years it seemed, superficially, that they had. From 1913 until 1919 there was no widespread anti-Japanese agitation. One reason was that during the First World War such agitation would have been inexpedient (and after the American declaration of war perhaps seditious), since the Japanese were also at war with Germany. But the "sleeping lion" of anti-Japanese emotion in California would reawaken, stronger than before, and would do so in a national climate of opinion much more conducive to ultimate success.

14

The Postwar Campaign Against Japanese Americans

CAREY McWILLIAMS

> *Carey McWilliams, now editor of* The Nation, *was for many years the most effective voice for racial justice in California. This work, written during World War II, helped alert Americans to the atrocity that Dean Eugene V. Rostow of Yale Law School would later call "our worst wartime mistake."*

The Postwar Campaign

DURING the 1915 and 1917 sessions of the California legislature attempts had been made to pass additional anti-Japanese measures; but these proposals were held in abeyance and later tabled when we found ourselves in the war as an ally of Japan. But on April 1, 1919, while the Peace Conference was in session in Paris, two California Senators sought to introduce a number of anti-Japanese bills. A cablegram was sent to the Secretary of State in Paris, asking his views on the advisability of pressing such legislation at the time. Mr. Lansing immediately replied that it would be particularly unfortunate to have the bills introduced and requested that they be withdrawn. But the moment the Treaty of Versailles was signed on June 28, 1919, a wave of anti-Japanese agitation swept California.

This renewed agitation differed, in important respects, from earlier movements. To an extent that had not previously been true, this agitation was anti-Japan rather than anti-Japanese. Elements that had never been previously interested now became violent partisans of the "anti" movement. This shift in opinion was largely due to Japanese action in Korea, Siberia, China, and Shantung. The publication of a number of books about the Korean situation contributed to the shift. Also various government reports dealing with Hawaii served to arouse general apprehension.

Organized labor, which had taken a leading part in all previous agitations, now began to dissociate itself from the anti-Japanese movement.

SOURCE: Carey McWilliams, *Prejudice—Japanese Americans: Symbol of Racial Intolerance* (New York, Little, Brown & Company, 1944), pp. 57-63. Reprinted with permission of the author.

After 1910 the Japanese had been driven from the cities toward the land. Now it looked as though they were going to be driven from the land back to the cities, and labor did not relish this possibility. The Federated Trades Council of Sacramento, on September 10, 1920, passed a resolution condemning anti-Japanese "propaganda now being spread by designing parties to the detriment of labor." In 1916 the American Federation of Labor failed, for the first time in years, to pass an anti-Oriental resolution. Speaking in California, Hugo Ernst, a leader of the San Francisco labor movement, had said: "This sort of resolution gets us nowhere. Why can't we face the question more squarely and organize the Japanese workers in our midst, which is the only solution to the question?" Walter Mac-Arthur, another influential labor leader, condemned the idea of "racial inferiority." "You can't charge the Japs with unassimilability," said Richard Caverly of the Boilermakers Union; "the same charge used to be directed against the lousy Irish." Despite labor's growing disaffection, however, the postwar anti-Japanese agitation was founded upon a broader popular base than at any previous period.

"The origin of the agitation which developed in 1919," write Tupper and McReynolds, "was a purely political move with an eye on the 1920 election." United States Senator James D. Phelan, a Democrat seeking re-election when every sign pointed to a Republican landslide, premised his entire campaign upon the issue of White Supremacy. Writing in the *Grizzly Bear* for February, 1920, he said: "Imagine a Japanese seeking the hand of an American woman in marriage! . . . If you knew," he said in the same article, "how these people raise their garden truck, you would never let a bite of it pass your lips." To aid the sorely pressed Senator, his colleagues arranged for the Committee on Immigration and Naturalization to hold hearings in California during the summer of 1920. The hearings were opened in San Francisco on July 12, 1920, by Senator Phelan himself. He testified that the "Japanese are an immoral people"; proceeded to confuse Buddhism and Shintoism; charged that California was headed toward "mongrelization and degeneracy"; claimed that mysterious threats had been made upon his life; and urged that the Japanese be ousted to save the state from the threat of Bolshevism! A man of great wealth, Senator Phelan financed the Anti-Asiatic League and the Oriental Exclusion League, both of which organizations were integral parts of his political machine.

After the Treaty of Versailles had been signed, the California legislators began to clamor for a special session so that they might pass the bills which had been tabled at the request of Mr. Lansing. Governor William D. Stephens refused to call a special session. The Native Sons immediately demanded his removal from office; renounced the opposition as "Jap-lovers," and railled their forces to save "California—the White

Man's Paradise." In an effort to sidetrack this agitation, Governor Stephens caused a special report to be prepared on the Japanese question. When this report (*California and the Oriental*) appeared in June, 1920, it was found to be a characteristically rabid document. It also appeared that the Governor himself had finally decided to mount the anti-Japanese bandwagon. Seeking to punish him, however, for his failure to call a special session of the legislature, the "anti" forces immediately placed two initiative measures on the November ballot: an alien poll-tax bill and a new Alien Land Act. Both measures were approved by decisive majorities: the Alien Land Act by a vote of 668,483 to 222,086.

The agitation accompanying the 1920 election and the campaign over these measures occasioned widespread resentment in Japan. In the autumn of 1920, the Marquis Okuma called a meeting in Tokyo to organize a publicity campaign against "the unlawful attitude of the California-Americans." Viscount Takahira Kato had said of the 1920 Alien Land Act: "We can never overlook this act." Students in Tokyo began to debate the question "Shall We Declare War against the United States?" and in this country Walter B. Pitkin raised the question: "Must We Fight Japan?" This 1920 agitation rapidly assumed national proportions. "The spread of the agitation throughout the country," observe Tupper and McReynolds, "encouraged the anti-Japanese agitators to renew their movement against the Japanese immigrant, and the old issues were once again brought to the front pages of the press." The California Oriental Exclusion League began to send speakers throughout the East and Middle West, and to cover the nation with its pamphlets and leaflets. Coming as it did, when the ink was scarcely dry on the Treaty of Versailles, this agitation did incalculable harm. It brought us, as a matter of fact, to the brink of war with Japan.

In point of virulence, the 1920 agitation far exceeded any similar demonstration in California. In support of the initiative measures, the American Legion exhibited a motion picture throughout the state entitled "Shadows of the West." All the charges ever made against the Japanese were enacted in this film. The film showed a mysterious room fitted with wireless apparatus by which "a head Japanese ticked out prices which controlled a state-wide vegetable market"; spies darted in and out of the scenes, Japanese were shown dumping vegetables into the harbor to maintain high prices; two white girls were abducted by a group of Japanese men only to be rescued, at the last moment, by a squad of American Legionnaires. When meetings were called to protest the exhibition of this scurrilous film, the meetings were broken up.

Two influential novels appeared which were planned as part of the campaign: *Seed of the Sun* (1921) by Wallace Irwin and *The Pride of Palomar* (1921) by Peter B. Kyne. The Irwin novel, I am informed, was prepared at the instigation of V. S. McClatchy. Both novels had appeared as serials in national publications of large circulation in 1920: the Irwin novel in the *Saturday Evening Post* and the Kyne novel in the *Cosmopolitan*. Both novels, according to Ruth Fowler, were long in active demand in the California public libraries. Mr. Cornelius Vanderbilt, Jr., sent copies of the Kyne novel to a list of important Americans and requested their comments. These were published in a pamphlet entitled *The Verdict of Public Opinion on the Japanese-American Question*. The Kyne novel was largely based upon Mr. Montaville Flowers' *The Japanese Conquest of American Opinion* (1917), and was dedicated to Mr. Flowers.

Here are some of the charges made against the Japanese in Mr. Kyne's novel: their manners are abominable; they are greedy, selfish, calculating, quarrelsome, suspicious, crafty, irritable, and unreliable; they have no sense of sportsmanship, no affection for their wives, and they have never shown the slightest nobility or generosity of spirit. These remarks were directed, of course, at immigrants living in America. "When a member of the great Nordic race," observes the hero of the novel, "fuses with a member of a pigmented race, both parties to the union violate a natural law." This hero, a Native Son, angrily argues with another character that "we ought to have Jim Crow cars for these cock-sure sons of Nippon." The book is one long paean of praise for the Anglo-Saxon copied almost verbatim from Homer Lea and Montaville Flowers. Amusingly enough, however, it is an Anglo-Saxon character who, in conspiracy with a Japanese, attempts to defraud the hero (who is part Mexican, but a "high-class" Mexican). "How about John Chinaman?" one character asks the hero. To this query he gives the stock California answer: "Oh, a Chinaman is different. He's a regular fellow—he appreciates the sanity of our position." When the Declaration of Independence is mentioned, the hero counters with the charge that that document was written by "sublimated jackasses."

Josiah Royce once observed, apropos of Anti-Oriental agitation in his native state of California, that "trained hatreds are particularly pathetic and peculiarly deceitful." By 1920 the people of California had been thoroughly trained to hate the Japanese and other Oriental people. Charges advanced against the Chinese in 1876—when the first Congressional committee inquired into the Oriental problem on the Coast—had been repeated, with scarcely a single modification, in every subsequent hearing or investigation. The people of California had listened to these charges; had heard them repeated by responsible public officials; had seen them in the newspapers and on the billboards; and had become familiar with them in every political campaign. For seventy-five years, writes Dr. Charles N. Reynolds, the people of California had "lived in an atmosphere of racial consciousness." Surveying the files of one small-town newspaper, Dr. Reynolds found 2877 news items about the Japanese, totaling 20,453 inches of space. The general attitude reflected in these items was that of "irritation verging on hostility." He also found that there were "peaks" and "depressions" in the amount of space devoted to the Japanese (which he was able to correlate with election years and periods of economic depression). "The almost complete disappearance of unfavorable news in the breaks between high levels," he wrote, "is eloquent proof of the fictitious character of the anti-Japanese movement."

The 1920 agitation in California was so violent that it overflowed, so to speak, and began to affect other groups. In the summer of 1920, roadside signs appeared in Fresno stating: "No Armenians Wanted"; and at the same time petitions were circulated, around Lodi, against the Armenians, Turks, Greeks, and Hindus, as well as against the Japanese. On the night of July 18, 1921, a band of several hundred white men, with the "apparent connivance of the police," rounded up fifty-eight Japanese laborers in Turlock, "placed them on board a train, and warned them never to return." The repercussions in Tokyo were instantaneous. "No recent development," wrote Louis Seibold, "has ever caused more excitement among the Japanese than the recent driving out of 700 Japs from the fruit section around Turlock, California. The leading newspapers of Tokio, Osaka, Kobe and Nagasaki seized upon the incident to demand from the United States an indemnity for the damage done to the feelings of the former subjects of the Mikado by the citizens of California." The Turlock "incident," notes Mr. Buell, was "a direct result of the campaigns of incitement against the Japanese which have featured in many California elections. The incident shows that the means employed by the Pacific Coast to 'solve' its Japanese problem merely increase the ill-feeling between the Oriental and the whites, and still further alienate the Japanese from American life." Later Japanese were driven out of the Merced area and still later from Hopland and other parts of the state.

These "incidents" in California in 1920 and 1921 had international significance. The Washington Naval Conference convened on November 12, 1921, and was in session through February, 1922. Prior agitation in California threatened to interfere with the plans for the conference. The people of Japan were certainly not in a position, in these years, to follow the devious diplomatic moves of their rulers; but as Mr. Buell has pointed out, the agitation in California "was perfectly comprehensible to the people of Tokyo." Surveying the work of the conference itself, Mr. Buell said: "As long as we continue this pin-pricking policy toward Japanese legally resident in this country, the Japanese in Japan will naturally be led to believe that the anti-Japanese agitation in the United

States is wholly illegitimate and caused by racial prejudice alone. More important still, they will be led to believe by the military party in Japan, that America's protests against Japanese imperialism in Asia are a mere mask behind which are hidden the 'real' designs of the United States in the Far east." The main reason for popular Japanese suspicion of American policy consisted in "our domestic policy toward the Japanese."

15

California's Discrimination Against Filipinos, 1927-1935

H. BRETT MELENDY

> *H. Brett Melendy, for many years a professor of history at San José State College, is now on the faculty of the University of Hawaii. Here he examines the oppression suffered by the least studied and the least upwardly mobile of all the Asian nationalities in California.*

WESTERN people are brought up to regard Orientals or colored peoples as inferior, but the mockery of it all is that Filipinos are taught to regard Americans as our equals. Adhering to American ideals, living American life, these are contributory to our feeling of equality. The terrible truth in America shatters the Filipinos' dream of fraternity.

I was completely disillusioned when I came to know this American attitude. If I had not been born in a lyrical world, grown up with honest people and studied about American institutions and racial equality in the Philippines I should never have minded so much the horrible impact of white chauvinism. I shall never forget what I have suffered in this country because of racial prejudice.[1]

Thus cried out Carlos Bulosan for Filipinos in 1937 against indignity and injustice. Those Filipinos, residing on the Pacific Coast during the 1920's and the 1930's were victims of anti-Asiatic hostilities which the western States had perfected over the years against Chinese, Japanese, and "Hindus." The basic motive of Asiatic discrimination was legislation leading to exclusion. Though the 1924 Immigration Act appeared to complete the exclusionist's program at the close of the 1920's, Californians became concerned about what they called the third Oriental invasion.

[1] Letter, Carlos Bulosan to Dorothy Babb, Los Angeles, Dec. 12, 1937, in Carlos Bulosan, *Sound of Falling Light: Letters in Exile*, ed. Dolores S. Feria (Quezon City, 1960), 191–192.

SOURCE: H. Brett Melendy, "California's Discrimination Against Filipinos, 1927–1935," in J. M. Saniel, ed., *The Filipino Exclusion Movement, 1927–1935—Occasional Papers No. 1* (Quezon City, Philippines: Institute of Asian Studies, University of the Philippines, 1967). Reprinted by permission of the author and the University of the Philippines.

Representing powerful circles in the state—including newspaper men, Congressmen, and elected state officials—California exclusionists constituted a vocal minority. They feared that as a consequence of a growing Filipino immigration, they were losing their fight for exclusion. On the other hand, those sympathetic with the Filipinos formed another minority group consisting of large scale agriculturalists (for economic reasons) and church leaders and educators (for social and moral reasons).

Actually, the large majority of Californians were apathetic to the Filipino problem which did not directly affect them. Whenever confronted with the problem, Californians, however, readily endorsed the exclusionist's programs of discrimination and exclusion legislation. Social, economic, and political harassment became part of the way of life for the California Filipino as labor groups and racists preached fear of economic competition, a lowering of American morality, miscegenation, and health hazards.[2]

Prior to the 1920's, Filipinos, coming to the United States primarily as students, were welcomed as disciples of democracy who would return to the islands to inculcate the American way of life among their own people.[3] This view changed after 1924. By then, an acute shortage of casual agricultural labor developed, resulting partly from the Immigration Act and from the failure of Californians to enforce the anti-alien land laws. Briefly, replacements had to be made for Japanese labor which was no longer available. Since white labor was not interested in filling up this void, large-scale American farmers turned again to foreign labor markets: Filipinos and Mexicans were induced to migrate. The labor scene was, however, changed during the depression. As the number of available white workers increased, racial antagonism against the Filipinos also markedly increased in California and Washington.

Having neither wives nor families in California, Filipino laborers migrating to the United States were quite young: either in their teens or in their early twenties.[4] The lack of social balance (not unique with this group) led the Filipinos later into conflict with the dominant white group when they associated with white girls, or gambled and fought among themselves.

Filipinos, like other immigrant groups, arrived in America as sojourners

[2] John H. Burma, *Spanish-Speaking Groups in the United States* (Durham: Duke Univ. Press, 1954), 141–145; California, Department of Industrial Relations, *Facts About Filipino Immigration Into California* (Sacramento: Special Bulletin No. 3, April, 1930), 12–13; Bruno Lasker, *Filipino Immigration to Continental United States and to Hawaii* (Chicago: Univ. of Chicago Press, 1939), 129–132.

[3] Carlos P. Romulo, *I Walked with Heroes* (New York: Holt, Rinehart and Winston, 1961), 130–154.

[4] Burma, *op. cit.*, 139–140; Lasker, *op. cit.*, 324–325; Maximo C. Manzon, *The Strange Case of the Filipinos in the United States* (New York: American Committee for Protection of Foreign Born, 1938), 7.

or "birds of passage," to earn money in order to return home as wealthy men. Most were, however, doomed to failure. The significant point is that Filipinos thought they would reside in California for but a short time, and made no serious effort at assimilation. Thus, they aided the exclusionists' argument that Filipinos made no effort to adapt themselves to the American way of life. Of course, these discriminators also made certain that Filipinos were not readily accepted by California society.[5]

Of all Asiatic groups, the Filipinos faced a most desperate and trying situation when confronted with discrimination. They had no governmental authority willing to speak for them as was the case (in varying degrees) for the Chinese, Japanese, or "Hindus." Technically classified as nationals, Filipino immigrants were neither fish nor fowl. During their residence in California, they were the United States Federal Government's unwanted wards. By definition in the 1924 Immigration Act, Filipinos were not considered aliens and were free to come to the United States. This proviso lasted until May 1, 1935 when the Filipino legislature accepted the Tydings-McDuffie Independence Act which provided an annual quota of fifty.[6] Filipinos, when traveling abroad, carried United States passports. Internally, they enjoyed only the most fundamental rights as described in the Insular Cases.[7]

Numerically, Filipinos never posed a threat to California or the United States. Exclusionists felt threatened primarily because Filipinos were from Asia. In 1920, there were 5,603 Filipinos in the United States with about 3,300 estimated to be in California.[8] By 1930, with increased demands for field workers, there were 45,208 in the United States with about 30,000 in California.[9] This significant increase caused alarm in California and won converts to the exclusionists' cause. By 1940, with the quota in effect after 1935 and the attending employment problems created by the depression, the number of Filipinos remained constant. In the

---

[5] Lasker, *op. cit.*, 326, 330; Manuel Buaken, *I Have Lived with the American People* (Caldwell, Idaho: Caxton Printers, 1948), 32–33, 45; Social Science Institute, Fisk University, "Orientals and Their Cultural Adjustment" (Social Science Source Documents #4, 1946), III.

[6] U.S. *Statutes at Large*, XLIII, Part I, 168; Garel A. Grunder and William E. Livezey, *The Philippines and the United States* (Norman, Okla.: Univ. of Oklahoma Press, 1951), 205, 223.

[7] Manzon, *op. cit.*, 5–6; Carey McWilliams, *Brothers Under the Skin* (rev. ed.; Boston: Little Brown & Co., 1951), 243.

[8] Calif. Dept. of Industrial Relations, *op. cit.*, 9.

[9] U.S. Bureau of the Census, *Sixteenth Census of the United States: 1940, Population, Characteristics of the Nonwhite Population by Race* (Washington, D.C.: Bureau of Printing, 1940), 2. California exclusionists claimed there were 60,000 Filipinos in the United States in 1930 with 50,000 in California. See U.S. Congress, House Committee on Immigration and Naturalization. *Hearings on Exclusion of Immigration from the Philippine Islands*, 71st Cong., 2nd Sess., 1930, 4.

United States, there were 45,563 with 31,408 residing in California.[10]

California's anti-Filipino opposition actually desired exclusion but this took time to implement since it required federal legislation. Meanwhile, discrimination techniques were employed to discourage Filipino immigration. These were supported by those Californians who believed that any Asiatics were bad for the State. Emory S. Bogardus—the leading sociologist studying the Filipino issue at the time—found that Caucasians holding favorable views based their opinions upon the Filipinos' educational ambitions, their willingness to do menial tasks, and their courteous and polite behavior when observed while working in hotels and restaurants. Unfavorable Caucasian views were based upon economic competition which displaced white workers as well as on the opposition of some farm employers who found Filipinos not capable of heavy farm work. Some agriculturists, who needed their labor, were unhappy because Filipinos were not docile, had a propensity to strike, and tended to be quarrelsome. A standard complaint also dealt with their aggressive attitudes toward white girls.[11]

In 1929, the Commonwealth Club of California studied Filipino immigration. Its study section reported that the Filipino's education did not fit him for American society. Admittedly based on incomplete evidence, the Filipino was found to be belligerent and a public health liability. Morally and socially, the Filipino did not improve life in the States. The absence of home life and Filipino women led him into undesirable associations with white women. The report further stated that Filipinos did not spend their wages properly, lived extravagantly, and engaged in gambling. The Commonwealth Club thus reinforced complaints of economic competition, improper sexual relationships, and problems of health, crime, and vice.[12]

During the depression years, hatred and fear of the Filipinos increased. In January, 1936, a San Francisco Municipal Court Judge unburdened himself during a case involving a Filipino:

It is a dreadful thing when these Filipinos, scarcely more than savages, come to San Francisco, work for practically nothing, and obtain the society of these girls. Because they work for nothing, decent white boys cannot get jobs.[13]

Carey McWilliams claimed that a Los Angeles Chamber of Commerce official denounced the Filipinos as "the most worthless, unscrupulous,

10 *Ibid.*, 4–5.
11 Emory S. Bogardus, "American Attitudes Towards Filipinos," *Sociology and Social Research*, XIV (1929), 59–69.
12 Commonwealth Club of California, "Filipino Immigration," *Transactions*, XXIV (1929), 312–320.
13 *San Francisco Chronicle*, Jan. 22, 1936, 13.

shiftless, diseased, semi-barbarians that ever came to our shores." [14] Perhaps, the viewpoint that gained the most widespread acceptance was stated by a Northern Monterey County Justice of the Peace in 1930. He first charged the Filipinos as possessing unhealthy habits and as destroying the wage scale for other nationalities. Secondly, Filipinos— little brown men attired like Solomon in all his glory—strutted around like cocks trying to attract young American and Mexican girls. Thirdly, Filipinos in America were but ten years removed from the loin and breechcloth. Lastly, they lived fifteen in one room and sustained themselves on rice and fish.[15] In short, the Filipino was destructive of American standards of labor and morality.

A Filipino, interviewed by the Social Science Institute of Fisk University, has summed up the reaction to this race hatred. He indicated that as a boy in the Islands, he had gained idealistic views about the United States. Upon arrival in San Francisco, he found himself considered different because of race and color. Once it had been determined that he was a Filipino, a definite attitudinal feeling of hostility developed. He added:

If I had the one chance of my life to express what I feel deepest about America and Americans, I would say that the white race is superior in either doing good or bad for others than any of the dark or colored races. The Americans can be the most generous people on earth towards other people and at the same time be unkind or unchristian in their dealings with the same, when they come face to face with each other.

The Americans are stupid when it comes to understanding foreign people because they think of themselves at their best and of the foreigners at their worst. They do not take any time to stop and think that foreigners, especially my people, have a different psychology and civilization.[16]

Economically, Filipinos were at the bottom of California's wage scale. Large farm operators used them because they had to, but did so reluctantly.[17] Filipinos, for their part, protested against unfair employment practices and defrauding of wages. Manual Buaken, a Filipino who en-

[14] McWilliams, *op. cit.*, 238.

[15] Buaken, *op. cit.*, 169; E. S. Bogardus, *Anti-Filipino Race Riots* (San Diego: Ingram Institute, May 15, 1930), 7–8.

[16] Social Science Institute, Fisk Univ., 112, 119.

[17] Interview, James Earl Wood with Paul Lewis, San Joaquin County Horticulture Commission, Feb. 15, 1930; James Earl Wood, "The Employer's Evaluation of Filipino Labor" in the James Earl Wood Collection; "Miscellaneous Printed Items Relating to Filipinos in California and the United States," Bancroft Library, Univ. of California, Berkeley; U.S. Congress, House Committee on Immigration and Naturalization, *Preliminary Hearing, Immigration from Countries of the Western Hemisphere*, 71st Cong., 2nd Session, 1930, 224–229.

dured the discrimination, charged that American farmers swindled Filipino farm hands regularly. He also reported that living conditions were always horrible. Consequently, many Filipinos preferred living and working in the cities.[18]

Bruno Lasker reported that small and rural community employers were influenced largely by non-economic motives. They claimed it was unwise to hire Filipinos where white women worked or where there was possible competition with white Americans. Many hotel and restaurant owners, conscious of customer prejudice, did not hire Filipinos for positions which would entail their meeting with the public.[19]

During the depression years, the fact that Filipinos were not citizens worked economic hardships. They were excluded from many federal relief projects.[20] M. C. Manzon wrote in 1938 that Filipinos were bewildered because of their uncertain citizenship status. Many of the Filipinos lost federal jobs. As the depression deepened, others were denied employment in private business for priority in hiring employees was extended to citizens.[21] Filipinos confronted economic discrimination throughout California. Out of this difficulty developed the movement for repatriation.

Filipinos were subjected to the usual social discrimination meted out to racial minority groups. Police harassment was common. Tennis courts, swimming pools, billiard parlors, barbershops, restaurants, and some churches were closed to them.[22] Unfortunately, these themes have been repetitive and familiar in United States history and need not be expanded here.

California's discrimination against minorities in real estate and housing has been of long standing. Therefore, Filipinos were forced to live in slum areas. Frequently, fifteen to twenty were compelled to live in one room.[23] Ironically, it was the Californians who forced the Filipinos into sub-standard living in urban areas and provided wretched housing on ranches and then attacked Filipinos for creating health problems and not living as Americans. Buaken best summarizes the feeling of Filipinos about the housing problem. After being denied, time and time again, a place of his own choosing, he wrote:

[18] Buaken, *op. cit.*, 87–88; Interview, James Wood with Mrs. Marcuello, Stockton, Feb. 7, 1930, James Earl Wood Collection, Bancroft Library.

[19] Lasker, *op. cit.*, 334.

[20] Manzon, *op. cit.*, 10; *San Francisco Chronicle*, Jan. 15, 1934, 10.

[21] *Ibid.*, 7–10.

[22] Bogardus, "Filipino Immigrant Attitudes," *Sociology and Social Research*, XIV (1930), 474; Bogardus, "The Filipino Immigrant Problem," *ibid.*, XIII (1929), 478; Buaken, *op. cit.*, 73–74, 94; Social Science Institute, Fisk Univ., 132.

[23] Burma, *op. cit.*, 144; U.S. Congress, House Committee on Immigration and Naturalization, *Hearings, To return to the Philippine Islands Unemployed Filipinos*, 72nd Cong., 2nd Sess., 1933, 8–9.

my personal pride was entirely subdued; I was wounded deeply in heart and soul for on that day I had tasted more pangs of life's bitterness and all the sordidness of this world than I [had] ever known before, and I learned what calamity and what tragic consequences race prejudice can inflict upon a man's life.[24]

The fear that Filipinos would wedge into California society led to social discrimination in order to keep them in their place.

A basic factor leading to social discrimination was the fear related to Filipino sexual desires and the danger these held for white women. Anti-Filipino spokesman saw America's future endangered by miscegenation. While exclusionists claimed this as a definite fact and blamed the Filipinos, there was another side to the problem. White men and women as well as Filipino operators—capitalizing upon the loneliness of Filipinos—proceeded to cheat them. For several years in Los Angeles, six major taxi dance halls, employing several hundred women, were devoted exclusively to the Filipino trade. Here was the costliest entertainment in the state—ten cents for each one minute dance. McWilliams estimated that in Stockton, the take on gambling and prostitution was about two million dollars a year.[25] Buaken felt that prostitution was a problem not so much because of Filipino aggressions as the seduction of Filipinos by white women. He claimed that "women professionals fleeced the innocent Filipino of his money by pretending that they loved him and so managed to cheat and deceive him." [26] White Californians, however, only saw their side of this problem.

The most violent form of discrimination against Filipinos came from white vigilante action, based upon a combination of economic and sex fears. California's first serious riot occurred at a carnival in Exeter on October 24, 1929 when a Filipino stabbed a white man. Prior to the incident, Filipinos had been abused in town, shoved off sidewalks, and molested by white transient workers. At the carnival, whites threw objects at Filipinos, particularly those in the company of white girls. This led to the aforementioned stabbing. An infuriated mob, estimated at 300, moved to the nearest ranch employing Filipinos and burned a barn. The Filipinos fled before the mob arrived.[27]

The most explosive riot occurred in the Watsonville agricultural area which depended upon a large number of transient farm workers. There, Filipinos had been subjected to various harassments. One January 10, 1930, the Northern Monterey [County] Chamber of Commerce, adopted anti-Filipino resolutions.

24 Buaken, *op. cit.*, 70.
25 McWilliams, *op. cit.*, 238–239.
26 Buaken, *op. cit.*, 178.
27 California Dept. of Industrial Relations, *op. cit.*, 73–74.

On January 11, a small Filipino club leased a dance hall from two Americans in Palm Beach—a few miles west of Watsonville on Monterey Bay. The Chamber of Commerce's resolutions set an attitudinal tone for the whites. The thought of Filipinos dancing with white girls angered Watsonville citizens and demonstrations commenced on Sunday (January 19) and lasted until early Thursday (January 23). On Monday, about 200 armed Americans formed hunting parties looking for Filipinos on the streets. On Tuesday, the dance hall was raided. The climax came the next evening, January 22, with considerable property destroyed, some Filipinos beaten, and one killed. A mob of 500 infuriated men and boys destroyed Filipino dwellings. Shooting indiscriminately into buildings, they killed the one young man. After the killing, community leaders belatedly formed a law and order group to oppose vigilance action and the rioting stopped.[28]

In August, 1930, a bundle of dynamite was thrown into a camp of 100 sleeping Filipinos near Reedley to protest the presence of some 500 Filipinos in the region. No one was hurt but it was reported that white laborers hated them for undercutting wages.[29] Mob actions to drive out Filipinos occurred in several localities, such as Imperial, Lake, and Sonoma Counties, during the next few years.[30]

The Filipino Labor Union had been formed to protect Filipinos from unfair employment practices. In August, 1934, about 3,000 Filipinos conducted a successful strike in the Salinas area lettuce fields and received a wage increase. But in early September, armed bands, comprised of some thirty vigilantes, moved into the fields and ousted about 500 Filipinos. An additional 300 left a short time later.[31]

The Filipinos moved to the Modesto-Turlock area where white labor saw them as a threat. Civic leaders met to lay plans to eliminate the Filipinos. On September 11, night riders ordered them to evacuate the Turlock district in two hours. Authorities claimed they feared drastic action against any who remained. Two days later the Board of Supervisors, while renouncing the idea of night riders, endorsed a stand that farmers hire only local white labor.[32]

The Filipinos, set upon from all sides as the depression deepened, found resentment increasing. They found it more difficult to work in communities, let alone live in them. Finally, they found themselves subject to violence.

---

[28] Buaken, *op. cit.*, 97–105; Bogardus, Anti-Filipino Race Riots, *op. cit.*, 5–17; Calif. Dept. of Industrial Relations, *op. cit.*, 75; *San Jose Mercury*, Jan. 11–23, 1930.

[29] *Fresno Republican*, Aug. 19, 1930, 9.

[30] Buaken, *op. cit.*, 105; *San Francisco Chronicle*, Aug. 16, 1931, 1; Jan. 23, 1934, 14; *Grizzly Bear*, LV (Sept., 1934), 21.

[31] Buaken, *op. cit.*, 106–107; *San Francisco Chronicle*, Sept. 6, 1934, 1.

[32] *San Francisco Chronicle*, Sept. 11, 1934, 15; Sept. 14, 1934, 10.

Legal or political discrimination had been actively used against other Asiatic groups. Since these laws were on the books, there was no need for extended legal enactment against the Filipinos. The only legislation aimed directly against them concerned mixed marriages.

Section 60 of the California Civil Code, enacted in 1901, forbade marriages of white persons with Negroes, Mongolians, or mulattoes.[33] On June 8, 1926, Attorney General U. S. Webb—a leading Asiatic exclusionist—ruled that Filipinos should be classified as Mongolians insofar as Section 60 was concerned. This was not a binding opinion and each county clerk continued to make his own interpretation as to the status of Filipinos.[34] A landmark case was that of Salvador Roldan v. Los Angeles County and L. E. Lampton, County Clerk. Roldan, in 1931, petitioned that Lampton be ordered to issue a marriage license so that he could marry a white girl. Both the superior court and the appellate court favored Roldan. The State Supreme Court in 1933 upheld the ruling, basing its views on an 1880 interpretation of the word—Mongolian. The court suggested that if the interpretation had changed, the matter should be decided by the legislature, not the courts.[35]

The 1933 California legislature had already been moving in this direction and amended Section 60 and 69 of the Civil Code. Section 60 then read, "All marriages of white persons with Negroes, Mongolians, members of the Malay race, or mulattoes are illegal and void." Section 69 required county clerks to ascertain the racial background of applicants for marriage licenses.[36] By 1937, the Western States of California, Oregon, Nevada, and Washington had laws forbidding marriages between whites and Filipinos.

Discrimination against Filipinos remained but a symptom of the larger issue: exclusion. From 1927 to 1929, the California State Federation of Labor conventions passed resolutions calling for Filipino exclusion. Labor gained support from the California Joint Immigration Committee, in turn supported by the American Legion, State Grange, Native Sons of the Golden West, and Federation of Labor.[37]

In 1929, the California legislature passed a resolution calling for Congressional enactment to restrict Filipino immigration because cheap labor

---

[33] California, *Statutes*, 34th Sess., 1901, 335.

[34] Commonwealth Club, *Transactions* (1929), 318–319; Nellie Foster, "Legal Status of Filipino Intermarriage in California," *Sociology and Social Research*, XVI (1932), 447–452.

[35] *San Francisco Chronicle*, March 30, 1933, 1.

[36] California, *Statutes*, 50th Sess., 1933, 561. California's miscegenation law came to an end in 1948 with the case, Perez v. Sharp. See *Calif. Reports*, 2nd Series, 1948, 711; Deering, *Annotations to Deering's Civil Code of California* (San Francisco: Bancroft-Whitney Co., 1950), I, 1962; California, *Statutes*, 1959, 2043.

[37] Lasker, *op. cit.*, v.

tended to destroy American ideals and racial unity.[38] The Commonwealth Club of California also endorsed Filipino exclusion.[39]

Richard Welch, a San Francisco Congressman, emerged in the 1928 Congress as California's leading spokesman for Filipino exclusion. In 1930, the House Committee on Immigration and Naturalization held hearings on his exclusion bill.[40] Exclusion is a story in itself. Robert Divine in his book, the *American Immigration Policy*, has ably detailed this issue and there is no need to describe the movement which culminated with Filipino independence and the establishment of the annual quota of fifty a year.[41]

The final aspect of exclusion and discrimination related to repatriation of Filipinos. Both exclusionist and humanitarian motives were interwoven. In 1931, the Philippine Society of California advocated the use of army transports to take Filipinos home. Through a survey, the society discovered that thousands of Filipinos were unemployed and anxious to return home. The society so informed California's senators and representatives. It hoped that voluntary return of unemployed Filipinos who had no money for passage would assuage the need for an exclusion law.[42]

In 1933, Congressman Samuel Dickstein of New York, Chairman of the House Committee on Immigration and Naturalization, introduced a joint resolution to provide for the return of unemployed Filipinos. The bills's purpose was summed up by Dickstein:

> The purpose of this resolution is to relieve cities, towns, and communities of the United States of the financial and other burdens incident to the care of unemployed and indigent natives of the Philippine Islands who are here and have fallen into their distressing condition since their arrival in the United States. This object is selfish in behalf of our own communities and humanitarian in behalf of these unfortunate Filipinos.[43]

After hearing witnesses, the committee recommended the resolution's passage.[44]

[38] California, *Senate Journal*, 48th Sess., 1929, 2690.

[39] Commonwealth Club, *Transactions* (1929), 320.

[40] *Congressional Record*, 70th Cong., 1st Sess., 9275; U.S. Congress, House, Committee on Immigration and Naturalization, *Hearings, Exclusion of Immigration from the Philippine Islands*, 71st. Cong., 2nd Sess.; *ibid.*, *Preliminary Hearing, Immigration from Countries of the Western Hemisphere*, 71st Cong., 2nd Sess., 205-234.

[41] Robert Divine, *American Immigration Policy*, 1924-1952 (New Haven: Yale University Press, 1957), 6, 70-76; Grunder and Livezey, *op. cit.*, 205.

[42] *San Francisco Chronicle*, Jan. 30, 1931, 41.

[43] U. S. Congress, House, Committee on Immigration and Naturalization, *Hearings, To Return to Philippine Islands Unemployed Filipinos*, 72nd Cong., 2nd Sess., 1933, 1.

[44] U. S. Congress, House, *Report No. 1926*, 72nd Cong., 2nd Sess., 1933.

But it was not until 1935, following the enactment of resolutions by Welch and Hiram Johnson, that provisions were made for repatriation. Those who returned to the islands could only reenter the United States as part of the immigration quota.[45] Unfortunately for California's exclusionists and humanitarians, the measure did not work. It had been hoped that several thousands of Filipinos would seize the opportunity for a free boat ride home. Only 2,190 were repatriated.[46] As late as 1939, Representative Welch asked for, and gained an extension of the repatriation law.[47]

The Filipinos in California suffered great personal and economic harm as a result of discrimination. They inherited the hatred that Californians held against all Asiatics and colored minorities in general. Individual Filipinos reacted differently to this treatment. Several of them became champions for Philippine independence. Others became greatly embittered as a consequence of their treatment. Others disproved the charges of exclusionists by being assimilated into American society.

---

[45] *Congressional Record,* 74th Cong., 1st Sess., 2337, 2994, 10046.
[46] McWilliams, *op. cit.,* 243.
[47] *Congressional Record,* 76th Cong., 1st Sess., 35, 2115, 9367, 9697, 10554.

16

The Testimony of Attorney General Earl Warren

A prime example of the hysteria that gripped California after Pearl Harbor is this testimony by the then state Attorney General, Earl Warren. Although Warren was not a key figure in the decision for evacuation, his attitude was all too typical of the California power structure. After the return of the Japanese in early 1945, Warren, then Governor, did help to prevent serious violence against them.

Testimony of Hon. Earl Warren

Attorney General WARREN. Mr. Chairman, we feel in California that it is a fortuitous circumstance that this committee is here at this particular time. We believe that there has been no time in our entire crisis when the need of clarification of the alien situation is as apparent as it is today. There are some things transpiring in our State at the present moment that are rather dangerous and we believe that there is only one way that they can be prevented, and that is by a speedy solution of the alien problem.

I had intended to present a prepared statement to the committee, but I have been working so diligently with the law enforcement officers since I received word from you in order to get the consensus of opinion from them that it has been impossible for me to do so.

The CHAIRMAN. We will hold our record open for you to send in a prepared statement within the next 10 days or 2 weeks. Will that be plenty of time within which to prepare it?

Attorney General WARREN. Thank you. I think that would be more informative to the committee than what I have to say at the present time.

The CHAIRMAN. Yes.

Attorney General WARREN. . . . We believe that the action that the President took yesterday was most wise and that it at least points the way to a real solution of our problem.

SOURCE: U. S. Congress, House, *Hearings before the Select Committee Investigating National Defense Migration*, Part 29, San Francisco Hearings, February 21, 1942 (Washington, D.C.; 1942), pp. 11009–11021.

The CHAIRMAN. If I may interrupt there, I might give you a little background of that recommendation to the President. The congressional delegations of Oregon, Washington, and California met almost daily trying to decide what recommendations we would make to the President on this alien problem. I have in mind Senators Downey, Johnson, Congressman Welch, Congressman Rolph. I mention them particularly because this is their district. They were in constant attendance and took deep interest. So, as the attorney general of the State of California, you know better than any of us the legal complications involved striking at any portion of our American citizenship. That Executive order yesterday was the recommendation, in almost the same words, of the Pacific coast delegation.

You may proceed now, Mr. Warren. I just wanted to give you a little background on that.

Attorney General WARREN. Yes. I am happy to have that; I had heard that from the press. We were following your action very closely and with great interest.

Alien Enemies As Problem for the Military

For some time I have been of the opinion that the solution of our alien enemy problem with all its ramifications, which include the descendants of aliens, is not only a Federal problem but is a military problem. We believe that all of the decisions in that regard must be made by the military command that is charged with the security of this area. I am convinced that the fifth-column activities of our enemy call for the participation of people who are in fact American citizens, and that if we are to deal realistically with the problem we must realize that we will be obliged in time of stress to deal with subversive elements of our own citizenry.

If that be true, it creates almost an impossible situation for the civil authorities because the civil authorities cannot take protective measures against people of that character. We may suspect their loyalty. We may even have some evidence or, perhaps, substantial evidence of their disloyalty. But until we have the whole pattern of the enemy plan, until we are able to go into court and beyond the exclusion of a reasonable doubt establish the guilt of those elements among our American citizens, there is no way that civil government can cope with the situation.

On the other hand, we believe that in an area, such as in California, which has been designated as a combat zone, when things have happened such as have happened here on the coast, something should be done and done immediately. We believe that any delay in the adoption of the necessary protective measures is to invite disaster. It means that we, too, will have in California a Pearl Harbor incident.

I believe that up to the present and perhaps for a long time to come the greatest danger to continental United States is that from well organized sabotage and fifth-column activity.

Opportunities for Sabotage

California presents, perhaps, the most likely objective in the Nation for such activities. There are many reasons why that is true. First, the size and number of our naval and military establishments in California would make it attractive to our enemies as a field of sabotage. Our geographical position with relation to our enemy and to the war in the Pacific is also a tremendous factor. The number and the diversification of our war industries is extremely vital. The fire hazards due to our climate, our forest areas, and the type of building construction make us very susceptible to fire sabotage. Then the tremendous number of aliens that we have resident here makes it almost an impossible problem from the standpoint of law enforcement.

A wave of organized sabotage in California accompanied by an actual air raid or even by a prolonged black-out could not only be more destructive to life and property but could result in retarding the entire war effort of this Nation far more than the treacherous bombing of Pearl Harbor.

I hesitate to think what the result would be of the destruction of any of our big airplane factories in this State. It will interest you to know that some of our airplane factories in this State are entirely surrounded by Japanese land ownership or occupancy. It is a situation that is fraught with the greatest danger and under no circumstances should it ever be permitted to exist.

I have some maps here that will show the specific instances of that character. In order to advise the committee more accurately on this subject I have asked the various district attorneys throughout the State to submit maps to me showing every Japanese ownership and occupancy in the State. Those maps tell a story, a story that is not very heartening to anyone who has the responsibility of protecting life and property either in time of peace or in war.

To assume that the enemy has not planned fifth column activities for us in a wave of sabotage is simply to live in a fool's paradise. These activities, whether you call them "fifth column activities" or "sabotage" or "war behind the lines upon civilians," or whatever you may call it, are just as much an integral part of Axis warfare as any of their military and naval operations. When I say that I refer to all of the Axis powers with which we are at war.

It has developed into a science and a technique that has been used most effectively against every nation with which the Axis powers are at war. It has been developed to a degree almost beyond the belief of our American citizens. That is one of the reasons it is so difficult for our people to become aroused and appreciate the danger of such activities. Those activities are now being used actively in the war in the Pacific, in every field of operations about which I have read. They have unquestionably, gentlemen, planned such activities for California. For us to believe to the contrary is just not realistic.

Unfortunately, however, many of our people and some of our authorities and, I am afraid, many of our people in other parts of the country are of the opinion that because we have had no sabotage and no fifth column activities in this State since the beginning of the war, that means that none have been planned for us. But I take the view that that is the most ominous sign in our whole situation. It convinces me more than perhaps any other factor that the sabotage that we are to get, the fifth column activities that we are to get, are timed just like Pearl Harbor was timed and just like the invasion of France, and of Denmark, and of Norway, and all of those other countries.

Invisible Deadline for Sabotage

I believe that we are just being lulled into a false sense of security and that the only reason we haven't had disaster in California is because it has been timed for a different date, and that when that time comes if we don't do something about it it is going to mean disaster both to California and to our Nation. Our day of reckoning is bound to come in that regard. When, nobody knows, of course, but we are approaching an invisible deadline.

The CHAIRMAN. On that point, when that came up in our committee hearings there was not a single case of sabotage reported on the Pacific coast, we heard the heads of the Navy and the Army, and they all tell us that the Pacific coast can be attacked. The sabotage would come coincident with that attack, would it not?

Attorney General WARREN. Exactly.

The CHAIRMAN. They would be fools to tip their hands now, wouldn't they?

Attorney General WARREN. Exactly. If there were sporadic sabotage at this time or if there had been for the last 2 months, the people of California or the Federal authorities would be on the alert to such an extent that they could not possibly have any real fifth column activities when the M-day comes. And I think that that should figure very largely in our conclusions on this subject.

Approaching an invisible deadline as we do, it seems to me that no time can be wasted in making the protective measures that are essential to the security of this State. And when I say "this State" I mean all of the coast, of course. I believe that Oregon and Washington are entitled to the same sort of consideration as the zone of danger as California. Perhaps our danger is intensified by the number of our industries and the number of our aliens, but it is much the same.

Gentlemen, it has become no longer a simple question of protecting life and property in this State, because people can't fight in the dark and you can't protect against things about which you don't know. We have all been good soldiers out here and we played the game. We have co-operated with the Federal authorities in every respect, and individual agencies have cooperated with us. As Chief Dullea told you, we work in complete harmony with the Federal authorities and I think that we have accomplished something, but we haven't scratched the surface and because of certain fundamental things.

In our civilian defense we are supposed as State and local officers to protect the lives and the property of our people whether it is in normal times or whether it is in times of great emergency. But when this emergency comes along we are going to have to deal with enemy aliens and those who are acting in concert with them.

Civilian Authorities Instructed Not to Investigate Subversive Activities

We don't know in this State who the enemy aliens are and it is not permitted for us to know. In the first place, the directive of the President (and I think wisely) at the outset of this situation placed the internal security in the hands of a Federal agency, the F. B. I. All local and State officers were instructed not to investigate subversive activities, but immediately upon the receipt of any information to turn it over to the F. B. I.

We have played the game in California. We have followed that directive, and everything we have had we have turned over to them. We have not made independent investigations concerning subversive activities or espionage matters or things of that kind. As a result, we don't have as local officers the pattern of the Axis plans for fifth column activities and sabotage.

In addition to that, we are not permitted to have the names, even, of the alien enemies in our midst. And at the present time every police station in this State, every sheriff's office, every law-enforcement agency can be flanked by aliens with weapons that we know absolutely nothing about.

Gentlemen, I say to you that if we expect local law enforcement officers to compete against a situation of that kind it is just like putting a blindfold over a man's face and asking him to go out and fight someone that he cannot see.

The CHAIRMAN. What is the objection to your not having that information?

Attorney General WARREN. I am afraid you will have to get that from the Department of Justice. The only information I have is what I gathered at the first Federal-State Conference that we had at Washington in August 1940. At that time there was discussion as to what should be done in these matters and it was thought that if local authorities started independently to investigate things of that kind they would develop perhaps into witch hunts in some instances. In other instances local authorities might destroy the pattern that the F. B. I. was working on. They might stumble into something that should not be disclosed at the time and in various ways might cause bungling in the counter-espionage work.

The CHAIRMAN. But we were not at war then.

Information on Registration of Aliens Not Available to Local Authorities

Attorney General WARREN. We were not at war at that time. Then the alien registration came along immediately after war was declared, and the local authorities then wanted to know who the aliens in their communities were, but they were not permitted to have their names.

The registration, as you know, is through the Post Office Department, and the Postal authorities have their instructions not to give that information to the local authorities.

The CHAIRMAN. Is that same procedure applicable throughout the United States?

Attorney General WARREN. Yes, sir; it is. Recently they had a second registration. It was thought at that time that it would be done through law-enforcement officers because of the tremendous problems that we have. But that registration also was made through the Postal authorities, and we were denied the right to get any information concerning aliens, even to ask them a question after they had registered with the Government.

We were investigating the alien land situation at the time and, of course, we wanted to know who the alien Japanese were. We have no way of knowing. We have almost 100,000 Japanese in California. The Census records show that 33,000 of them are aliens and 66,000 are American-born. But we have no way on earth of knowing who the 33,000 are and who the 66,000 are. Still we are obliged to protect life and property against any activities in which they may engage during the war.

We believe that that information should be made available to the law-enforcement officers and that they never can be of substantial help to any Federal agency that is charged with the solution of the alien problem unless they do have it.

The CHAIRMAN. You see, that is the very object of these hearings. I did not know that.

Attorney General WARREN. I am sure that very, very few people in the country realize it. Maybe some know about it, but they have never thought of the significance of it. But if our civilian defense effort is to be what our Government wants it to be, if we are to assume our full responsibilities for protecting life and property in time of emergency, then we must have some tools to work with. We have at the present time absolutely none, and I say that without any reflection upon any agency. They have all been helpful within the limits of their instruction.

So that is one of the things that led us to the conclusion that it was entirely a military problem and entirely a military decision as to what we do with these aliens. The fact that so many of them are citizens makes the situation far more dangerous.

Potential Danger from American-Born Japanese

I want to say that the consensus of opinion among the law-enforcement officers of this State is that there is more potential danger among the group of Japanese who are born in this country than from the alien Japanese who were born in Japan. That might seem an anomaly to some people, but the fact is that, in the first place, there are twice as many of them. There are 33,000 aliens and there are 66,000 born in this country.

In the second place, most of the Japanese who were born in Japan are over 55 years of age. There has been practically no migration to this country since 1924. But in some instances the children of those people have been sent to Japan for their education, either in whole or in part, and while they are over there they are indoctrinated with the idea of Japanese imperialism. They receive their religious instruction which ties up their religion with their Emperor, and they come back here imbued with the ideas and the policies of Imperial Japan.

While I do not cast a reflection on every Japanese who is born in this country—of course we will have loyal ones—I do say that the consensus of opinion is that taking the groups by and large there is more potential danger to this State from the group that is born here than from the group that is born in Japan.

Mr. ARNOLD. Let me ask you a question at this point.

Attorney General WARREN. Yes, Congressman.

Mr. ARNOLD. Do you have any way of knowing whether any one of this group that you mention is loyal to this country or loyal to Japan?

Many American-Born Japanese Educated in Japan

Attorney General WARREN. Congressman, there is no way that we can establish that fact. We believe that when we are dealing with the Caucasian race we have methods that will test the loyalty of them, and we believe that we can, in dealing with the Germans and the Italians, arrive at some fairly sound conclusions because of our knowledge of the way they live in the community and have lived for many years. But when we deal with the Japanese we are in an entirely different field and we cannot form any opinion that we believe to be sound. Their method of living, their language, make for this difficulty. Many of them who show you a birth certificate stating that they were born in this State, perhaps, or born in Honolulu, can hardly speak the English language because, although they were born here, when they were 4 or 5 years of age they were sent over to Japan to be educated and they stayed over there through their adolescent period at least, and then they came back here thoroughly Japanese.

The CHAIRMAN. There are certain Japanese schools here, are there not?

Attorney General WARREN. Then we have the Japanese school system here. There is no way that we know of determining that fact.

I had together about 10 days ago about 40 district attorneys and about 40 sheriffs in the State to discuss this alien problem. I asked all of them collectively at that time if in their experience any Japanese, whether California-born or Japan-born, had ever given them any information on subversive activities or any disloyalty to this country. The answer was unanimously that no such information had ever been given to them.

Now, that is almost unbelievable. You see, when we deal with the German aliens, when we deal with the Italian aliens, we have many informants who are most anxious to help the local authorities and the State and Federal authorities to solve this alien problem. They come in voluntarily and give us information. We get none from the other source.

Does that answer your question, Congressman?

Mr. ARNOLD. That answers it fully.

Attorney General WARREN. There is one thing that concerns us at the present time. As I say, we are very happy over the order of the President yesterday. We believe that is the thing that should be done, but that is only one-half of the problem, as we see it. It is one thing to take these people out of the area and it is another thing to do something with them after they get out. Even from the small areas that they have left up to the present time there are many, many Japanese who are now roaming around the State and roaming around the Western States in a condition that will unquestionably bring about race riots and prejudice and hysteria and excesses of all kind.

I hate to say it, but we have had some evidence of it in our State in just the last 2 or 3 days. People do not want these Japanese just loaded from one community to another, and as a practical matter it might be a very bad thing to do because we might just be transposing the danger from one place to another.

So it seems to me that the next thing the Government has to do is to find a way of handling these aliens who are removed from any vital zone.

In the county of Tulare at the present time and in the county of San Benito and in other counties there are large numbers of the Japanese moving in and sometimes the suggestion has come from the place that they leave, that they ought to go to this other community. But when they go there they find a hostile situation. We are very much afraid that it will cause trouble unless there is a very prompt solution of this problem.

Vigilantism

My own belief concerning vigilantism is that the people do not engage in vigilante activities so long as they believe that their Government through its agencies is taking care of their most serious problem. But when they get the idea that their problems are not understood, when their Government is not doing for them the things that they believe should be done, they start taking the law into their own hands.

That is one reason why we are so happy that this committee is out here today because we believe that it will help us solve this problem quickly, which is just as important as to solve it permanently.

The CHAIRMAN. We are certainly in a position to get the word right to the heads when we get back to Washington.

Attorney General WARREN. Yes, sir.

The CHAIRMAN. We can give them the facts that you are just giving us. We are the parties that can transmit them. We can get the word there anyway.

Attorney General WARREN. Yes. There has been a lot of talk of how it would disturb the agricultural situation in the State to move the Japanese. I think that is a very debatable question and I think that the records of the Department of Agriculture or the Government will show that it is not as great a problem as it is generally supposed to be. We have seen some very fantastic figures as to what part the Japanese labor plays in California agriculture. I think the facts will not support those figures, and this is one thing that I think should be borne in mind by your committee: That we have a great many large Japanese agricultural operators in this State, and when they operate on a large scale they use exactly the same kind of help that white operators use. In other words, when their crops are to be harvested they don't necessarily harvest them with

Japanese. They harvest them with Filipinos and Mexicans and even white people. There is one thing this year that makes it even less desirable to have the Japanese on the land, and that is the fact that the Filipinos and the Mexicans have resolved that they will not harvest crops for Japanese. So they might have their crops on the ground and still they would not be harvested. If those people don't work for them, I have an idea that probably white people won't work for them, either.

The CHAIRMAN. We are going to have a representative from the Department of Agriculture to get those figures.

Japanese Land Ownership

Attorney General WARREN. Yes. I merely made that observation.

Now, gentlemen, I have some maps which show the character of the Japanese land ownership and possessory interests in California. I will submit them at the time I submit a formal statement on the subject. These maps show to the law enforcement officers that it is more than just accident, that many of those ownerships are located where they are. We base that assumption not only upon the fact that they are located in certain places, but also on the time when the ownership was acquired.

It seems strange to us that airplane manufacturing plants should be entirely surrounded by Japanese land occupancies. It seems to us that it is more than circumstance that after certain Government air bases were established Japanese undertook farming operations in close proximity to them. You can hardly grow a jackrabbit in some of the places where they presume to be carrying on farming operations close to an Army bombing base.

Many of our vital facilities, and most of our highways are just pocketed by Japanese ownerships that could be of untold danger to us in time of stress.

So we believe, gentlemen, that it would be wise for the military to take every protective measure that it believes is necessary to protect this State and this Nation against the possible activities of these people.

Mr. ARNOLD. During the past years have the Japanese been shrewd investors when it comes to buying property in cities? Could they have bought this land near these airplane factories because of shrewdness in their investment ability?

Attorney General WARREN. Yes, that could be, Congressman.

Mr. ARNOLD. I mean, does the history of the past 50 years show any shrewdness in that respect?

Attorney General WARREN. The Japanese have been good farming operators. They have competed on very favorable terms with our white farmers.

Mr. ARNOLD. What I mean is, you say some of this farming land surrounding factories is not very productive. It might increase in value because of the large industry. Have they shown ability in the past to invest where land values go up?

Attorney General WARREN. I have no knowledge of that, Congressman. I would be inclined to doubt it because of the limited right they have to buy land in this State. You know, we have an alien land law which prevents them from owning agricultural lands; but it has been honored more in the breach than in the observance in recent years because of the fact that they have placed the ownership in the names of their California-born children. They have not been speculators in lands as far as I know.

Mr. ARNOLD. One thing you are sure of—it just couldn't have happened that way?

Pattern of Japanese Land Ownership

Attorney General WARREN. We don't believe that it could in all of these instances, and knowing what happened at Pearl Harbor and other places we believe that there is a pattern to these land ownerships in California and possessory interests in California.

The CHAIRMAN. In the last few years have purchases by these native-born Japanese increased in the surroundings close to these aircraft factories?

Attorney General WARREN. Yes, sir.

Mr. SPARKMAN. I was interested in your whole statement. As you were discussing it, I thought of testimony that was given before the House Military Affairs Committee, of which I am a member, by a French officer who was in the French Army prior to, and at the time of, the French capitulation. He told us of the difficulties that the French had in their own villages; that always their strategy was given away; the enemy found out about it. Their final solution to the problem was simply, when they started operating in a territory, to evacuate everybody, citizens and all. Of course, that was the field of battle.

Attorney General WARREN. Yes, sir.

Mr. SPARKMAN. Your thought is that this, too, is a possible combat area?

Attorney General WARREN. Yes, sir.

Mr. SPARKMAN. And those in charge of operations should have the authority to evacuate all whom they feel should be evacuated for the defense of the area?

Attorney General WARREN. Precisely. And regardless of citizenship or alienage.

Mr. SPARKMAN. And is it your understanding that the Executive order of yesterday gave such authority to the military commander?

Attorney General WARREN. That is the way I read the newspaper report and that is the only thing that I have. The newspapers stated that specifically.

Mr. SPARKMAN. I do want to add a word to what the chairman said. I am sure you people out here know it, but your congressional delegation in both Houses of Congress has been very much on the alert in discussing and making plans for the defense of this area. A week, 10 days, or 2 weeks ago, this very recommendation was made to the President and, as I read the order, it follows out almost word for word the recommendation that was made by your congressional delegation.

I have noticed suggestions in newspaper stories. I noticed a telegram this morning with reference to the civil rights of these people. What do you have to say about that?

Attorney General WARREN. I believe, sir, that in time of war every citizen must give up some of his normal rights.

Evacuation As Military Problem

I believe that no good citizen should object to it. I do believe, however, that it should be done by proper authority and not by sporadic action on the part of agencies that do not function according to the law. That is the reason that I believe that this is a military problem and not a problem in civil government. We have had instances in this State where extra-legal action has been taken with regard to these very people, without regard to our statutes or our constitution or the Constitution of the United States. Now, I think, that is bad.

Mr. SPARKMAN. May I say there, when you say "without regard" you don't consider this as being without regard of Constitution, because isn't it true that the Constitution makes provision for just such things?

Attorney General WARREN. You mean the action the President took yesterday?

Mr. SPARKMAN. Yes.

Attorney General WARREN. I think that is entirely in keeping with it and that is why I commend it so highly. That is why I believe so sincerely in it because it does transfer the solution of this problem to the military authorities who are charged with the defense of this area and, therefore, have the right morally and legally and every other way to take any protective measures that are necessary to insure the security of the area.

The CHAIRMAN. In other words, there are two alternatives—the suspension of the writ of habeas corpus, or martial law. Is that right?

Attorney General WARREN. Yes, sir.

The CHAIRMAN. We are putting them all on the same footing. I think, like you, that it is absolutely constitutional. But if we took it direct, we would be in the courts for the duration of the war fighting that thing out. Is that not so?

Attorney General WARREN. Yes.

Authority for Exclusion of Persons from Military Areas

The CHAIRMAN. Well, we haven't the time to fight it out in the courts. That is the way we feel. Isn't that right?

Attorney General WARREN. Yes. There was a time in the Civil War— I don't have the name of the case in mind at the moment, but I have it available—where the War Department through the commander of the Army, declared certain areas to be danger zones and directed that only those who were given permits were entitled to enter and move about. Then Congress fortified that situation by declaring it in a statute to be a danger zone. When it went to the Supreme Court, the Supreme Court did not sustain the military commander but it did sustain the action of Congress in declaring it to be a zone of danger in which those things could be done by the military.

It may be in this situation that if there is any question about the right of the military to do it, Congress could draw a line so far in from the coast and say that, because of the world conditions and the things that are confronting us, that constituted an area in which the military could do certain things.

The CHAIRMAN. When you prepare your final paper, will you give us that citation? That will be very valuable to us.

Orderly Movement of Evacuees Required

Attorney General WARREN. I will be very happy to do it.

Mr. SPARKMAN. General, you do believe that these people who are evacuated ought to be moved with some system or some order?

Attorney General WARREN. I believe it must be.

Mr. SPARKMAN. In other words, you don't believe that the order should be simply given, "Get out," and then leave it to them to get out?

Attorney General WARREN. No, sir; I think that the Government must provide some solution to that problem, because if we don't, it is not only going to entail hardship on the people who are told to move but it is going to entail hardship on every community to which they go.

We have in California 109,000 enemy aliens. How many of those will be moved out none of us knows, but assuming that a substantial portion of them is moved out and just put on the road indiscriminately. It would be an unspeakable situation for our country.

There must be a solution for them. There must be some resettlement program.

Mr. SPARKMAN. That, too, should be handled by the Army, in your opinion?

Attorney General WARREN. I believe that is a problem of civil government. I believe that the problem of the Army would be to say, "You cannot come into this area because we don't believe that it is consistent with the security of the area." But once out of the area, it seems to me that it would be a problem of civil government to relocate and resettle those people, unless they were dangerous people that the Army wanted to intern or otherwise keep under surveillance. But if they were just doing it as a protective measure, not knowing whether as individuals they were dangerous or not, it would seem to me that it is more of a resettlement program than an Army problem.

Mr. SPARKMAN. You would divide the evacuees into two groups, then: One would be those considered to be dangerous?

Attorney General WARREN. Yes, sir.

Mr. SPARKMAN. The other group simply those who were not desirable in a particular defense area and yet not considered necessarily dangerous?

Attorney General WARREN. Yes, sir. I think we must.

In one situation the military would be in charge, and in the other situation it would be the civil government.

The CHAIRMAN. Don't you see right away the problem is looming before us as to where they are going to go as the evacuation increases in the Pacific Coast States? It may run into hundreds of thousands of people. So we will have to feel out—probably this committee will do it— as to where they are going to go; that is, what States, whether Nebraska, Kansas, and so on. For instance, if it were the other way around, and if you evacuated three or four hundred thousand into California, I don't know how we would take care of them here, don't you see.[1]

Attorney General WARREN. That is correct. And even in California, that is a problem. A community of Japanese moved out of one city in our State and just moved over a little range of hills and started moving into another community. There was a tremendous uproar there and it hasn't subsided yet. Every time you move them en masse you create big problems not only for them but for the communities to which they go.

Review of Hardship Cases

Mr. SPARKMAN. In the mayor's statement he made some mention, I believe, of the hardship cases that might arise.

Attorney General WARREN. Yes, sir.

Mr. SPARKMAN. Would you agree with [t]his panel to the effect that

---

[1] See pp. 27–30, House Report 1911, preliminary report by this committee.

there should be some tribunal that could review hardship cases and perhaps give permits or licenses to reenter?

Attorney General WARREN. Well, Congressman, I don't believe that there should be any civil panel that would review the action of the military commander taken as a protective measure.

Mr. SPARKMAN. I didn't say "civil tribunal." I simply said "a tribunal."

Attorney General WARREN. I believe this: That the Army is in the very nature of things not equipped to know or to find out by itself who is loyal and who is not loyal among all of these hundreds of thousands of aliens that we have. I believe that it calls for the assistance of all the local authorities. For instance, when we are dealing with Italians in San Francisco, most of them came here years ago. They have been in established lines of business, and I believe by their conduct through the years the local authorities could come pretty close to telling the Army who at least would unquestionably be loyal. I think that the Army would probably call upon the local authorities and set up some agency for advising them and helping them on that subject. But I wouldn't have any council to which a man could appeal from the decision of the military commander in a situation like this.

Mr. SPARKMAN. I didn't intend to imply that. The point I was trying to get is this. I agree with you that final decisions should rest with those who are charged with responsibility for defending the area. That, of course, is the military.

Attorney General WARREN. Yes, sir.

Mr. SPARKMAN. The point I was trying to get at is this: Do you think that there ought to be flexibility in the order so as to permit those people whom the military command believed to be hardship cases and worthy cases to allow them to reenter under a permit or a license?

Attorney General WARREN. I do without question. There are thousands of people who are in this State who are nationals of countries with which we are at war, who would be just as loyal to this country as you and I. I think they can be ascertained.

17

Why It Happened Here

ROGER DANIELS

> *This selection, first delivered to a symposium on the twenty-fifth anniversary of the relocation and sponsored by the Extension Division of the University of California, Los Angeles, draws heavily on the research findings of Stetson Conn, now the United States Army's Chief Military Historian. For an expanded treatment see Roger Daniels,* Concentration Camps, USA: Japanese Americans and World War II, *New York, Holt, Rinehart and Winston, 1971.*

WRITING in *Harper's* Magazine in September, 1945, constitutional law specialist Eugene V. Rostow unhesitatingly characterized the evacuation and incarceration of the West Coast Japanese as "our worst wartime mistake." Two decades of scholarship have merely rung the changes on that indictment. Professor A. Russell Buchanan writing on World War II in the authoritative New American Nation Series argued that it was "the most widespread disregard of personal rights since . . . slavery." Most educated persons today would echo these sentiments; in addition, most Americans seem to have changed their basic attitudes toward the Japanese. This dramatic change of image is perhaps best reflected in a pair of Gallup polls which asked a cross-section of Americans to characterize Japanese. In 1942, the image was negative: the five most frequently mentioned adjectives were "treacherous," "sly," "cruel," "warlike" and "hard-working." In 1961 the same question drew a quite positive set of adjectives: "hard-working" moved to the top, followed by "artistic," "intelligent" and "progressive," with a residual "sly" ranking fifth.

With this highly favorable image, in part at least a result of the magnificent and well-publicized performance of Japanese-American troops during the war plus a reaction against wartime excesses, it is almost impossible for the generations that have come to maturity since the war to comprehend how it was possible for such an undemocratic act to occur in this country under the most liberal government it had ever known. When one tries to explain to students that it was one of the most popular wartime acts, many react with stunned disbelief. This essay has a dual burden:

to tell first of all, what happened here and how it happened, and then to try to place the wartime evacuation into a more long-range historical perspective.

First of all I would like to try to convey something of the feeling of the weeks after Pearl Harbor in Los Angeles: much of the material presented will be drawn from the pages of the Los Angeles *Times*. The result would be much the same had almost any other California newspaper been used: the *Times* was not especially prejudiced against Japanese (by 1941 California standards that is) and was more moderate than many papers. The predominant feeling that one gets from reading the press of that period is one of near hysteria. Hawaii, which had actually been attacked, was relatively calm. California, thousands of miles from the scene of operations, was nervous and trigger happy. The paranoid style in California life is not as recent as some would have us believe. A thousand movies and stories and reminiscences have recorded the solemn mood with which the nation reacted on that "day of infamy" in 1941. Yet, at Gilmore Field, the *Times* informs us

Eighteen thousand spectators at the Hollywood Bears-Columbus Bulldogs football game . . . jumped to their feet and cheered wildly when the public address system announced that a state of war existed between Japan and the United States.

In its first editorial reaction, the *Times* announced that California was a "zone of danger": and invoked the ancient vigilante tradition of the state by calling for

alert, keen-eyed civilians [who could be] of yeoman service in cooperating with the military and . . . civilian authorities against spies, saboteurs and fifth columnists. We have thousands of Japanese here. . . . Some, perhaps many, are . . . good Americans. What the rest may be we do not know, nor can we take a chance in the light of yesterday's demonstration that treachery and double-dealing are major Japanese weapons.

Day after day, throughout December, January, February, and March, the *Times* and the rest of the California press spewed forth racial venom against the Japanese. The term "jap," of course, was standard usage. Japanese were also "Nips," "yellow men," "mad dogs" and "yellow vermin," to name only a few of the choicer epithets. Individual columnists and bylined writers in the *Times* added their bit. Ed Ainsworth cautioned his readers

to be careful to differentiate between races. The Chinese and Koreans both hate the Japs more than we do . . . . Be sure of nationality before you are rude to anybody.

Just after a series of murderous and sometimes fatal attacks on Japanese residents by Filipinos, a *Times* sports page feature was headlined:

FILIPINO BOXERS NOTED FOR COURAGE, VALOR

Columnist Lee Shippey, who often stressed that *some* Japanese were alright, prophetically suggested, on New Year's Day, that there be established

a number of big, closely guarded, closely watched truck farms on which Japanese-Americans could earn a living and assure us a steady supply of vegetables.

If a Nazi had suggested doing this with Poles, Shippey undoubtedly would have called it a slave labor camp. But the palm for *shrecklichkeit* must go to Westbrook Pegler, a major outlet of what Oswald Garrison Villard once called "the sewer system of American journalism." Taking time off from his vendettas with Eleanor Roosevelt and the American Labor Movement, Pegler proposed, on December 9, that every time the Axis murdered hostages

the United States could raise [them] 100 victims selected out of [our] concentration camps [for German Bundists, Italian Fascists and] many alien Japanese.

I shall conclude this brief survey of incitement to racial violence by our supposedly responsible press by quoting a few headlines, none of which had any basis in fact and all of which heightened local hysteria and made people believe that military or paramilitary Japanese activists were all around them:

JAP BOAT FLASHES MESSAGE ASHORE
ENEMY PLANES SIGHTED OVER CALIFORNIA COAST
TWO JAPANESE WITH MAPS AND ALIEN LITERATURE
    SEIZED
JAP AND CAMERA HELD IN BAY CITY
VEGETABLES FOUND FREE OF POISON
FOOD PLOT FEARS SPIKED
CHINESE ABLE TO SPOT JAP
MAP REVEALS JAP MENACE
    Network of Alien Farms Covers
    Strategic Defense Areas Over Southland
JAPS PLAN COAST ATTACK IN APRIL
    WARNS CHIEF OF KOREAN SPY BAND

In short, any reading of the wartime California press—or for that matter viewing the wartime movies that still pollute our television channels—shows clearly that while a distinction was continually being made between "good" and "bad" Germans—a welcome change from World War I—few distinctions were ever made between Japanese. The evil deeds of Nazi Germany were the deeds of bad men: The evil deeds of Tojo's Japan were the deeds of a "bad" race. While the press was throwing fuel on the fires of racial animosity, other faggots were contributed by politicians, federal officials, and, above all, the military. The Governor of California, Culbert L. Olson, a liberal Democrat, had insisted, before Pearl Harbor, that Japanese Americans should enjoy all their rights and privileges even if war with Japan came, and correctly pointed out that equal protection under the law was a "basic tenet" of American government. But Olson's constitutional scruples were a casualty of Pearl Harbor: on December 8, the Governor told the press that he was thinking of ordering all Japanese, alien and citizen, to observe house arrest "to avoid riot and disturbance."

The Federal Department of Justice, working partially through the F.B.I. and calling on local law enforcement officials for assistance, began round-ups of those they considered "dangerous" enemy aliens. Throughout the nation this initial round-up involved about 3,000 persons, half of whom were Japanese, most of them living in California. In other words, the federal authorities responsible for counter-espionage thought that some 1,500 persons of Japanese ancestry or nationality constituted a danger to the nation. This was slightly over 1 per cent of the country's Japanese population. It might be useful to give the 1940 census figures. There were, in the continental United States about 127,000 Japanese, fewer than one-tenth of 1 per cent of the total population; 113,000 of these (almost 90 per cent) lived in the three Pacific states and Arizona, while 94,000 (almost 75 per cent) lived in California. Almost two-thirds of the total were native-born citizens. The nearly 1,500 who were initially rounded up were almost universally of the Issei or immigrant generation —and thus enemy aliens—and usually community or organizational leaders. The government, acting as it so often does on guilt by association, automatically pulled in the officers and leading lights of a number of Japanese organizations and religious groups. Many of these were perhaps "rooting" for the emperor rather than the president and thus technically subversive, but most of them were rather elderly and inoffensive gentlemen and not a threat to anything. This limited internment, however, was a not too discreditable performance for a wartime government security agency, but it must be noted that even at this restrained level the government acted much more harshly, in terms of the numbers interned, toward Japanese nationals than toward German nationals, and more harshly toward Germans than Italians. It should also be noted, however, that more than a few young Nisei leaders applauded this early round-up and contrasted their own native son loyalty to the presumed disloyalty of many of the leaders of the Issei or immigrant generation.

In addition to the selective round-up of enemy aliens, the Justice Department also announced the sealing off of the Mexican and Canadian borders to "all persons of Japanese ancestry, whether citizen or alien." Thus by December 8, 1941, that branch of the federal government particularly charged with protecting the rights of our citizens was willing to single out one ethnic group for invidious treatment. Other national civilian officials discriminated in other ways: even Fiorello La Guardia, who was for a time director of the Office of Civilian Defense as well as Mayor of New York, pointedly omitted mention of the Japanese in two public statements calling for decent treatment of enemy aliens and suggesting presumptive loyalty for Germans and Italians. Seventeen years earlier La Guardia had been one of three Congressmen to speak openly in favor of continued Japanese immigration, but in December, 1941, he could find nothing good to say about Japanese.

Even more damaging were the mendacious statements of Frank Knox, Roosevelt's Secretary of the Navy. On December 15, in a story that made front pages all over the country, Secretary Knox, returning from a quick inspection of the damage at Pearl Harbor, spoke of "treachery" there and insisted that much of the disaster was caused by "the most effective fifth column work that's come out of this war, except in Norway." The disaster at Pearl Harbor, as is now generally acknowledged, was caused largely by the unpreparedness and incompetence of the local military commanders, as Knox already knew. But the secretary probably didn't want the people to lose faith in their Navy, so the Japanese population of Hawaii—and indirectly all Japanese Americans—was made the scapegoat on which to hand the big lie. (Knox, it should be remarked, as a Chicago newspaper publisher in private life had a professional understanding of these matters.)

But the truly crucial role was played by the other service, the United States Army. The key individual, initially at least, was John L. De Witt, in 1941 a Lieutenant General and Commander of both the Western Defense Command and 4th Army, with headquarters at San Francisco's Presidio. Despite these warlike titles De Witt was essentially an administrator in uniform, a staff officer who had specialized in supply and had practically nothing to do with combat during his entire Army career. Serving under him, in December, 1941, as a Corps Commander and in charge of the defense of Southern California was a real fighting man, the then Major General Joseph W. Stilwell, the famed "Vinegar Joe" of the heartbreaking Burma campaigns. His diary of those hectic days gives an accurate and pungent picture of the hysteria and indecisiveness that prevailed at De Witt's headquarters.

Dec. 8—Sunday night "air raid" at San Francisco. . . . Fourth Army kind of jittery.

Dec. 9— . . . Fleet of thirty-four [Japanese] ships between San Francisco and Los Angeles. Later—not authentic. . . .

Dec. 11 [Phone call from 4th Army] "The main Japanese battle fleet is 164 miles off San Francisco." I believed it, like a damn fool. . . .

Of course [the 4th Army] passed the buck on this report. They had it from a "usually reliable source," but they should never have put it out without check.

Dec. 13 Not content with the above blah, [the 4th] Army pulled another at ten-thirty today. "Reliable information that attack on Los Angeles is imminent. A general alarm being considered." . . . What jackass would sound a general alarm [which would have meant warning all civilians to leave the area] under the circumstances? The [4th] Army G-2 is just another amatuer, like all the rest of the staff. Rule: the higher the headquarters, the more important is *calm*.

Dec. 18 [An unidentified subordinate commander in the Long Beach-Torrance area wanted Stilwell to evacuate all Japanese from Terminal Island and to take other measures against the civilian population] "We talked to midnight," Stilwell wrote, "by which time he was pretty well calmed down."

Dec. 19 [Stilwell tries to soothe the fears of an Air Corps Lt. Col. in charge of a bombing range in the Mohave Desert] ". . . he was fearful of a parachute attack that would come in off carriers or from a secret base in Lower California, and murder them all. Or Japs from Los Angeles could sneak up and sabotage everything. . . . (P.S. The colonel has seen some suspicious signaling with flashlights)

This situation has produced some strange cases of jitters. Common sense is thrown to the winds and any absurdity is believed.

The wild, farcial and fantastic stuff that G-2 Fourth Army pushes out!

Just before Christmas Stilwell was transferred to Washington; shortly after his arrival there he noted that Lieutenant General Lesley J. McNair, Deputy Commander, Army Ground Forces had told him that "De Witt has gone crazy and requires ten refusals before he realizes it is 'No.' "

It was in this panic-ridden, amateurish Western Defense Command atmosphere that some of the most crucial decisions about the evacuation were made. Before discussing them, I should point out that the nearest Japanese aircraft during most of December were attacking Wake Island, more than 5,000 miles west of San Francisco, and any major Japanese surface vessels or troops were even farther away. In fact, elements of the Luftwaffe over the North Atlantic were actually closer to California than any Imperial Japanese planes. But despite the patent absurdity of these fears, it is axiomatic that misconceptions, when acted upon, may become more significant than the reality that they distort.

The official Army history of the evacuation—written by Stetson Conn, a perceptive civilian historian in the office of the Chief of Military History —gives us additional insights into General De Witt's confusion. On December 19, De Witt formally proposed to the War Department that alien Japanese fourteen years of age and older be removed from the West Coast and that these individuals "be held under restraint after removal . . . in order to preclude their surreptitious return." De Witt felt that these 40,000 persons constituted an immediate and potential menace to vital measures of defense. (De Witt's language in this message was enemy aliens, Germans, Italians, and Japanese; the number he proposed evacuating however, was the number of alien Japanese.)

A week later, the Provost Marshal General of the War Department, Major General Allen W. Gullion, the Army's top cop, a service intellectual who had once read a paper to an International Congress of Judicial Experts on the "present state of international law regarding the protection of civilians from the new war technics," telephoned De Witt and told him that he (Gullion) had just been visited in Washington by a representative of the Los Angeles Chamber of Commerce who asked that all Japanese in the Los Angeles area be rounded up. De Witt was opposed to this and told General Gullion that:

I'm very doubtful that it would be common sense procedure to try and intern 117,000 Japanese in this theater. . . . An American citizen, after all, is an American citizen. And while they all may not be loyal, I think we can weed the disloyal out of the loyal and lock them up if necessary.

At about the same time De Witt opposed a pet Army project—to have control over enemy aliens transferred from the Justice Department to the War Department. This was apparently instigated in the Provost Marshal General's office by an empire-building lawyer in uniform, Major Karl R. Bendetsen. He and his chief, General Gullion, continually pushed General De Witt to adopt their point of view. Engaged in a bureaucratic battle with Attorney General Francis Biddle to transfer the enemy aliens from civilian to military control, from due process to martial law, they apparently felt they could win only if a field commander declared that such a transfer was a military necessity.

General De Witt, not a strong character, as we have seen, soon got the message. By mid-January he was telling the War Department that any raid on the West Coast would be accompanied by "a violent outburst of coordinated and controlled sabotage." On January 24 he told General Gullion that:

The fact that nothing has happened so far is more or less ominous in that I feel that in view of the fact that we have had no sporadic attempts at sabotage there is control being exercised and when we have it it will be on a mass basis.

The next day the "quickie" investigation of Pearl Harbor conducted by the Roberts Commission was released. One of its erroneous conclusions was that there had been widespread espionage by Japanese residents in the Islands. On January 27 De Witt met with Governor Olson of California and told Washington afterwards that "the best people in California" wanted all the Japanese out. Two days later De Witt saw California Attorney General Earl Warren, a Republican who was then preparing his campaign that would defeat Olson in November. Warren, the General told Washington, was in thorough agreement with the Governor that the Japanese population should be removed from the coastal areas. In this same conversation, De Witt, for the first time joined the growing consensus for a mass evacuation of aliens and citizens, and came around to the Provost Marshal's view that the military should have charge of enemy aliens, at least within the Western Defense Command. In the same conversation, Bendetsen told De Witt that, without authorization from his civilian chiefs, he was meeting with California and other Western congressmen and reporting De Witt's new views to them. The legislators were organizing under the aegis of Hiram W. Johnson, California's senior Senator who organized a similar *ad hoc* steering committee in the 1920's to get Japanese exclusion. What Bendetsen was actually doing was telling the Western Congressmen that the way to get what both he and they wanted—the removal of all Japanese from the West Coast—was to undercut the Attorney General Francis Biddle, a civil libertarian but not, in this instance, a fighter. Biddle was also being undercut by one of his own subordinates, Tom C. Clark, a future justice of the Supreme Court, who was the Justice Department's coordinator for enemy aliens on the West Coast.

In early February, De Witt told Washington that what the California authorities really wanted was to move the Japanese to interior agricultural areas of the state to avoid the possible influx of Mexicans and Negroes to replace them if they were completely removed. De Witt thought that this proposal was consistent with "military necessity" as he understood it. By this time the Provost Marshal's proposal had drifted up the chain of command to the civilian leadership of the department—Secretary of War Henry L. Stimson and his Assistant Secretary, John J. McCloy. Both of these men were Eastern Establishment Republicans brought into the administration as a unity move. On February 3, the civilians, in the words of General Mark Clark, were "pretty much against" the mass evacuation of the Japanese "and they are also pretty much against interfering with citizens unless it can be done legally." Despite the apparent disavowal by their civilian chiefs, Gullion and Bendetsen continued to assume, correctly as it turned out, that they would get their way in the end.

On February 6, Gullion and Bendetsen rejected De Witt's California-oriented suggestions about resettlement within the state—in the words of the key Provost Marshal memorandum on the subject because it contained "too much of the spirit of Rotary" and ignored "the necessary cold-bloodedness of war." Instead Gullion and Bendetsen formally recommended to the civilian Assistant Secretary McCloy that all alien Japanese be interned east of the Sierra Nevadas with as many citizen members of their families as would voluntarily accompany them, and the exclusion of the remaining citizen Japanese from precisely those areas of the West Coast where most of them lived. The next day, February 7, Stimson and McCloy who only four days previously were "pretty much against it," had somehow become converted to the Bendetsen-Gullion view. Perhaps they had become convinced that it was "pretty much legal." At any rate, by February 7 McCloy had decided to send Lieutenant Colonel Bendetsen (he had just been promoted) to the West Coast "to confer with General De Witt in connection with the mass evacuation of all Japanese." Three days later, Attorney General Biddle, who made a poor fight in a good cause, indicated that he was ready to throw in the sponge, but insisted that the Army would have to do its own dirty work.

The conflict at the Cabinet level necessitated an appeal to the Commander-in-Chief, whose final approval would have been needed in any event. On Wednesday, February 11, 1942—the real day of infamy as far as the Constitution was concerned—Stimson and McCloy sent Franklin D. Roosevelt a brief memorandum that listed four alternatives and is worth quoting in full:

1. Is the President willing to authorize us to move Japanese citizens as well as aliens from restricted areas?
2. Should we undertake withdrawal from the entire strip De Witt originally recommended, which involves a number of over 100,000 people, if we included both aliens and Japanese citizens?
3. Should we undertake the intermediate step involving, say 70,000, which includes large communities such as Los Angeles, San Diego, and Seattle?
4. Should we take any lesser step such as the establishment of restricted areas around airplane plants and critical installations, even though General De Witt states that in several, at least, of the large communities this would be wasteful, involve difficult administration problems, and might be a source of more continuous irritation and trouble than 100 per cent withdrawal from the area?

President Roosevelt refused to choose. After a brief telephone call the decision making power was passed to two men who had never been elected to any office. "We have *carte blanche* to do what we want as far as the President is concerned," McCloy telephoned Bendetsen at the Presidio. According to the Assistant Secretary, Roosevelt's only qualification was "Be as reasonable as you can."

Why did Roosevelt do it? No historian can ever answer, definitively, this kind of question, but every historian worth his salt must at least try. Nothing anyone can say in explanation, however, can expiate; no doctrine of historical relativism can absolve Franklin Roosevelt. But the student of history must also try to understand the forces that were at work. February, 1942, was not a good time for the United States. The Japanese had landed on the island of Singapore on February 8, on New Britain on February 9, and were advancing rapidly in Burma. Roosevelt was concerned, first of all, with winning the war, and secondly with unity at home, so that he, unlike Wilson, could win the peace with the advice and consent of the Senate. He could read the congressional signs well and knew that cracking down on the Japanese Americans would be popular both on Capitol Hill and with the nation at large. And the last thing he wanted was a rift with establishment Republicans such as Stimson and McCloy. So do what you think you have to do to win the war, he told the civilian spokesmen for the military. And one can imagine him on the phone in the great Oval office where so much of our history has been made, that leonine head lifting up and with the politician's charm and equivocation, saying "Be as reasonable as you can." Thus do great and good men do evil acts in the name of good. The closest historical analogy that comes to mind is Lincoln's amoral insistence, at the start of the Civil War, that preservation of the union was central and slavery peripheral to the nation's war aims. But the very centrality of slavery slowly but surely asserted itself despite the politicians and the war for the union did become in Mrs. Howe's prophetic words, a "fight to make men free."

But the 110,000 Japanese who were eventually sent to ten God-forsaken camps in the name of a fictitous military necessity remained merely an incident of global war. Outside the West Coast the internment received very little notice and I suspect that during the war years most Americans east of the Rockies were only vaguely aware of it. The Japanese went quietly and voluntarily, as they had been counseled to do by most of their leaders. Schedules were posted and published, and they went, in the same quiet law-abiding manner in which they had lived their lives up to then. But were they being law-abiding? Was the evacuation, necessary or not, legal? Stimson and McCloy had been satisfied that it was "pretty much legal," the President signed the executive orders, Congress had passed ratifying legislation and appropriated money, but what would the Supreme Court say? In the months ahead the Court had three separate chances to strike down the legality of the evacuation, but instead the Court merely "struck out" as far as civil liberties were concerned.

The first case, *Hirabayashi,* involved curfew violation. Gordon Hira-bayashi, a native-born American, was arrested and convicted for refusing to obey a curfew order by General De Witt. In a decision handed down on June 21, 1943—North Africa had been liberated but we were still fighting in the Solomons—the court upheld the General rather than the citizen. Chief Justice Harlan Fiske Stone, speaking for a non-dissenting but uneasy Court, argued that:

We cannot close our eyes to the fact demonstrated by experience, that in time of war residents having ethnic affiliations with an invading enemy may be a greater source of danger than those of a different ancestry.

The second and third cases—*Korematsu* and *Endo*—were handed down during Christmas week of 1944, when final victory in the war seemed assured. Fred Korematsu had simply refused to report to a designated point for evacuation, and so was arrested. The Court refused to judge. Justice Hugo Black, writing for the majority, insisted that:

Korematsu was not excluded from the Military area because of hostility to him or his race. He was excluded because we are at war with the Japanese Empire, because the properly constituted military authorities feared an invasion of our West Coast and felt constrained to take proper security measures, because they decided that the military urgency of the situation demanded that all citizens of Japanese ancestry be segregated from the West Coast temporarily and finally, because Congress, reposing its confidence in this time of war in our military leaders—as inevitably it must—determined that they should have the power to do just this. There was evidence of disloyalty on the part of some, the military authorities considered that the need for action was great, and time was short. We cannot—by availing ourselves of the calm perspective of hindsight—now say that these actions were unjustified.

In a pithier concurrence, Justice William O. Douglas simply stated:

We cannot sit in judgment on the military requirements of that hour.

Three justices, however, did so sit and found the judgment bad. Owen J. Roberts, Frank Murphy, and Robert L. Jackson all dissented sharply with their brethren. Justice Murphy, probably stated it best when he simply and bluntly characterized Black's majority decision as a "legalization of racism."

The third case involved Mitsuye Endo, a twenty-two-year-old native daughter of undisputed loyalty with a brother in the United States armed forces. She went off to camp, as ordered, but on July 13, 1942, she filed for a writ of *habeas corpus.* Two years and four months later—she was still in camp—the Court ordered her release but refused to inquire into the constitutional question of how she got there, much to the disgust of

Justices Murphy and Roberts. Thus, if anyone asks you about the legal
status of concentration camps requested by the military, established by
executive order, and eventually sanctioned by Congress, tell him simply
to go quietly and file for a writ of *habeas corpus* upon his arrival—but
warn him that he may have to wait a long time on the docket.

The Supreme Court thus made obeisance to the doctrine of "military
necessity," itself a dubious extra-legal criterion, but there was no "military
necessity." As we now know, our top military planners did not fear an
invasion of the West Coast in 1942, and the Japanese high command never
even contemplated one. Is this just the exercise of what Justice Black
called the "calm perspective of hindsight?" No, it is not; there was ample
evidence available at the time, most glaringly in the differential treatment
given Hawaii and the West Coast. The West Coast was a war zone only
by virtue of proclamation; Hawaii had been struck by war, and would
certainly have been occupied as a necessary prelude to any invasion of
the continental United States. In Hawaii persons of Japanese ancestry
constituted roughly one-third of the population; yet there was no military
necessity to round them up. Without the crutch of "military necessity,"
the shaky legal underpinnings of the evacuation collapsed completely,
and we are left with Justice Murphy's bitter analysis—racism legalized.

This, then, is how it happened here; but there remains the even bigger
question of *why* it happened. The real answer to that question, far
beyond the scope of this essay, must be sought in both the American
racist tradition, in which, in the words of Chief Justice of the United
States Roger B. Taney in 1857, non-whites "had no rights which the
white man was bound to respect," and in the special California racist
tradition, which nearly exterminated the Indians, systematically despoiled
Spanish-speaking Californians after the American conquest, and, shortly
after the beginnings of immigration from China during the Gold Rush,
began nearly a century of consistent anti-Oriental behavior. By the 1920's
the chief enemy was the Japanese. One dedicated opponent of the Japanese could argue:

The Japanese are less assimilable and more dangerous as residents in this country than any other people. . . . With great pride of race they have no idea
of assimilating in the sense of amalgamation. They do not come here with any
desire or any intent to lose their racial or national identity. They come here
specifically and professedly for the purpose of colonizing and establishing here
permanently the proud Yamato race. They never cease being Japanese. . . .
In pursuit of their intent to colonize this country with that race they seek to
secure land and to establish large families. . . . They have greater energy and
greater determination, and greater ambition than the other yellow and brown
races. . . . California regards herself as a frontier State. She has been making
for 20 years the fight of the nation against the incoming of alien races

whose peaceful penetration must in time with absolute certainty drive the white race to the wall, and prior to that time inevitably provoke international trouble across the Pacific.

Added to these fears about Japanese immigrants, there was that phenomenon known as the "yellow peril"—the fear of invasion by armed Oriental hordes. This started out as almost pure fantasy: the first yellow peril books in the 1870's and 1880's feared China, in the nineteenth century a victim rather than a predator. After 1895 it was clear to most that Japan was the real power in the Far East, and when, in 1905, with shots that were truly heard around the world Japan defeated a European power, Czarist Russia, the yellow peril literature began to proliferate. Literally hundreds of books, most of them utterly devoid of any literary or intellectual merit, were written on this theme; there were also movies, articles, and even whole pulp magazines devoted to imaginary invasions. In the popular press, particularly the papers of William Randolph Hearst, the shrill warnings about the menace of Japan became an integral part of editorial policy. By the end of World War I, the threat of a coming Pacific War, a war of the races, was part of the conscious intellectual equipment of almost all Americans. When, in the 1930's Japan began the truly atrocious phase of her imperial expansion into East Asia, the fantasy image seemed to merge with the historical reality.

In short, as the winter of 1941 approached the American mind was ready to believe anything—literally anything—about Japan and her people. Fear and contempt, as we have seen, were strangely mixed. When, after a stunning and unfair blow, Japan scored success after success, it is not at all surprising that men were able to convince themselves that the evacuation was necessary. Naturally, the overwhelming majority of Americans who were aware of it, approved it, and would have approved worse. It has even been argued that the evacuation was a good thing, because it prevented the mass violence against Japanese Americans that many feel would surely have come. Perhaps. It seems to me, however, that using our prejudice to distort due process was, in some ways at least, worse than the mob violence that might have occurred but didn't. The evacuation did more than commit a legal atrocity against 110,000 innocent people; measured against the total human cost of World War II that wasn't so very much. As the late Morton Grodzins put it, the evacuation gave "precedent and constitutional sanctity for a policy of mass incarceration under military auspices. . . . That . . . betrayed all Americans."

Who was responsible for this betrayal? The question of responsibility has been argued back and forth, and will be again. California pressure groups—the American Legion, the Native Sons and Daughters of the Golden West, the State Grange, the state Federation of Labor, all played their role, as did politicians. General De Witt, the Army, Secretary Stimson, and President Roosevelt have all been blamed. It can also be argued that history itself was really responsible. But men make history, and surely the names of all the leading culprits have been mentioned in this essay. But nearly unnoticed in all this has been the rather Prussian tradition in America that in wartime generals should become the arbiters of all things. The great French war leader, Georges Clemenceau, once said that "War is too important to be left to the generals." No American war leader could say such a thing publicly. But for this particular military atrocity, however, I would amend the statement to read: "Wartime decisions of military necessity are too important to be formulated by second rank bureaucrats." Clearly Bendetsen and his chief Gullion shaped policy and set the stage for the betrayal that was executed by their superiors. Bendetsen, who received the Distinguished Service Medal from a grateful nation for efficiently incarcerating his fellow Americans, admitted (perhaps the right word is boasted) that he "conceived method, formulated details and directed" the mass evacuation of the West Coast Japanese. America has so far been spared from the man on horseback; perhaps what it really has to fear is the middle-echelon manipulator behind a desk.

PART III
Mexican Americans:
From "Greasers" to Chicanos

> Yankee hatred has diminished and grown less overt. As one Anglo observed, the Mexican-American of California lives in "a kind of limbo; neither accepted nor rejected." The Americano finds the Mexican-American amiable and anxious to please, but does not understand him in his "displaced status." Some Anglo-Saxons at least experience a sense of guilt toward the Negro for past oppressions; toward the Spanish-speaking, few feel any similar sentiments or any vivid emotion at all.
>
> Leonard Pitt, *The Decline of the Californios*
> (1966)

AMERICANS arriving in the California mining districts in 1849 and 1850 were confronted with competition from other miners, particularly Mexicans already living in California and those emigrating from the northern Mexican province of Sonora. Fearing that these and other aliens would drastically diminish the supply of gold, Americans adopted various exclusionary devices, including the Foreign Miners' Tax of 1850 (see Selection 18). Unlike the Chinese, who often paid the tax, Mexicans adamantly refused. "Yankee" miners then joined forces with tax collectors to insure that the tax would be paid and that no Mexican without a license would work the mines.

The Treaty of Guadalupe Hidalgo, which marked the end of the Mexican War, conferred American citizenship upon those Mexicans who wished to remain in California. But in their furious haste to drive out the offensive "foreigners," Anglos made no distinction between Californios and Sonoran Mexicans. The American nativist movement of 1848–1853 thus provided a legacy of arguments and rationalizations subsequently used in a virulent anti-Chinese crusade of the second half of the nineteenth century. By early 1854, in fact, Mexican immigration had virtually ceased, and for several decades thereafter Orientals bore the brunt of racial prejudice and discrimination in California.

At the same time a second generation of Californios were victims of an irreversible process of "Americanization." One consequence of this process was the dividing of large Mexican ranchos and estates into farms and towns by land speculators, financiers, and railroad developers. Although it is difficult to determine the precise amount of rancho land ultimately devoured by American settlers, estimates run as high as twenty to twenty-five per cent.

It was during the land boom of the 1880s that large landowners in the San Joaquin and Imperial valleys began to import seasonal farm workers from Mexico. Indeed, the history of inequities suffered by Californians of Mexican descent is closely related to the state's unique agricultural system. This system, always dependent upon a large, mobile supply of inexpensive farm labor, has attracted thousands of unskilled aliens to the state. Throughout the late nineteenth and early twentieth centuries, Mexicans were generally of lesser numerical importance as farm laborers than Orientals. It was not until after World War I, as the Oriental labor supply continued to diminish, that Mexicans surpassed other minorities as field workers. Mexican farm laborers were far from docile during the 1920s and 1930s. There are several examples of Mexican efforts to organize for their own protection, perhaps the most significant of which was the Imperial Valley cantaloupe workers' strike of 1928 (see Selection 19).

During World War II there was a marked shift of Mexicans to the cities, particularly to Los Angeles. Attracted by higher-paying jobs, access to education, welfare, and other urban amenities, they found discrimination and deprivation as well. (See Selection 21.) Los Angeles residents who most actively opposed the newly arrived Mexicans were themselves newcomers, such as the civilian defense workers from the South and Southwest and the sailors who participated in the brutal week-long zoot-suit riots of 1943. (See Selection 20.) This migration to the cities, in addition to heavy wartime enlistments among Mexicans and the evacuation of the entire Japanese population of the Pacific Coast (see Part II), drastically reduced the agricultural labor supply in California. Sugar-beet growers were the first formally to protest this shortage. Supported by small farmers and the Grange, the growers prevailed upon the federal government to request from Mexico the importation of 100,000 temporary farm workers, known as *braceros*. An informal agreement in 1942 between the United States and Mexico was formalized in 1951 under Public

Law 78, which gave the Secretary of Labor the authority to recruit Mexican workers for employment in the United States. In the peak year of 1957, California imported 192,438 *braceros*. For the next several years their number declined and eventually Congress, under pressure from labor unions and various liberal organizations, terminated Public Law 78 as of December 31, 1964, although problems involving border crossings, legal and illegal, continue.

In subsequent years the story of Mexican American farm labor in California has been dominated by the bitter, prolonged strike-boycott against table grapes. Begun in the vineyards of Delano in September, 1965, this strike-boycott grew slowly and steadily until its impact was felt around the world. The Delano Grape Strike came to a dramatic conclusion on July 29, 1970, when, after nearly five years of organized struggle, suffering, and sacrifice, farm workers and twenty-six Delano growers signed an agreement. The first and most obvious accomplishment of the strike-boycott was a modest increase in farm workers' wages (from $1.10 an hour and $.15 a box in 1965 to $1.80 an hour and $.20 a box in 1970, to be increased to $2.05 an hour in 1972). A second and perhaps equally important result was the reversal of the growers' position on farm labor legislation. Initially hostile to such legislation, growers later hired a public relations firm to publicize the need for a federal farm labor law. A third consequence was the weakening of the growers' once-united front against the farm workers' union (the AFL-CIO United Farm Workers Organizing Committee, led by Cesar Chavez), the most effective union of its kind in American history.

Whereas the battle of *la huelga* largely involves California farm workers (about two-thirds of whom are Mexican Americans), it is also symbolic of the broader struggle for full equality being waged by this Spanish-speaking minority. Despite the numerical significance of Mexican Americans, who constitute approximately 12 per cent of California's total population, they are as yet underrepresented in governmental positions, politics, the professions, and business. Recent studies show that the Californian of Mexican descent lives today on a smaller per capita income than any comparable group in the population. Mexican Americans have nevertheless been slow to develop militant leadership and to engage in aggressive political action. Whereas the obstacles to organized participation in political life are great (see Selection 22), the situation began to change dramatically in the late 1960's. The distinguished Mexican American journalist

Ruben Salazar spoke to this issue in one of his columns immediately prior to his tragic death. In an article about a "Chicano Voting Rights Act" (in the Los Angeles *Times* on August 7, 1970), Salazar, who was killed by Los Angeles law men in the violent action that broke up a war protest march of 15,000 *Chicanos* on August 29, 1970, pointed to a growing political unity among Mexican Americans. According to Salazar, "*Chicano* unity, which means political power, is more important to [*Chicanos*] than who gets elected." It is becoming increasingly clear that the white power structure in the future will have to contend with a more militant, aggressive, and united *Chicano* community (see Selection 24).

18

"Greasers" in the Diggings
LEONARD PITT

In his book, The Decline of the Californios: A Social History
of Spanish-Speaking Californians, 1846–1890 *(1966), Leonard
Pitt examines the painful process by which native Californians
born of Spanish-speaking parents lost their numerical supremacy,
land, political influence, and cultural dominance. In an important
chapter entitled* " 'Greasers' in the Diggings: Californians and
Sonorans Under Attack," *reprinted here in its entirety, Pitt
treats the gold rush as the first real conquest of California and
establishes a link between the misfortunes of nineteenth-century
Californios and the disadvantaged social status of contemporary
Mexican Americans.* "The modern predicament of the Mexican-
American jelled a century ago, from 1849–1885," *Pitt asserts,*
"and not after the turn of the century, as some suppose."

WHY did the Spaniards and Mexicans fail to discover gold before
1848? What would have happened to them had they done so?
These are two of the "iffiest" questions in all of California history.

The Mexicans had, in fact, discovered minor deposits of gold in southern California more than a decade prior to the historic Coloma discovery,
but they did miss the big find in the Sierra. The causes of their oversight
include a fear of Indian attack in the interior and a decision to hug the
coast for protection; no population pressure ever drove them inward.
The Spanish tradition of looking for signs of *oro* among the Indians, as
in Hernán Cortés' conquest of the Aztecs, also played a role, although
a negative one, for the California Indians did not manipulate gold. Another cause may have been that the contentment of rancho life after 1834
had sapped the rancheros' energy necessary to explore new territory.
Or perhaps the trouble was, simply, bad luck: Captain Gabriel Moraga's
forty-six expeditions before 1820 had brought him near, if not directly
atop, the Mother Lode, yet no gleam caught his eye. The Spanish Americans generally did not want for daring as explorers or for skill as miners;
centuries of experience in both had equipped them ideally for the fateful
discovery they somehow failed to make.

SOURCE: Leonard Pitt, *The Decline of the Californios: A Social History of Spanish-
Speaking Californians, 1846–1890* (Los Angeles and Berkeley: University of Cali-
fornia Press, 1966), pp. 48–68. Originally published by the University of California
Press; reprinted by permission of The Regents of the University of California.

As to what might have been their history had they chanced upon the Sierra gold, the possibilities are numerous. They range from the attainment of genuine cultural maturity and political independence to an even more crushing defeat than the one they received after 1849. Perhaps California would have become one of the most populous and heavily defended places in the Spanish Empire or in the Mexican Republic. The Californios might have had genuine Mexican military support in a war with the Yankees, and thus also a better treaty settlement. Conquest by a European power would not have been entirely out of the question either. The answer, of course, depends upon *when* one supposes the gold to have been discovered: the earlier the better for the Californios, from the standpoint of the growth of Yankee expansionism in the 1840s. One suspects, however, that Manifest Destiny somehow was bound to triumph along the Pacific Coast and eventually convert California into a Yankee province.

The Californios themselves scarcely ever engaged in such ruminations, for they were not a people to pine over lost opportunities and were faced with realities that gave them enough food for thought. The discovery of gold in 1848 made an enormous impact on them—the greatest in their brief experience: it brought them riches, for one thing; it threw them together with other Latin Americans, for another; and, most important, it opened them to full-scale Yankee penetration and conquest.

As news of the discovery spread in 1848, Californios speedily converged on the Sierra from all directions and, in a sense, made up for lost time. The experience of the Angeleños was typical. With Don Antonio Coronel taking on the function of patrón, the thirty Californios, Sonorans, and Indian servants had good luck from the outset. They immediately enticed some mountain tribesmen to accept baubles in exchange for gold nuggets and, after spying out the Indians' trove and plying them with more trinkets, they obtained their digging labor into the bargain. In one day Antonio himself ended up with 45 ounces of gold; Dolores Sepúlveda found a 12-ounce nugget; and Señor Valdez discovered a boulder buried only 3 feet down which had once blocked the flow of an ancient alluvial stream and produced a towelful of nuggets in a short time. He sold his claim to Lorenzo Soto, who took out a whopping 52 pounds of gold in eight days and then sold it to Señor Machado, who also became rich. Even a Sonoran servant became fabulously wealthy overnight.

In all, about 1,300 native Californians mined gold in 1848, the year of the bonanzas. If they had missed the opportunity to discover Sierra gold in the past, they did not do so now; nearness to the placers gave them the head start on the thousands of prospectors still getting their wits together for the voyage halfway around the world. The Californios had additional advantages in knowing precisely where and how to find gold and in gladly pooling their resources and dividing their labor. As a result, the organized Californians, though less numerous than the 4,000 individualistic Yankees in the mines that year, probably extracted as much gold as they. Coronel, a struggling Mexican schoolteacher, had pocketed enough gold to become a prominent landowner, viticulturist, and community leader. He and many other Californios resolved to make a second expedition the next year. They dismissed the news that a few Californios had been harried from their claims by fist-swinging Oregon Yankees, who refused to acknowledge that the Treaty of Guadalupe Hidalgo granted some Mexicans full citizenship: in 1848 "everything ended peacefully."

In the year that followed, the story changed drastically. Coronel's return trip to the mines began badly, with a near-fatal brawl in a Sonoma saloon. One day he and *compadre* Juan Padilla were waiting for the wet January weather to clear, when a former Bear Flagger began to bully Padilla for having served as Bernardo García's henchman in the wartime atrocity against Cowie and Fowler. Padilla insisted that the charge was a lie, and the American replied with an assault. After a severe beating, Pedilla lay in an upstairs room, hovering near death for several weeks, while below his accuser continued to threaten his life. Only Coronel's good reputation and the intercession of friendly Americans restrained the former Bear Flagger.

After nursing his friend back to life, Coronel returned to the Sierra. He fell in among Chileans, Mexicans, and Germans doing well at dry diggings until confronted with posters declaring that foreigners had no right to be there and must leave the mines at once; resistance would be met by force. Although his threat never materialized, excitement mounted. In a nearby camp, a Mexican gambler's tent had been raided, and some Yankees accused five foreigners of stealing 5 pounds of gold. Coronel's associates doubted the accusation against at least one apparently honorable man and raised 5 pounds of gold to offer as ransom. Coronel conferred with a Yankee delegation and gave them the gold. The delegates then retired to consider the offer but never re-emerged from the drunken and agitated crowd, which by then numbered into the hundreds. The money did no good; all five prisoners were convicted and flogged at once, and two of them, a Frenchman and a Chilean, were charged with a previous murder and robbery. Guilty or not, the pair scarcely understood enough of the proceedings to reply to the accusations. When Coronel next saw them they were standing in a cart, lashed together back to back and pinned with a note warning away defenders such as might come from Coronel's camp. A horse then jolted the cart from under the men, and California had witnessed its first lynching. The incident resulted, Coronel thought, from a declining gold supply and the Yankees' increasing jealousy of successful Spanish Americans.

As quickly as possible Don Antonio led his group away from the newly named "Hangtown," and resettled in the remote northern mines. But even there a hundred gringos appeared with the gruff announcement that the entire riverbed belonged exclusively to Americans who would tolerate no foreigners. Furious, some of Coronel's people who had reached the limit of their endurance planned armed resistance, even at the cost of their lives, but Coronel held back and sadly announced, "For me gold mining is finished."

By July many other Californios had cause to echo Coronel's words. As the only true native-born citizens they did have a legitimate place in the mines, yet they knew no way to convince 100,000 hostile strangers of this truth. Fisticuffs or hand combat simply was not the Californians' style. Consequently, one of them carried into the field of combat a safe-conduct pass, signed by the army's secretary of state, which certified him as a bona fide citizen deserving of every right and privilege, of every lawful aid and protection. What good the pass did is not recorded, but the attacks mounted. For most Californios, the best answer was to go home and stay there: "Don't go to the mines on any account," one *paisano* advised another. Out of pride, which prevented them from being converted into aliens by Yankee rogues and upstarts, few Californians ventured back into the maelstrom after 1849.

Musing over the gold rush from a safe distance, the Californians once more concluded that outsiders were, by and large, despicable. Mariano Vallejo said of the forty-niners without sparing and nationality, "The good ones were few and the wicked many." Hugo Reid ticked off the list of troublemakers:

vagabonds from every quarter of the globe. Scoundrels from nowhere, rascals from Oregon, pickpockets from New York, accomplished gentlemen from Europe, interlopers from Lima and Chile, Mexican thieves, gamblers of no particular spot, and assassins manufactured in Hell for the expressed purpose of converting highways and biways into theatres of blood; then, last but not least, Judge Lynch with his thousand arms, thousand sightless eyes, and five-hundred lying tongues.

The Californians now simply reverted to their customary circular logic, which held that evil came from outsiders, that outsiders were mostly evil, and that evil mothered evil. In no other way could they explain the ugly behavior of so many people, especially Americanos.

After a century of slow population growth, during which the arrival of twenty-five cholos or fifty Americans seemed a momentous occasion, suddenly and without warning, California faced one of the swiftest, largest, and most varied folk migrations of all time. More newcomers now arrived each day in California than had formerly come in a decade. Briefly told, the story of the Californians in the gold rush is their encounter with 100,000 newcomers in the single year of 1849—80,000 Yankees, 8,000 Mexicans, 5,000 South Americans, and several thousand miscellaneous Europeans—and with numbers that swelled to a quarter million by 1852. Even assuming the goodwill of every last one of these strangers, they outnumbered the Californians ten and fifteen times over and reduced them to feelings of insignificance.

It is the destiny of ethnic groups in the United States to be thrown together with people of "their own kind" whom they neither know nor particularly like—perhaps even despise. This was the lot of the Californios in 1849, with the massive migration of Latin Americans. It was bad enough that by 1850 the Mexican cholos outnumbered the 15,000 Californios; even worse, angry Yankees simply refused to recognize any real distinctions between Latin Americans. Whether from California, Chile, Peru, or Mexico, whether residents of twenty years' standing or immigrants of one week, all the Spanish-speaking were lumped together as "interlopers" and "greasers." In this molding, the Californians, who had always kept aloof from cholos and earlier had won some grudging respect from the Yankees, lost most heavily. Their reputation as a people more heroic, handsome, and civilized than other "Spaniards" now dissolved. Their proximity to the greasers between 1849 and 1852 put them in actual jeopardy of their lives. In essence then, the Latin-American immigrants were a sort of catalyst whose presence caused the sudden and permanent dissolution of the social elements.

The biggest waves of Latin Americans came from Chile and northern Mexico. The Chileans excelled in baking and bricklaying and other skills and thus found themselves in especially great demand in California. They settled down at the foot of San Francisco's Telegraph Hill, in a place called "Little Chile," or went into the mines to dig, until expelled by the Yankees.

Even more prominent and numerous were the northern Mexicans. Distinguishable from other Latin Americans by their billowy white pantaloons, broad sandals, and sombreros, the "Sonoranians" or "Sonorans," as the Yankees called them, first entered the Sierra late in 1848, after either trudging across the Colorado deserts or sailing via Mazatlán. Some had sojourned in California earlier; in 1842, well before the advent of James Marshall, a Sonoran had discovered gold near San Fernando Mission. More visibly mestizo, less consciously Spanish than the Californians, they seemed "primitive" by local standards. Apache raiders kept them from their own mines and pastures, so that the Sonorans pounced on the California discovery as a panacea. The northern Mexican patróns themselves encouraged the migration of the peons by sponsoring expeditions of twenty or thirty underlings at a time, giving them full upkeep in return for half of their gold findings in California. The migration included so broad a spectrum of the population of Sonora and Sinaloa and was so large and continuous throughout 1850, that it compelled the governors of northern Mexico to admonish repeatedly about the dangers of life on gringo soil.

The Sonorans came on swiftly, heedless of any warnings, knowing that they had vital services to offer California—as prospectors and hired hands, as supply merchants and mule skinners, also as monte gamblers and prostitutes. The leading merchants of Altar and Horcasitas, Sonoran towns near the international boundary, stripped their shelves in the spring of 1849, loaded up every available pack animal, and scurried for the mines. There they sold everything they had brought, dug some gold, and shortly left their followers to return to Sonora for new stock or for quick investment in Mexican securities—much of this accomplished before most of the Yankee Argonauts had even arrived.

Sonorans gravitated mainly toward the San Joaquin River tributaries, called the "southern mines" or "dry diggings," especially near a spot named in their honor, Sonora. Here they introduced Yankees to many of the rudimentary mining techniques that typified the early gold rush era. Sonorans somehow could probe the topsoil with knives and bring up nuggets, or work the *batea* (pan) to great advantage. Where water was scarce and quartz plentiful, as in the southern mines, they had the endurance to sit for hours and winnow dirt in their serapes, sometimes using their own gargantuan breath if the wind died down. They could also improvise the *arastra* (mill), consisting of a mule harnessed to a long spoke treading in a circle and grinding ore under a heavy, flat boulder. Others eventually caught on to those techniques and machines and later surpassed them, but the Sonorans' sixth sense for finding gold and their willingness to endure physical hardship gave them great advantages. Talent made them conspicuously "lucky"—and, therefore,—subject to attack by jealous Yankees.

Although the Californios quietly withdrew from the Sierra and left the field to the Mexicans and the Yankees, the scene in the mines deserved their closest attention. For, the mines became the staging ground for widespread attacks on their ranchos and pueblos, the rehearsal place for broad-scale assaults on the Spanish-speaking.

The problem of precisely how to react to the remaining "Spaniards" made the Yankees squirm. They shifted from violence to legislation, from legislation to litigation, and back again to violence. Some wished to exploit, others to expel, and still others to control the Latin Americans. On occasion, some Yankees even proposed allowing them completely free access to the mines.

It would have given small comfort to Coronel, Vallejo, Reid, and other Californios to learn that good and decent men had inspired the purge trials of the winter and spring of 1849. Yet, in truth, a great deal of antiforeigner agitation originated from the most reputable new citizens—army officers, lawyers, merchants, clergy, and public officials. It is a fact that the first organized and officially sanctioned outburst against Spanish Americans came from three hundred "white-collar" Yankees. While stranded in Panama in January, 1849, on their way to San Francisco, they heard distressing rumors that "foreign plunderers" from all over the Pacific littoral had already siphoned off $4 million worth of gold in California; how much remained for "true citizens" thus was problematic. On a slight provocation, the Yankees called a public meeting to deal sternly with the interlopers. No less a dignitary than the justice of the Oregon Territory presided over the gathering, and in the background hovered General Persifor F. Smith, traveling to Monterey to take charge of the army. Smith drafted a circular declaring that, in California, he would "consider everyone who is not a citizen of the United States, who enters upon public land and digs for gold as a trespasser." This declaration won him three hundred vows of support.

The miners, who twice confronted Coronel with the charge that "foreigners" had "no right" to dig gold, were simply enforcing Smith's hastily improvised "doctrine of trespass." In April, vigilantes at Sutter's Mill drove away masses of Chileans, Mexicans, and Peruvians; and during a similar purge along the Sacramento River on the Fourth of July lives were lost, property was destroyed, and foreigners' goods were sold at auction. More than a thousand victims, mainly Chileans, came pouring down into San Francisco shortly afterward, many of them embarking for home. "General Smith is blamed by everyone as the sole cause of the outrage."

Smith beat a hasty retreat when he discovered that the consequences of the plunderers' activities had been grossly overrated: gold was still plentiful, and most of the dust already exported from California had found its way into the hands of American supply merchants. His successor, Brigadier General Bennet Riley, rode through the mines trying to undo some of the damage caused by the doctrine of trespass by telling Americans that technically all diggers were guests on government land, and that thereafter none should be denied access to its bounty.

Resentment against the "greasers" mounted, however, a product of deep and abiding feelings of nationalism, racism, and despair over the debasement of free labor. The nationalism was partly a hangover from the war. Some men imagined seeing "whole battalions, armed to the teeth . . . moving through the heart of Mexico . . . gotten up by the great capitalists and friends of Santa Anna . . . rising in one solid mass whose cry is 'California's recovery or death!' " Yankee veterans unhappy in the diggings and nostalgic for army comradery saw in the coming of the "greasers" the pretext for a "muss," whether for mayhem or for merriment. Northern Europeans—the Irish in particular—and Australians became implacable foes of the Spanish Americans, more so perhaps than many native-born citizens of the United States. The notorious San Francisco gang, the "Hounds," for example, which was staffed by former New York Volunteers and Australians, took particular delight in attacking the Chileans who came to San Francisco after fleeing enemies in the mountains.

The forty-niner's xenophobia also stemmed from fear of unfair economic competition. Back home, one could normally see who became rich, how rich, and by what means; a community could use institutional means to regulate the process and keep it fair. But on the periphery of civilization, controls broke down: men sometimes prospered by unfair means; the population upsurge, the ceaseless shuffling of men from camp to camp, and their scrambling for the top of the social ladder defied control by ordinary methods. Thus the forty-niner improvised new devices, even vigilante justice.

Fear of economic competition had some basis in reality. Sonoran peddlers marched into the mines and sold 10,000 pack mules in three years, thereby depressing the prices of mules (from $500 to $150 a head in a matter of weeks) and of freight rates (from $75 to $7 per hundredweight in two months). This reversal of fortunes evoked no complaint from the Yankee miners, who could buy onions, potatoes, and other supplies all the more cheaply and had come to associate Mexican mule bells with savory cooking odors and a few cheap comforts of life; but it brought, in 1850, a pained outcry from Stockton entrepreneurs, who sought mass expulsion of their business rivals. Moreover, when the Mexicans set to work as peons in the employ of their patróns, they did make themselves the target of the prospectors. Miners who began muttering against the Mexicans and plotting violence felt keenly conscious that the Spanish Americans were cheapening the value of labor.

The treatment of immigrant Spanish Americans in the mines hinged also on the slavery question. They came into California precisely when the Yankees felt most irritated on this score and could see most clearly the parallels between Negroes and their masters, on the one hand, and peons and patróns, on the other. Yankee prospectors ejected from the mines with equal vigor any combination of bondsmen and masters. In July a prominent Texan, Thomas Jefferson Green, and his slaves were unceremoniously tossed out of Rose Bar on the Yuba River. The prospectors put into effect a local code prohibiting the mining operations of all master-servant teams, whatever their relationship. Three months later this provision cost the life of a Chilean and led to the ear cropping and whipping of Chileans and Mexicans who tried to oppose it.

With California's entry into the Union as a free state, the plight of the Spanish Americans in the mines worsened momentarily. Their protagonists proclaimed that, if slaves were prohibited from the mines, then so should be the "refuse population from Chile, Peru and Mexico and other parts of the world [who are] . . . as bad as any of the free negroes of the North, or the worst slaves of the South." The apparent inconsistency in immigration policy annoyed both the friends and the enemies of slavery. In the first California legislature, nativists freely categorized the Pacific immigrants as a race whose morality and intelligence stood "but one degree above the beasts of the field." The State Assembly, in no uncertain terms (by a vote of twenty-two to two), asked Congress to bar from the mines all persons of foreign birth, *even* naturalized citizens.

This extreme nativism soon brought about its own backlash. A fraction of the entrepreneurs in the mines began to worry less about the alleged dangers of unlimited immigration or of competition from "foreign capitalists" and more about the "disaggregated, fractioned, broken up" techniques of mining; more about the possibilities of investing capital and hiring Mexican laborers, and less about expelling the interlopers. Usually outshouted at public meetings and outvoted in the legislature, this Yankee faction nonetheless had on its side the logic of economy and the ear of a few outspoken politicans who began a campaign to exploit, rather than exclude, aliens.

Advocates of this new position were most numerous and effective in the southern mines. There, the Sonorans evicted from the northern placers late in 1849 found relative safety, hiring themselves out to Yankees who maintained loaded pistols, "cool eyes . . . [and] steady nerves" against possible opposition by other Yankees. The Yankee patróns especially appreciated the Sonorans' skill and willingness to work for a daily wage of a dollar in food and a fraction of gold. "Greasers" worked speedily, when prompted, although work itself—and riches or savings— bored them, and gambling, drinking, dancing, and indolence cut down their work time. The argument ran as follows: The American, "with all his impatience of control, his impetuous temperament, his ambitions and yearning will . . . [never] be content to deny himself the pleasure of civilized life in the states for the sake of $4.00 to $3.00 per day, to develop the resources of the dry diggings"; the Mexican, on the other hand, is "milder in spirit, more contented to endure, more willing to suffer, more weak spirited, if you please," but for those very reasons he is the man for the job. Although a mere "hewer of wood and drawer of water," he would unlock California's wealth much as the Negro had done in the South. American freight shippers at the same time learned that the Mexican *arrieros* (mule skinners) were the most reliable of hired hands— skillful, proud of their work, and sure to get the pack train through the worst blizzard, over the toughest mountain trail. A genuine paternal fondness sometimes linked the arriero and his new Yankee patrón.

Yankee tradesmen of the southern mines came to see the Spanish Americans as particularly good customers. It occurred to them that, in contrast with the stingy Yankee who saved his money and sent it home, the Latin American invariably wanted to take home goods, not money; he spent all he had. Just as the Spaniard's eccentric work habits could be turned to the operator's profit, so could his spendthrift tendencies be turned to the advantage of the merchant. General Riley discovered that "Americans, by their superior intelligence and shrewdness in business, generally contrived to turn to their own benefit the earnings of Mexicans, Chileans and Peruvians."

The tension between Yankee and Latin-American miners climaxed in the Foreign Miners' Tax Law of 1850, one of the most original if benighted laws ever passed in a California legislature.

Thomas Jefferson Green, its author, boasted that he personally could "maintain a better stomach at the killing of a Mexican" than at the crushing of a body louse. A Texan, he had come to this opinion in a Mexican prison while brooding over the failure of a filibustering expedition. After a harrowing escape from the prison, Green published an account of his exploits, together with a tirade against all things Mexican (and Negro) and a proposal that the United States swallow up all of Mexico. He had come to California in the hope of using slaves to plant cotton, although the episode at the Yuba River smashed that idea completely. Because he had served in three Southern legislatures, however, and had a good reputation among Southerners, he easily won election as state senator from Sacramento.

Green had legendary powers of persuasion, even over men who disliked his social ideals. It was he who always gained adjournment of the California Senate to "more comfortable surroundings"—namely, his own bar—and thus earned his colleagues the sobriquet, "Legislature of the Thousand Drinks." In his tax bill—a kind of personal rejoinder to the men who had expelled him from Rose Bar for attempting to use Negro bondsmen—he proposed to issue mining permits to foreigners at a cost of $20 monthly (he later reduced it to $16). The tax, he thought, would bolster the bankrupt state treasury by $200,000 each month and would also encourage Yankee operators to buy licenses for their operatives, and to employ them "at a fair rate . . . until the labor is performed according to contract." The law would delight Americans no end and discourage mob action, or what Green grandly called "the interruption of the stronger power which is in the people." This possibility so neatly wrapped up all the nagging problems of labor competition, foreign monopolies, taxation, bondage, immigration, and mob violence that the

Assembly passed it nineteen to four and the Senate seven to four; the latter house, by a vote of eleven to two, also gave Green a special commendation for originating so "splendid" a plan.

Although later condemned as an intemperate and malicious act, "conceived in drink and brought forth in jollity," the Foreign Miners' Tax Law actually had quite sober intentions. Its main difficulty was that instead of flatly trying to either exploit, expel, or give free rein to the foreign-born, it tried to straddle the issue. It promised something for everybody: the prospector would be able to evict all "unprotected" aliens, the operator would be able to undercut the "agents of foreign bankers" who sponsored immigration, the government would receive money to pay its bills (among them, the expense vouchers of the legislature), the collectors would make a commission of $3 on each permit sold, and the immigrants themselves could claim the protection of the law if they paid their tax. On the face of it, one could hardly have asked for a more equitable solution.

Yet the Foreign Miners' Tax Law hardly worked that way at all. In Tuolumne County, where most of the potential taxpayers were entrenched, the impost caused outright defiance. Printed posters immediately denounced the tax and implored its intended victims to "put a bridle in the mouths of that horde who call themselves citizens of the United States, thereby profaning that country." Two French radicals, schooled in the Revolution of 1848, engineered a rebellion and for its success needed the cooperation of the Mexicans. Although the Mexicans were gun-shy, they nevertheless went to tell the Yankees what was on the mind of all non-Yankees. An impressive array of 4,000 "aliens"— mostly Mexicans—congregated on the outskirts of Sonora on Sunday, May 19, to consider proper action against the law, which was to take effect the next day. To the collector's face the delegation flatly declared that the foreign-born might pay $3 or even $5 monthly, but not $20— a token sum for protection against rowdies, but not an entire fortune monthly. When the collector held his ground and demanded the full amount, most foreigners fled the town. One remaining Mexican threatened the sheriff, or so it seemed to the bystander who killed him with a bowie knife. Local officials prohibited merchants from selling supplies to any foreign miners and spread an alarm to nearby camps to call up reinforcements for the forthcoming "war" at the county seat.

One hundred and fifty war veterans promptly stopped work at Mormon Gulch, selected a captain, put on the remains of their uniforms, and, with regimental colors high, marched to Sonora for action. Sonora received them warmly with fulsome speeches, food, and free liquor. By nightfall the town seethed with inevitable rumors of Mexican incendiarism, assassination, and massacre. Officers posted pickets, stored weapons, and briefed the men for the next day's action. Sonora was under martial law.

Next morning, into the diggings marched four hundred Americans —a moving "engine of terror"—heading for Columbia Camp, the foreigners' headquarters. They collected tax money from a few affluent aliens and chased the rest away, with a warning to vacate the mines. One trooper recalls seeing "men, women and children—all packed up and moving, bag and baggage. Tents were being pulled down, houses and hovels gutted of their contents; mules, horses and jackasses were being hastily packed, while crowds were already in full retreat." The posse finally arrested the two "hot-headed Frenchmen . . . of the red republican order," who started everything, fined them $5 for "treason," and dismissed them. Thus ended the "muss." The men liquored up for the road, hoisted the Stars and Stripes to the top of a pine tree, fired off a salute, and headed for home. Next day, about five hundred French and German forty-eighters stormed into Sonora shouting revolutionary slogans and vowing to liberate the Frenchmen. Upon hearing that the pair had been freed, the would-be liberators dispersed sheepishly.

Sonora had just about recovered from the excitement of this "French Revolution" when a new attack broke over the heads of the Spanish-speaking. A series of robberies and violent deaths came to light near town in which the victims were Yankees and the murder weapons *riatas;* this made it easy to blame "foreigners of Spanish-American origin." Next, a Sonoran and his three Yaqui Indian retainers were caught burning two bodies and would have been lynched, but for the timely intervention of the justice of the peace and the sheriff, who remanded the prisoners to the district court. On the morning of the court trial (July 15), the Mormon Gulch veterans again descended on Sonora in military order and spoiling for action. Informed that the prisoners might be hirelings of a "notorious Mexican chief" at Green Flat, they marched there, rounded up practically every male in sight, herded them back to Sonora, and literally corralled them for safekeeping overnight. In the morning, the justice of the peace investigated the "caze of murther against 110 Greasers . . . captured by 80 brave Americans," but, having determined that the Mexicans were innocent newcomers, he let them go. After a momentary riot scene in the courtroom, the Sonoran, on bended knees, convinced the jury that he and his Indians had killed no one but had accidentally discovered the bodies and were trying to dispose of them according to Yaqui burial custom. The crowd dispersed grudgingly.

Unhappily, another gruesome death, uncovered the very next day, again made Sonora the prey of every rumor incriminating Latin Americans. Since all previous measures had failed to stop the atrocities, it was proposed to cleanse the hillsides thoroughly of every Spanish American with the least tinge of "evil." The present emergency demanded that "all Mexicans should suffer for a few." The "better element" of Yankees in the southern mines, who normally recoiled from drastic measures, now feared that their territory was fast acquiring the reputation of a bandit refuge, which was bad for business, and felt impelled to join the broadside attack. Outshouting one dissenting voice, a large public meeting in Sonora voted to force all foreigners to deposit their arms with Americans and apply for permits of good conduct. All Latin Americans, except "respectable characters," were given fifteen days in which to depart. The Mormon Gulch veterans set to work enforcing these dicta with gusto.

The screening plan to expel the "obnoxious" Spanish Americans worked well. It reduced the danger of *bandido* attack and frightened off economic rivals. Between May and August, from five to fifteen thousand foreign-born diggers scattered from the southern mines. Mexicans went elsewhere looking for surcease of trouble but were dogged everywhere; eventually, they came streaming out of the Sierra, some showing signs of "pinching want." Even those who paid the extortionate $20 found that it bought very little protection, for if the collector neglected his monthly rounds their certificates lapsed, and if the Americans of one county refused to honor permits bought in another, the Spanish-speaking had little recourse but to leave. They knew that they alone of all foreign miners were being subjected to the tax: when they taunted the collectors to tax Irishmen, Frenchmen, and other Europeans they received no satisfactory reply. Masqueraders posing as collectors came into Mexican camps, solemnly tore up valid permits, and demanded money for new ones; when rebuffed, they auctioned off the victim's dirt and installed in his claim a "loyal citizen." One imposter carried off his charade so well at Don Pedro's Bar that he convinced a posse to help him chase away forty peons and their patrón and killed two Mexicans in the action, before his identity was uncovered.

Even when seeking an escape from California, Mexicans found the Americans lying in wait for them. On the Colorado River, a United States Army lieutenant had express orders "to make all Soronans passing out of California with gold, pay a duty . . . and for my trouble, to put the whole of it in my pocket." A troop of California militiamen blandly confiscated from homebound Sonorans more than a hundred "stolen" mules and horses, ignoring the brand marks proving ownership and compelling the Mexicans to walk 300 miles, including 100 miles across desert.

In the preceding year misunderstanding, fear, and hatred had created an atmosphere so hostile to "Sonorans" as to sanction fraud and murder. Nonetheless, the argument for both protecting and exploiting the foreign miners once more gathered strength. The earliest and most effective counterattack against prejudice was made by the San Francisco Vigilance Committee of 1849, which summarily expelled the "Hounds" from town and made amends to the Chileans who had been tormented by them. Thereafter many individuals took up the cause, speaking in behalf of civil law or laissez-faire competition or on grounds of simple revulsion against mob violence. Among those spokesmen were judges, editors, lawyers, a sheriff, a brigadier general, merchants, mine operators, and the French consul. Several sympathetic collectors ceased selling permits. Even the state attorney general disliked the tax so thoroughly that he refused to defend the collector prosecuted in the California Supreme Court and ignored the governor's threat to prosecute him for dereliction of duty.

Xenophobia had injured its perpetrators as well as its victims. As Mexicans fled the southern mines in 1850, the profits of Yankee merchants plunged alarmingly. Eight-dollar crowbars in one afternoon dropped to fifty cents; a plot of land worth several thousand dollars went begging "for a few bits." Out of sheer dollars-and-cents self-interest, if nothing else, businessmen collected money, hired a lawyer to sue the local collector, and circulated a mass petition asking the governor to lower the impost to $5; all but one merchant signed the document. In July and August, after the second wave of expulsions caused retail losses as high as $10,000 a day in three southern counties, merchants who had helped expel the "evil characters" during the bandit scare became aware that *all* Mexicans were fleeing, not merely the undesirables. A crowd gathered at Georgetown, down the road from Sonora, and went on record as denouncing antiforeigner vigilantes and as supporting civil law. As a result the Stockton *Times* reported that the screening plan enforced at Mormon Gulch and elsewhere was "speedily held in contempt."

These forces had planned to persuade the governor to reduce the tax, the legislature to repeal it, or, best of all, the courts to nullify it. In the state Supreme Court they pleaded that it infringed the exclusive right of the federal government to govern federal lands and abridged the protection granted to aliens by the state constitution and by two treaties with Mexico. Neither of these arguments, however, swayed the high tribunal, which advanced a philosophy of states' rights in all matters relating to the federal government. Two Southern attorneys convinced the court that a state (1) could rightfully tax federal lands, unless specifically prohibited from doing so, and (2) had police powers to defend itself against undesirables. The court, in effect, agreed with the author of the tax act, Green, who had grandly declared that congressional inaction on the California mines had thrown the state back onto "universal laws . . . higher, greater, and stronger than the written constitution." Gratuitously, the court added that even had the law violated a treaty—which had not been demonstrated—it might still be valid, for state laws could take precedence over treaties. Thus, the Spanish Americans had unknowingly become the victims of the imponderable and pervasive sectional controversies of the day.

Notwithstanding its new judicial seal of approval, the tax was a practical failure, as even its original supporters admitted. The Mexican was not the Negro slave; California was not Texas. The governor, aware that the tax was reaping more resentment than revenue, cut the rate to $20 for four months. Even after this corrective, however, the state obtained only $30,000 instead of an expected $2,400,000. The collector in a county that had 15,000 potential taxpayers, sold only 525 permits and was so harassed on his job that he resigned. By 1851 Stockton's leading citizens had developed such loathing for the tax—"a law for the killing of children to get their fat"—that they decided to rally the entire county and lobby in the state capital to obtain its repeal. This they accomplished early in 1851.

The tax had failed to make the state wealthy, to prevent mob action, and to convert immigrants into hirelings as promised. It had eliminated the Latin Americans already in California and curtailed new immigration, a result that did not altogether fill the original bill. Now, having pushed the tax aside, the boosters of the foreign miners hoped to summon them back and make amends. The Yankees had a sudden vision that with the law gone, tens of thousands of Latin Americans would come flooding out of Mexico and Chile and the California towns and wash up into the southern mines, thus opening a new era in gold mining.

That dream failed to materialize, however, since the Spanish Americans by now mistrusted the Yankees and suspected that gold was giving out. They withdrew to Los Angeles and other villages or returned home, informing their countrymen of the dangers of venturing forth into California. Of course, small parties of Spanish Americans continued to enter the diggings, rummaging about on their own hook and staying alert to the possibility of trouble. The one lone Mexican patrón who dared bring in peons in 1852 stood out so conspicuously that he became the center of an international incident. His case made the complete circuit to Mexico City, Washington, and back to California. The district attorney investigated it for the United States Secretary of War, who determined that, although the crowd of Americans who stopped the Mexican was "wholly unprincipled and deserving of punishment," Mexican nationals should seek reparations in the state courts, since the federal government took no responsibility for riots. Thereafter, no patrón was courageous or indiscreet enough to enter the mines, and the Yankee triumph over "foreign capitalists" and "slaves" was complete.

In the long view of California history, the Mexican miners represent merely a link in a long chain of migrants who reach across the "Spanish borderland." They unwittingly followed the trail blazed by the Spanish soldier Juan Bautista Anza and used later by Mexican cholos and colonists. They foreshadowed the coming of the "wetbacks" and the braceros in the twentieth century. As ever, the Mexicans met with mixed success in California, often defeat. They did find some gold, but had to fight for every ounce. That they escaped Yankee bondage was perhaps the most fortunate thing that happened to them.

The migration of the Mexican forty-niners affected the Californios in two ways: for one thing, it put the Yankees in an ugly frame of mind toward all the Spanish-speaking, including the native-born; for another, it sent the newcomers into the established old communities of California, where they fused imperceptibly with those born there. This tended to break down the old and somewhat artificial distinction between "native Californians" and "Mexicans." The fusion went on continuously thereafter.

The Mexican newcomers had, however, one major advantage over their California-born brethren; whereas they could ultimately evade the gringo enemy by returning home, the Californios, attacked on their own soil, could not.

19

Huelga, 1928 Style

CHARLES WOLLENBERG

Carey McWilliams has explained that, "By 1930 the myth of the docility of Mexican labor had been thoroughly exploded." Mexican sugar-beet workers struck in Ventura in 1903, and in 1912 Mexican field workers attempted to establish a union of grape-pickers at Fresno. One of the most significant examples of Mexican efforts to organize for their own protection was the Imperial Valley cantaloupe workers' strike of 1928. Charles Wollenberg, who teaches at Laney College in Oakland, California, examines the 1928 strike as a precursor of recent farm labor struggles in Delano, the Imperial Valley, and Salinas. His article serves to remind us that the conflict between Mexican agricultural workers and their employers in rural California is one of long duration.

THE Imperial Valley cantaloupe worker's strike of 1928 has been all but ignored by California historians. As a labor dispute, it is dwarfed in scope and drama by the Wheatland strike of 1913 and the virtual class warfare of the 1930's. Unlike these more spectacular conflicts in California's fields, the 1928 strike was a purely local affair, staged by Imperial Valley workers with little or no aid from outside organizations. It was broken easily, in part because of organizational weaknesses, but primarily through threats and force by the valley's growers and law enforcement officials. Neverthless, the strike stands as an important event in California history. It was the first attempt at a major work-stoppage organized by Mexican farm workers in modern California. It is important to note that this attempt occurred nearly forty years before the current struggle in Delano and nearly fifteen years before the beginning of the formal *bracero* program. The strike of the Imperial cantaloupe workers in 1928 is part of a long and sometimes bitter heritage of conflict between Mexican agricultural workers and their employers in rural California. The basic economic and social conditions that caused the Imperial Valley strike already were well established in 1928, and the

SOURCE: Charles Wollenberg, *"Huelga, 1928 Style: The Imperial Valley Cantaloupe Workers' Strike," Pacific Historical Review*, 38 (February 1969), pp. 45-49, 52-58. Copyright © 1969 by the Pacific Coast Branch, American Historical Association. Reprinted by permission of the author and the Branch.

Delano *Huelga* indicates that these conditions still exist in California's fields.

During the first week of May 1928, the Imperial Valley was preparing for the harvest of the cantaloupe, its most valuable crop. As early as April 26, the first crate of ripe melons was shipped out of the valley, destined for President Calvin Coolidge at the White House. On May 4 another crate was sent to Washington, this time addressed to Senator Hiram Johnson, leader of the fight for congressional approval of the Boulder Dam Project, a cause dear to the hearts of Imperial growers. By May 5 the valley had filled its first railroad car with ripe melons. Extensive harvesting was expected to begin on Monday, May 7. Work would continue until the middle of July, by which time more than fourteen thousand carloads of Imperial cantaloupes would have been shipped to all parts of the United States.

But on many of the valley's ranches extensive harvesting did not, in fact, begin on May 7. At the Sears Brothers Ranch near Brawley, about half the crew of Mexican field laborers refused to work unless they were paid a piece-work wage of fifteen cents per standard crate of melons. Since the harvesters already had been contracted to work at a thirteen and one-half cent rate, the employer, E. L. Sears, turned down the demand for higher wages. The rebels tried to prevent the other workers from going into the fields. A confused, bilingual argument ensued and, eventually, Sears sent for the county sheriff. The strikers were dispersed, and four of them were arrested for disturbing the peace. Similar incidents occurred at other Imperial Valley ranches that Monday morning, and by afternoon knots of excited Mexicans were discussing the day's events on the street corners and in the pool halls of the valley's towns. On Tuesday the eighth and Wednesday the ninth few field workers reported for harvest duty. The local press reported that between two and three thousand workers were idle.

At the time, Imperial County's agriculture was dependent on Mexican labor. During the first decade of the twentieth century, extensive irrigation projects had opened Imperial desert land to cultivation. The original agricultural pioneers of those years had utilized American Indian, "white," and Oriental labor. Between 1910 and 1920, there was a steady increase in acreage under cultivation, particularly in crops (melons, lettuce, and cotton) which needed a large labor force. While World War I created a substantial growth in the demand for these crops, it also created a shortage of native agricultural labor. By this time, Chinese and Japanese were moving into occupations that were more lucrative than field work. Thus, by 1910, Imperial growers were being forced to look to Mexico as a new source of labor. A revolutionary upheaval had created social and political chaos in some parts of Mexico, conditions that helped to stimulate migration to the United States. By 1920 Mexicans dominated the valley's harvest work and, at the time of the 1928 strike, persons of Mexican descent comprised about ninety percent of Imperial County's field labor force.

Although the valley's Mexican population originally came to the United States as temporary migrants, by 1928 the great bulk of that population had become year-around residents of Imperial County. About twenty thousand people, one-third of the county's total population, were persons of Mexican descent. Virtually all economically active Mexicans living in the valley were field laborers. Some of them spent a few weeks each year in other agricultural regions of California and the Southwest, but they lived most of the year in Imperial Valley towns and worked most of the year in Imperial Valley fields. During the height of the harvest season for the area's two major crops, lettuce and cantaloupes, the resident work-force was supplemented by some temporary migrants from elsewhere. But most, if not all, of the workers who struck in 1928 were residents of Imperial County.

The major employers of agricultural labor in the valley were large landholders—either individuals or corporations which owned or leased large holdings. Such growers needed big work crews, and rather than take the trouble to hire great numbers of workers directly, the growers utilized the services of labor contractors. Contractors were often men of Mexican descent who organized work crews, collected wages from employers, and distributed the money to workers. In return for these services, contractors normally were allowed to deduct for themselves one-half cent per standard crate of melons from the pay of their workers. They distributed wages at the end of each workweek, withholding the first week's pay until the end of the harvest. Thus, after the last work-week, the contractor owed the workers two weeks' pay. When the workers tried to collect this last installment, it was not uncommon for the contractor to disappear.

Uncollected wages was not the only difficulty Mexican workers experienced. Dr. Paul S. Taylor of the University of California made a thorough study of the valley's Mexican population in 1927. He found that the average Mexican field worker earned only six to eight hundred dollars per year. Such a worker housed his family in a one or two-room shack, usually on the outskirts of one of the valley's towns. Most of the Mexican dwellings had no plumbing or sanitation facilities. Mexican children in most Imperial County communities attended segregated elementary schools.

By 1928, then, Mexican workers had become an integral part of the Imperial Valley's economic and social system. They provided the growers with a source of cheap labor, and organizations representing growers acted energetically to protect this labor source. The federal immigration laws of the 1920's allowed Mexican nationals to enter and live in the United States, providing they paid fees amounting to about eighteen dollars on entry. An estimated seventy-five percent of the Mexicans living in the Imperial Valley in 1926 had not paid these fees and thus were illegal residents of the United States. When it was rumored that the Immigration Service was planning to deport such persons, the Associated Labor Bureau, an employment agency founded by and for Imperial growers, began a campaign to "persuade" Mexican workers to pay their fees retroactively. The deportations never occurred, but many workers were forced to pay immigration fees through involuntary wage deductions.

In the early months of 1928, growers faced another threat to their supply of Mexican labor. Legislation applying the 1924 immigration quota system to Mexico and the rest of the Western Hemisphere was introduced by Congressman John Box of Texas. Imperial County's Western Growers Protective Association joined with similar organizations in California, Arizona, and Texas to fight the Box bill. The association's executive secretary, Calexico banker Chester Moore, spent six weeks in Washington lobbying against the measure. In the middle of March 1928, Moore happily reported that the Box bill was buried in committee and would remain that way for the rest of the 1928 congressional session.

While Imperial County growers were exerting pressure to protect their labor force, the county's Mexican workers were organizing a union. The original idea of the union seems to have come from Carlos Ariza, Mexican vice consul at Calexico. In his official position, Ariza received many complaints from workers about defaulting contractors and poor working conditions. In early 1928 he decided that a union might protect the workers' interests, and discussed his idea with members of the valley's Mexican community. In the middle of April, these discussions led to the formation of the Union of United Workers of the Imperial Valley. On April 22 Ariza, now a private attorney, filed incorporation papers for the new organization. Offices were established in Brawley and El Centro, dues were set at one dollar per month, and an executive committee was chosen. By the time of the strike, the union claimed a membership of 2,754 persons, all of Mexican descent.

. . . .

The valley's growers seemed to be psychologically unprepared for a strike of Mexican laborers. Many employers had come to believe that "their" Mexicans were content and peaceful. One California rancher had testified before a congressional committee in February 1928 that a Mexican worker "never causes trouble except when he indulges in intoxicants." Dr. Bloch concluded that Imperial growers considered their

Mexican workers to be "bovine and tractable individuals." Thus, it was not difficult for many Imperial Valley residents to believe that the strike had been caused by alien forces which had subverted the passive, happy workers.

One grower claimed that "agitators or communists or whatever they are . . . have come with their comrade stuff and with threats have intimidated the workers." Imperial County Sheriff Charles L. Gillett believed that the strike had been caused by "reds and radicals." An Imperial Valley *Press* headline declared: "Radicals to Blame." The Imperial Valley *Farmer* warned that "agitators" might be planning "dangerous and violent acts." And from the Los Angeles *Times* came a report that "I. W. W. members are in back of the movement." (Later the *Times'* headline writer forgot about the Wobblies and decided that "Agitators from Old Mexico" had caused the disturbance.)

In spite of the frequency of such charges, there is no evidence indicating that the Imperial Valley strike was fomented by "outside agitators" or members of radical organizations. A spokesman for the workers claimed that "we are not a bunch of Bolsheviks or I. W. W.'s." He and his fellow laborers had organized a union to gain "better wages for the benefit of our families." Dr. Bloch accepted these claims; moreover, the local press, which gave extensive coverage to the legal hearings of "agitators" who were arrested as a result of the strike, made no mention of any attempt by the County District Attorney to prove that the defendants were members of radical organizations or that they were non-residents of the Imperial Valley.

Such questions, however, must have seemed academic to most Imperial County growers on May 8. Their major concern was to persuade workers to return to the fields. On that day anonymous leaflets, reportedly printed in "illiterate Spanish," appeared throughout the valley. They warned the workers to "be careful." "If you fail to cooperate, the same men who have given their time and money to get you into this country and protect you here, the same men, will turn against you." Some of the leaflets contained alleged copies of telegrams in which Texas and Arizona employment agencies assured Imperial Valley growers that "thousands" of new workers could be brought to California within thirty-six hours.

Along with these threats came action by Imperial County's law enforcement officials. Perhaps the attitude of these public servants was best summarized by District Attorney Elmer Heald: "Imperial Valley melon growers have millions of dollars invested in a highly perishable crop, and every resource of law enforcement machinery is to be used in harvesting the crop." On Tuesday, May 8, the County Board of Supervisors ordered Sheriff Gillett to "arrest agitators." Gillett also was given authority to add forty deputies to his staff, which he did, in part, by swearing in field bosses from some of the largest ranches. The sheriff also told Mexican workers in the Imperial Valley that, if they were not satisfied with conditions in the United States, they could go back to Mexico. Both Gillett and Heald warned that trouble-makers would be referred to the United States Immigration Service for possible deportation.

Sheriff Gillett believed that "Mexicans are excitable and if idle will gather into groups to their own detriment as well as hindering work in the fields." Given these premises, the sheriff's tactics were obvious: he would see to it that Mexicans in the Imperial Valley neither "remained idle" nor "gathered into groups." On Tuesday, May 8, Gillett arrested about thirty Mexicans for "loitering about the streets of El Centro." Learning that the union was planning a membership meeting in Brawley that evening, he announced that he would be "chairman of that meeting." One half hour after the sheriff arrived at the gathering, "there were few Mexicans left in the vicinity." On May 13, a Mexican newspaper distributor in Brawley was arrested for allegedly writing on his billboard, "Forty-eight Mexicans in jail—What for?—Nothing."

Dr. Bloch could not resist injecting a bit of subtle humor into his official report when he described the activities of Imperial County's sheriff. "Prompted by an intuitive sense of justice and spurred on by the requirements of the occasion, . . . [Gillett] sallied forth immediately to bring order out of the chaos which threatened to engulf the land of the cantaloupes." And, indeed, Gillett's zeal did at times lead him into embarrassing situations. On the afternoon of May 8, he saw a group of Mexicans gathering outside the county courthouse in El Centro. Fearing the worst, the sheriff arrested the group, only to discover that it was a delegation of workers invited to discuss the crisis with District Attorney Heald. On the evening of May 10, Gillett entered the Martinez Pool Hall in Westmoreland and ordered patrons to vacate the premises. The patrons, led by Mrs. Francisca Rodriguez, responded by throwing the sheriff into the street. Gillett recovered his dignity, gathered reinforcements, and returned to arrest four persons, including Mrs. Rodriguez. The sheriff later claimed there had been one thousand people in the pool hall; Mrs. Rodriguez put the figure at six.

But if Gillett's actions sometimes were humorous, they were also effective. By May 11, at least fifty persons of Mexican descent had been arrested. The offices of the Union of United Workers had been closed for the duration of the emergency, and so were five pool halls frequented by a Mexican clientele. All "congregations of foreigners" in the Imperial Valley were prohibited. The sheriff claimed to have a "secret service" operating in the valley's Mexican neighborhoods in order to identify agitators and troublemakers. Louis Bloch concluded that "the Sheriff's decisiveness in rounding up and incarcerating actual and potential disturbers of the peace undoubtedly had the effect of stopping a movement which might have resulted in an effective general strike and in heavy losses to the growers."

During the week of May 14, as the cases of arrested workers came up for hearing, attention shifted from Gillett to District Attorney Elmer Heald. In some instances, prisoners may have been released after a night or two in jail, without formal charges being brought against them. However, by Monday, May 14, there were still about fifty workers in custody on charges of vagrancy and disturbing the peace. Bail had been set at between $250 and $1,000, and there is no indication that any prisoners had been able to post bond. But Elmer Heald had no intention of keeping Imperial County's jails filled with harvest workers. He wished only that the Mexicans would go back to work and stay out of trouble. Thus the prisoners were offered six-month suspended sentences if they would plead guilty and promise to return to the fields. As Heald explained, "if the judge would hold them on bail, they would enter pleas of guilty next day and would go to work and behave themselves."

In view of the high bail schedules, many workers had no choice but to accept Heald's offer. However, on the fifteenth, Alfred Blaisdell, a Calexico attorney hired by the Mexican consulate, entered the case on behalf of the defendants. Blaisdell advised his clients to refuse the prosecutor's terms, and on May 15 and 16 Blaisdell instituted *habeus corpus* proceedings in an attempt to free the prisoners. He argued that the trials had been delayed too long and bail set too high. He also suggested that Gillett and Heald be cited for contempt of court. On the fifteenth Blaisdell was unable to obtain freedom for several prisoners held in Brawley. But on the sixteenth he did win the release of thirty-three prisoners in Westmoreland. The decision was hardly a landmark for civil liberties. Justice of the Peace F. T. Cook decided that the city of Westmoreland no longer could afford to feed thirty-three prisoners.

By the time of the hearings, the strike had been broken. Harvest work seems to have been seriously hampered from Monday, May 7, to Thursday, May 10. On Saturday, the twelfth, the Imperial Valley *Press* reported "all quiet in labor circles," and the Brawley *News* announced that "the strike, so-called, seems to have passed into history." The growers do not appear to have sustained major losses as a result of the workstoppage. An unusual spell of cool weather kept the melons from ripening too quickly and, by the time that temperatures rose on the twelfth, the strike had been broken. By May 18 more than one hundred and fifty carloads of melons a day were being shipped by rail out of the valley. Between the first and twenty-third of May, a total of 1,855 carloads left the valley, a record harvest for that period.

Yet, from the workers' point of view, the strike was not a complete failure. On Saturday, May 12, the Brawley *News* proudly claimed that the conflict had ended "with no yielding on the part of the employer." However, another article on the same page admitted that S. A. Gerrard, one of the valley's largest growers, had "reached a compromise with the workers." Dr. Bloch found that most growers eventually agreed to pay the fifteen-cent per crate wage originally requested by the union. But most of the other requests were ignored, and in no case was the union recognized as a bargaining agent.

Dr. Bloch, himself, played a major role in informing the state government of the difficulties encountered by Imperial Valley workers. His report to the Bureau of Industrial Relations emphasized the inequities of the contract system. During December of 1928, Bloch and bureau chief W. J. French came to the Imperial Valley to persuade growers to readjust their labor arrangements. A joint grower-bureau committee wrote a "standard picking agreement," which all growers were encouraged to use during the 1929 harvests. The agreement's most important features were those calling for the elimination of withheld wages and the direct distribution of wages to the workers by growers rather than by contractors.

The strike also strengthened the position of those who wished to limit further immigration of Mexicans into the United States. After learning of the disturbance in the Imperial Valley, Congressman Box reaffirmed his conviction that, since "Mexico is by far the most bolshevistic country in the Western Hemisphere," Mexicans "constitute a bad element to have imported into the United States." Although the Box bill had been killed for the 1928 congressional session, its supporters planned to try once more in 1930 (a try that would again fail).

By the beginning of 1929, an informed observer such as Dr. Bloch could be cautiously optimistic about the future of Mexican farm workers in the Imperial Valley. The state government had taken action to alleviate some of the workers' difficulties. Federal restriction of Mexican immigration certainly would have improved the bargaining position of the valley's resident Mexicans. And workers had shown a willingness to form labor unions and strike for better wages and working conditions.

But Bloch could not foresee the events which, for the next thirty-seven years, would weaken the ability of Mexican field workers to improve their economic and social positions in California. The depression of the 1930's created a disastrous drop in wage rates and caused the introduction of hundreds of thousands of Anglo workers into the field labor market. Violent strikes organized by outside radical groups occurred in the valley during the thirties but were not successful. World War II helped create the bracero program, which gave California growers a government guarantee of cheap migrant labor from Mexico. Not until

Congress ended the importation of braceros in 1965 did anything approximating the agricultural labor situation of the 1920's return to rural California. Perhaps, then, it is no accident that in September of 1965 Mexican workers in Delano again walked out of California fields.

This paper has sought to emphasize that the conflict between California farmers and their Mexican workers has a heritage of more than forty years. In spite of the pioneering published works of writers such as Paul S. Taylor and Carey McWilliams, current events in Delano too often are treated as if they have no historical perspective. If we are to understand fully the Delano conflict, we also must understand the role that people of Mexican descent have played in rural California for more than a generation. We must know more about the organizations and institutions that were developing in the *barrios* of California towns during the twenties. We must have a better understanding of the part Mexican workers played in the great agricultural strikes of the 1930's. Certainly we should be studying the impact of the bracero program upon resident Mexican laborers in the forties and fifties. And we need studies of past conflicts between Mexicans and other ethnic groups engaged in field labor. Finally, the entire history of Mexican field labor must be placed within the context of the larger story of migrant workers and agricultural development on California's fields.

20

Zoot-Suiters and Mexicans

RALPH H. TURNER and SAMUEL J. SURACE

No action in recent California history—with the notable exception of the incarceration of Japanese Americans during World War II—surpasses in discriminatory intensity the vicious assaults by Anglo-Americans on Mexican Americans in that same period. Both the "Sleepy Lagoon" murder case of 1942 and the "Zoot Suit" riots of 1943 testify to the second-class citizenship enjoyed by Mexican Americans at that time. In this selection, Ralph Turner and Samuel Surace describe the role of the media in the development of hostile consciousness toward Mexicans. In the presentation of unfavorable symbols to describe certain groups of people, those people can thereby be removed from the constraints of the conventional moral order so that extra-legal action can then be directed against them. Thus to label Mexican Americans "zoot-suiters" and "pachucos" in Los Angeles in 1943 was to provide a rallying point for hostile crowd behavior, and was to encourage a wave of brutal anti-Mexican assaults. Readers interested in a similar phenomenon with respect to "Hippies" may wish to consult Michael E. Brown's informative article, "The Condemnation and Persecution of Hippies," in Trans-action *(September, 1969).*

THE purpose of this paper is to test a hypothesis concerning the symbols with which a hostile crowd designates the object of its action. The hypothesis is that hostile crowd behavior requires an unambiguously unfavorable symbol, which serves to divert crowd attention from any of the usual favorable or mitigating connotations surrounding the object. The hypothesis has been tested by a content analysis of references to the symbol "Mexican" during the ten-and-one-half-year period leading up to the 1943 "zoot-suit riots" in Los Angeles and vicinity.

SOURCE: Ralph H. Turner and Samuel J. Surace, "Zoot-Suiters and Mexicans: Symbols in Crowd Behavior," *American Journal of Sociology*, 62 (July 1956), pp. 14-20. Reprinted with permission of the University of Chicago Press and the authors.

Theory and Hypothesis

The hypothesis under examination is related to two important characteristics of crowd behavior. First, crowd behavior is *uniform* behavior in a broad sense, in contrast to behavior which exposes the infinitely varied attitudes of diverse individuals. Many attitudes and gradations of feeling can be expressed in a group's actions toward any particular object. However, the crowd is a group expressing *one* attitude, with individual variations largely concealed.

In non-crowd situations uniform behavior may be achieved by majority decision, acceptance of authority, or compromise of some sort. But crowd behavior is not mediated by such slow and deliberate procedures. Within the crowd there is a readiness to act *uniformly* in response to varied suggestions, and, until such readiness to act has spread throughout the crowd's recruitment population, fully developed and widespread-acting crowd behavior is not possible.

The response in the community to shared symbols is crucial to this uniformity of action. Ordinarily, any particular symbol has varied connotations for different individuals and groups in the community. These varied connotations prevent uniform community-wide action or at least delay it until extended processes of group decision-making have been carried out. But, when a given symbol has a relatively uniform connotation in all parts of the community, uniform group action can be taken readily when the occasion arises. To the degree, then, to which any symbol evokes only one consistent set of connotations throughout the community, only one general course of action toward the object will be indicated, and formation of an acting crowd will be facilitated.

Second, the crowd follows a course of action which is at least partially sanctioned in the culture but, at the same time, is normally inhibited by other aspects of that culture. Mob action is frequently nothing more than culturally sanctioned punishment carried out by unauthorized persons without "due process." Support of it in everyday life is attested to in many ways. Organizations such as the Ku Klux Klan and other vigilante groups act as self-appointed "custodians of patriotism" and are fairly widely accepted as such. The lynching of two "confessed" kidnapers in California in 1933 was given public sanction by the then governor of the state on the grounds of its therapeutic effect on other would-be criminals. The legal system in America implicitly recognizes these supports by including statutes designed to suppress them.

Hostile acting crowd behavior can take place only when these inhibiting aspects of the culture cease to operate. Conflict between the norms sanctioning the crowd's action and the norms inhibiting it must be resolved by the neutralization of the inhibiting norms.

There is normally some ambiguity in the connotations of any symbol, so that both favorable and unfavorable sentiments are aroused. For example, even the most prejudiced person is likely to respond to the symbol "Negro" with images of both the feared invader of white prerogatives and the lovable, loyal Negro lackey and "mammy." The symbol "bank robber" is likely to evoke a picture of admirable daring along with its generally unfavorable image. These ambiguous connotations play an important part in inhibiting extreme hostile behavior against the object represented by the symbol.

The diverse connotations of any symbol normally inhibit extreme behavior in two interrelated ways. First, the symbol evokes feelings which resist any extreme course of action. A parent, for example, is normally inhibited from punishing his child to excess, because affection for him limits the development of anger. Pity and admiration for courage or resolute action, or sympathy for a course of action which many of us might like to engage in ourselves, or charity toward human weakness usually moderate hostility toward violators of the mores. So long as feelings are mixed, actions are likely to be moderate.

Second, the mixed connotations of the symbol place the object *within the normative order*, so that the mores of fair play, due process, giving a fair hearing, etc., apply. Any indication that the individual under attack respects any of the social norms or has any of the characteristics of the in-group evokes these mores which block extreme action.

On the other hand, unambiguous symbols permit immoderate behavior, since there is no internal conflict to restrict action. Furthermore, a symbol which represents a person as outside the normative order will not evoke the in-group norms of fair play and due process. The dictum that "you must fight fire with fire" and the conviction that a person devoid of human decency is not entitled to be treated with decency and respect rule out these inhibiting norms.

We conclude that a necessary condition for both the uniform group action and the unrestricted hostile behavior of the crowd is a symbol which arouses uniformly and exclusively unfavorable feelings toward the object under attack. However, the connotations of a symbol to the mass or crowd do not necessarily correspond exactly with the connotations to individuals. The symbol as presented in the group context mediates the overt expression of attitudes in terms of sanction and the focus of attention. The individual in whom a particular symbol evokes exclusively unfavorable feelings may nevertheless be inhibited from acting according to his feelings by the awareness that other connotations are sanctioned in the group. Or the individual in whom ambivalent feelings are evoked may conceal his favorable sentiments because he sees that only the unfavorable sentiments are sanctioned. He thereby facilitates crowd use of the symbol. Furthermore, of all the possible connotations attached to a symbol, the individual at any given moment acts principally on the basis of those on which his attention is focused. By shielding individuals from attending to possibly conflicting connotations, the unambiguous public symbol prevents the evocation of attitudes which are normally present. Thus, without necessarily undergoing change, favorable individual attitudes toward the object of crowd attack simply remain latent. This process is one of the aspects of the so-called restriction of attention which characterizes the crowd.

While unambiguous symbols are a necessary condition to full-fledged crowd behavior, they may also be a product of the earlier stages of crowd development. In some cases sudden development of a crowd is facilitated by the pre-existing linkage of an already unambiguous symbol to the object upon which events focus collective attention. But more commonly we suspect that the emergence of such a symbol or the stripping-away of alternative connotations takes place cumulatively through interaction centered on that object. In time, community-wide interaction about an object takes on increasingly crowd-like characteristics in gradual preparation for the ultimate crowd action. It is the hypothesis of this paper that *overt hostile crowd behavior is usually preceded by a period in which the key symbol is stripped of its favorable connotations until it comes to evoke unambiguously unfavorable feelings.*

The "Zoot-Suit Riots"

Beginning on June 3, 1943, Los Angeles, California, was the scene of sporadic acts of violence involving principally United States naval personnel, with the support of a sympathetic Anglo community, in opposition to members of the Mexican community which have come to be known as the "zoot-suit riots." "Zooter" referred mainly to two characteristics. First, zoot suits consisted of long suit coats and trousers extremely pegged at the cuff, draped full around the knees, and terminating in deep pleats at the waist. Second, the zooters wore their hair long, full, and well greased.

During the riots many attacks and injuries were sustained by both sides. Groups of sailors were frequently reported to be assisted or accompanied by civilian mobs who "egged" them on as they roamed through downtown streets in search of victims. Zooters discovered on city streets were assualted and forced to disrobe amid the jibes and molestations of the crowd. Street-cars and busses were stopped and searched, and zooters found therein were carried off into the streets and beaten. Cavalcades of hired taxicabs filled with sailors ranged the East Side districts of Los Angeles seeking, finding, and attacking zooters. Civilian gangs of East

Side adolescents organized similar attacks against unwary naval personnel.

It is, of course, impossible to isolate a single incident or event and hold it responsible for the riots. Local, state, and federal authorities and numerous civic and national groups eventually tried to assess blame and prevent further violence. The most prominent charge from each side was that the other had molested its girls. It was reported that sailors became enraged by the rumor that zoot-suiters were guilty of "assaults on female relatives of servicemen." Similarly, the claim against sailors was that they persisted in molesting and insulting Mexican girls. While many other charges were reported in the newspapers, including unsubstantiated suggestions of sabotage of the war effort, the sex charges dominated the precipitating context.

Method

In the absence of any direct sampling of community sentiment in the period preceding the riots, it is assumed that the use of the symbol "Mexican" by the media of mass communication indicates the prevalent connotations. Any decision as to whether the mass media passively reflect community sentiment, whether they actively mold it, or whether, as we supposed, some combination of the two processes occurs is immaterial to the present method. Ideally we should have sampled a number of mass media to correct for biases in each. However, with the limited resources at our disposal we chose the *Los Angeles Times*, largest of the four major newspapers in the Los Angeles area. It is conservative in emphasis and tends away from the sensational treatment of minority issues. In the past a foremost romanticizer of Old Mexico had been a prominent member of the *Times* editorial staff and board of directors.

In order to uncover trends in the connotation of the symbol under study, one newspaper per month was read for the ten and one-half years from January, 1933, until June 30, 1943. These monthly newspapers were selected by assigning consecutive days of the week to each month. For example, for January, 1933, the paper printed on the first Monday was read; for February, the paper printed on the first Tuesday was read. After the seven-day cycle was completed, the following months were assigned, respectively, the *second* Monday, the *second* Tuesday, etc. To avoid loading the sample with days that fell early in the first half of the month, the procedure was reversed for the last half of the period. Then, to secure an intensive picture of the critical period, consecutive daily editions were read for one month starting with May 20, 1943, through June 20, 1943. This covered approximately ten days before and after the period of violence. Any editorial, story, report, or letter which had reference to the Mexican community or population was summarized, recorded, and classified. The articles were placed in five basic categories: favorable themes, unfavorable themes, neutral mention, negative-favorable mention, and zooter theme.

1. *Favorable:* (*a*) Old California Theme. This is devoted to extolling the traditions and history of the old rancheros as the earliest California settlers. (*b*) Mexican Temperament Theme. This describes the Mexican character in terms of dashing romance, bravery, gaiety, etc. (*c*) Religious Theme. This refers to the devout religious values of the Mexican community. (*d*) Mexican Culture Theme. This pays homage to Mexican art, dance, crafts, music, fifth of May festivities, etc.

2. *Unfavorable:* (*a*) Delinquency and Crime Theme. This theme includes the specific mention of a law violator as "Mexican," associating him with marihuana, sex crimes, knife-wielding, gang violence, etc. (*b*) Public Burden Theme. This attempts to show that Mexicans constitute a drain on relief funds and on the budgets of correctional institutions.

3. *Neutral:* This is a category of miscellaneous items, including reports of crimes committed by individuals possessing obvious Mexican names but without designation of ethnic affiliation.

4. *Negative-Favorable:* This category consists of appeals which *counter* or *deny* the validity of accusations against Mexicans as a group. For example: "Not all zoot-suiters are delinquents; their adoption by many was a bid for social recognition"; "At the outset zoot-suiters were limited to no specific race. . . . The fact that later on their numbers seemed to be predominantly Latin was in itself no indication of that race" (*Los Angeles Times,* July 11, 1943, Part I, p. 1).

5. *Zooter Theme:* This theme identifies the zooter costume as "a badge of delinquency." Typical references were: "reat pleat boys," "long coated gentry," coupled with mention of "unprovoked attacks by zoot-suited youths," "zoot-suit orgy," etc. Crime, sex violence, and gang attacks were the dominant elements in this theme. Almost invariably, the zooter was identified as a Mexican by such clues as "East Side hoodlum," a Mexican name, or specific ethnic designation.

If the hypothesis of this paper is to be supported, we should expect a decline in the favorable contexts of the symbol "Mexican." The change should serve to produce the type of symbol suggested by the hypothesis, a symbol dominated by unambiguously unfavorable elements.

Findings

The favorable and unfavorable themes are reported alone in Table 20-1 for the ten and one-half years. The table by itself appears to negate our hypothesis, since there is no appreciable decline in the percentage of favorable themes during the period. Indeed, even during the last period the mentions appear predominantly favorable, featuring the romanticized

TABLE 20-1. FAVORABLE AND UNFAVORABLE MENTION OF "MEXICAN"
DURING THREE PERIODS

Period	Favorable Themes	Unfavorable Themes	Percentage Favorable
January, 1933—June, 1936	27	3	90
July, 1936—December, 1939	23	5	82
January, 1940—June, 1943	10	2	83
Total	60	10	86

TABLE 20-2. DISTRIBUTION OF ALL THEMES BY THREE PERIODS

Period	Percentage Favorable	Percentage Unfavorable	Percentage Neutral	Percentage Negative-Favorable	Percentage Zooter	Total Percentage	Total Number
January, 1933—June, 1936	80	9	11	0	0	100	34
July, 1936—December, 1939	61	13	23	3	0	100	38
January, 1940—June, 1943	25	5	32	8	30	100	40

Mexican. However, there is a striking decline in the total number of articles mentioning the Mexican between the second and third periods. Treating the articles listed as a fraction of all articles in the newspapers sampled and using a subminimal estimate of the total number of all articles, the *t* test reveals that such a drop in the total number of articles mentioning Mexicans could have occurred by chance less than twice in one hundred times. We conclude, then, that the decline in total favorable and unfavorable mentions of "Mexican" is statistically significant.

While the hypothesis in its simplest form is unsubstantiated, the drop in both favorable and unfavorable themes suggests a shift away from *all* the traditional references to Mexicans during the period prior to the riots. If it can be shown that an actual substitution of symbols was taking place, our hypothesis may still be substantiated, but in a somewhat different manner than anticipated.

From the distribution of all five themes reported in Table 20-2 it is immediately evident that there has been no decline of interest in the Mexican but rather a clear-cut shift of attention away from traditional references. The straightforward favorable and unfavorable themes account for 89, 74, and 30 per cent of all references, respectively, during the three periods. This drop and the drop from 61 to 25 per cent favorable mentions are significant below the 1 per cent level. To determine whether this evidence confirms our hypothesis, we must make careful examination of the three emerging themes.

The *neutral* theme shows a steady increase throughout the three periods. While we have cautiously designated this "neutral," it actually consists chiefly of unfavorable presentations of the object "Mexican" without overt use of the symbol "Mexican." Thus it incorporates the unfavorable representation of Mexican, which we assume was quite generally recognized throughout the community, without explicit use of the symbol.

The *negative-favorable* theme, though small in total numbers, also increased. At first we were inclined to treat these as favorable themes. However, in contrast to the other favorable themes, this one documents the extent of negative connotation which is accumulating about the symbol "Mexican." By arguing openly against the negative connotations, these articles acknowledge their widespread community sanction. When the implicitly favorable themes of romantic Mexico and California's historic past give way to defensive assertions that all Mexicans are not bad, such a shift can only reasonably be interpreted as a rise in unfavorable connotations.

The most interesting shift, however, is the rise of the *zoot-suit* theme, which did not appear at all until the third period, when it accounts for 30 per cent of the references. Here we have the emergence of a new symbol which has no past favorable connotations to lose. Unlike the symbol "Mexican," the "zoot-suiter" symbol evokes no ambivalent sentiments but appears in exclusively unfavorable contexts. While, in fact, Mexicans were attacked *indiscriminately* in spite of apparel (of two hundred youths rounded up by the police on one occasion, very few were wearing zoot suits), the symbol "zoot-suiter" could become a basis for unambivalent community sentiment supporting hostile crowd behavior more easily than could "Mexican."

It is interesting to note that, when we consider only the fifteen mentions which appear in the first six months of 1943, ten are to zooters, three are negative-favorable, two are neutral, and none is the traditional favorable or unfavorable theme.

In Table 20-3 we report the results of the day-by-day analysis of the period immediately prior, during, and after the riots. It shows the culmination of a trend faintly suggested as long as seven years before the riots and clearly indicated two or three years in advance. The traditional favorable and unfavorable themes have vanished completely, and three-quarters of the references center about the zooter theme.

From the foregoing evidence we conclude that our basic hypothesis and theory receive confirmation, but not exactly as anticipated. The

TABLE 20-3. DISTRIBUTION OF ALL THEMES FROM MAY 20 TO JUNE 20, 1943

Theme	Percentage of All Mentions *
Favorable	0
Unfavorable	0
Neutral	3
Negative-favorable	23
Zooter	74
Total	100

* Total number = 61.

simple expectation that there would be a shift in the relative preponderance of favorable and unfavorable contexts for the symbol "Mexican" was not borne out. But the basic hypothesis that an unambiguously unfavorable symbol is required as the rallying point for hostile crowd behavior is supported through evidence that the symbol "Mexican" tended to be displaced by the symbol "zoot-suiter" as the time of the riots drew near.

The conception of the romantic Mexican and the Mexican heritage is deeply ingrained in southern California tradition. The Plaza and Olvera Street in downtown Los Angeles, the Ramona tradition, the popularity of Mexican food, and many other features serve to perpetuate it. It seems quite probable that its force was too strong to be eradicated entirely, even though it ceased to be an acceptable matter of public presentation. In spite, then, of a progressive decline in public presentation of the symbol in its traditional favorable contexts, a certain ambivalence remained which prevented a simple replacement with predominantly unfavorable connotations.

Rather, two techniques emerged for circumventing the ambivalence. One was the presenting of the object in an obvious manner without explicit use of the symbol. Thus a Mexican name, a picture, or reference to "East Side hoodlums" was presented in an unfavorable context. But a far more effective device was a new symbol whose connotations at the time were exclusively unfavorable. It provided the public sanction and restriction of attention essential to the development of overt crowd hostility. The symbol "zoot-suiter" evoked none of the imagery of the romantic past. It evoked only the picture of a breed of persons outside the normative order, devoid of morals themselves, and consequently not entitled to fair play and due process. Indeed, the zoot-suiter came to be regarded as such an exclusively fearful threat to the community that at the height of rioting the Los Angeles City Council seriously debated an ordinance making the wearing of zoot suits a prison offense.

The "zooter" symbol had a crisis character which mere unfavorable versions of the familiar "Mexican" symbol never approximated. And the "zooter" symbol was an omnibus, drawing together the most reprehensible elements in the old unfavorable themes, namely, sex crimes, delinquency, gang attacks, draft-dodgers, and the like and was, in consequence, widely applicable.

The "zooter" symbol also supplied a tag identifying the object of attack. It could be used, when the old attitudes toward Mexicans were evoked, to differentiate Mexicans along both moral and physical lines. While the active minority were attacking Mexicans indiscriminately, and frequently including Negroes, the great sanctioning majority heard only of attacks on zoot-suiters.

Once established, the zooter theme assured its own magnification. What previously would have been reported as an adolescent gang attack would now be presented as a zoot-suit attack. Weapons found on apprehended youths were now interpreted as a building-up of arms collections in preparation for zoot-suit violence. In short, the "zooter" symbol was a recasting of many of the elements formerly present and sometimes associated with Mexicans in a new and instantly recognizable guise. This new association of ideas relieved the community of ambivalence and moral obligations and gave sanction to making the Mexicans the victims of widespread hostile crowd behavior.

21

The Segregation of Mexican-American School Children in Southern California

W. HENRY COOKE

In March, 1945, some Mexican American families applied for a federal injunction against segregating Spanish-speaking children in certain Orange County schools. The court agreed, ordering a permanent injunction in February, 1946. The ruling, upheld in higher courts, found this form of segregation unconstitutional eight years before Brown vs. Board of Education (1954). Despite these rulings, de facto segregation flourishes in California. In Los Angeles, 80 per cent of Mexican Americans and Afro-Americans attend largely segregated schools. Recent (1970) rulings in Los Angeles and Houston, Texas, have insisted that Mexican Americans are an "identifiable ethnic minority group" and therefore fall under the Brown ruling. In California and the Southwest generally, however, the segregated conditions described in this selection still prevail.

SCHOOLS for "Mexicans" and schools for "Americans" have been the custom in many a Southern California city. It mattered not that the "Mexicans" were born in the United States and that great numbers of them were sons and daughters of United States citizens. It has been the custom that they be segregated at least until they could use English well enough to keep up with English-speaking children. Neither did it matter that many of them had a command of English nor that there was no legal basis for their segregation. Under a law, enacted in 1885 and amended in 1893, it has been possible to segregate Indians and Mongolians in California's public schools. To many an administrator this included "Mexicans." This pattern was followed principally because the majority groups in the local communities wanted it done that way. Since the spring of 1947, a new legal situation has maintained: it is not now legal in California to segregate any ethnic group. And yet the practice still continues in many cities. This fact needs explanation. But first, just what is meant by "racial segregation" as applied to schools?

SOURCE: W. Henry Cooke, "The Segregation of Mexican-American School Children in Southern California," *School and Society*, 67 (June 5, 1948), 417–421. Reprinted with permission of The Society for the Advancement of Education, Inc.

Segregation as a school policy does not come about by accident. If it exists, there must be intent to separate children between schools or into school groups on the basis of race, national origin, or religion. This sometimes takes the form of an action by a school board providing that all students of a named ethnic group be registered in a given school. In other instances a school board approves the drawing of zone boundaries in such a way as to throw all families of a certain ethnic group into homogeneous areas. When neither of these two methods seems feasible, a policy of transfer of students from zone to zone brings about the same result. Few, if any, cases of segregation of Mexican-Americans have been absolute in nature, for the parents who have had sufficient influence could usually have an exception made for their children. Once made for an elder child, it usually held for all of the succeeding children of the family. Thus it is that the question of privilege raised its head—privilege as between Mexican and Mexican, as well as between Mexican and "Anglo."

As a general thing, segregation comes from and leads to discrimination. This is true in Southern California where Mexican-Americans are involved just as it is in the Southern states where Negroes are the principal minority people. To be sure, it is not necessarily true that policies of discrimination originate in the schools; they grow out of habits in community life. They are the result of the social process by which the majority group or groups seek to protect themselves, their culture, and their property values from all deteriorating influences from the outside. Despite the polyglot nature of America, and especially of Western America, their habits have persisted from one generation to another and have been carried from state to state. A group of low-income workers of Caucasian ancestry who "invade" a California county or township is likely to be excluded for a time, at least, from the economic and social opportunities enjoyed by the older Caucasian population of that region. But if the "invading" low-income workers speak a foreign language, have dark skin, or practice a strange religion, they are likely to be considered dangerous to the majority group and its standards of culture. Employment may be restricted for them generation after generation, churches may not be open to their worship, city parks with plunges and other apparatus will be closed, and even the public schools will not welcome them. One does not need to go far to find instances in which, in time of peace, they have been intimidated, attacked, and driven out of the region.

With the Mexican-Americans there has never been the sense of danger there was during the war with the Japanese peoples. The Mexican people came to the United States as agricultural laborers, their wages were traditionally low as compared with American standards, although not with Mexican levels. They found habitat in the edges of California towns where land was cheap, and they built simple and inadequate buildings.

Often there would be no sewers in the section they chose and few taps for running water were opened. Many people lived upon small pieces of property that should have housed but one family each. Two decades ago they were hesitant about investing more of their earnings in residences because they harbored the idea that they would soon go back across the border. The fact is that they have stayed in very large numbers, and relatively few of them have left their "colonies" to live in better conditions, although the numbers have been increasing in recent years.

The characteristics of all Mexican-Americans have been set in the minds of most citizens by the descriptions of these early peasants who spoke a foreign tongue and lived unto themselves in ways that seemed uninviting or even squalid. It did not look like discrimination twenty-five years ago to furnish these people with a school and a teacher or two. The building did not have to be much to be better than their homes. The teacher might have been just anybody who would go "down there"; no results were to be expected. Mexican people were roving workers who were a charge upon any school district.

Today these conditions have changed in that the Mexican-Americans have become established as permanent residents in very large numbers. A third generation is now growing up in the once temporary shacks. New houses have been built that would do credit to any worker family. A sizable percentage of Mexican-American young people have become educated, have been around the world with the American armed forces, and want to be accepted in the larger community. Many of the first-generation people and virtually all of the second and third generation speak English. Organizations for their own improvement and integration exist among them. They are now in large numbers "Americans" in every sense of the word. In addition, the whole country is awakening to the injustices under which many backward and colonial peoples have lived. We are more conscious of civil rights for all members of society than we once were. What was once winked at in California can now justly be called discrimination.

That an "Anglo" who was young and intelligent as a business man should be driven out of his new home in a Southern California city because his wife was of Mexican ancestry, although born in that same city and educated in its high school, is an evidence of discrimination. The neighbors waited upon him and he had to sell his home. That a schoolteacher who took her class to a motion picture theater had to divide them so that the "whites" sat in their proper sections and the "Mexicans" in theirs, is evidence of discrimination. When a probation officer finds on his hands a Mexican-American boy who is so brilliant that he gets ahead of his classes and gets into trouble and when this officer tries to place the boy in employment and finds the jobs that are suited to his caliber closed to him because he is a Mexican, there is evidence of discrimination. When a vice-principal of a high school admits that he does not urge Mexican boys to seek varied employment as other boys do because he knows that they cannot do anything more than work in the groves, there is discrimination. When a city council refuses to let Mexican-American boys and girls swim in the public plunge and when it places at the entrance of the bathhouse a red sign reading FOR WHITE RACE ONLY and when it admits through its city clerk that this is for the purpose of keeping out "Mexican" children, it is both ignorance and discrimination.

Many instances of this kind could be cited from California. And yet this state is better than some of its neighbors in that it has adequate laws that prohibit these practices. They continue because communities demand them. The point of this article is not to review the whole field of discrimination, but to study this phenomenon within the public schools—the place above all others where it should not exist.

On the brighter side of the picture several facts can be set forth. The large city school systems of the state have all abolished the segregation of Mexican-Americans and, with the exception of a few vestiges of segregation by zoning or transfer, the segregation of all-ethnic groups. Some of these cities have staff members detailed to work upon a better integration and understanding throughout all their schools. This does not mean that all teachers are yet convinced of the values of mixing all students in the schools, but it does reveal an administrative policy that will in time have its effect. In these cities teachers of Negro, Mexican, or Chinese backgrounds are finding their places upon teaching staffs. One large city has five Negro building principals and another has a director of intercultural education. Other cities have committees working on intergroup relationships. In a number of smaller cities where the segregation of Mexican-Americans has been a tradition, the school boards have definitely abolished the policy and the practice. In most cases they aroused a clamor of opposition from parents of the majority group, but by tactful handling this has subsided. Some parents sent their children outside of these progressive districts for their schooling in order to avoid having their children sent to the "Mexican school" or to avoid intermingling of their offspring with Mexican-Americans. A number of these changes came about because the administrators realized that segregation was good for neither the English- nor the Spanish-speaking children and that the best type of community could come from having all students learn and play together. Other administrators persuaded their school boards to change to integration because of the danger of lawsuits against them such as four districts in Orange County had had to fight. Certain county superintendents of schools have been working to educate school boards in their jurisdiction to the values of integration and to the dangers of continued segregation.

The work of supervisors and the influence of county meetings and institutes have begun to show results in counties that could be named. In other counties changes are overdue. A school district seventeen miles from the residence of the writer of this article has established a full-fledged segregated school plan within the past year. A brief review of the legal situation that this district has ignored will be helpful.

It was during the late years of the war, when perhaps one fifth of all nonmetropolitan schools still practiced segregation of Mexican-Americans in one form or another, that four school districts in Orange County, California, were faced with a suit because of their policies of segregating Mexican-American children. A few parents and an organized group of Mexican-Americans, called the LULACS, initiated the action and supported it to try to clear up certain glaring malpractices in these four districts.[1] That malpractices existed, probably in conformity to social demand, even the defense briefs did not deny. That many educational practices of commendable nature were usual, the prosecution admitted. The school trustees in the four districts that were sued no doubt knew that segregation existed under their administration, just as many school trustees know that it still exists in their districts. That it was without clear legal sanction everyone in authority probably knew. That the "Anglo" section of their districts demanded it was also believed by trustees. Their course of action was not easy to determine. The lawsuit answered many questions.

The legal action was instituted in a Federal court in a demand for an injunction against the four school districts. The parties of the prosecution claimed their rights under the Fourteenth Amendment which guarantees equal protection of the law to all citizens of the United States. The arguments are summarized as follows:

The plaintiffs, being citizens of the United States and of Mexican or Latin descent, charged on behalf of their minor children that the school-district officials in Westminster, Garden Grove, El Modeno, and Santa Ana followed a concerted policy and design of class discrimination against persons of Mexican or Latin descent or extraction in the operation of their elementary schools. They charged that this resulted in the denial of the equal protection of the laws to such class of persons because the children of Mexican descent are excluded from "attending, using, enjoying, and receiving the benefits of the education, health, and recreation facilities of certain schools within their respective districts and systems," while "other schools are maintained, attended, and used exclusively and for persons and children purportedly known as White or Anglo-Saxon children."

[1] League of United Latin American Citizens.

An injunction against the rules, regulations, customs, and usages that required this practice was asked. It was conceded by all parties that there was no question of racial discrimination in the action, for the Mexican-Americans are considered to be Caucasians. The segregation was in terms of English-speaking *versus* non-English-speaking children either explicitly or tacitly. It extended through the fifth grade in one of the districts cited, through the sixth in a second, and through the eighth grade in the other two. There was no argument about the technical facilities and physical conveniences offered to children of Mexican descent. The whole issue turned upon the question: Does the official action of the defendant district-school agencies in three of the districts and do the usages and practices described in the fourth district named operate to deny or deprive equal protection of the laws to the so-called non-English-speaking children of Mexican ancestry or descent within such school districts; do these actions affect in similar manner the English-speaking children of like ancestry?

All four of the school districts responded in their defense by stating that there was no substantial Federal question involved in the complaints; that the complaint did not show any deprivation of rights under any law, ordinance, or custom secured by the Constitution of the United States and that therefore the Federal court lacked jurisdiction. The respondents denied that there was unusual treatment of the Spanish-speaking children, denied that they were given inferior facilities, accommodations, or quality of instruction. The Santa Ana board affirmed that the proportion of Mexican-American children in each of its fourteen elementary schools corresponded almost exactly with the proportion of Spanish-speaking families in each school zone. The other three boards explained that Mexican-American children were put into separate schools only until they could learn English and matters of personal hygiene and then were integrated with other children of the districts.

Despite the provisions of the School Code relating to Indians and Mongolians, Judge Paul J. McCormick of the United States District Court expressed the opinion that segregation of pupils of Mexican ancestry was not permitted either under the Constitution or under the Statutes of California; that it was not possible to single out a class for segregation.[2] The educational advantage of students of Mexican ancestry commingling with other students is so important to the school system that the state has provided for it regardless of the citizenship of the parents, he said. Distinctions of class are similar to those based upon race or ancestry, which, according to the United States Supreme Court "by their very nature are odious to a free people whose institutions are founded upon the doctrine of equality."

[2] Southern District of California, Central Division.

Judge McCormick said further:

Our conclusions in this action, however, do not rest solely upon what we conceive to be the utter irreconcilability of the segregation practices in the defendant school districts with the public educational system authorized and sanctioned by the laws of the State of California. We think such practices clearly and unmistakably disregard rights secured by the supreme law of the land.

"The equal protection of the laws" pertaining to the public-school system in California is not provided by furnishing in separate schools the same technical facilities, textbooks, and courses of instruction to children of Mexican ancestry that are available to the other public-school children regardless of their ancestry. A paramount requisite in the American system of public education is social equality. It must be open to all children by unified school association regardless of lineage.

He went on to say that the only possible grounds upon which one can justify segregation is that of language difficulty determined by the testing of individual children, but that this educational separation could be made only for the lower grades and not up to the sixth or eighth grades. The evidence showed that Mexican children in segregated schools learned English less effectively than those in mixed schools. The injunction was ordered on March 21, 1946. The Court allowed costs to the plaintiffs and decreed that segregation of pupils of Mexican descent as done by the defendants was arbitrary and discriminatory and in violation of the plaintiffs' constitutional rights.

The case was appealed by the four school districts enjoined. The United States Circuit Court of Appeals for the Ninth District through the opinion of Judge Albert Lee Stephens affirmed the decision of the Federal District Court.[3] The legal basis for his opinion was that the violation of a state law by administrative officials constitutes a denial of equal protection of the laws under the provisions of the Fourteenth Amendment of the United States Constitution. The state law in California provided for segregation of Indians and certain Mongolians, and it not only did not provide for the segregation of Mexicans but it expressly admitted these children, even though they should live across the border in Mexico. The appellate court did not decide the case upon the racial nature of the Mexican-Americans. Judge Denman of the Court of Appeals in a concurring of opinion wrote in part:

Here the regulation shows "on its face" the denial of equal protection of the California laws, prevention of which is the very purpose of that Amendment [The Fourteenth Amendment to the United States Constitution]. Here

[3] Westminster School District, et al. vs. Mendez, et al., 161 Federal Reporter (second series), p. 774 ff.

the "intent" so to deny such protection by the enforcement of the regulation is proclaimed in the briefs to this court.

Since the applicable criterion is whether the segregation regulation of each district is discriminatory and not fair on its face, it is pertinent that they clearly fail even to give equal facilities to the children in the two classes.

The teacher of a class of both English- and non-English-speaking pupils is not the same facility to the English-speaking pupils that the same teacher would be to a class made up entirely of those speaking English. There is diverted to the teaching of English to the Spanish-speaking pupils much of the teacher's professional energy and time which otherwise would be given to an English-speaking class.

The judge went on to say that those students of Mexican background who could speak English were discriminated against in a segregated school by the impaired facility of the teacher, occupied with the teaching of English to their classroom associates who had less ability in English. This was a strong point and was going beyond the position of the trial court on the question of equal facilities.

With the judgment of the United States District Court affirmed by the United States Circuit Court, the officials of the four Orange County school districts mentioned were legally stopped in their segregative policies, practices, customs, and usages as these applied to Mexican-Americans as of April 14, 1947.

Certain observations can be made as a result of these decisions:

1. The segregation of Mexican-Americans in public schools is not a racial matter as would be the segregation of Negroes or Chinese students. The Mexican background is recognized as Caucasian; but that was not a significant point in this case. The segregation of these children was a violation of state law and therefore a denial of equal protection of the laws.

2. The essence of "equal protection of the laws" was held by Judge McCormick to be social equality in relation to public education.

3. The decisions were based upon rights under the United States Constitution as well as under the State Constitution and California statutes. This has implications for Mexican-American segregation in other states.

4. The court recognized the fact that Spanish-speaking children learn English more readily in mixed than in segregated schools. This undercuts one of the principal educational reasons put forward for the existence of segregated schools.

5. The idea of "equal facilities" includes more than similar school plants and equally equipped teachers. The teaching task itself in the presence of groups with language handicaps was included as a factor in teaching effectiveness.

At about the time of the decision of the United States Court of

Appeals, the California legislature dropped from the Educational Code of the State Sections 8003 and 8004, which had been the basis for the segregation of Indians and Mongolians, thus making it legal to segregate *no* ethnic group in the state's public schools. Under these conditions it is noteworthy that twenty-five or more districts in one of the larger counties still continue to segregate Mexican-Americans and that numerous districts in other counties likewise follow the older custom. They are certainly facing an early change.

22

Colonialism: The Case of the Mexican Americans *

JOAN W. MOORE

Joan Moore is a sociologist on the faculty of the University of California, Riverside. Here she examines the concept of "colonialism" as it applies to Mexican Americans living in three "culture areas": New Mexico ("classic colonialism"), Texas ("conflict colonialism"), and California ("economic colonialism"). The concept of "colonization" itself is extremely useful in understanding the historical and contemporary conditions of the Mexican Americans.

A MERICAN social scientists should have realized long ago that American minorities are far from being passive objects of study. They are, on the contrary, quite capable of defining themselves. A clear demonstration of this rather embarrassing lag in conceptualization is the current reassessment of sociological thought. It is now plain that the concepts of "acculturation," of "assimilation," and similar paradigms are inappropriate for groups who entered American society not as volunteer immigrants but through some form of involuntary relationship.

The change in thinking has not come because of changes within sociology itself. Quite the contrary. It has come because the minorities have begun to reject certain academic concepts. The new conceptual structure is not given by any academic establishment but comes within a conceptual structure derived from the situation of the African countries. In the colonial situation, rather than either the conquest or the slave situation, the new generation of black intellectuals is finding parallels to their own reactions to American society.

This exploration of colonialism by minority intellectuals has met a varied reaction, to say the least, but there have been some interesting attempts to translate these new and socially meaningful categories into proper academic sociologese. Blauner's (1969) article in this journal is

SOURCE: Joan W. Moore, "Colonialism: The Case of the Mexican Americans," *Social Problems*, 17 (Spring 1970), pp. 463–472. Reprinted by permission of the author and *Social Problems*.

* I would like to thank Carlos Cortes for his very helpful comments on an earlier draft of this paper.

one of the more ambitious attempts to relate the concept of "colonialism" as developed by Kenneth Clark, Stokely Carmichael and Eldridge Cleaver to sociological analysis. In the process, one kind of blurring is obvious even if not explicit: that is, that "colonialism" was far from uniform in the 19th Century, even in Africa. In addition, Blauner (1969) makes explicit the adaptations he feels are necessary before the concept of colonialism can be meaningfully applied to the American scene. Common to both American internal colonialism of the blacks and European imperial expansion, Blauner argues, were the involuntary nature of the relationship between the two groups, the transformation or destruction of indigenous values, and, finally, racism. But Blauner warns that the situations are really different: "the . . . culture . . . of the (American black) colonized . . . is less developed; it is also less autonomous. In addition, the colonized are a numerical minority, and furthermore they are ghettoized more totally and are more dispersed than people under classic colonialism."

But such adaptations are not needed in order to apply the concept fruitfully to America's second largest minority—the Mexican Americans. Here the colonial concept need not be analogized and, in fact, it describes and categorizes so accurately that one suspects that earlier "discovery" by sociologists of the Mexican Americans, particularly in New Mexico, might have discouraged uncritical application of the classic paradigms to all minorities. The initial Mexican contact with American society came by conquest, not by choice. Mexican American culture was well developed; it was autonomous; the colonized were a numerical majority. Further, they were and are less ghettoized and more dispersed than the American blacks. In fact, their patterns of residence (especially those existing at the turn of the century) are exactly those of "classic colonialism." And they were indigenous to the region and not "imported." [1]

In at least the one state of New Mexico, there was a situation of comparatively "pure" colonialism. Outside of New Mexico, the original conquest colonialism was overlaid, particularly in the 20th century, with a grossly manipulated voluntary immigration. But throughout the American Southwest where the approximately five million Mexican Americans are now concentrated, understanding the Mexican minority requires understanding both conquest colonialism and "voluntary" immigration. It also requires understanding the interaction between colonialism and voluntarism.

In this paper I shall discuss a "culture trait" that is attributed to Mexi-

---

[1] "Indigenous" by comparison with the American blacks. Spanish America itself was a colonial system, in which Indians were exploited. See Olguín (1967), for an angry statement to this effect.

can Americans both by popular stereotype and by social scientists—that is, a comparatively low degree of formal voluntary organization and hence of organized participation in political life. This is the academic form of the popular question: "What's wrong with the Mexicans? Why can't they organize for political activity?" In fact, as commonly asked both by social scientist and popular stereotype, the question begs the question. There is a great deal of variation in three widely different culture areas in the Southwest. And these culture areas differ most importantly in the particular variety of colonialism to which they were subjected. In the "classically" colonial situation, New Mexico, there has been in fact a relatively high order of political participation, especially by comparison with Texas, which we shall term "conflict colonialism," and California, which we shall term "economic colonialism." [2]

New Mexico

An area that is now northern New Mexico and parts of southern Colorado was the most successful of the original Spanish colonies. At the beginning of the war between the United States and Mexico, there were more than 50,000 settlers, scattered in villages and cities with a strong upper class as well as a peasantry. There were frontier versions of Spanish colonial institutions that had been developing since 1600. The conquest of New Mexico by the United States was nearly bloodless and thus allowed, as a consequence, an extraordinary continuity between the Mexican period and the United States period. [3] The area became a territory of the United States and statehood was granted in 1912.

Throughout these changes political participation can be followed among the elite and among the masses of people. It can be analyzed in both its traditional manifestations and in contemporary patterns. In all respects it differs greatly in both level and quality from political participation outside this area. The heritage of colonialism helps explain these differences.

On the elite level, Spanish or Mexican leadership remained largely intact through the conquest and was shared with Anglo leadership after the termination of military rule in 1851. The indigenous elite retained con-

[2] Of course, we are not arguing that colonialist domination—or for that matter the peculiar pattern of voluntary immigration—offers a full explanation of this complex population, or even of the three culture areas which are the focus of this selection. Mexican Americans and the history of the region are far too complexly interwoven to pretend that any analytic thread can unravel the full tapestry. For other theses, see the analyses developed in Grebler *et al.* (1970).

[3] This account draws on González (1967); Lamar (1966); Holmes (1964); and Donnelly (1947). Paul Fisher prepared a valuable analytic abstract of all but the first of these sources while a research assistant. I have used his document extensively here.

siderable strength both in the dominant Republican party and in the state legislature. They were strong enough to ensure a bilingual provision in the 1912 Constitution (the only provision in the region that guarantees Spanish speakers the right to vote and hold office). Sessions of the legislature were—by law—conducted in both languages. Again, this is an extraordinary feature in any part of the continental United States. Just as in many Asian nations controlled by the British in the 19th century, the elite suffered little—either economically or politically.

On the lower-class level, in the villages, there was comparatively little articulation of New Mexican villages with the developing urban centers. What there was, however, was usually channeled through a recognized local authority, a *patrón*. Like the class structure, the *patrón* and the network of relations that sustained him were a normal part of the established local social system and not an ad hoc or temporary recognition of an individual's power. Thus political participation on both the elite and the lower-class levels were outgrowths of the existing social system.

Political participation of the elite and the *patrón* system was clearly a colonial phenomenon. An intact society, rather than a structureless mass of individuals, was taken into a territory of the United States with almost no violence. This truly colonial situation involves a totally different process of relationship between subordinate and superordinate from either the voluntary or the forced immigration of the subordinate—that is, totally different from either the "typical" American immigrant on the eastern seaboard or the slave imported from Africa.

A final point remains to be made not about political participation but about proto-political organization in the past. The villages of New Mexico had strong internal organizations not only of the informal, kinship variety but of the formal variety. These were the *penitente* sects and also the cooperative associations, such as those controlling the use of water and the grazing of livestock.[4] That such organizations were mobilized by New Mexican villagers is evidenced by the existence of terrorist groups operating against both Anglo and Spanish landowners. González (1967) mentions two: one functioning in the 1890's and one in the 1920's. Such groups could also act as local police forces.

Let us turn to the present. Political participation of the conventional variety is very high compared to that of Mexican Americans in other states of the Southwest. Presently there is a Spanish American in the United States Senate (Montoya, an "old" name), following the tradition of Dennis Chavez (another "old" name). The state legislature in 1967 was almost one-third Mexican American. (There were no Mexican Ameri-

---

[4] González (1967:64) concludes that *moradas*, or *penitente* organizations, "were found in most, if not all, of the northern Spanish settlements during the last half of the 19th Century and the first part of the 20th."

can legislators in California and no more than six percent in the legislature of any other Southwest state.) This, of course, reflects the fact that it is only in very recent years that Mexican Americans have become a numerical minority in New Mexico, but it also reflects the fact that organized political participation has remained high.

Finally, New Mexico is the locus of the only mass movement among Mexican Americans—the *Alianza Federal de Mercedes*, headed by Reies Tijerina. In theme, the *Alianza*, which attracted tens of thousands of members, relates specifically to the colonial past, protesting the loss of land and its usurpation by Anglo interests (including, most insultingly, those of the United States Forest Service). It is this loss of land which has ultimately been responsible for the destruction of village (Spanish) culture and the large-scale migration to the cities.[5] In the light of the importance of the traditional village as a base for political mobilization, it is not really surprising that the *Alianza* should have appeared where it did. In content the movement continues local terrorism (haystack-burning) but has now extended beyond the local protest as its members have moved to the cities. Rather than being directed against specific Anglo or Spanish landgrabbers, it has lately been challenging the legality of the Treaty of Guadalupe Hidalgo. The broadening of the *Alianza's* base beyond specific local areas probably required the pooled discontent of those immigrants from many villages, many original land grants. It is an ironic feature of the *Alianza* that the generalization of its objectives and of its appeal should be possible only long after most of the alleged landgrabbing had been accomplished.

Texas

Mexican Americans in Texas had a sharply contrasting historical experience. The Mexican government in Texas was replaced by a revolution of the American settlers. Violence between Anglo-American settlers and Mexican residents continued in south Texas for generations after the annexation of Texas by the United States and the consequent full-scale war. Violence continued in organized fashion well into the 20th Century with armed clashes involving the northern Mexican *guerilleros* and the U.S. Army.

This violence meant a total destruction of Mexican elite political participation by conquest, while such forces as the Texas Rangers were used to suppress Mexican American participation on the lower status or village levels. The ecology of settlement in south Texas remains somewhat

---

[5] González (1967:75) analyses the *Alianza* as a "nativist" movement, and suggests that its source is partly in the fact that "*for the first time* many elements of Spanish-American culture are in danger of disappearing" (emphasis added).

reminiscent of that in northern New Mexico: there are many areas that are predominantly Mexican, and even some towns that are still controlled by Mexicans. But there is far more complete Anglo economic and political dominance on the local level. Perhaps most important, Anglo-Americans outnumbered Mexicans by five to one even before the American conquest. By contrast, Mexicans in New Mexico remained the numerical majority for more than 100 years after conquest.

Texas state politics reflect the past just as in New Mexico. Mexican Americans hold some slight representation in the U.S. Congress. There are two Mexican American Congressmen, one from San Antonio and one from Brownsville (at the mouth of the Rio Grande river), one of whom is a political conservative. A minor[ity] representation far below the numerical proportion of Mexican Americans is maintained in the Texas legislature.

It is on the local level that the continued suppression is most apparent. As long ago as 1965 Mexican Americans in the small town of Crystal City won political control in a municipal election that electrified all Mexican Americans in Texas and stirred national attention. But this victory was possible only with statewide help from Mexican American organizations and some powerful union groups. Shortly afterward (after some intimidation from the Texas Rangers) the town returned to Anglo control. Some other small towns (Del Rio, Kingsville, Alice) have recently had demonstrations in protest against local suppressions. Small and insignificant as they were, the demonstrations once again would not have been possible without outside support, primarily from San Antonio. (The most significant of these San Antonio groups have been aided by the Ford Foundation. The repercussions in Congress were considerable and may threaten the future of the Ford Foundation as well as the Mexican Americans in Texas.)

More general Mexican American political organizations in Texas have a history that is strikingly reminiscent of Negro political organization. (There is one continuous difference: whites participated in most Negro organizations at the outset. It is only very recently that Anglos have been involved with Mexicans in such a fashion. In the past, Mexicans were almost entirely on their own.) Political organization has been middle class, highly oriented toward traditional expressions of "Americanism," and accommodationist. In fact, the first Mexican American political association refused to call itself a political association for fear that it might be too provocative to the Anglo power structure; it was known as a "civic" organization when it was formed in Texas in the late 1920's. Even the name of this group (LULAC or the League of United Latin American Citizens) evokes an atmosphere of middle-class gentility. The second major group, the American G.I. Forum, was formed in an atmosphere of greater protest, after a Texas town had refused burial to a Mexican American soldier. In recent years, increasing politicization has been manifested by the formation of such a group as PASSO (Political Association of Spanish Speaking Organizations). But in Texas, throughout the modern period the very act of *ethnic* politics has been controversial, even among Mexican Americans.[6]

California

The California transition between Mexican and American settlement falls midway between the Texas pattern of violence and the relatively smooth change in New Mexico. In northern California the discovery of gold in 1849 almost immediately swamped a sparse Mexican population in a flood of Anglo-American settlers. Prior to this time an orderly transition was in progress. Thus the effect was very much that of violence in Texas; the indigenous Mexican elite was almost totally excluded from political participation. A generation later when the opening of the railroads repeated this demographic discontinuity in southern California the Mexicans suffered the same effect. They again were almost totally excluded from political participation. The New Mexico pattern of social organization on a village level had almost no counterpart in California. Here the Mexican settlements and the economy were built around very large land holdings rather than around villages. This meant, in essence, that even the settlements that survived the American takeover relatively intact tended to lack internal social organization. Villages (as in the Bandini rancho which became the modern city of Riverside) were more likely to be clusters of ranch employees than an independent, internally coherent community.

In more recent times the peculiar organization of California politics has tended to work against Mexican American participation from the middle and upper status levels. California was quick to adopt the ideas of "direct democracy" of the Progressive era. These tend somewhat to work against ethnic minorities.[7] But this effect is accidental and can hardly be called "internal colonialism," coupled as it was with the anti-establishment ideals of the progressive era. The concept of "colonialism," in fact, appears most useful with reference to the extreme manipulation of Mexican immi-

---

[6] This discussion draws on Guzman (1967) and Cuéllar (1970).

[7] Fogelson (1967) gives a good picture of political practices which had the latent consequence of excluding Mexicans from Los Angeles politics—a fact of great importance given the very large concentrations of Mexican Americans in that city. Political impotence in Los Angeles has affected a very significant fraction of California's Mexican Americans. Harvey (1966) gives a broader picture of California politics.

gration in the 20th Century. Attracted to the United States by the hundreds of thousands in the 1920's, Mexicans and many of their U.S.-born children were deported ("repatriated") by welfare agencies during the Depression, most notably from California. (Texas had almost no welfare provisions; hence no repatriation.) The economic expansion in World War II required so much labor that Mexican immigration was supplemented by a contract labor arrangement. But, as in the Depression, "too many" were attracted and came to work in the United States without legal status. Again, in 1954, massive sweeps of deportations got rid of Mexicans by the hundreds of thousands in "Operation Wetback." New Mexico was largely spared both waves of deportation; Texas was involved primarily in Operation Wetback rather than in the welfare repatriations. California was deeply involved in both.

This economic manipulation of the nearly bottomless pool of Mexican labor has been quite conscious and enormously useful to the development of California extractive and agricultural enterprises. Only in recent years with increasing—and now overwhelming—proportions of native-born Mexican Americans in the population has the United States been "stuck" with the Mexicans. As one consequence, the naturalization rate of Mexican immigrants has been very low. After all, why relinquish even the partial protection of Mexican citizenship? Furthermore the treatment of Mexicans as economic commodities has greatly reduced both their motivation and their effectiveness as political participants. The motivations that sent Mexican Americans to the United States appear to have been similar to those that sent immigrants from Europe. But the conscious dehumanization of Mexicans in the service of the railroad and citrus industries in California and elsewhere meant an assymmetry in relationship between "host" and immigrant that is less apparent in the European patterns of immigration. Whatever resentment that might have found political voice in the past had no middle class organizational patterns. California was structurally unreceptive and attitudinally hostile.

Thus in California the degree of Mexican political participation remains low. The electoral consequences are even more glaringly below proportional representation than in Texas. There is only one national representative (Congressman Roybal from Los Angeles) and only one in the state legislature. Los Angeles County (with nearly a million Mexican Americans) has no Supervisor of Mexican descent and the city has no Councilman of Mexican descent. Otherwise, the development of political associations has followed the Texas pattern, although later, with meaningful political organization a post-World War II phenomenon. The G.I. Forum has formed chapters in California. In addition, the Community Service Organization, oriented to local community political mobilization, and the Mexican American Political Association, oriented to state-wide political targets, have repeated the themes of Texas' voluntary association on the level of the growing middle class.

How useful, then, is the concept of colonialism when it is applied to these three culture areas? We argue here that both the nature and extent of political participation in the state of New Mexico can be understood with reference to the "classical" colonial past. We noted that a continuity of elite participation in New Mexico from the period of Mexican rule to the period of American rule paved the way for a high level of conventional political participation. The fact that village social structure remained largely intact is in some measure responsible for the appearance of the only mass movement of Mexicans in the Southwest today—the *Alianza*. But even this movement is an outcome of colonialism; the expropriation of the land by large-scale developers and by federal conservation interests led ultimately to the destruction of the village economic base—and to the movement of the dispossessed into the cities. Once living in the cities in a much closer environment than that of the scattered small villages, they could "get together" and respond to the anti-colonialist protests of a charismatic leader.

Again following this idea, we might categorize the Texas experience as "conflict colonialism." This would reflect the violent discontinuity between the Mexican and the American periods of elite participation and the current struggle for the legitimation of ethnic politics on all levels. In this latter aspect, the "conflict colonialism" of Texas is reminiscent of black politics in the Deep South, although it comes from different origins.

To apply the colonial concept to Mexicans in California, we might usefully use the idea of "economic colonialism." The destruction of elite political strength by massive immigration and the comparative absence of local political organization meant a political vacuum for Mexican Americans. Extreme economic manipulation inhibited any attachment to the reality or the ideals of American society and indirectly allowed as much intimidation as was accomplished by the overt repression of such groups as the Texas Rangers.

To return to Blauner's use of the concept of "internal colonialism:" in the case of the Mexicans in the United States, a major segment of this group who live in New Mexico require no significant conceptual adaptation of the classic analyses of European overseas colonialism. Less adaptation is required in fact than in applying the concepts to such countries as Kenya, Burma, Algeria, and Indonesia. Not only was the relationship between the Mexican and the Anglo-American "involuntary," involving "racism" and the "transformation . . . of indigenous values," but the culture of the Spanish American was well developed, autonomous, a majority numerically, and contained a full social system with an upper and middle as well as lower class. The comparatively non-violent conquest was really almost a postcript to nearly a decade of violence between the United States and Mexico which began in Texas.

The Texas pattern, although markedly different, can still be fitted under a colonialist rubric, with a continuous thread of violence, suppression, and adaptations to both in recent political affairs.

The Mexican experience in California is much more complicated. Mexicans lost nearly all trace of participation in California politics. Hence, there was no political tradition of any kind, even the purely negative experience in Texas. Then, too, the relationship between imported labor and employer was "voluntary," at least on the immigrants' side. The relationships were much more assymmetrical than in the "classic colonial" case.

If any further proof of the applicability of the idea of "colonialism" were needed, we have the developing ideology of the new *chicano* militants themselves. Like the black ideologies, *chicanismo* emphasizes colonialism, but in a manner to transcend the enormous disparities in Mexican American experience. Thus one of the latest versions of the ideology reaches out to a time *before* even Spanish colonialism to describe the Southwestern United States as "Aztlán"—an Aztec term. "Aztlán" is a generality so sweeping that it can include all Mexican Americans. Mexican Americans are the products of layer upon layer of colonialism and the overlay of American influence is only the most recent. That the young ideologues or the "cultural nationalists" (as they call themselves) should utilize the symbols of the first of these colonists, the Aztecs (along with Emiliano Zapata, the most "Indian" of Mexican revolutionaries from the past), is unquestionably of great symbolic significance to the participants themselves. But perhaps of more sociological significance (and far more controversial among the participants) is the attempt to legitimate *chicano* culture. This culture comes from the habits, ideas, and speech of the most despised lower-class Mexican American as he has been forced to live in a quasi-legal ghetto culture in large Southwestern cities. These symbols are all indigenous to the United States and are neither Mexican, nor Spanish, nor even Aztec. But they *do* offer symbols to all Mexican Americans, after a widely varying experience with Americans in which, perhaps, the ideologues can agree only that it was "colonialist."

REFERENCES

BLAUNER, ROBERT 1969 "Internal colonialism and ghetto revolt." *Social Problems* 16 (Spring, 1969): 393–408.

CUÉLLAR, ALFREDO 1970 "Perspective on politics." In Joan W. Moore with Alfredo Cuéllar, *Mexican Americans*. Englewood Cliffs, N.J.: Prentice-Hall, Inc.

DONNELLY, THOMAS C. 1947 *The Government of New Mexico*. Albuquerque: The University of New Mexico Press.

FOGELSON, ROBERT M. 1967 *The Fragmented Metropolis: Los Angeles, 1850–1960.* Cambridge, Mass.: Harvard University Press.

GONZÁLEZ, NANCIE L. 1967 *The Spanish Americans of New Mexico: A Distinctive Heritage.* Advance Report 9. Los Angeles: University of California, Mexican American Study Project.

GREBLER, LEO *et al*, 1970 *The Mexican American People.* New York: Free Press.

GUZMÁN, RALPH 1967 "Political socialization." Unpublished manuscript.

HARVEY, RICHARD B. 1966 "California politics: Historical profile." In R. B. Dvorin and D. Misner (eds.), *California Politics and Policies.* Reading, Mass.: Addison-Wesley, Inc.

HOLMES, JACK E. 1964 Party, Legislature and Governor in the Politics of New Mexico, 1911-1963. Ph.D. Dissertation, Chicago: University of Chicago.

KITANO, HARRY H. L. 1968 *The Japanese Americans.* Englewood Cliffs, N.J.: Prentice-Hall, Inc.

KUPER, LEO AND M. G. SMITH (eds.) 1969 *Pluralism in Africa.* Berkeley and Los Angeles: University of California Press.

LAMAR, HOWARD ROBERTS 1966 *The Far Southwest, 1845–1912: A Territorial History.* New Haven: Yale University Press.

OLGUÍN, JOHN PHILLIP 1967 "Where does the 'justified' resentment begin?" New Mexico Business offprint, July 1967.

SÁNCHEZ, GEORGE I. 1940 *Forgotten People.* Albuquerque: The University of New Mexico Press.

23

The Schizoid Heritage

LEONARD PITT

> *The focus of this brief selection by Leonard Pitt is on the
> conflict between the romantic heritage of the Spaniard (per-
> sonified until a few years ago by Leo Carrillo playing the gui-
> tar on horseback in fiestas and rodeos) and the contemporary
> reality of the Mexican—between the mythical past and the
> painful present. Those who venture to Los Angeles' Olvera
> Street in order to gain an awareness of the plight of the Mexi-
> can American in California would do much better to visit the
> Delano grape fields or an East Los Angeles barrio. "Live people
> constitute a forgotten minority," writes Pitt, "while the mythi-
> cal ones are remembered only too well."*

CALIFORNIA today sees the Spanish-speaking as living at once in
two disharmonious worlds, one mythic, the other real. The mythic
would emphasize the "Spanish" past—carefree, unchanging, and enveloped
in a religious aura; the other is a "Mexican" world—disagreeable, mun-
dane, potentially violent. The twain rarely meet, except on public occasions such as the commemoration of Cinco de Mayo and September
Sixteenth or of the founding of the city of Los Angeles. Then the
"Spaniards" mount white horses to lead the "Mexicans." On one ludi-
crous occasion, the Olvera Street fiesta committee selected a descendant
of Cortés to serve as the Mexicans' *padrino*, or parade marshal—like
choosing a descendant of King George III to lead a Fourth of July cele-
bration, mused one wry Mexican-American. From this sort of event
strangers sometimes mistakenly conclude that today's aristocratic Californios are the true spokesmen of the Mexican-American community,
which is far from the truth.

One August week in 1963 the Los Angeles *Times* gave a particularly
good display for what may be called the "schizoid heritage." Luckily, the
editor segregated the items concerned into the news columns and the
society section, or they might have been doubly hard to reconcile.

SOURCE: Leonard Pitt, *The Decline of the Californios* (Los Angeles and Berkeley:
University of California Press, 1966), pp. 291–296. Originally published by the University of California Press; reprinted by permission of The Regents of the University
of California.

A headline on August 5, 1963, blazed that "LATINS HERE . . . PROTEST BRACERO LAW"; that is, that Mexican-Americans denounced the importation of Mexican nationals in a system that "takes advantage of hunger and hardship in Mexico to provide for recruitment of a captive, docile and exploitable foreign farm labor force." That same issue also noted that a Mexican-American "CROWD FORCES DEPUTIES TO FREE PRISONERS"; that is, that a crowd twice attacked sheriff's deputies attempting to arrest juveniles in a gang fracas, whereupon assailants beat one deputy and freed his prisoners, and later were arrested for resisting an officer and violating the antilynch law. Vice President "JOHNSON URGES LATIN CITIZENS TO REPORT BIAS," the *Times* noted three days later. Johnson suggested to 1,000 leading Mexican-Americans that "perhaps you have not been successful in making your needs known," and should report cases of discrimination more urgently—"I mean facts, not mere grumblings."

On August 7, on the other hand, a mere two days later, readers of the society section of the *Times* learned of the opening of the "OLD SPANISH DAYS FIESTA" at Santa Barbara. The five-day annual festivities, timed to meet the August moon, included parades, speeches, and tableaux commemorating the 250th anniversary of the birth of Father Serra, as well as a costume breakfast, a "cocktail fiesta," garden tours, performances of the Mexican Folklorica Ballet, and the opening of a "Spanish market place." The event represented the "apogee of the summer social season" in Santa Barbara and was attended by tens of thousands, including the lieutenant governor of the state.

The romantic heritage gives every indication of continuing indefinitely, despite an unprecedented debunking from sociologists, school-teachers, and historians and a decimation in the ranks of the romantics. Leo Carrillo personified the romantic tradition until a few years ago, and with valid license, having been born into a venerable local family at the Los Angeles Plaza in 1880. He spoke Spanish well, played the guitar, rode horseback, took part in fiestas and rodeos, listened carefully to the conversation of his elders and transmitted their oral tradition masterfully, read a good deal of local history, and wrote his autobiography with a deep sense of ancestral pride. The smiling, waving Carrillo perched on a lavishly bridled horse was an inevitable part of any southern California parade for two decades. But Carrillo was the last figure who could legitimately personify the Spanish past—although many considered him a mere creation of Hollywood—and his death in 1961 left a gap in the front ranks of many Los Angeles parades.

Mexican-Americans cannot lightly accept or dismiss this "fantasy heritage," for it seems to reproach them for failing to meet impossibly high standards. (Thus it was probably the sight of Carrillo in a parade that prompted a Mexican-American labor leader to swear that if he met the horse-and-rider combination again, he would spit in the horse's eye.) The Mexican-American discovers that "Anglos" are far less kindly disposed toward the living Mexican-Americans than toward the imaginary Californios, and he claims that Yankees fawn over the clay caballeros sold in Olvera Street but tend to show contempt for the people who sell them. Live people constitute a forgotten minority, while the mythical ones are remembered only too well.

After 1900 the living bearers of Spanish-American culture, the Mexicans, created a new stir in the Southwest. They supplied an important source of agricultural and industrial labor, more important than that of the 1850's. Those Americans who had mistaken the rancheros' demise by about 1885 for the extinction of an entire people had to review their thinking. Droves of wetbacks flocked across the border to work in fields and orchards and on the railroads. In both world wars growers imported tens of thousands of *braceros* yearly to work in the Imperial and San Joaquin valleys of California, and as far east as the Mississippi River and as far north as the Dakotas. Mexican-Americans served in the armed forces, sometimes with distinction. Despite ugly wartime incidents such as the Sleepy Lagoon case and the Pachuco [zoot suit] Riots in Los Angeles, that city acquired so many Spanish-speaking residents as to qualify for a time as the second-largest Latin-American city (next to Mexico City) in the Western Hemisphere.

By 1964 the Spanish-speaking in California numbered close to 2,000,000 (1,426,538 by the 1960 census). They were the state's largest and most rapidly growing minority and about 80 percent urbanized and native born. Even immigration figures reached astonishing levels: 5,400 Mexicans came to the United States monthly in the 1950's, 58,000 residents had been waiting for years to obtain permanent visas, 350,000 have entered legally from 1953 to 1959, and untold thousands have done so illegally. Most of the immigrants came to the Los Angeles area; some 260,000 Mexican-Americans lived within the city limits, 577,000 in the county, more than 700,000 in the metropolitan area. In San Fernando, 28 percent of the population in 1960 or 4,400, had Spanish surnames, which compared very favorably with the percentage in 1880.

The Mexican-American of today finds himself in some situations altogether new and different from those known to his ancestors a century ago. The "patina of romantic mis-information" which surrounds his culture is a major factor unknown a hundred years ago. The frontier is gone, of course, along with the lynchings, although the ritualistic aspects of the Sleepy Lagoon trial and the Pachuco riots during World War II (and the more recent booking of a Mexican-American for violating the anti-lynch law) strike some familiar notes. The land problem has subsided (although the instance of a Yankee who gained possession of Señor Arguëllo's valid claim to all of downtown Tiajuana, Mexico, is a bizarre reminder of things long past).

Unhappily, the closing of the frontier has also obliterated the "Mexicanized gringo," the Californios' sometime friend and mentor, who had eased their acculturation. The twentieth-century gringo sees fewer and more sordid glimpses of Spanish-American culture than his forefathers did in the 1850's. In the pathetic border towns he visits he sees few amenities comparable to the rancho fiesta. In most of Los Angeles he lives worlds apart from the town's "Serape Belt" and can spend his entire lifetime seeing few Mexican-Americans other than Olvera Street vendors and the occasional Spanish-speaking gardener or delivery boy.

At the same time, Yankee hatred has diminished and grown less overt. As one Anglo observed, the Mexican-American of California lives in "a kind of limbo; neither accepted nor rejected." The Americano finds the Mexican-American amiable and anxious to please, but does not understand him in his "displaced status." Some Anglo-Saxons at least experience a sense of guilt toward the Negro for past oppressions; toward the Spanish-speaking, few feel any similar sentiments or any vivid emotion at all.

The Spanish-speaking find themselves, however, in the presence of astonishing continuities and depressing parallels with the past. Francisco P. Ramirez, Reginaldo del Valle, and Antonio Coronel would find their community in 1964 in an all too deplorable condition. The lack of a local Spanish-language newspaper for a vast Spanish-speaking audience would give Ramirez an unhappy reminder of the day he closed up *El Clamor Público* in 1859. Lack of education among Mexican-American youths weighs down upon most of them like an incubus and prevents them from competing for decent jobs. Three-quarters of the youths dropped out of high school in 1950, and the same number in 1960; in short, there has been no progress in that respect. Serious crime and law enforcement problems still strain the mutually exclusive patience of youth and of officers of the law. Young men and women still feel displaced, resentful at the dominant group and thus inclined toward occasional irrational outbursts.

The Spanish-speaking community continues to reinforce itself numerically from the old country. And the newcomers still fan out into the ghettos, which still run in the same general direction as before, east of Olvera Street. The braceros of the 1960's remind one of the Mexican miners of the 1850's. Moreover, the linkup between the Negro problem and the Mexican problem in 1964 is partly a reversion to an earlier time, when the dominant race first debated the fate of dark-skinned laborers of all nations.

Numerically, the Mexican-Americans today have regained the losses of the Californios; the relative strength of the Spanish-speaking presently exceeds that of the 1880's. But lack of an effective political leadership still hobbles the community much as it did then. Mexican-American leaders could not "deliver the vote" in 1960 as well as they did in 1870.

Because the modern predicament of the Mexican-American jelled a century ago, from 1849 to 1885, and not after the turn of the century, as some suppose, the resolution of these problems looks all the more difficult. Problems ten decades old will not respond quickly to reform; urban and industrial life confound simple problems; a great city will find it hard to shake off the troubles it bypassed as a village. But there is a final hopeful note: If the 1960's find the legendary Spanish heritage in a virile condition, so do they witness a new stirring among those who prefer to cope with the real, though less pleasant, heritage of the past hundred years.

24

Chicano Militancy in California: A Quest for Identity and Power

CARLOS MUÑOZ, JR.

Professor Carlos Muñoz, Jr., is a political scientist at the University of California, Irvine. Born in the barrio *of El Paso, Texas, and raised in the* barrios *of East Los Angeles, Muñoz is today one of the most respected young Chicano intellectuals in the Southwest. He played a role in the development of the Chicano Student Movement in Southern California, and served as the department chairman of the first program of Mexican American Studies in the country. His academic interests are in political sociology, political theory, and philosophy. In this original essay he links the emergence of the Chicano Power Movement to Anglo racism and oppression.*

> We seek our basic, God-given rights as human beings. Because we have suffered—and are not afraid to suffer—in order to survive, we are ready to give up everything, even our lives, in our fight for social justice. We shall do it without violence because that is our destiny.
>
> Delano Proclamation (September, 1965)

> Mexican Americans . . . are reminding us all of the very powerful roots of our personality, of the very wide extension of our cultural image and of the community of action that is required if that identity is to become something more than a passing reference in celebrations.
>
> Carlos Fuentes (1968)

THE dramatic emergence of the Chicano Power Movement in California during the latter part of the 1960's has been interpreted by some as the "awakening of the sleeping giant." To those who have long ignored the existence of the state's largest oppressed minority and the second largest in the nation, it seemed that Chicanos had finally decided to break away from their "traditional passivity and apathy." The farm labor struggle spearheaded by Cesar Chavez and Chicano-organized urban political protest caught the dominant Anglo society by surprise. For it had appeared that Chicanos had been "content in almost somnambulant torpor" with their life of poverty and second-class citizenship.

Until the late 1960's social scientists and others had analyzed the plight of Chicano America from within the framework of concepts such as "culture of poverty" and "lower class culture." Such concepts, for the most part, only resulted in placing the blame for the problems of the poor on the poor themselves. Chicanos were "disadvantaged" and politically powerless basically because the majority happened to be poor. In more recent years some have recognized that, like Black people, Chicanos have also been victims of white racism. We are still lacking, however, analyses that go beyond mere description to critical inquiry about the reasons for Chicano powerlessness.

Prior to the development of the Chicano Power Movement, the systematic exclusion of Chicanos from the democratic process had been mainly attributed to three factors. First, there has always been a lack of Chicano unity in the barrios. Secondly, the Chicano community has failed to develop an aggressive leadership that can give the Chicano "political clout." And thirdly, the Mexican cultural tradition does not encourage the young to strive for success in the "approved Protestant Ethic" fashion. As was the case with analyses based on the culture of poverty paradigm, such conventional perspectives of Chicano powerlessness overlook the sources and root causes of the plight of Chicano America.

The oppression of Chicano America in general, and its political powerlessness in particular, cannot be fully understood without a proper historical perspective and critical analysis of Anglo capitalist society vis-à-vis the Chicano experience. Unfortunately, the history of the Mexican people in Anglo America remains to be written. While some historians have touched upon such history, few have provided critical analysis of the origin and nature of the issues that have been raised by Chicano Power. Even radical historians have not challenged the writings of those who have written the history of the Southwest from the perspective of the "winning side." The period of the Mexican-United States War of 1846 is crucial to Chicano history for it marked the beginning of Anglo oppression in the barrios and the decline from power for Chicanos. The past is the key to the present and the future.

Contemporary Chicano militancy does not mark the first time that cries of protest and rebellion have been heard in the barrios of Chicano America. Contrary to the myth that Chicanos have lain dormant and have been complacent in the face of Anglo racism and oppression, Chicano history is full of episodes of militant protest. During the post Mexican-United States War period Chicano militancy manifested itself in the form of armed guerrilla warfare. Many of the Mexican "bandits" of that period were in truth Chicano revolutionaries intent on regaining their lands stolen by Anglo invaders and on rectifying many of the social injustices perpetrated upon Chicanos by Anglo colonizers.

This interpretation of history has not been written. Anglo historians have in general not gone beyond, in historian Jack Forbes' words, "the romance and mythology of the supposed westward movement of the pioneers." The history of the Southwest has not been viewed for what it was, a military conquest of a land and a people which parallels closely "the German march eastward against the Poles." And as Forbes has put it,

the United States conquest of the Southwest [was] a very real case of aggression and imperialism . . . it involved not only the military phase of immediate conquest, but the subsequent establishment of a colonial society, a rather complex colonial society because there was not one single colonial office to administer the Mexican American people.

After the Chicano guerrilla period came Chicano involvement in militant labor organizations. The early 1900's were marked with union political activity throughout the agricultural and mining areas of the Southwest. Chicanos were participants in that activity and in some cases provided the actual leadership in the efforts to organize the workers against agricultural and mining capital. Chicano political activity later evolved into the more conventional type of voluntary associations, which while not conforming to the Anglo patterns of such associations nevertheless did fulfill many of the same objectives.

It can be asked at this point why it is that given past political involvement by Chicanos, the barrios, until the late 1960's, remained politically leaderless. Much of the answer to this question lies in the fact that Chicano militant leadership was brutally oppressed. Chicano leaders were either murdered through Anglo vigilante action or assassinated. Many were also "deported" back to Mexico. The leadership that did not meet tragic fate was successfully coopted into the Anglo political institutions by Anglo power structures. In addition, the colonial situation never provided the basis for mass militant action against the Anglo oppressor. As Albert Memmi, the Tunisian writer, has argued in *The Colonizer and the Colonized*, "To observe the life of the colonizer and the colonized is to discover rapidly that the daily humiliation of the colonized, his objective subjugation, are not merely economic."

According to Memmi, it is colonial racism that eventually allows for the demise of an indigenous people. Such racism contributes to the development of a system which serves to perpetuate the interest of the colonizer at the expense of the colonized. In the case of the Chicano in the Southwest, a psychological subjugation eventually took place among the masses which, in the final analysis, put the "giant to sleep." But while the masses never participated in large scale rebellion or protest against the colonizer, there has always been conflict in the barrios, conflict which has been generated by Anglo racism and institutions.

The Chicano militancy of the late 1960's is new for several reasons. First, it is directly challenging Anglo institutions and power structures. Secondly, it has generated a cultural renaissance which has given impetus to the rekindling of a spirit deeply rooted in the revolutionary cultural tradition of the Mexican people. Thirdly, and very significantly, it has challenged the traditional assimilationist and accommodationist Chicano "power structures" to move toward a position more in accord with the objectives of Chicano liberation and self-determination in the barrios.

The development of the Chicano Power Movement in California, as elsewhere in the nation, is intimately connected to the fact that we are living in an age of protest. The winds of revolution touched the barrios, especially the young people of those barrios who, as with youth throughout the world, see the need for radical social change as imperative to the welfare of the poor. Like all movements for social change, the Chicano movement was sparked by certain events which served as catalysts for political mobilization.

The single most important event was the organization of the migrant farm workers in Delano, California. Much has already been said and written about Cesar Chavez and the struggle he leads. But while the farm worker movement is technically a labor movement, the psychological impact that it has had throughout Chicano America can never be overestimated. More specifically, the thought and the person of Cesar Chavez was and continues to be a guiding light of the Chicano movement. While other militant Chicano leaders have emerged, none has yet reached the stature of Chavez in the eyes of the Chicano masses. The Chavez model of political organization and action remains the most viable because it rests upon a strong philosophical foundation which Chavez has extracted from the thought of Gandhi and Martin Luther King.

The greatness of Chavez perhaps lies in the fact that he does not identify himself as a "Chicano leader." He is not a self-proclaimed radical, but the movement he leads has definite radical directions. For his movement has directly challenged California monopoly capital. And while in itself the movement will not cause Agri-business to release from its grip on California political power, the fact is that the immorality and decadence of monopoly capital has been exposed to the general public.

As Cesar Chavez himself has stated, the farm worker movement is not a Chavez movement. It is rather a poor peoples' movement whose objectives go beyond the mere acquisition of more equitable wages and better living conditions for the migrant worker. By its very nature it is a struggle for social justice and human liberation. And because of Chavez, the Gandhian philosophy of nonviolence pervades the Chicano Movement. And because of Chavez, Chicano Power is on the move in the urban barrios.

The second most significant event in the development of contemporary Chicano militancy in California occurred in March of 1968 in the barrios of East Los Angeles. Thousands of Chicano students staged a dramatic walk out from the predominantly Chicano high schools. This event was the first massive urban demonstration in the history of Chicano America. It generated other similar organized protests in other states. The schools became the foremost symbol of oppression and the prime source of Chicano powerlessness.

The student demonstration, coupled with the arrests two months later of thirteen Chicano community leaders for their alleged role in the walk-outs (they were indicted for conspiracy to disturb the peace and disrupt the state educational process), awakened the total Chicano community to the need for political action against the Anglo power structure. Leaders of traditional Chicano community organizations were challenged to respond to the issue directly. One leading conservative Chicano banker (who played a significant role in the election of Governor Reagan in 1966) made a public demand to the mayor of Los Angeles for immediate investigations of the arrests and imprisonment of the thirteen Chicanos and indicted the educational system for its failure to respond to the needs of Chicano students and the community.

This event had a profound impact on the politics of the barrio and on community organization. Many of the previously formed new organizations were given further impetus to develop and other new and more militant grass roots organizations developed almost over night to provide new political leadership in the barrios. These organizations led statewide challenges to the Anglo power structures which control the educational, economic, and political institutions that directly affect barrio life.

The student demonstrations also contributed to the strengthening of the Chicano Student Movement which had emerged a year before on the college and university campuses throughout the state. The movement had gone by the name of United Mexican American Students (UMAS) and had already established itself as a new political force to be reckoned with in the Chicano community. A month before the dramatic demonstrations, UMAS had taken control of the first political barrio convention sponsored by the new Congress for Mexican American Unity in East Los Angeles. For the first time in the contemporary life of the barrio, the political accent was on Chicano youth. Chicano students became the focus for political organizational efforts.

The Student Movement has since become the *Movimiento Estudiantil Chicano de Aztlan* (MECHA) as a consequence of the emergence of a cultural nationalist ideology which has been generated by the cultural renaissance made possible by contemporary Chicano militancy. The nationalist concept of Aztlan took form at a youth conference held in Denver, Colorado, in 1969. It was agreed upon by the delegates attending from throughout the nation that all future political action would be predicated upon the "Plan Espiritual de Aztlan." The plan is in essence the Chicano declaration of independence from Anglo oppression and for Chicano liberation. It also calls for a new identity for Chicano America. It reads in part:

In the spirit of a new people that is conscious not only of its proud historical heritage, but also of the brutal "Gringo" invasion of our territories. We, the Chicano inhabitants and civilizers of the northern land of Aztlan, from whence came our forefathers, reclaiming the land of their birth and consecrating the determination of our people of the sun, declare that the call of our blood is our power, our responsibility, and our inevitable destiny.

The plan outlines a three-point program for political action by establishing the theme that "Chicanos must use their nationalism as the key or common denominator for mass mobilization and organization." The plan goes on to state that, "Once we are committed to the idea and philosophy of *El Plan de Aztlan*, we can only conclude that social, economic, cultural, and political independence is the only road to liberation from oppression, exploitation and racism."

In California, the overwhelming majority of Chicano youth organizations have adopted Aztlan as part of their "letterhead." The community at large appears to be moving in the direction outlined by the cultural nationalist ideology. It remains to be seen whether the central thrust of the Chicano Power Movement will become cultural nationalism. In terms of Chicano politics, however, that ideology has apparently been endorsed in some circles. *La Raza Unida Party* has been formed as a Chicano alternative to the Anglo political parties in California. The creation of this Chicano party is in keeping with the Plan de Aztlan: "Political liberation can only come through an independent action on our part, since the two party system is the same animal with two heads that feeds from the same trough. Where we are a majority we will control; where we are a minority we will represent a pressure group; nationally, we will represent one party, La Familia de La Raza."

The decade of the 1960's was a time of protest. The decade of the 1970's will be a time for the quest of Chicano identity and power.

PART IV
The Black Experience
in the Golden State

An idea has long prevailed that prejudice is invincible, and to such an extent has it gained credence that it is looked upon as a self-evident proposition. The whites, from a natural love of arbitrary rule, yield to its seductive influences, and the blacks succumb before its baneful power; liberal men deplore its existence, but take no measures to eradicate the evil; the vicious rejoice in the power it gives them to oppress a race already borne to the earth with cruelty and injustice, and endeavor to perpetuate it; all classes, without examining into it or analyzing the subject, take it for granted that it is instinctive, therefore invincible. Hence, between irresolute friends and virulent foes, we suffer all the indignities which prejudice can heap upon us.

The Pacific Appeal (April 26, 1862), an early
black newspaper in California

As noted earlier, the few blacks in nineteenth and early twentieth century California experienced relatively higher status than the chief targets of the state's racists. Governor Hiram Johnson, while denouncing the Japanese, campaigned for black votes. But it must not be imagined that blacks had full citizen status, although the state's statute book did not discriminate. (See Selection 25.) The migration of large numbers of blacks to California in the 1930s, followed by even more migration during the war and postwar years, began to produce minighettoes in Los Angeles, Oakland, and San Francisco and racial tensions in defense plants. During the years that followed the war, blacks developed some political influence, electing a congressman, state legislators, and local officials. Clearly oppression was not total, and as long as black aspirations remained confined to the ghettoes, white resistance was not aggressive.

In 1964 the illusion of black-white harmony was shattered. An initiative campaign, sponsored by California real estate brokers, placed the patently unconstitutional Proposition No. 14 on the ballot. It would not only have repealed the state's ineffective Fair Housing Law but would also have put a bar against any future such law into the state Constitution. It passed overwhelmingly, and, although it was later negated by the courts, blacks in the state got the message: stay in the ghetto and do not attempt to get out. It is probably not entirely a coincidence that the Watts riots occurred the very next year. (See Selections 27 and 28.)

Not surprisingly, increasing rather than lessening social tension has followed. School board elections have been carried by backlash candidates where white liberals, however inadequate, once prevailed. Most California cities—Berkeley is a notable exception—have resisted meaningful school integration. (See Selections 30 and 31.) The state's ghettoes—whether or not they have exploded into violence—have become more sharply defined, more tightly hemmed in by the nooselike white suburbs that surround them. The major black bid for significant political power in 1969 saw Los Angeles Councilman Thomas Bradley defeated by the incumbent Samuel Yorty in an election campaign that the winner deliberately pitched at the lowest common denominator—a naked appeal to white racial solidarity.

These actions have produced reactions. Black nationalist and extremist movements, always present in the ghettoes, have gained support and publicity, but always much more of the latter than the former. That some of these groups have advocated a kind of black racism cannot be denied, although the media and frightened liberals —not to mention J. Edgar Hoover—pay far too much attention to these phenomena. What has to be remembered is that while any kind of racism is sheer nonsense, there is a distinct functional difference, in our society, between white racism and black: the first is a means of oppression, the second a response to it.

25

Negro Rights Activities in Gold Rush California

RUDOLPH M. LAPP

During the late 1840s and 1850s, blacks were generally denied access to ownership of land in the Far West and were prohibited from voting and holding office, as well as from testifying against whites in courts of law. Rudolph M. Lapp, a leading authority on the early history of blacks in California, teaches at the College of San Mateo. In this article, Lapp discusses the struggles of blacks against discrimination in early California.

LONG before the Civil War free Negroes were active in movements to improve the position of their people in American society. Recent events of this kind are actually a continuum of earlier, lesser known efforts. The nineteenth century free Negro also had his detractors and his supporters. His struggles were marked by some successes and many defeats. Little has been written of the leadership he developed, the campaigns he conducted, and the frustrations he endured. While the greatest part of this story is set in the eastern states of the North, the Gold Rush brought a chapter of it to California.

The Negro population of Gold Rush California was not large. They comprised roughly 1 percent of the population. The significance of their story is not in their number but rather in the moral force that the Negroes were able to exert and the courage they displayed. Above all, the account of Negro organization and their struggles against often insurmountable odds testifies to the inaccuracy of the belief that the American Negro did little on his own behalf.

In the spring of 1850 the *Daily Alta* of San Francisco stated that in their opinion most forty-niner Negroes had become free. The 1850 census supported this view, of course, since slavery was declared illegal in the 1849 state constitution and there was no provision for enumerating slaves on the census forms. The census merely states there were 962 Negroes in the state at that time.

SOURCE: Rudolph M. Lapp, "Negro Rights Activities in Gold Rush California," *California Historical Society Quarterly*, 45 (March 1966), pp. 3–20. Reprinted by permission of the author and the California Historical Society.

Future research may provide a more precise statistic on how many of the 962 California Negroes were slaves or free men.

The fact, however, of a significant number of Negroes in a slave condition in a state that had excluded the 'peculiar' institution provided the setting for the first of what can be called Negro rights struggles in California. Had every Negro who came to California with the promise of freedom been granted that freedom and had every slave who came to the state without freedom commitments not had any freedom thoughts of his own, there would not be any story. But masters did try to break their promises, and slaves did decide to strike for freedom in Gold Rush California.

The fugitive slave fights in the early months and years did not seem to be associated with carefully laid plans by well organized groups. Rather they were a blend of personal courage, aid from unknown free Negroes, and legal help from local sympathetic lawyers and judges. Perhaps the most important catalytic agent in every case was the free Negro who told his black brother that in California he had a legal chance for freedom. One of the earliest cases occurred in San Jose in February, 1850. It came to the attention of the authorities as a street brawl in which a white man was beating a Negro with a club. Cries of shame were reported from the crowd, and the marshal took both parties into custody. The court proceedings revealed that the white man claimed the Negro as his slave and complained that his contact with the free Negroes of San Jose had spoiled him to the point where he refused to be obedient property and leave the city with his master. The Alcalde ruled in favor of the master. With the assistance of the local authorities, the Negro was spirited away in time to avoid a writ that several friendly lawyers brought too late to the alcalde.

Cornelius Cole, the venerable early Californian, thought in later days that he and Judge Crocker were the only members of the legal profession in Sacramento who came to the defense of the Negro. His memory was not too good in this matter because there were others that he was associated with in court cases. In Sacramento only a few months after the unhappy San Jose case, another street brawl involving a Negro named Charles resulted in another fugitive slave case. In this instance the judge set the Negro free. He pointed out to the presumed master that the laws passed before as well as after the American conquest of California made Charles a free man. One of the attorneys for the Negro was Joseph Winans who was to be involved again in fugitive slave matters and to become one of the outstanding members of the legal fraternity in the state. He has been described as the "first scholar of the Bar."

The next important case occurred in a court in San Francisco in March, 1851. A Missourian had brought to the mines a "yellow boy," as the newspapers described him, named Frank who decided in the atmosphere of the Sierras to run away. His master tracked him down and had him confined preparatory to returning to Missouri. In San Francisco legal aid was provided by attorney S. W. Holladay, and a writ was presented to Judge Morrison to set him free. Judge Morrison, after a few days' deliberation, set Frank free claiming that California laws supported his decision and that the National Fugitive Slave Law was not involved. His reasoning was that Frank did not come to California as a fugitive. His running away activities began within the boundaries of the state which were not offenses in California law. The judge must have had a sardonic sense of humor, for he continued in his decision to pour a bit of salt on the wounded feelings of the proslavery listeners. It seems that in the course of interrogation Frank had stated that he had been a slave in Missouri. The judge calmly rejected this bit of testimony because the California state legislature had only the year before made Negro testimony illegal in civil and criminal cases! This case was notable in another way. It seems that the Negro community of San Francisco was noticeably involved in its outcome. This may have been the first stimulus to active organization.

It soon became apparent that slave owners who were tarrying too long in California were in danger of losing their property. If the word got around, Judge Morrison's court could become quite busy.

In the first month of 1852 a champion for the slave owner emerged. He was Assemblyman Henry A. Crabb, a southern aristocrat, who gained a tragic fame a few years later by losing his life in a Sonoran filibustering adventure. Crabb introduced a fugitive slave bill in January, 1852, that gave white men arbitrary powers in returning Negroes whom they claimed as slaves in Southern states. Assemblyman Ellis of San Francisco had the suspicious feeling that a portion of this bill was so written in order to allow slavery to establish itself in California through the back door. Crabb's bill did not sharply define any limits on how long a slave owner might remain in California. Ellis' amending proposals were rejected. When the unchanged bill reached the senate, it faced more formidable opposition. Here David Broderick voiced his apprehensions. He feared that the bill did nothing to protect the Negro who came to California with the promise of freedom from a callously capricious former owner or from some white man with the talents of a Negro kidnapper. Through much of April, 1852, the senate debated the bill with Broderick gaining strong but not quite sufficient support. The bill was passed fourteen to nine with Broderick in the minority.

It was not too long before Broderick's fears were realized. In April of the following year the first publicly noted attempt to return a free Negro girl to slavery was reported in the *Daily Alta*. The attempt took place in Auburn, California, but fortunately a local lawyer was the custodian of the young woman's freedom papers and could produce them in court. The claimant was the son of the man who freed the girl, and he professed not to know of his father's action. In Gold Springs, Tuolumne County, a Negro named Stephen Hill, who had been free long enough to accumulate property to the value of $4,000, was imprisoned by men claiming to be agents of his former owner. They managed to destroy his freedom papers too. He was taken to Stockton where a daring escape was managed. Some years later a letter from a white man to the *Daily Alta* suggested that this escape involved a great deal of Caucasian collusion.

It was inevitable that the constitutionality of Crabb's Fugitive Slave Act would be tested. The opportunity arose in what is called the Perkins Case. A Mississippian named Perkins claimed through agents that three Negroes working in Placer County, two of them bearing the name Perkins, were his fugitive property. A justice of the peace and then a county judge gave the three Negroes to Perkins' agent. In the meantime support was rolling up for the trio. Enlisted in their cause were lawyers Joseph Winans, Joseph Zabriskie, and Cornelius Cole. This battery of legal talent managed to temporarily rescue the three Negroes from a ship that was about to leave San Francisco. The case was brought directly to the state supreme court. The proslave court upheld the entire California Fugitive Slave law. It even upheld that section of the law that corroded the genuinely free Negro's right to maintain his freedom. In 1855 that feature of the law was allowed to lapse, and the California Negro was in a slightly less uncertain status.

The odious section of the state's fugitive slave law may have been allowed to lapse because it might have been believed that by 1855 the problem no longer existed. But its lapse may also be due to changes in public sentiment. The Methodist Minister M. C. Briggs of San Francisco noted in a letter, "There has been a manifestly growing change in public sentiment in this state, in respect of slavery." Just before the Frémont presidential campaign, a Missourian wrote to his brother from Columbia saying, "The Blue Bellied Yankees are every day getting a stronger hold." In 1857 even the San Francisco YMCA reflected sympathy for the Negro. They criticized the exclusion of Negroes practiced by certain eastern YMCA's.

It was apparent that the California Negro had a growing number of friends in the white population, especially in San Francisco and Sacramento. These were found largely in the very young Republican Party. Of equal importance was the growing sturdiness of their own organizations and their determination to act. A German observer noted that wealthy California Negroes had become "especially talented" in stealing slaves to freedom. He added that they "exhibit a great deal of energy and intelligence in saving their brothers."

In 1855 the California Negroes had a general marshalling of their forces through the meeting of the First Colored Convention. It was mainly concerned with the right of testimony in civil and criminal cases where white men were also involved. That the denial of this right was a tragic handicap soon became apparent through the fugitive slave experience. But as this issue gradually declined in importance, the problem of protection of life and property rose. The need for testimony rights was a clear requirement for manhood as well as for livelihood. The Negro whose wife or daughter was raped by a white man, without white witnesses, had no recourse to justice. The Negro who was robbed in open daylight in his shop was also defenseless if no white witness would agree to testify in his behalf. There is also scattered evidence that Negro farmers in California were ejected from lands they had cultivated because they could not testify to their ownership. At the heart of this testimony issue was the California Negro's modest prosperity and ability to accumulate material goods in spite of handicaps. At this first convention one of the delegates announced that the property of the California Negro population was worth over three and one-half million dollars. In all societies propertied classes have insisted on legal and political protection commensurate with their wealth.

The struggle for the right of testimony began several years before this statewide convention. It had its beginnings in a number of incidents in San Francisco. A Negro barber had been murdered by a white man who was never brought to justice because only Negro testimony was available. One of the most capable Negro leaders, Mifflin Wistar Gibbs, was humiliated when a white man came into the boot and shoe shop that Gibbs was a partner in and, in a series of shabby maneuvers, virtually stole an expensive pair of boots while beating Peter Lester, Gibbs' partner. These, plus other factors, brought about the organization of the Franchise League in 1852 which was primarily a San Francisco organization.

The first effort of the league was a petition campaign to change the law in regard to Negro testimony. It was directed at the state legislature and it gathered names from whites as well as Negroes. The assembly received this petition in March, 1852, in the most insulting fashion. Assemblyman Cannay from Placer County presented the petition for Assemblyman Ellis from San Francisco in his absence. There were those in the assembly who shouted that it should not even be read. Assemblyman Hinchman pleaded for politeness in the matter. Assemblyman Crabb, the slave-catcher's friend, said that if Negroes only were associated with this petition it should not even be heard. It was finally heard, and then it was moved that a petition from "such a source" should not be officially received. Hinchman's vote was the only one for receiving the petition.

One year later almost the same scene was repeated. The Franchise

League had assembled another round of petitions, and these were presented by Assemblyman Meredith. One member of the assembly proposed that the petition be thrown out of the window. Patrick Cannay, who was chairman this time, ruled him out of order and was sustained. He needed to be sustained several times during that session when he had to rule out of order one insulting frivolity after another. Motions to reject and not to file the petition were passed almost unanimously. In referring to the behaviour of the assembly, the San Francisco *Daily Alta* wrote, "Our doughty Assembly may possibly have laid themselves liable to the severest censure by the remarkable course pursued in this matter."

Despite these depressing prospects, the Franchise League proceeded to organize the first statewide Negro convention for the following year, 1855. Perhaps the league drew its hope from looking to New England. While five northern states did prohibit Negro testimony in cases where white men were involved, none of them was in New England. It may also have drawn strength from the activities of its colored convention compatriots in the East with whom its members were in correspondence. Many of these members had had organizational experience in the Eastern Negro rights movements.

The work of this convention produced even more petitions during the following months. More whites expressed their wish for justice to the Negro. In 1856 petitions were presented to the state legislature from San Francisco, Sacramento, and El Dorado counties to change the testimony laws. Support for such a change even came from the San Francisco County Grand Jury. All petitions were referred to the Judiciary Committee where they died. The Judiciary Committee was evidently not impressed with the fact that nearly three hundred lawyers had also given support to this legal reform proposal.

The convention movement was not disheartened however. It prepared for another round and another convention in 1856. The year had seen more white friends enter the struggle. In fact, a great deal of its approach involved an appeal to the self-interest of white men: there were times when white men needed Negro testimony. A United States Circuit Court in San Francisco could not prosecute a seaman for killing a mate on the high seas because the only witness was a Negro.

As one colored convention delegate put it:
I may see the assassin plunge the dagger to the vitals of my neighbor. . . . I may overhear the robber or incendiary plotting the injury or utter ruin of my fellow-citizen. . . . The robbery may follow, the conflagration may do its work, and the author of the evil may go unpunished because only a colored man saw the act or heard the plot. Under these circumstances who are not really injured and lose by the law? . . . is it not evident that the white citizen is an equal sufferer with us? When will the people of this state learn that justice to the colored man is justice to themselves?

The 1856 Colored Convention was to be the biggest of the three before the Civil War. Sixty-one delegates came from seventeen counties. There were men of great ability, talent, and education at this gathering. The topic of education loomed up as a competitor to the issue of testimony. The California Negro community was sufficiently stabilized to be concerned about the education of its children. The white school systems in the state showed virtually no interest in Negro children at this time. These children obtained their basic education through the work of the churches and especially the efforts of one man, Jeremiah B. Sanderson, a Bedford, Massachusetts, Negro who was in effect the scribe for all the Colored conventions. With evidence of regret, however, the 1856 convention kept itself mainly to the single issue of testimony.

The resulting petition campaign rolled up another wave of strong white support. Petitions were presented to the assembly the following year from seven counties: San Francisco, Sacramento, and five mountain counties. San Francisco alone presented a petition with five-hundred signatures. But in the assembly nothing happened.

While the testimony law had to wait until the Civil War before it was reformed, some judges in San Francisco were beginning to receive Negro testimony despite the state law. In an assault case in 1858 the defendant's lawyer tried to set aside an indictment because the injured party was a Negro and his testimony was thereby rendered invalid. The judge in the case so interpreted existing law as to accept the Negro's testimony. He claimed in his decision that he was in accordance with "the common-law, and with the principles of justice and humanity." The jury sustained the judge. As a result of this case a police court shortly afterwards ruled in favor of a Negro woman in an assault and battery case. A few weeks later an old Negro woman was able to obtain justice against a white man who had beaten her.

The Third Colored Convention that met in 1857 was a bit smaller than the previous one, and must have taken place in an atmosphere of depression. The Dred Scott decision had been handed down that year, and in the California assembly there was talk of anti-Negro immigration legislation. The Dred Scott decision had produced additional problems for Negro farmers. As a result of this decision the United States Land Office denied pre-emption rights to Negroes. This convention was, in addition, distracted by internal problems. Forgetting to heed the requirement that minority groups must be perfect in all things, members of the convention movement permitted themselves the luxury, granted only to Caucasians, of jealousies and pettiness. They were never to be quite free of this difficulty.

The subsequent months saw another petition campaign. In spite of technical difficulties in assembling the petitions from some of the far-flung counties and the inadequate funds sent from those areas, a respectable showing was made. San Francisco and Sacramento counties came through very well as usual. Eighteen-hundred signatures were sent to the assembly from San Francisco alone. A San Francisco newspaper noted that "the number of petitions favoring the repeal of the statute disqualifying Negroes and Mulattoes from giving evidence . . . causes them [the assemblymen] no little uneasiness." The petitions were again buried in committee.

Some unfriendly assemblymen could find new excuses to be antagonistic to the Negro in 1858. This was the year of the famous Archy fugitive slave case.

While the fugitive slave problem was virtually nonexistent in California by 1858, the Archy case occurred because of the dull-wittedness of his owner in bringing him to California. It took on spectacular dimensions because of the supreme court's decision that legally Archy deserved his freedom. But out of kindness to his master, the court also decided he must return to slavery. The press all over the state roared in ridicule, and the Negro community, especially in San Francisco, was thoroughly aroused. The minute details of the Archy case make for another story. Suffice it to say, that the aggressive concern and involvement of San Francisco Negroes offended the tender sensibilities of some of the assemblymen. It is not clear whether the militancy of Bay Area Negroes had much to do with the rejection by the assembly of the testimony petitions, but it did have some bearing on a legislative attempt to register all free Negroes in California and bar future colored immigration into the state. Referring to the Archy excitement in San Francisco, State Senator Merritt in support of antifree Negro immigration legislation stated that "he becomes insolent and defiant, and, if in sufficient numbers, would become dangerous, as evidenced by recent occurrences in one of our cities."

This was not the first effort to prevent Negro immigration to California. An attempt that died had been made at the constitutional convention. Assemblyman Crabb, who incidentally in the year of Archy's freedom was on his way to meet his own fate in Sonora, announced in 1852 that he would introduce a bill to prevent future Negro immigration into California. It was not until 1857 that such a bill almost became a law. By a thirty to thirty-two vote the bill was defeated in the assembly.

The year 1858 was a painfully dramatic one for California Negroes. There was to be another more serious attempt to prevent Negro immigration and to label the Negro a proscribed class. Many were to despair of legal relief and to begin to think of leaving the country. The only bright spot in that year was the astonishing victory of Archy at the hands of a federal official who was a Southerner!

The 1858 attempt to bar Negro immigration moved along more successfully than previous efforts. While feelings about the Archy case were discernible, there may have been other factors as well at play. The latter half of the 1850's in California was a period of some economic distress, and the cities and towns had increasing numbers of former miners seeking work. An antagonistic sentiment was rising against Chinese and Negroes. At almost the same time that the anti-Negro Immigration bill was running its course through the legislature, an Anti-Chinese bill of the same kind was on its way.

The anti-Negro immigration bill was introduced in the assembly in March of 1858. Its provisions were harsh on Negroes who were in violation of the bill as well as white men who unwittingly hired Negroes who were subject to its exclusion provisions. The unwillingness of the assemblymen to modify the penalties on white employers of Negroes in violation of this act lends strength to the view that the legislators had the general problem of employment on their minds. Efforts to penalize a slave-owner who brought a Negro into the state after the effective date of the law were, however, defeated. The assemblymen were in no mood for moderation whenever this bill was up for discussion. A partial explanation for this impatience may be that this bill seemed to come to the floor repeatedly in the late afternoons or in the evening and that this session was in its last days. The bill was finally passed overwhelmingly in the assembly and sent to the senate.

Uneasiness about this bill was more evident in this body. An attempt to postpone consideration indefinitely was defeated nine to seventeen. State Senator Bell attempted to introduce safeguards for California Negroes temporarily out of the state or members of their immediate families on their way to California. He won a temporary delay on this point, but the Judiciary Committee by a three to two vote rejected his suggestion. Maneuvering came to an end with the passage of the bill twenty-one to eight. But the maneuvering bore fruit. The senate included some minor revisions that required the bill's return to the assembly for approval. The very impatient and partially drunk assembly had, however, in the meantime adjourned. The bill therefore died.

Had this bill passed, at least two very influential newspapers, the Sacramento *Daily Union* and the San Francisco *Daily Evening Bulletin*, thought that it would be unenforceable. As it worked its way through the legislature, these newspapers reported the proceedings with undisguised distaste. In their view it was unnecessarily harsh to the Negro. The *Daily Evening Bulletin* defended the California Negroes by making a case for them—with some logic—as the best of the free Negro group in the United States. It saw some merit in preventing future immigration of Negroes but pleaded for more kindness in treating the resident population. At least one outstanding leader of the San Francisco Negro community took a thanks-but-no-thanks view of this kind of support. Mifflin Wistar Gibbs wrote to the *Evening Bulletin* defending free Negroes everywhere in the United States. He said, in part:

I appeal with pride to the history of the free colored people for the last twenty years in every free state in the Union. . . . During all that time, notwithstanding they have been subjected to the most unjust enactments and coerced by rigorous laws, pursued by a prejudice as unrelenting as inhuman, disregarded by the Church, and persecuted by the State—they have made steady progress, upward and onward, in oral and intellectual attainments.

I admit the right of a family or a nation to say who, from without, shall be a component part of its household or community; but the application of this principle should work no hardship to a colored man, for he was born in the great American family, and is your black brother—ugly though he may be—and is interested in its weal or woe, is taxed to support it, and having made up his mind to stay with the family, his right to the benefit of just government is as good as that of his pale face brother who clamors for his expatriation.

Even as Gibbs wrote this ringing statement he must have been having doubts about remaining in the country of his birth. His letter appeared in the first week of April, 1858, and in the days that followed Negroes in San Francisco were conducting indignation meetings and talking about going to Canada. The anti-immigration bill seemed certain of passage, and there was excitement to the north due to the Frazier River Gold Rush.

Accident in history played its part. Due to the Frazier River fever, the British officials in Victoria found it necessary to expand governmental functions. This required a building program that called for a large group of laborers. The gold rush had created a severe labor shortage in Victoria. British sea captains who knew about California and San Francisco events were in touch with Victoria officials and things began to happen. At one of the April Negro mass meetings in San Francisco the audience was informed that they would be welcome in Victoria and that there was employment and land.

The result was an exodus of several hundred California Negroes led by a number of leaders of the convention movement, including the author of the previous statement, Mifflin Wistar Gibbs. The convention movement lost another leader in Peter Lester who was Gibbs' business partner. He is the same man who was beaten while they were being robbed and could get no justice because of the testimony laws. Lester had his own special grief during the weeks before he decided to join his partner in the Victoria migration. His daughter, who was apparently very light-skinned, was accepted into an all-white public school after examination by the board of education in San Francisco. This was found offensive to some school officials, and an agonizing debate resulted. The board resolved its problem at the expense of Peter Lester's daughter. This was too much for the Lester family, and they headed for Victoria. There were other parents with daughters like Lester's who had also applied to the white schools. Some of them too must have joined the Victoria exodus. Most of the group settled in Victoria, but some went to the gold fields of British Columbia. For many this was a vast improvement in their situation. The Negro community of Victoria might have been much larger today if it had not been for the developments of the Civil War just a few years later. Like most of the American Negroes who fled to Canada in the 1840's and 1850's the Victoria Negro community returned in great numbers to their native land. Gibbs, who became an elective official in Victoria, returned to the United States and received recognition for his abilities in the postwar period. Among his official positions was the post of municipal judge of Little Rock, Arkansas.

With the departure of the contingent to Victoria in 1858, the convention movement seemed to fall into spiritual and organizational doldrums. There was no convention that year, and frustration produced accentuated internal bickering. Defeat was in the air notwithstanding that the anti-immigration legislation never became law. An effort at independent Negro journalism had just expired in spite of great sacrifices by its editor. In November, 1858, the executive committee of the convention movement issued a report in which it announced that after much thought it had decided not to call for another testimony petition until there was a change of political administration in California. This, of course, could only mean that the Negro felt that his fortunes lay with an eventual Republican victory. It is interesting to note that in this mood of depression Negro leadership turned faintly to recourses suggested more forcefully nearly forty years later when the American Negro was experiencing the bitter fruits of home rule in the South. Foreshadowing Booker T. Washington, the executive committee report advised that

> Pecuniary prominence, in a country so diversified as this, takes precedence over intellectual, and it should be our highest aim to seek the end we have marked out, through that mode which has formed a superiority. . . .

But the report does not call for surrender. It agrees to conduct another petition campaign if the California Negro community responds with sufficient vigor and funds. This does not seem to have been the case before 1860.

The fortunes of the California Negro began to rise with the opening of the next decade. The cause of the convention movement was assisted tremendously by national developments as well as human factors. 1860 saw the arrival in California of the Reverend Thomas Starr King, who gave Negro causes as well as other causes a great deal of support. In the same year one of the major figures in Negro journalism came to California, and a Negro press was soon born again on the West Coast: Peter

Bell had been associated with the Negro press in the East since its beginnings in the 1830's and was a very sophisticated and worldly journalist.

Bell was a fine addition to the leadership group in the California convention movement. While the exodus to Victoria had resulted in the loss of Gibbs and Lester, the leadership of the 1850's had at all times contained an unusual group of men. Gibbs had worked with Frederick Douglass in the antislavery movement in the East. William H. Yates, who was the president of the first California Colored Convention and was associated with all the subsequent conventions, bought his own freedom in Washington, D.C., as a young man. Becoming a porter in the United States Supreme Court, he experienced an unusual intellectual exposure. When he moved to New York, he became a Mason and was an active anticolonizationist. He came to California in 1851 and became an employee of the California Steamship Navigation Company. As a chief steward he plied the waters of San Francisco Bay and was undoubtedly able to function as a unifying agent in the convention movement.

William H. Hall, who was president of the Second Colored Convention, had an equally interesting career before coming to California. In Washington, D.C., he was the fund raiser for a monument for Benjamin Banneker. In New York he too became a Mason and was active in that state in the campaign for Negro suffrage in the 1840's. Abner Francis was a correspondent of Fred Douglass as were others in the convention movement. William Newby had also been a western contributor to Frederick Douglass' paper. He was one of the founders of the first California Negro paper, *The Mirror of the Times*. His ability was recognized by the French government, and he was asked in 1858 to be the private secretary to the French Consul General in Haiti. New Bedford-born Jeremiah B. Sanderson was on the same platform with Frederick Douglass when the latter was discovered by William Lloyd Garrison. Most, if not all, of the printed proceedings of the California Colored Conventions are in his handwriting. William Wells Brown's *The Black Man*, published during the Civil War, which was a review of distinguished Negroes in America included Sanderson as the only Western Negro. Sanderson had worked with Douglass as well as with the Eastern Negro leaders, Brown and William C. Nell. His great competence made him the foremost Negro teacher in California. He was the most indefatigable worker in organizing schools for Negro children and gained begrudging financial support from boards of education.

Most of these men were born free or had achieved freedom at an early age back East. There were many who were active in the California convention movement who did not attain the prominence of the aforementioned but were of its flesh and bone. A most interesting group are those whose early years in California were absorbed with the back-breaking business of buying themselves and their families out of slavery in the East and paying for their passage to California. They should also be remembered.

In 1863 the State Legislature of California revised the testimony laws, and the Negro was, at last, relieved of this disability. The previous year had seen the defeat of many opponents of Negro testimony, and the assemblymen who tried to reform the law in 1862 were now successful. By the time of the Fourth Colored Convention in 1865, Negro leadership was turning itself to the problems of education and suffrage.

When victory had at last been gained in the matter of testimony, Peter Bell, now the editor of the Negro paper, *The Pacific Appeal*, wrote:

we should be more guarded than ever against committing any acts that might be construed by the enemies of our advancement, as a consequence of the repeal of those unjust laws. . . . We should be patient and conciliating. . . .

And then he added with a remarkable quality of objectivity:

we must not always suppose that every offense that may be committed against us is altogether in consequence of our color.

Early in 1864, editor Bell felt optimistic and wrote:

A new era has already dawned and it is with yourselves to decide as to whether you or your children shall be made capable of assuming the responsible positions which already await you. The Federal Government and the good and intelligent among the American people, are endeavoring to help you.

Peter Bell had no way of knowing in 1864 that many generations of white Americans were yet to come who would try to freeze the Negro in his subordinate position in American life by telling him that he was trying to move too fast.

26

"Willie Stokes at the Golden Gate"
WILSON RECORD

During World War II thousands of blacks migrated to the San Francisco Bay Area seeking employment in the giant shipyards and government installations. Many blacks experienced enormous difficulties finding jobs, and even those who were eventually employed encountered intense hostility and discrimination from whites. The personal history of Willie Stokes symbolizes the plight of these blacks.

IN June of 1941 Willie Stokes, a 27-year-old Negro farm laborer, was working on a cotton plantation in Desha county, Arkansas. It was in the flat bottom lands with the Mississippi all muddy and mighty wide just to the east. For each "can to can't" day he worked, he received credit to the amount of $1.25 at the plantation store. He was "allowed" to use a small plot of ground for a garden and was provided a two-room, windowless shack in which he lived with his wife and two children. His "understanding" with the planter provided that he could gather off the place "enough wood to cook with."

In June of 1943 Willie Stokes was working as a welder in Yard Number 2 of the Kaiser Shipbuilding Company in Richmond, California, just across and up the bay from San Francisco. On a clear day, he could see the giant red tiers of the Golden Gate Bridge towering above the brown hills and on beyond, the city, its buildings all white in the mid-day sun. For each eight-hour day he worked he was paid ten dollars—in cash. Nominal deductions were made for social security payments and health and medical fees.

He bought his price-controlled groceries from a big supermarket down on Cutting Boulevard near San Pablo Avenue. He paid a moderate rent for a four-room apartment in the conveniently located government housing project. This included lights, gas and hot and cold running water. His cooking was done with gas on a neat white range.

In June of 1946 Willie Stokes was working as a laborer in a small chemical plant on the outskirts of Richmond. He unloaded trucks, swept floors and sometimes cleaned the large heavy vats. For each eight-hour

SOURCE: Wilson Record, "Willie Stokes at the Golden Gate," *The Crisis*, 56 (June 1949). Reprinted by permission of the author and *The Crisis*.

day he worked, he was paid $6.40. He continued to live in the government housing project. He still bought his groceries at the big supermarket, but the prices were much higher, and his weekly check was considerably smaller than at the shipyard.

He was no longer able to save anything from his pay. Another child, arriving during the preceding year, had added to the cost of "getting enough for my folks to eat." Unless he worked a full week ends didn't meet, and he had to draw on his meager savings. His wife was a good cook; she kept the stove all neat and white.

In June of 1947 Willie Stokes wasn't working anywhere; he had been unemployed for seven months. At first he "made do" on unemployment compensation checks. They were gone in a few weeks and weren't enough "even when they did come." Then he used the remaining three dollars in savings. One by one, as the weeks went by and he was unable to find a job, he cashed the war bonds bought through pay deductions during 1944 and 1945. The man at the bank told him he ought to hold onto the bonds. He didn't tell him what to use for money.

Lived by Borrowing

Later he borrowed money from friends, expecting that "some job would turn up soon." To repay them he sold his car. Once when I talked with him he had just returned from the offices of the Contra Costa County Department of Public Welfare where he had filed an application for indigent relief. He confided that the pantry wasn't exactly empty, but there was very little to cook on the neat white gas range.

Willie Stokes is not an exception. He is an example. He is an example of what is happening to many of the thousands of Negroes who migrated to the San Francisco Bay Area during the war years and later, seeking jobs in the giant shipyards and government installations—supply depots, shipping centers, training stations and repair yards. If you talk with the Negroes over in East Oakland, or in Fillmore District in San Francisco, or in South Berkeley, or down by the Santa Fe tracks in Richmond, or in any of the segregated housing projects scattered through the Bay Area, the story will be repeated many times. Variations in small details occur, but the central pattern is constant.

It is a pattern of migration, employment in war production industries at relatively high wages, intermittent employment at lower wages during a transition period, and finally frequent and prolonged unemployment attended by an exhaustion of unemployment compensation benefits, cash savings and war bonds, and in numerous cases the indigent relief roles. This is not to suggest that all Negro workers in the area are unemployed. But conservative estimates indicate that at least one third of all Negroes in

the Bay Area labor force are unable to find jobs. With total unemployment in the state exceeding 400,000 at present, Negroes can anticipate
even more difficulty in finding work. The problem can be stated in a
simple equation: Willie Stokes multiplied by 20,000.

In 1940 when Willie Stokes was a farm laborer in Arkansas, there were
less than 20,000 Negroes in the entire San Francisco Bay Area, which
included six heavily-populated counties and such cities as San Francisco,
Oakland, Berkeley and Richmond, Alameda and Vallejo. By 1944 this
number had increased to more than 65,000. In 1947 it stood at an estimated 103,000, the result of continued movement of war workers, veterans, and other Negro migrants. At present the total is estimated at
120,000. This gain of more than 500 percent within a nine-year period
resulted in the addition of some 100,000 Negroes to the Bay Area population. In 1940 Negroes made up only a little more than one per cent of
the total population. But in 1947 they were an estimated 6 per cent of an
overall total of almost 2,000,000.

The Negro population of San Francisco increased from less than 5,000
to more than 40,000. That of Oakland from less than 9,000 to an estimated
45,000. In Richmond there were less than 300 Negroes in 1940, but more
than 14,000 in 1949. The Negro population of Berkeley doubled during
this period and now exceeds 7,000.

Like Willie Stokes, many of the Negro war workers (and later, veterans) came to the San Francisco Bay Area directly from farms in the
South and Southwest. But even more came from the small towns and cities
where they had worked as laborers, porters, janitors, domestic servants,
truck drivers, railroad section hands, freight handlers, machine operators,
craftsmen and craftsmen's helpers.

A recent study of unemployed Negroes in Richmond disclosed that
approximately 30 per cent had migrated directly from farms, 50 per cent
from smaller towns and cities and the remaining 20 per cent from larger
cities such as Dallas, New Orleans, Memphis, Little Rock, St. Louis and
Tulsa. No recent conclusive studies of states of origin of the present
Negro population in the Bay Area have been done. However, estimates
based on previous reports and spot surveys suggest that as much as 65 per
cent of the in-migrants since 1940 have come from the four West-South-
Central states of Arkansas, Louisiana, Oklahoma and Texas.

When Willie Stokes arrived in Richmond during the early part of 1943,
he went to the home of a friend, also from Desha county, who had moved
to Richmond the year before. They "doubled up" until Willie Stokes was
able to secure an apartment unit in the emergency housing project about a
month later. By the end of June he was able to send for his wife and
children, who made the long trip out by bus over Highway 66.

On the day after his arrival Willie Stokes reported to Employment
Service. The offices were crowded, and long lines of men and women

stood patiently before the reception windows waiting their turns for interviews. At the reception window a middle-aged woman, wearing horn-rimmed glasses and perched on a high stool, wrote his name on a paper and gave him a card directing him to report to Yard Number 2 of the Kaiser Shipbuilding Company within 48 hours. He went to work as a "laborer," and his first job was unloading steel plates from flat cars. Within a few days, however, he was being trained to use the torch and rod, and by the end of June he was reclassified as a "welder" and his pay increased.

All Kinds of Workers

There were all kinds of workers in the shipyard: whites, Negroes, Mexicans, Chinese, and even Indians. He could recognize the "poor whites," the "red necks" and the "Oakies" and "Arkies." If he was elated at the prospects of doing war work at good pay, he was awed and a little frightened by the size of the ships, the yards stretching for miles along the bay, the noise and the people hurrying everywhere. He was bewildered by the strange teeming city and its people. He did not know what to expect or what was expected of him. But he realized that he was not alone, that there were thousands like him in the yard, that thousands more would come.

Thousands more were working in the government installations, Army Port of Embarkation, Quartermaster Supply Depot, Navy Supply Base, Naval Air Station, San Francisco Medical Depot, Benecia Arsenal and the Navy Ammunition Depot. A much smaller number of Negroes found employment in some of the little iron and steel plants. A number of jobs, particularly for Negro women, opened in the canning and food processing industries. The chemical, petroleum and electrical equipment firms in the Bay Area employed some Negroes. More than a thousand found platform jobs and other jobs in the San Francisco Municipal Railway System.

Total Negro employment in the Bay Area, at its war-time peak in November, 1944, was more than 40,000. Acute labor shortages made jobs for Negroes in shipbuilding and government installations. With the exception of transportation, warehousing and a few smaller industries, Negroes like Willie Stokes found employment only on an "emergency, temporary and duration" basis. They were in industries born of war and doomed to collapse with its end.

On the job, Willie Stokes kept to himself and the small group that made up his all-Negro welding crew. There were stories of fights and outbreaks between Negroes and whites in the yard. He didn't want any trouble. He wanted to do his work, get his pay and stay on the job as long as he possibly could. He knew all too well that it was a chance that he might never have again.

He knew, too, that his chances for promotion beyond a welder were not good, that there were many jobs in which no Negroes, not even the well-educated ones, were employed. For the most part, they worked as laborers in a dozen basic "hull," rather than "outfitting" trades, as welders, burners, chippers, scalers, sheet-metal workers, carpenters, riggers and helpers. He knew of no Negro foremen or supervisors, although a few were used as "pushers" and straw bosses. No Negroes worked as technicians or in clerical and office jobs.

He knew that even had there been opportunity for advancement, his lack of education and experience would have handicapped him. In school he had completed only the third grade, attending classes held in a one-room building that was used for a church on Sundays. It was never open for more than five months during the year; only three or four, if the picking season ran late.

He had never worked off a farm before. He knew how to drive trucks and tractors, to service them with gas and oil, and do minor repairs, but that was the extent of his acquaintance with machinery. He doubted if he could learn to read a blueprint or do fine precision welding. He knew that and accepted it. But he believed, as did thousands of his fellow Negroes in the industry, that given the chance and the time, he could do all right. The chance never came. It might have, but it never did. The time ran out, quickly.

When Willie Stokes went to work in the Kaiser yards in Richmond, he was required to join a union. This meant the payment of an initiation fee and monthly dues as long as he worked. Like most of the workers from the South, and particularly the Negroes, Willie Stokes had never before belonged to a union. Back in Arkansas, about eight or ten years ago, some of the wage hands and sharecroppers in Crittenden and St. Francis counties had organized a union. Whites and Negroes could belong. They held meetings in the small churches and out-of-the-way school houses, and some of the preachers were organizers. Willie Stokes never joined, but once he attended a meeting and read some of the mimeographed handbills. The people went out on strike during one of the chopping seasons. Some of them were driven off the land; others were beaten and thrown in jail. The strike was broken.

Shipyard Union

The shipyard union which Willie Stokes was required to join was the United Brotherhood of Boilermakers and Iron Shipbuilders and Helpers of America, AFL. But actually, neither he nor any of the other Negroes were bona fide members. They belonged to an "auxiliary," a separate, second-class adjunct of the parent, "white only," organization. He could attend meetings and pay dues. But he could not vote for officers; he had no voice in its affairs or its relations with the company. He did not know much about unions, but he knew jim-crow, segregation, discrimination, and second-class citizenship when he saw it.

Yet he paid his dues in much the same manner as he took a rear seat on a bus in Memphis or removed his hat when a white lady passed him on the street. He did not protest, but regarded the payments as a necessary bribe for the privilege of working at a job that paid more than he ever dreamed. That was not the attitude of a noted Negro artist, Joe James, down at the Marinship Company. With the support of a large committee of fellow workers in the yard, he refused to pay dues to the jim-crow auxiliary, and upon being discharged by the company carried the matter to the Supreme Court of California. The court ruled that a closed shop was contrary to public policy when the union discriminated in admitting racial minorities. The enforcement of that decision was another matter.

During 1944 employment in the shipbuilding industry in the Bay Area began to decline. This was due to reduced operations in the major construction yards. But Negro employment in this industry and in government installations increased. Willie Stokes didn't exactly understand what was happening. Negroes were usually the last to be hired and the first to be laid off. But gradually it became clear to him. The white workers were leaving, returning to their home states or seeking employment in the peace-time industries in the area. Negroes had no such opportunities. Willie Stokes couldn't leave the shipyard for other employment; there were no other jobs; that was why he remained until the bitter end and the discharge slip.

In January, 1944, the shipbuilding industry in the Bay Area employed some 240,000 people. About 24,000 or roughly 10 per cent were Negroes. By January of 1945 employment in shipbuilding had dropped to 200,000, but of this number more than 26,000 were Negroes. By July of 1945 less than 150,000 persons were employed in shipbuilding, and Negro employment had dropped to less than 20,000. In September of 1945, just two months later, Negro employment in shipbuilding had fallen precipitously to less than 12,000. This downward trend continued on into 1946 until the number of Negroes in the industry was an insignificant portion of the total in the labor force.

Over in the East Bay Area, one large ship construction firm employed more than 25,000 persons during its peak operations in 1944. Some 20 per cent, or about 5,000 were Negroes. After V-J Day, Negro employment was reduced to about 2,000. In early 1946 less than 300 Negroes found employment in that yard. A small shipyard farther down the bay employed approximately 1,500 Negroes in 1944, but less than half that number in 1945, and only a handful in 1946.

Up in Richmond the Kaiser yards employed more than 47,000 workers in December of 1944, of whom more than one fourth, or about 12,000, were Negroes. One of these was Willie Stokes, who had worked steadily in different yards for eighteen months. After V-J Day employment at Kaiser declined rapidly. By early 1946 less than 9,000 persons were working there, and total Negro employment was insignificant compared to what it had been at peak.

Willie Stokes could see the end coming, the closing of the shipyards, his loss of a job. He was apprehensive and hopeful all at the same time. But he could do nothing about it. A few of his friends had loaded up their cars and headed back South. They went the way they came, down the Central Valley and into Bakersfield, on to Highway 66 and through the Mohave Desert, and then the long drive across Arizona and New Mexico, back into the red hills of Oklahoma, the Brazos bottoms of Texas, the cane fields of Louisiana, and the flat cotton lands of eastern Arkansas or the hill country to the north. But not Willie Stokes, and not the thousands like him who would never go back, who were in California to stay—for better or for worse—and for a long time.

Willie Stokes believed that he might be able to find a job as a laborer or longshoreman when his job in the shipyard ended. During the war, a great many Negroes had found such jobs down on the docks in Oakland or across the bay in San Francisco. He thought something might be found in one of the government establishments. He even speculated that there might be something right in Richmond, a steady job close to his home.

On November 22, 1945, Willie Stokes received his dismissal notice. He had seen hundreds of them handed out in recent months. He had expected it any day and recognized it immediately. He knew it was coming, and yet it was hard to believe that it could actually happen to him. But there it was, with his name and badge number, the blank spaces all filled in and neatly initialed at the bottom. In a way he was glad; there would no longer be the long nights of worrying and waiting.

He had thought about what he would do on the day he was fired. Maybe he would put his wife and kids in the car and drive down to Los Angeles for a vacation. Perhaps he would take off a month and drive back to Arkansas, show the people in Desha county that Willie Stokes had done all right out in California. It would be good to see some of his relatives again and have a long talk with old Cleo Jones. Maybe on a Sunday he would put on his new suit and go to the little unpainted church over by the levee. As he looked at the discharge slip, he realized that he would do none of these things.

He picked up the lunch box, slung the worn woolen jacket over his shoulder, and made for the ramp that led up over the railroad tracks and down to the bus stop across the street. He lived some two miles away and he was tired, but he decided to walk. He wanted to think. When he got home he showed the discharge slip to his wife. She had expected it, too, and indicated no surprise.

Among the Unemployed

On the following Monday Willie Stokes reported to the offices of the Employment Service. Long lines again crowded in front of the reception windows. But they were waiting to collect unemployment benefit checks. Few were being referred out to jobs. A sign above one of the windows read "Veterans Only," and before it waited a long line of younger men, some of them still wearing old army pants, greasy field jackets and the heavy GI shoes. He recognized from a glance some Negroes from Louisiana who lived near him in the housing project. He nodded slightly, and they nodded in return. Several men with whom he had worked on his last shift were ahead of him in the line.

In the large, squared-off space behind the counters were perhaps a hundred chairs, neatly arranged in rows and each occupied by what appeared to be a former shipyard worker. Some still wore their identification badges, others their plastic safety helmets, pushed back on their heads. At either side of the waiting areas were neat rows of desks at which sat the interviewers.

When it came his turn for an interview, Willie Stokes was motioned to the desk of a young man who wore a neat, double-breasted grey suit with a discharge button in the lapel. He was asked many questions: Where was he born? When did he move to California? How long had he worked in the shipyards? And so on. Finally, he was told that there were no openings. There were few demands for welders, and only the most experienced were being hired. No laborers were needed; in fact, there was a surplus, particularly now that the harvest and canning seasons were coming to a close.

If his wife cared to work as a cook or housekeeper, a few jobs were open. They didn't pay much, but might be worth investigating. A laborer's job might turn up later on, but the prospects in the Bay Area and in the state were not at all good he was told.

He was given a new card with his name at the top and his social security number written in little squares. He was told to report at least once each week and to promptly answer any summons to report for referral to a job.

The next day Willie Stokes began looking for a job in the government installations. One of his neighbors who worked at the Naval Air Station down at Alameda told him he might get a job there. Turnover, particularly among white workers, had been increasing, and Negroes were being hired to fill these places. But he found no job.

It was true, these establishments had greatly increased their employment of Negroes in 1945, but by December of that year they had passed peak employment; they were slowly reducing their work force in the early months of 1946. In 1944 one large military supply base employed some 3,000 Negroes. In 1945 this number had increased to a little over 5,000, but by 1946 it had been reduced to less than 4,000.

Another shipping and embarkation center had employed some 2,000 Negroes in 1945, but in 1946 it was employing only about half that number. One of the smaller ammunition depots afforded employment to an estimated 250 Negroes in 1945, but in 1946 not more than 10 per cent of that number were still working. Some estimates place the number of Negroes employed in government installations in the Bay Area in 1945 as high as 35 per cent of total Negro employment. After that time it declined, numerically and as a percentage. This was especially the case after early 1946. Willie Stokes didn't know much about figures and statistics. He knew that a lot of people couldn't find jobs.

During the following week he reported twice to the offices of the Employment Service, but he was not referred to a job. He collected the first of his unemployment compensation checks and was told to keep reporting back each week on the designated day. On the other days he "just about wore the car out" looking for a job. He went down to the south end of the bay, over into San Francisco. He went up the bay as far as Martinez and Vallejo and even up to Napa. He stood at the gates of flour mills and soap factories, oil refineries and the shipyards. He waited in the employment offices of the little steel mills and the iron and pipe factories, of the trucking firms and the machinery manufacturers. And with him waited hundreds of other men, many of them Negroes, former welders and scalers, shipfitters and burners. Once they were classed as essential skilled workers in a vital industry; now they were surplus common laborers, essential to no one.

Sometimes he never got inside the gate for an interview. Sometimes there were huge signs reading "No Help Wanted" and occasionally one that read "No Colored Need Apply." In the employment office of one of the small steel companies, he was interviewed by a polite elderly man. He was asked about his war-time experience, his education, his work in Arkansas. The man was sympathetic, but he held out little chance for a job for Willie Stokes.

"You have little education," he said, "and in most cases your war-time experience will mean very little. During the war, wage costs weren't too important and the system of classification and grading by skills was all out of whack. They would call a man a welder who a month before had never seen a torch, and they paid him as a welder, too. They could afford to do it. The government was footing the bill and needed the ships. That's why it won't mean very much to have worked as a welder. I mean it isn't very likely to help you get a job now. Jobs out here require a lot of skill and experience, and many of you people from the South don't have it. Maybe you could learn in time . . . I guess you could."

He took from a desk drawer, perhaps, a hundred completed application forms like the one Willie Stokes had completed. "You see these cards," he said. "They are filled out by Negroes . . . about a hundred in all. Every one of these men has had a high school education and has worked in shipbuilding for at least two years. Most of them have had some other plant experience as well. We are going to hire some Negroes soon, a dozen perhaps. Of course, we are going to select the best ones we can get. We have to do it. It's good business. I am afraid we can't be of much help to you. If you could arrange to go to school or take vocational training or get some kind of apprenticeship training, you might qualify sometime, but that would take quite a while."

Willie Stokes walked out of the office, on past the line of applicants still waiting for interviews. It was funny almost. One day you were an essential skilled worker in a vital industry (they said that in the speeches every time they launched a ship) and the next you were a surplus unskilled laborer, essential to no one.

Some of the other people in the employment offices were hardly as polite. "We don't hire any colored people here," he was told by a clerk in the office of a machinery manufacturing company, not even during the war when there was a shortage, and we don't intend to start now." And at another place it was a different story, but it all added up to the same thing. "All our workers are referred by the union," said the clerk at the information desk. "You will have to be a member of the union and approved by the business agent before you can work here. But if I were you, I wouldn't bother about going to them; they won't take in any of you colored people." In the office of one of the large freight hauling companies in the East Bay Area, he was told again. "We get our drivers through the union, but the local that we contract with wouldn't let one of you colored boys behind a wheel."

Seeking Employment

Sometimes he would be the first in the lines forming before the gates in the morning. He would see the white workers who had arrived later called into the office for interviews. After completing an application form he was told not to wait, that the company would send him a letter "in case we need you." Such were the stories that Willie Stokes heard at the employment offices day after day. It was nothing new. He had heard similar ones all his life back in Desha county, Arkansas; they just sounded a bit strange when told with a western brogue rather than a southern accent.

During the last week of December, 1945, Willie Stokes received a notice to report to the office of the Employment Service to see about a job. He reported on the following morning and again talked with the young veteran in the double-breasted grey suit. "Out north of Richmond here, there is a small chemical plant that yesterday placed an order for two Negro laborers," the young interviewer said. "The jobs pay only eighty cents an hour and I don't know just what kind of work you will do. It may last for several months or, again, it may be only a few days. If you care to go out and check on it, I will give you a referral card." Willie Stokes nodded quickly. The interviewer gave him the card with the address of the company and the name of the man to see.

When he went to the plant Willie Stokes was wearing a clean pair of overalls and a new blue denim cap. He wanted to get that job. He could stop drawing money out of the bank. He got the job. At the end of the first week he drew a check for $30.38. It wasn't very much; it wasn't welder's pay. But it was more than the unemployment compensation checks, and it was a job. It wasn't too far from his home. It might be steady; he might get a wage increase.

Willie Stokes worked in the chemical plant for almost a year, with an occasional layoff. In December, 1946, about one third of all workers in the plant were laid off; he was one of them. There followed again the fruitless visits to the various plants of the year before. Willie Stokes, formerly an essential skilled worker in a vital industry, a responsible and upright citizen, was becoming a problem. People made studies and held conferences to determine what should be done about him and the thousands like him all up and down the West Coast. If Willie Stokes and his kind had "gone back where they came from," the problem would have been solved; it could have been exported like raisins or oranges. But Willie Stokes was not for export. He was in California to stay, like the Chinese and the Mexicans and the Filipinos and the Oakies and Arkies.

Down in Oakland in 1947 no less than seventy-five persons a day were filing applications for temporary indigent relief. Almost one half of these were Negroes, yet they were only an estimated 10 per cent of the population. In Alameda City, Negroes made up at least 25 per cent of the unemployed, although they were only a little more than 5 per cent of the population. Up in Vallejo, Negroes were in more dire circumstances perhaps than anywhere else in the Bay Area. Their numbers had increased from a little over 1,000 to more than 9,000 in the period 1940–1947. During the war most of them found employment in nearby government installations. But after 1945 employment dropped from approximately 45,000 to less than 15,000 in 1947. Some 4,000 Negro workers remained in Vallejo, but almost half could find no employment.

On April 25, 1947, the Pacific Coast Board of Inter-governmental Affairs, a body composed of leading Federal and State executives in California, Oregon and Washington, held its seventh regular meeting in San Francisco. The problem of Willie Stokes—the problem of Negro unemployment—was prominent on the agenda. The facts presented were numerous; the discussion was long and earnest. The difficulties inherent in the whole matter were probably best summarized by a representative of the United States Employment Service when he said: "The short and immediate term outlook for Negro employment is not at all good. . . . If, as seems increasingly probable, we were to experience a significant recession, the lot of the West-Coast Negro, already serious, may become little short of desperate. . . . As long as Negroes are commonly regarded as marginal labor, they will suffer very heavy unemployment when sufficient white labor is available."

It is now February, 1949, and Willie Stokes has had only casual employment for almost two years. During last August he worked for one month on a construction job, and in December he worked for a couple of weeks as a pick-and-shovel man on a cable-laying gang. He worked as a migrant farm laborer during the last harvest season. His wife hires out for house work several days each week. Somehow he manages to get by, or at least he keeps a place to live and a little to eat.

The children don't have good clothes to wear to school like during the war. But that isn't so noticeable now; there are a lot of people like Willie Stokes and a lot of children like his in Richmond and up in Vallejo and down in Oakland and over across the bay in San Francisco.

Sometimes he wonders about returning to Arkansas. But this doesn't concern him for very long. He knows that he will never go back. He probably couldn't find a job in Desha county Arkansas, even if he wanted to go back. Things are bad; they are very bad for Willie Stokes and his family out in California. But they will stay; there are good reasons. In California his children go to the same schools as other children. They go for nine months during the year. The buildings are new and warm and well lighted. He can ride on a bus without having to take a rear seat marked "colored." He can attend any movie and take any seat he likes; no climbing the long flights of stairs to the uppermost stuffy balcony. He can walk down the street without having to move toward the curb when a white man passes. He isn't required, on perhaps pain of beating or arrest, to say "ma'am" to the woman clerks in the stores.

Western "Freedom"

He can vote by registering and going to the polls, and no night-shirt Klansmen are going to try to stop him. It isn't likely that he will be clubbed by bullying white policemen "just for the hell of it," thrown in jail and then charged with "disturbing the peace." When he works he knows that he will be paid in cash, get all that is coming to him. His children can use the library like any other children. He can join the local chapter of the NAACP or some unions or a local anti-discrimination committee without fear of violent reprisal at the hands of law and order.

These are ordinary rights due any citizen. And yet they have a special meaning for Willie Stokes. He never had them before. They are things that money and a job alone cannot give. They are things that poverty and unemployment cannot take away. That is why Willie Stokes is in California to stay. That is why thousands like him will never go back to Arkansas, Louisiana, Oklahoma or Texas or "where they come from." That is why, in part, Negroes will continue to pour into the state, swelling the number already crowded into its teeming cities. Willie Stokes is not alone. Reliable estimates indicate that at least 85 per cent of the Negroes migrating to the West Coast since 1940 have remained there.

Negroes on the West Coast face a very uncertain future. The most important and immediate problems are employment and housing. Related to these are health, welfare and education and innumerable difficulties with which the general public is only remotely acquainted. But the potential resources of the community and of the Negro group itself suggest that eventually Negroes can achieve a more wholesome and complete adjustment in the Bay Area than they have in any of the larger urban-industrial centers.

Numerous interracial groups are active throughout the Bay Area. Some are sponsored by churches, some by organizations such as the Young Women's Christian Association. Still others are supported by veterans' groups or by trade unions and trade union councils or central bodies. Local city officials, aware of certain problems in Negro-white relations in their communities, have established official or quasi-official bodies to make studies and develop race relations programs. Some two years ago in Richmond, representatives of the American Council on Race Relations were invited to conduct training courses on minority group problems for the police force.

Some of the trade unions, particularly the affiliates of the Congress of Industrial Organizations in the automobile, canning, shipping and steel industries in the area, stress non-discrimination in employment and admission to unions. Working with Negro groups and employers, they have widened job opportunities for Negroes. Whatever one may think of the left-wing tendencies of the Bridges-controlled International Longshoremen and Warehouse Workers Union, the fact remains that through it Negroes have obtained a fair break in job opportunities and union participation. Even in some of the die-hard affiliates of the American Federation of Labor, there is a growing awareness of the importance of absorbing rather than alienating the Negro worker in the Bay Area. For example, the Alameda and Francisco Central Labor Councils helped establish in San Francisco a branch of the Jewish Labor Committee, whose purpose is to combat prejudice and discrimination among trade unions and trade-union members.

Group Consciousness

A significant group consciousness is developing among Bay-Area Negroes. Instead of isolated individuals or families from Arkansas, Louisiana, Oklahoma or Texas, they are becoming communities of people in the compact cities. A more mature and hard-headed Negro leadership, capable of directing the frustrations and aggressiveness of individuals into more constructive channels of political and economic action, is emerging. These leaders stand out in sharp contrast to some of the Uncle Toms and handkerchief heads on the one hand and the hide-bound racial chauvinists on the other.

Thus Willie Stokes and those like him are not helpless in the face of the pressing problems of unemployment, housing shortages, discrimination in unions and the multiple forms of race prejudice. But the resources of the community and of the Negro group are hardly sufficient to cope with the most immediate and important of these. The positive developments are small when placed against the almost overpowering needs of 90,000 recent Negro migrants to the Bay Area.

While some programs are presently in operation, their results will not be significant for a number of years, and the immediate need of Willie Stokes and his people is a job today and tomorrow. In the absence of Federal or State legislation outlawing discrimination in job opportunities, the prospects for rapid progress are not good. It can be anticipated that discrimination on racial grounds will become more pronounced if the present high rate of unemployment increases.

The development of new industries, an increase in demand for semi-skilled and unskilled workers would possibly lead to an absorption of the Negro unemployed. But there is the real probability that the solution would be only temporary. Increases in Negro employment would more than likely induce more in-migration to the San Francisco Bay Area. For mechanization of southern agriculture is going to force more Negroes off the farms. This was demonstrated immediately after the war when Negro shipyard workers from Portland, Seattle, and Vancouver, instead of returning to their home states, migrated into the Bay Area where reductions in the Negro employment were not as drastic as in Oregon and Washington. It is for this reason that no long-term solution to the problem of Negro unemployment in the area is anticipated.

But Willie Stokes and his people are in the Bay Area to stay. They may find few jobs, and then only the "hot, heavy and dirty" ones or perhaps those in the menial and service occupations. They may have to "double up" with friends and relatives in the already over-crowded Negro communities and public housing projects. But they will be joined by in-laws, parents, aunts and uncles. As a prominent sociologist recently pointed out, "The Negro is now the number one minority group and the number one minority group problem on the West Coast and in the Bay Area." The sooner the community realizes it, the sooner something can be done. The Bay Area need not be another Chicago or Detroit. Willie Stokes will try to prevent it.

27

Watts: Before the Riot

PAUL BULLOCK

*This selection is drawn from a research project on the Watts
community directed by Paul Bullock, a white economist from
the Institute of Industrial Relations at UCLA. The report, comprised largely of the views of the black residents of Watts, is
a useful antidote to the McCone Commission's official version.
Here Bullock traces the origins of Watts and describes the
increasing ghettoization of that community prior to the insurrection of 1965.*

WHATEVER may be the stereotypes created by national magazines
and the other mass media, Watts is in no sense a completely unified
and homogeneous community. The hostile delinquent, the aggressive
nationalist, the "middle-class" homeowner, the college-bound youngster,
the hustler, the conventional politician, the welfare recipient, the hard-
core unemployed, and the hard-working employed are all represented,
and only a journalist with a superficial view and a pressing deadline
would dare to suggest that any one group symbolizes the "community."
The one common bond is skin color, but even here we must recognize
the presence of Mexican-Americans, now dwindling in number but still
noticeable in some neighborhoods.

In the early days of Los Angeles, the area now known as Watts was part
of a large ranch, El Rancho Tajuata. When the original owner died, his
estate was divided into many parcels to accommodate his heirs. In those
days, land in California was easily acquired—legally and illegally—from
its Mexican owners, and a number of Americans benefited.

Two subsequent building booms, the first in 1885–88 and the second
in 1900–1910, hastened the growth of Tajuata, still an unincorporated
area in the county of Los Angeles. Twenty-five-foot lots sold at a dollar
down and a dollar a week. Land speculation, largely associated with the
building of railroads and of Henry Huntington's Pacific Electric transportation system, eventually led to further settlement of the area, close
to the city but not in it. A major spur of the Pacific Electric tracks ran

SOURCE: Paul Bullock, ed., *Watts: The Aftermath—An Inside View of the Ghetto
by The People of Watts* (New York: Grove Press, Inc., 1969), pp. 11–19. Reprinted
by permission of Grove Press, Inc.

north and south through Tajuata, which was a junction for tracks running to Long Beach and San Pedro.

With the construction of the Pacific Electric railroad came the immigration of poor Mexican laborers, most of them employed by the railroad. By this time the heirs of the original owner had sold the land to subdividers. The PE decided to build a station on the old ranchland and acquired the necessary property from several Anglo subdividers, among whom was Julia A. Watts. The railroad men called it the Watts Station, and the growing settlement became known, unofficially, as Watts. Even then the cheap land and the corruption gave Watts something of a local reputation. One resident, a white American who had lived in Watts for many years, commented:

> A dollar down and a dollar a week became a by-word. This, with the politics and vice which abounded among the white inhabitants, caused Watts to be used as a joke in the theaters and on the streets. A spite deal sold the first land to the Negroes in the southern part of Watts. . . .

Whatever the nature of this "spite deal" may have been, it is certain that some time before the first World War the southern edge of Watts became a Negro ghetto. Locally known as "Mudtown," this rustic community served as a port of entry for Negroes immigrating from the South. In his 1931 novel, *God Sends Sunday*, the distinguished author Arna Bontemps described the early black settlements in Los Angeles:

> In those days, fifteen or twenty years ago, Negroes were not plentiful in the far West. Least of all were they to be seen in rural parts. A few of them, to be sure, had come as early as the historical gold rush with the forty-niners, working in personal service. Others had followed the conquest of the frontier. But the number had remained small until the great transcontinental railway lines established important terminals in Los Angeles and in San Francisco. Then the real immigration began. First, the railroad men, Pullman porters and dining car waiters, brought their families; hearing the rumors of attractive working conditions, their friends followed. Still the tendency was for them to remain in the larger centers and particularly in the location of the train yard.
>
> The small group in Mudtown was exceptional. Here, removed from the influence of white folks, they did not acquire the inhibitions of their city brothers. Mudtown was like a tiny section of the deep south literally transplanted. . . .
>
> The streets of Mudtown were three or four dusty wagon paths. In the moist grass along the edges cows were staked. . . . Ducks were sleeping in the weeds, and there was on the air a suggestion of pigs and slime holes. Tiny hoot-owls were sitting bravely on fence posts while bats hovered overhead like shadows. . . .

If early Mudtown was like a section of the South transplanted, it would not remain so for long. Mudtown was a part of Watts, both geographically and commercially. As the population grew, and as the Anglo and Mexican inhabitants of Watts moved toward political self-determination, the Negro community became less isolated. Incorporated as a separate city in 1907, Watts was the scene of unending political turmoil as the Anglos sought to maintain their control of community affairs. When industrial development associated with World War I encouraged further immigration from the South, mainly from Texas, Louisiana, and Mississippi, the black newcomers settled either in Watts or in the Central Avenue ghetto to the north, closer to downtown. The expanding Watts ghetto, however, remained surrounded by Anglo communities, existing as a Negro island in an otherwise "lily white" and often hostile sea. Indeed, until World War II, Watts itself retained its racially heterogeneous character, its population divided about equally among Anglos, Mexicans, and Negroes.

The internal politics of Watts became more troubled in the twenties. The Ku Klux Klan, already a force in the Compton area just to the south, schemed to gain control of city government through the use of recall petitions and devices to split the Negro community. Its plans were thwarted by unwelcome publicity, but it remained active. The political difficulties in the small town, coupled with water shortages which could only be overcome through the Owens Valley Aqueduct project, led, in 1926, to the abandonment of cityhood and annexation to the city of Los Angeles.

Its absorption into Los Angeles, however, did not destroy Watts' identity as a community. Anyone familiar with Los Angeles knows that it is not one city but, rather, a series of distinct communities: one lives in Pacific Palisades, or San Pedro, or Eagle Rock, or Highland Park, or Bel Air, each technically a "neighborhood" within Los Angeles. Watts, of course, had a further claim to distinction: it contained a high proportion, though still a minority, of Negroes. Except for the Central Avenue area and a small middle-class Negro community along West Jefferson Boulevard to the north and west, Negroes in Los Angeles were to be found only in Watts, and, even then, mainly in the southern part of the community below 103rd Street. Northern Watts remained dominated by Anglos and Mexicans. Before World War II, the Mexican and Negro inhabitants were of lower economic status; in 1938, a writer commissioned by the Works Progress Administration (WPA) noted, somewhat snobbishly, that a low grade of labor was demanded by the manufacturing plants which had located on the eastern edge of Watts, and that this fact, plus the impact of the depression, had changed the character of the community. He also noted the mixture of good and poor dwellings in the area, a characteristic which remains in evidence today.

During World War II, the population of Los Angeles boomed and Watts was no exception. Many of the immigrants were Negroes drawn by the lure of jobs in the war industries, and they encountered a critical housing problem when they entered this thoroughly segregated city.

Tens of thousands moved into "Little Tokyo," vacated by the Japanese, but other thousands had to find accommodations in the traditionally segregated Central Avenue and Watts ghettos. Some of those who had decent jobs bought or built pleasant homes, many of which are still visible in the western part of Watts below 103rd Street and just east of Central Avenue. But many others moved into deteriorating or substandard housing, absentee owned, and several hundred more located in public housing projects built by the federal government in the Watts area.

The construction of the public housing projects, which became all-Negro though they were supposedly interracial, accelerated the ghettoization of the community. Three projects were built during the war, and a fourth, William Nickerson Jr. Gardens, was finished in 1955. The earliest—Hacienda Village (1942)—is the most attractive, with trees shading its single-story units. It was constructed as a permanent project, and its designers (Richard Neutra, Paul Williams, and Welton Becket) are now among the most prominent architects in California. Jordan Downs (September, 1944) and Imperial Courts (May, 1944) were semi-permanent projects for war workers, which were later converted into permanent units. Like Nickerson Gardens, they are massive and conventional two-story structures.

By 1946, Negroes represented almost two-thirds of the population of Watts, twice their proportion in 1940. Writing during the war, sociologist Lloyd H. Fisher noted the increasing tension in the community. Watts elementary schools were interracial both in teaching staff and student bodies, but the only high school (actually a combined junior and senior high), David Starr Jordan, was predominantly Negro because Anglo youngsters were encouraged to go elsewhere for their high school education. The nearby junior college in the all-white city of Compton discouraged Jordan High graduates from attending it. Fisher observed a lack of confidence in the police force, the absence of an interracial church, and a lack of leadership and organization within the community. In short, he detected all the major elements which were to explode into violence twenty years later.

Nor was Fisher alone in his observations. In a book on the Los Angeles Youth Project, published in 1949, Duane Robinson described the Watts area in terms which, in essence, were equally applicable fifteen years hence:

> This area is surrounded by strong Anglo-American communities which in the past have manifested discriminatory practices—even physical aggression. The Latin-American residents are disturbed by the rapidly growing Negro majority. The native Negroes are disturbed by the incoming "southern"

Negroes, many of whom have imported and are supporting the approximately eighty churches in the area, ranging from magnificent edifices to tattered tents. Recreational and other facilities are hopelessly overwhelmed. There is no sizable building facility for recreation in the entire area.

Even some bureaucrats and public officials seemed aware that something was amiss in Watts. In a report on conditions of blight in the central area of the city of Los Angeles, the City Planning Commission, in 1947, concluded that Watts was

an obsolescent area in which all the social and physical weaknesses of urban living are to be found. Some streets are unpaved, others have fine concrete roadways and ornaments; some structures seem about to fall apart, while next to them exist new, standard buildings. In some areas, a great number of twenty-five foots lots stand vacant, while in others six or more dwellings are crowded into a similar parcel. Recreational facilities in certain sections are few in number and limited in area. Schools are located in places where the maximum walking distance, rather than the minimum, is required of a great number of children. The shopping district on 103rd Street has little provision for off-street parking, and during busy hours the street is cluttered with double parked vehicles and is almost closed to traffic movement. Some of the worst interracial conflicts occurring in the past decade were in this area. The low rental pattern, the low assessed value of property, the high disease and delinquency rates, all reflect the blighted character of this district.

Clearly, every evidence of social pathology in Watts was a matter of public knowledge as early as 1947. But no action was forthcoming, or even suggested. After its incisive analysis of the problems in the area, the City Planning Commission offered no concrete plan for their alleviation. The conditions which breed riots had already emerged, conservatively speaking, a generation ago. In the light of such public indifference to deprivation and deterioration, the wonder is not that a riot eventually exploded in the area but, rather, that the residents were patient for so long.

The 1950's saw a few changes in Watts, but the movement of the community remained primarily the same, and was perhaps accelerated. In the first half of the decade, the Nickerson Gardens project was completed and both Jordan Downs and Imperial Courts were converted to permanent units, and by the decade's end over a third of the total population lived in public housing. Inevitably, the actual population density in the projects far exceeded the earlier projections, and the streets and yards swarmed with children. Large families were often crammed into relatively small quarters. The percentage of young people under the age of twenty-five rose to a little more than sixty per cent in 1960, and the proportion of homeowners dropped markedly as the projects expanded. The construction of a modern junior high school—Edwin Markham—

improved the school system in a physical sense, but the dropout (or pushout) rate at Jordan High School was depressingly high. Anglos virtually disappeared, though a very few remain even today, and the Mexican-American percentage of total population dropped to less than eleven per cent, concentrated mostly in the eastern section.

As the community entered the 1960's, the forces of social and economic disorganization became stronger and more pervasive than ever. In a 1959 study, the Welfare Planning Council had noted that there was still no master plan for the Watts area, nor was there any current program of planning or activity even in regard to parks and schools. Its analysis has a familiar ring:

> Preoccupation with earning a living for many persons in this area reduces their interest in preparation for or acceptance of leadership of youth groups. This condition, however, does not mean that there is no leadership; rather, it means that it is harder to locate and recruit. The continual immigration of persons from different sections of the country makes it difficult to stabilize and stimulate interests in long range projects or even in the immediate social problems as related to youth. Compounded upon these factors is that most of the residents in this area are employed outside the area which poses a transportation problem of taxing even more the inadequate public transportation system of the area. This hinders the chance of developing a strong feeling of community responsibility with so much of the residents' time spent outside the area.

As the summer of 1965 approached, the character of the Watts community had been fixed inexorably by the events of the previous two decades. The previously separated ghettos—Watts, Central Avenue, and West Jefferson—had now been amalgamated by the vast increase in black population and outflow of Anglos during the 1940's and 1950's, creating a massive, segregated area in the heart of the county which stretches from the western part of the city of Compton on the south to the lower part of downtown Los Angeles; and from Alameda Street on the east to the pleasant, middle-class (and occasionally integrated) Crenshaw-La Brea district on the west. Alameda Street, still the site of the railroad tracks, remains an impenetrable "Berlin Wall," which has always separated the Negro ghetto from the lily-white and decidedly unfriendly communities of South Gate, Huntington Park, Lynwood, and Bell. Thus, the direction of the ghetto's expansion is predominantly westward, and it is now merging into, and possibly transforming, an area which has been largely Jewish in population.

In the postwar years, the development of Los Angeles' complex freeway system further compounded the isolation of those Negroes who remained in the poorest section of the ghetto. The Harbor Freeway, linking downtown Los Angeles with the coastal communities of Wilmington and San

Pedro, bisects the huge central ghetto, leaving what are, in effect, two distinct Negro settlements. The area to the east of the freeway, which includes Watts, is predominantly poor, with a few middle-class enclaves, while the area to the west is predominantly middle-class, with a few low-income enclaves. In the hills above Crenshaw Boulevard, on the western edge of what was later defined as the riot "curfew zone," an integrated high-income community contains impressive homes, often with swimming pools, inhabited by Negro professionals and businessmen. In the West Adams area, an extension of the early West Jefferson middle-class ghetto, the neighborhoods differ from those in the Anglo areas only in the darkness of the residents' complexions.

Even the area east of the Harbor Freeway would not be adjudged a "slum" by those accustomed to the rat-infested tenements of Eastern cities. Single-family dwellings still predominate, though probably a third of the population of Watts itself (narrowly defined as the area between 92nd Street on the north and Imperial Highway on the south, Central Avenue on the west and Alameda Street on the east) still lives in public housing. At the corner of Central Avenue and 103rd Street, on the western edge of Watts, Will Rogers Park gives the visitor a favorable first impression, with its spacious lawns, baseball diamonds, tennis courts, swimming pool, and large gymnasium. However, programs at the park are limited, partly because its administrators are fearful of "incidents." About a mile further to the southeast, the famous Watts Towers, fashioned by Italian immigrant Simon Rodia out of steel, cement, and fragments of bottles, shells, and glassware, rise majestically on a small plot of land at the end of a street which leads into the abandoned PE right-of-way.

Then, as now, as the observer moves from one neighborhood to another, he is invariably impressed by the diversity in the physical appearance of Watts. The neat, attractive, and well-maintained houses on Zamora or Pace Avenue south of 103rd—many of them owned by residents who came to Los Angeles during the 1940's—would do credit to the most status-conscious suburb. Nearby are two of the imposing public housing projects, Hacienda Village to the north, and Nickerson Gardens, to the south. The other two projects provide living space for about 5,000 persons in other sections of Watts. Elsewhere, shabby absentee-owned houses contrast sharply with better-maintained residences on the same block or around the corner, the latter attesting to the earnest but probably futile efforts of the inhabitants to preserve some semblance of pride in their aging homes. Just across Central Avenue, on 94th and 95th Streets, a neighborhood of handsome homes attracts thousands of visitors every December to its imaginative display of outdoor Christmas decorations.

As one ventures into still other neighborhoods, new and more mixed impressions come to the fore. Small and usually dilapidated churches, of religious denominations, are everywhere, challenged in number only by the many liquor stores. The main business center is along 103rd Street, with dozens of dingy stores offering their wares at prices and terms well in excess of those charged in Anglo neighborhoods. On the eve of the riot, the only new construction in sight was the still-unfinished Doctors' Building, the iron framework being raised by an all-white crew of building craftsmen. At the other end of 103rd, near Alameda, marijuana and pills of all varieties are readily available on and off the campus of David Starr Jordan High School. In a corner lot adjoining Jordan Downs project, the dropouts and delinquents of the "parking lot gang" terrify the rest of the community.

Watts is characterized by one-parent households. It is a community of young people, the yards and streets filled with children, the classrooms overflowing. The observer is impressed by their apparent health and handsomeness: the boys are muscular and lively, the girls well-developed and neatly dressed. The older teen-agers search desperately for "kicks," a respite from the boredom and frustration of a ghetto in which there is nothing to do. Many of the youngsters carry their most prized possession —a "box" (radio)—from which "soul" sounds blare incessantly. Thousands of them will rarely see the world outside the ghetto, except perhaps in jail. The whites they know are policemen, probation officers, merchants, and teachers, and the relationship is often uneasy or hostile.

28

The McCone Commission Report

*The August, 1965, revolt in the black ghetto of Los Angeles—
usually called the Watts riots after a tiny portion of that fifty
square mile ghetto—forms a nodal point in not only the racial
history of California but of the whole nation. The usual "blue
ribbon" commission—like those appointed after nearly every
massive racial incident in the twentieth century—sat, sifted the
evidence, and wrote its report. Its chairman, and the man responsible for the final form of the report, was John J. McCone,
an establishment Republican businessman who had headed the
Central Intelligence Agency and had no expertise and little
visible sympathy for the dispossessed, as the report shows. Much
criticized, and rightly so, it was the first such commission, however, to advocate "compensatory" rather than "equal" treatment
for disadvantaged minorities. It made modest recommendations,
almost none of which have been followed by either Sam Yorty's
Los Angeles or Ronald Reagan's California.*

The Crisis—An Overview

THE rioting in Los Angeles in the late, hot summer of 1965 took six
days to run its full grievous course. In hindsight, the tinder-igniting
incident is seen to have been the arrest of a drunken Negro youth about
whose dangerous driving another Negro had complained to the Caucasian
motorcycle officer who made the arrest. The arrest occurred under rather
ordinary circumstances, near but not in the district known as Watts, at
seven o'clock on the evening of 11 August, a Wednesday. The crisis ended
in the afternoon of 17 August, a Tuesday, on Governor Brown's order to
lift the curfew which had been imposed the Saturday before in an extensive area just south of the heart of the City.

In the ugliest interval, which lasted from Thursday through Saturday,
perhaps as many as 10,000 Negroes took to the streets in marauding bands.
They looted stores, set fires, beat up white passersby whom they hauled
from stopped cars, many of which were turned upside down and burned,
exchanged shots with law enforcement officers, and stoned and shot at
firemen. The rioters seemed to have been caught up in an insensate rage

SOURCE: *Violence in the City—An End or a Beginning?* (Los Angeles: Governor's
Commission on the Los Angeles Riots, 1965), pp. 1-9.

of destruction. By Friday, the disorder spread to adjoining areas, and ultimately an area covering 46.5 square miles had to be controlled with the aid of military authority before public order was restored.

The entire Negro population of Los Angeles County, about two thirds of whom live in this area, numbers more than 650,000. Observers estimate that only about two per cent were involved in the disorder. Nevertheless, this violent fraction, however minor, has given the face of community relations in Los Angeles a sinister cast.

When the spasm passed, thirty-four persons were dead, and the wounded and hurt numbered 1,032 more. Property damage was about $40,000,000. Arrested for one crime or another were 3,952 persons, women as well as men, including over 500 youths under eighteen. The lawlessness in this one segment of the metropolitan area had terrified the entire county and its 6,000,000 citizens.

Sowing the Wind

In the summer of 1964, Negro communities in seven eastern cities were stricken by riots.* Although in each situation there were unique contributing circumstances not existing elsewhere, the fundamental causes were largely the same:

—Not enough jobs to go around, and within this scarcity not enough by a wide margin of a character which the untrained Negro could fill.

—Not enough schooling designed to meet the special needs of the disadvantaged Negro child, whose environment from infancy onward places him under a serious handicap.

—A resentment, even hatred, of the police, as the symbol of authority.

These riots were each a symptom of a sickness in the center of our cities. In almost every major city, Negroes pressing ever more densely into the central city and occupying areas from which Caucasians have

*   SUMMARY OF 1964 RIOTS

City	Date	Killed	Injured	Arrests	Stores Damaged
New York City	July 18–23	1	144	519	541
Rochester	July 24–25	4	350	976	204
Jersey City	August 2–4	0	46	52	71
Paterson	August 11–13	0	8	65	20
Elizabeth	August 11–13	0	6	18	17
Chicago (Dixmoor)	August 16–17	0	57	80	2
Philadelphia	August 28–30	0	341	774	225

moved in their flight to the suburbs have developed an isolated existence with a feeling of separation from the community as a whole. Many have moved to the city only in the last generation and are totally unprepared to meet the conditions of modern city life. At the core of the cities where they cluster, law and order have only tenuous hold; the conditions of life itself are often marginal; idleness leads to despair and finally, mass violence supplies a momentary relief from the malaise.

Why Los Angeles

In Los Angeles, before the summer's explosion, there was a tendency to believe, and with some reason, that the problems which caused the trouble elsewhere were not acute in this community. A "statistical portrait" drawn in 1964 by the Urban League which rated American cities in terms of ten basic aspects of Negro life—such as housing, employment, income—ranked Los Angeles first among the sixty-eight cities that were examined. ("There is no question about it, this is the best city in the world," a young Negro leader told us with respect to housing for Negroes.)

While the Negro districts of Los Angeles are not urban gems, neither are they slums. Watts, for example, is a community consisting mostly of one and two-story houses, a third of which are owned by the occupants. In the riot area, most streets are wide and usually quite clean; there are trees, parks, and playgrounds. A Negro in Los Angeles has long been able to sit where he wants in a bus or a movie house, to shop where he wishes, to vote, and to use public facilities without discrimination. The opportunity to succeed is probably unequaled in any other major American city.

Yet the riot did happen here, and there are special circumstances here which explain in part why it did. Perhaps the people of Los Angeles should have seen trouble gathering under the surface calm. In the last quarter century, the Negro population here has exploded. While the County's population has trebled, the Negro population has increased almost tenfold from 75,000 in 1940 to 650,000 in 1965. Much of the increase came through migration from Southern states and many arrived with the anticipation that this dynamic city would somehow spell the end of life's endless problems. To those who have come with high hopes and great expectations and see the success of others so close at hand, failure brings a special measure of frustration and disillusionment. Moreover, the fundamental problems, which are the same here as in the cities which were racked by the 1964 riots, are intensified by what may well be the least adequate network of public transportation in any major city in America.

Looking back, we can also see that there was a series of aggravating events in the twelve months prior to the riots.

—Publicity given to the glowing promise of the Federal poverty program was paralleled by reports of controversy and bickering over the mechanism to handle the program here in Los Angeles, and when the projects did arrive, they did not live up to their press notices.

—Throughout the nation, unpunished violence and disobedience to law were widely reported, and almost daily there were exhortations, here and elsewhere, to take the most extreme and even illegal remedies to right a wide variety of wrongs, real and supposed.

—In addition, many Negroes here felt and were encouraged to feel that they had been affronted by the passage of Proposition 14—an initiative measure passed by two-thirds of the voters in November 1964 which repealed the Rumford Fair Housing Act and unless modified by the voters or invalidated by the courts will bar any attempt by state or local governments to enact similar laws.

When the rioting came to Los Angeles, it was not a race riot in the usual sense. What happened was an explosion—a formless, quite senseless, all but hopeless violent protest—engaged in by a few but bringing great distress to all.

Nor was the rioting exclusively a projection of the Negro problem. It is part of an American problem which involves Negroes but which equally concerns other disadvantaged groups. In this report, our major conclusions and recommendations regarding the Negro problem in Los Angeles apply with equal force to the Mexican-Americans, a community which is almost equal in size to the Negro community and whose circumstances are similarly disadvantageous and demand equally urgent treatment. That the Mexican-American community did not riot is to its credit; it should not be to its disadvantage.

The Dull Devastating Spiral of Failure

In examining the sickness in the center of our city, what has depressed and stunned us most is the dull, devastating spiral of failure that awaits the average disadvantaged child in the urban core. His home life all too often fails to give him the incentive and the elementary experience with words and ideas which prepares most children for school. Unprepared and unready, he may not learn to read or write at all; and because he shares his problem with 30 or more in the same classroom, even the efforts of the most dedicated teachers are unavailing. Age, not achievement, passes him on to higher grades, but in most cases he is unable to cope with courses in the upper grades because they demand basic skills which he does not possess. ("Try," a teacher said to us, "to teach history to a child who cannot read.")

Frustrated and disillusioned, the child becomes a discipline problem. Often he leaves school, sometimes before the end of junior high school. (About two-thirds of those who enter the three high schools in the center of the curfew area do not graduate.) He slips into the ranks of the permanent jobless, illiterate and untrained, unemployed and unemployable. All the talk about the millions which the government is spending to aid him raise his expectations but the benefits seldom reach him.

Reflecting this spiral of failure, unemployment in the disadvantaged areas runs two to three times the county average, and the employment available is too often intermittent. A family whose breadwinner is chronically out of work is almost invariably a disintegrating family. Crime rates soar and welfare rolls increase, even faster than the population.

This spiral of failure has a most damaging side effect. Because of the low standard of achievement in the schools in the urban core and adjacent areas, parents of the better students from advantaged backgrounds remove them from these schools, either by changing the location of the family home or by sending the children to private schools. In turn, the average achievement level of the schools in the disadvantaged area sinks lower and lower. The evidence is that this chain reaction is one of the principal factors in maintaining de facto school segregation in the urban core and producing it in the adjacent areas where the Negro population is expanding. From our study, we are persuaded that there is a reasonable possibility that raising the achievement levels of the disadvantaged Negro child will materially lessen the tendency towards de facto segregation in education, and that this might possibly also make a substantial contribution to ending all de facto segregation.

All Segments of Society

Perhaps for the first time our report will bring into clear focus, for all the citizens to see, the economic and sociological conditions in our city that underlay the gathering anger which impelled the rioters to escalate the routine arrest of a drunken driver into six days of violence. Yet, however powerful their grievances, the rioters had no legal or moral justification for the wounds they inflicted. Many crimes, a great many felonies, were committed. Even more dismaying, as we studied the record, was the large number of brutal exhortations to violence which were uttered by some Negroes. Rather than making proposals, they laid down ultimatums with the alternative being violence. All this nullified the admirable efforts of hundreds, if not thousands, both Negro and white, to quiet the situation and restore order.

What can be done to prevent a recurrence of the nightmare of August? It stands to reason that what we and other cities have been doing, costly, as it all has been, is not enough. Improving the conditions of Negro life will demand adjustments on a scale unknown to any great society. The programs that we are recommending will be expensive and burdensome. And the burden, along with the expense, will fall on all segments of our society—on the public and private sectors, on industry and labor, on company presidents and hourly employees, and most indispensably, upon the members and leaders of the Negro community. For unless the disadvantaged are resolved to help themselves, whatever else is done by others is bound to fail.

The consequences of inaction, indifference, and inadequacy, we can all be sure now, would be far costlier in the long run than the cost of correction. If the city were to elect to stand aside, the walls of segregation would rise ever higher. The disadvantaged community would become more and more estranged and the risk of violence would rise. The cost of police protection would increase, and yet would never be adequate. Unemployment would climb; welfare costs would mount apace. And the preachers of division and demagoguery would have a matchless opportunity to tear our nation asunder.

Of Fundamental and Durable Import

As a Commission, we are seriously concerned that the existing breach, if allowed to persist, could in time split our society irretrievably. So serious and so explosive is the situation that, unless it is checked, the August riots may seem by comparison to be only a curtain-raiser for what could blow up one day in the future.

Our recommendations will concern many areas where improvement can be made but three we consider to be of highest priority and greatest importance.

1. Because idleness brings a harvest of distressing problems, employment for those in the Negro community who are unemployed and able to work is a first priority. Our metropolitan area employs upwards of three millions of men and women in industry and in the service trades, and we face a shortage of skilled and semi-skilled workers as our economy expands. We recommend that our robust community take immediate steps to relieve the lack of job opportunity for Negroes by cooperative programs for employment and training, participated in by the Negro community, by governmental agencies, by employers and by organized labor.

2. In education, we recommend a new and costly approach to educating the Negro child who has been deprived of the early training that

customarily starts at infancy and who because of early deficiencies advances through school on a basis of age rather than scholastic attainment. What is clearly needed and what we recommend is an emergency program designed to raise the level of scholastic attainment of those who would otherwise fall behind. This requires pre-school education, intensive instruction in small classes, remedial courses and other special treatment. The cost will be great but until the level of scholastic achievement of the disadvantaged child is raised, we cannot expect to overcome the existing spiral of failure.

3. We recommend that law enforcement agencies place greater emphasis on their responsibilities for crime prevention as an essential element of the law enforcement task, and that they institute improved means for handling citizen complaints and community relationships.

The road to the improvement of the condition of the disadvantaged Negro which lies through education and employment is hard and long, but there is no shorter route. The avenue of violence and lawlessness leads to a dead end. To travel the long and difficult road will require courageous leadership and determined participation by all parts of our community, but no task in our times is more important. Of what shall it avail our nation if we can place a man on the moon but cannot cure the sickness in our cities?

29

The Watts "Manifesto" and The McCone Report

BAYARD RUSTIN

Among the many trenchant criticisms of the McCone Com-
mission Report, none had more moment or impact than this
one by Bayard Rustin, a veteran strategist, tactician, and gadfly
of the civil rights movement. Director of the A. Philip Randolph
Foundation—the AFL-CIO's token contribution to the civil
rights movement—he helped develop the $100 billion freedom
budget or black "Marshall Plan," which has stirred liberal hopes
but found negligible congressional support.

THE riots in the Watts section of Los Angeles last August continued for six days, during which 34 persons were killed, 1,032 were injured, and some 3,952 were arrested. Viewed by many of the rioters themselves as their "manifesto," the uprising of the Watts Negroes brought out in the open, as no other aspect of the Negro protest has done, the despair and hatred that continue to brew in the Northern ghettoes despite the civil-rights legislation of recent years and the advent of "the war on poverty." With national attention focused on Los Angeles, Governor Edmund G. Brown created a commission of prominent local citizens, headed by John A. McCone, to investigate the causes of the riots and to prescribe remedies against any such outbreaks in the future. Just as the violent confrontation on the burning streets of Watts told us much about the underlying realities of race and class relations in America— summed up best, perhaps, by the words of Los Angeles Police Chief William Parker, "We're on top and they're on the bottom"—so does the McCone Report, published under the title *Violence in the City—An End or a Beginning?*, tell us much about the response of our political and economic institutions to the Watts "manifesto."

Like the much-discussed Moynihan Report, the McCone Report is a bold departure from the standard government paper on social problems. It goes beyond the mere recital of statistics to discuss, somewhat sym-

SOURCE: Bayard Rustin, "The Watts 'Manifesto' and the McCone Report," *Commentary* (March 1966), pp. 2–8. Reprinted by permission of the author and *Commentary*. Copyright © 1966 by the American Jewish Committee.

pathetically, the real problems of the Watts community—problems like unemployment, inadequate schools, dilapidated housing—and it seems at first glance to be leading toward constructive programs. It never reaches them, however, for, again like the Moynihan Report, it is ambivalent about the basic reforms that are needed to solve these problems and therefore shies away from spelling them out too explicitly) Thus, while it calls for the creation of 50,000 new jobs to compensate for the "spiral of failure" that it finds among the Watts Negroes, the McCone Report does not tell us how these jobs are to be created or obtained and instead recommends existing programs which have already shown themselves to be inadequate.*The Moynihan Report, similarly, by emphasizing the breakdown of the Negro family, also steers clear of confronting the thorny issues of Negro unemployment as such.

By appearing to provide new viewpoints and fresh initiatives while at the same time repeating, if in more sophisticated and compassionate terms, the standard white stereotypes and shibboleths about Negroes, the two reports have become controversial on both sides of the Negro question. On the one hand, civil-rights leaders can point to the recognition in these reports of the need for jobs and training, and for other economic and social programs to aid the Negro family, while conservatives can find confirmed in their pages the Negro penchant for violence, the excessive agitation against law and order by the civil-rights movement, or the high rates of crime and illegitimacy in the Negro community; on the other hand, both sides have criticized the reports for feeding ammunition to the opposition. Unfortunately, but inevitably, the emphasis on *Negro* behavior in both reports has stirred up an abstract debate over the interpretation of data rather than suggesting programs for dealing with the existing and very concrete situation in which American Negroes find themselves. For example, neither report is concerned about segregation and both tacitly assume that the Civil Rights Acts of 1964 and 1965 are already destroying this system. In the case of the McCone Report, this leaves the writers free to discuss the problems of Negro housing, education, and unemployment in great detail without attacking the conditions of de facto segregation that underly them.

The errors and misconceptions of the McCone Report are particularly revealing because it purports to deal with the realities of the Watts riots rather than with the abstractions of the Negro family. The first distortion of these realities occurs in the opening chapter—"The Crisis: An Overview"—where, after briefly discussing the looting and beatings, the writers conclude that "The rioters seem to have been caught up in an insensate rage of destruction." Such an image may reflect the fear of the white community that Watts had run amok during six days in August, but it does not accurately describe the major motive and mood of the riots, as subsequent data in the report itself indicate. While it is true that Negroes in the past have often turned the violence inflicted on them by society in upon themselves—"insensate rage" would perhaps have been an appropriate phrase for the third day of the 1964 Harlem riots—the whole point of the outbreak in Watts was that it marked the first major rebellion of Negroes against their own masochism and was carried on with the express purpose of asserting that they would no longer quietly submit to the deprivation of slum life.

This message came home to me over and over again when I talked with the young people in Watts during and after the riots, as it will have come home to those who watched the various television documentaries in which the Negroes of the community were permitted to speak for themselves. At a street-corner meeting in Watts when the riots were over, an unemployed youth of about twenty said to me, "We won." I asked him: "How have you won? Homes have been destroyed, Negroes are lying dead in the streets, the stores from which you buy food and clothes are destroyed, and people are bringing you relief." His reply was significant: "We won because we made the whole world pay attention to us. The police chief never came here before; the mayor always stayed uptown. We made them come." Clearly it was no accident that the riots proceeded along an almost direct path to City Hall.

Nor was the violence along the way random and "insenate." Wherever a store-owner identified himself as a "poor working Negro trying to make a business" or as a "Blood Brother," the mob passed the store by. It even spared a few white businesses that allowed credit or time purchases, and it made a point of looting and destroying stores that were notorious for their high prices and hostile manners. The McCone Report itself observes that "the rioters concentrated on food markets, liquor stores, clothing stores, department stores, and pawn shops." The authors "note with interest that no residences were deliberately burned, that damage to schools, libraries, public buildings was minimal and that certain types of business establishments, notably service stations and automobile dealers, were for the most part unharmed." It is also worth noting that the rioters were much more inclined to destroy the stock of the liquor stores they broke into than to steal it, and that according to the McCone Report, "there is no evidence that the rioters made any attempt to steal narcotics from pharmacies . . . which were looted and burned."

This is hardly a description of a Negro community that has run amok. The largest number of arrests were for looting—not for arson or shooting. Most of the people involved were not habitual thieves; they were members of a deprived group who seized a chance to possess things that all the dinning affluence of Los Angeles had never given them. There were innumerable touching examples of this behavior. One married couple in their sixties was seen carrying a couch to their home, and when its weight became too much for them, they sat down and rested on it until they could pick it up again. Langston Hughes tells of another woman who was dragging a sofa through the streets and who stopped at each intersection and waited for the traffic light to turn green. A third women went out with her children to get a kitchen set, and after bringing it home, she discovered they needed one more chair in order to feed the whole family together; they went back to get the chair and all of them were arrested.

If the McCone Report misses the point of the Watts riots, it shows even less understanding of their causes. To place these in perspective, the authors begin by reviewing the various outbursts in the Negro ghettoes since the summer of 1964 and quickly come up with the following explanations: "Not enough jobs to go, around, and within this scarcity not enough by a wide margin of a character which the untrained Negro could fill. . . . Not enough schooling to meet the special needs of the disadvantaged Negro child whose environment from infancy onward places him under a serious handicap." Finally, "a resentment, even hatred, of the police as a symbol of authority."

For the members of the special commission these are the fundamental causes of the current Negro plight and protest, which are glibly summed up in the ensuing paragraph by the statement that "Many Negroes moved to the city in the last generation and are totally unprepared to meet the conditions of city life." I shall be discussing these "causes" in detail as we go along, but it should be noted here that the burden of responsibility has already been placed on these hapless migrants to the cities. There is not one word about the conditions, economic as well as social, that have pushed Negroes out of the rural areas; nor is there one word about whether the cities have been willing and able to meet the demand for jobs, adequate housing, proper schools. After all, one could as well say that it is the *cities* which have been "totally unprepared" to meet the "conditions of *Negro* life," but the moralistic bias of the McCone Report, involving as it does an emphasis on the decisions of men rather than the pressure of social forces, continually operates in the other direction.

The same failure of awareness is evident in the report's description of the Los Angeles situation (the Negro areas of Los Angeles "are not urban gems, neither are they slums," the Negro population "has exploded," etc.). The authors do concede that the Los Angeles transportation system is the "least adequate of any major city," but even here they fail to draw the full consequences of their findings. Good, cheap transportation is essential to a segregated working-class population in a big city. In Los Angeles a domestic worker, for example, must spend about $1.50 and 1½ to 2 hours to get to a job that pays $6 or $7 a day. This both discourages efforts to find work and exacerbates the feeling of isolation.

A neighborhood such as Watts may seem beautiful when compared to much of Harlem (which, in turn, is an improvement over the Negro section of Mobile, Alabama)—but it is still a ghetto. The housing is run-down, public services are inferior, the listless penned-in atmosphere of segregation is oppressive. Absentee landlords are the rule, and most of the businesses are owned by whites: neglect and exploitation reign by day, and at night, as one Watts Negro tersely put it, "There's just the cops and us."

The McCone Report, significantly, also ignores the political atmosphere of Los Angeles. It refers, for example, to the repeal in 1964 of the Rumford Act—the California fair-housing law—in these words: "In addition, many Negroes here felt and were encouraged to feel that they had been affronted by the passage of Proposition 14." Affronted, indeed! The largest state in the Union, by a three-to-one majority, abolishes one of its own laws against discrimination and Negroes are described as regarding this as they might the failure of a friend to keep an engagement. What they did feel—and without any need of encouragement—was that while the rest of the North was passing civil-rights laws and improving opportunities for Negroes, their own state and city were rushing to reinforce the barriers against them.

The McCone Report goes on to mention two other "aggravating events in the twelve months prior to the riot." One was the failure of the poverty program to "live up to [its] press notices," combined with reports of "controversy and bickering" in Los Angeles over administering the program. The second "aggravating event" is summed up by the report in these words:

Throughout the nation unpunished violence and disobedience to law were widely reported, and almost daily there were exhortations here and elsewhere, to take the most extreme and illegal remedies to right a wide variety of wrongs, real and supposed.

It would be hard to frame a more insidiously equivocal statement of the Negro grievance concerning law enforcement during a period that included the release of the suspects in the murder of the three civil-rights workers in Mississippi, the failure to obtain convictions against the suspected murderers of Medgar Evers and Mrs. Violet Liuzzo, the Gilligan incident in New York, the murder of Reverend James Reeb, and the police violence in Selma, Alabama—to mention only a few of the more notorious cases. And surely it would have been more to the point to mention that throughout the nation Negro demonstrations have almost invariably been non-violent, and that the major influence on the Negro community of the civil-rights movement has been the strategy of discipline and dignity. Obsessed by the few prophets of violent resistance, the

McCone Commission ignores the fact that never before has an American group sent so many people to jail or been so severely punished for trying to uphold the law of the land.

It is not stretching things too far to find a connection between these matters and the treatment of the controversy concerning the role of the Los Angeles police. The report goes into this question at great length, finally giving no credence to the charge that the police may have contributed to the spread of the riots through the use of excessive force. Yet this conclusion is arrived at not from the point of view of the Watts Negroes, but from that of the city officials and the police. Thus, the report informs us, in judicial hearings that were held on 32 of the 35 deaths which occurred, 26 were ruled justifiable homicides, but the report —which includes such details as the precise time Mayor Yorty called Police Chief Parker and when exactly the National Guard was summoned —never tells us what a "justifiable homicide" is considered to be. It tells us that "of the 35 killed, one was a fireman, one was a deputy sheriff, and one was a Long Beach policeman," but it does not tell us how many Negroes were killed or injured by police or National Guardsmen. (Harry Fleischman of the American Jewish Committee reports that the fireman was killed by a falling wall; the deputy sheriff, by another sheriff's bullet; and the policeman, by another policeman's bullet.) We learn that of the 1,032 people reported injured, 90 were police officers, 36 were firemen, 10 were National Guardsmen, 23 were from government agencies. To find out that about 85 per cent of the injured were Negroes, we have to do our own arithmetic. The report contains no information as to how many of these were victims of police force, but one can surmise from the general pattern of the riots that few could have been victims of Negro violence.

The report gives credence to Chief Parker's assertion that the rioters were the "criminal element in Watts" yet informs us that of the 3,438 adults arrested, 1,164 had only minor criminal records and 1,232 had never been arrested before. Moreover, such statistics are always misleading. Most Negroes, at one time or another, have been picked up and placed in jail. I myself have been arrested twice in Harlem on charges that had no basis in fact: once for trying to stop a police officer from arresting the wrong man; the second time for asking an officer who was throwing several young men into a paddy wagon what they had done. Both times I was charged with interfering with an arrest and kept overnight in jail until the judge recognized me and dismissed the charges. Most Negroes are not fortunate enough to be recognized by judges.

Having accepted Chief Parker's view of the riots, the report goes on to absolve him of the charge of discrimination: "Chief Parker's statements to us and collateral evidence, such as his fairness to Negro officers, are

inconsistent with his having such an attitude ['deep hatred of Negroes'].
Despite the depth of feeling against Chief Parker expressed to us by so
many witnesses, he is recognized even by many of his vocal critics as a
capable Chief who directs an efficient police force and serves well this
entire community."

I am not going to stress the usual argument that the police habitually
mistreat Negroes. Every Negro knows this. There is scarcely any black
man, woman, or child in the land who at some point or other has not
been mistreated by a policeman. (A young man in Watts said, "The riots
will continue because I, as a Negro, am immediately considered to be a
criminal by the police and, if I have a pretty woman with me, she is a
tramp even if she is my wife or mother.") Police Chief Parker, however,
goes beyond the usual bounds. He does not recognize that he is prejudiced,
and being both naïve and zealous about law and order, he is given to a
dangerous fanaticism. His reference to the Negro rioters as "monkeys,"
and his "top . . . and bottom" description of the riots, speak for themselves, and they could only have further enraged and encouraged the
rioters. His insistence on dealing with the outbreak in Watts as though
it were the random work of a "criminal element" threatened to lead the
community, as Martin Luther King remarked after the meeting he and I
had with Chief Parker, "into potential holocaust." Though Dr. King and
I have had considerable experience in talking with public officials who do
not understand the Negro community, our discussions with Chief Parker
and Mayor Samuel Yorty left us completely nonplussed. They both denied, for example, that there was any prejudice in Los Angeles. When we
pointed to the very heavy vote in the city for Proposition 14, they replied,
"That's no indication of prejudice. That's personal choice." When I asked
Chief Parker about his choice of language, he implied that this was the
only language Negroes understood.

The impression of "blind intransigence and ignorance of the social
forces involved" which Dr. King carried away from our meeting with
Chief Parker is borne out by other indications. The cast of his political
beliefs, for example, was evidenced during his appearance last May on
the Manion Forum, one of the leading platforms of the radical right, in
which (according to newspaper reports) he offered his "considered
opinion that America today is in reality more than half pagan" and that
"we have moved our form of government to a socialist form of government." Such opinions have a good deal of currency today within the
Los Angeles police department. About a month before the riots, a leaflet
describing Dr. King as a liar and a Communist was posted on the bulletin
board of a Los Angeles police station, and only after the concerted efforts
of various Negro organizations was this scurrilous pamphlet removed.

Certainly these were "aggravating factors" that the McCone Report

should properly have mentioned. But what is more important to understand is that even if every policeman in every black ghetto behaved like
an angel and were trained in the most progressive of police academies,
the conflict would still exist. This is so because the ghetto is a place where
Negroes do not want to be and are fighting to get out of. When someone
with a billy club and a gun tells you to behave yourself amid these terrible
circumstances, he becomes a zoo keeper, demanding of you, as one of
"these monkeys" (to use Chief Parker's phrase), that you accept abhor-
rent conditions. He is brutalizing you by insisting that you tolerate what
you cannot, and ought not, tolerate.

In its blithe ignorance of such feelings, the McCone Report offers as
one of its principal suggestions that speakers be sent to Negro schools to
teach the students that the police are their friends and that their interests
are best served by respect for law and order. Such public-relations gim-
micks, of course, are futile—it is hardly a lack of contact with the police
that creates the problem. Nor, as I have suggested, is it only a matter of
prejudice. The fact is that when Negroes are deprived of work, they
resort to selling numbers, women, or dope to earn a living; they must
gamble and work in poolrooms. And when the policeman upholds the
law, he is depriving them of their livelihood. A clever criminal in the
Negro ghettos is not unlike a clever "operator" in the white business
world, and so long as Negroes are denied legitimate opportunities, no
exhortations to obey the rules of the society and to regard the police as
friends will have any effect.

This is not to say that relations between the police and the Negroes
of Watts could not be improved. Mayor Yorty and Police Chief Parker
might have headed off a full-scale riot had they refrained from denouncing
the Negro leaders and agreed to meet with them early on. Over and over
again—to repeat the point with which we began—the rioters claimed
that violence was the only way they could get these officials to listen to
them. The McCone Commission, however, rejects the proposal for an
independent police review board and instead recommends that the post
of Inspector General be established—under the authority of the Chief of
Police—to handle grievances.

The conditions of Negro life in Watts are not, of course, ignored by
the McCone Report. Their basic structure is outlined in a section entitled
"Dull, Devastating Spiral of Failure." Here we find that the Negro's
"homelife destroys incentive"; that he lacks "experience with words and
ideas"; that he is "unready and unprepared" in school; and that, "unprepared and unready," he "*slips* into the ranks of the unemployed" (my
italics).

I would say, *is shoved*. It is time that we began to understand this
"dull, devastating spiral of failure" and that we stopped attributing it to

this or that characteristic of Negro life. In 1940, Edward Wright Bakke described the effects of unemployment on family structure in terms of the following model: The jobless man no longer provides, credit runs out, the woman is forced to take a job; if relief then becomes necessary, the woman is regarded even more as the center of the family; the man is dependent on her, the children are bewildered, and the stability of the family is threatened and often shattered. Bakke's research dealt strictly with white families. The fact that Negro social scientists like E. Franklin Frazier and Kenneth Clark have shown that this pattern is typical among the Negro poor does not mean, then, that it stems from some inherent Negro trait or is the ineluctable product of Negro social history. If Negroes suffer more than others from the problems of family instability today, it is not because they are Negro but because they are so disproportionately unemployed, underemployed, and ill-paid.

Anyone looking for historical patterns would do well to consider the labor market for Negroes since the Emancipation. He will find that Negro men have consistently been denied the opportunity to enter the labor force in anything like proportionate numbers, have been concentrated in the unskilled and marginal labor and service occupations, and have generally required wartime emergencies to make any advances in employment, job quality, and security. Such advances are then largely wiped out when the economy slumps again.

In 1948, for example, the rates of Negro and white unemployment were roughly equal. During the next decade, however, Negro unemployment was consistently double that of whites, and among Negro teenagers it remained at the disastrously high figure which prevailed for the entire population during the Depression. It is true that the nation's improved economic performance in recent years has reduced the percentage of jobless Negroes from 12.6 per cent, which it reached in 1958 (12.5 per cent in 1961) to roughly 8.1 per cent today. Despite this progress, the rate of Negro unemployment continues to be twice as high as white (8.13 per cent as against 4.2 per cent). In other words, job discrimination remains constant. These statistics, moreover, conceal the persistence of Negro youth unemployment: in 1961, 24.7 per cent of those Negro teenagers not in school were out of work and it is estimated that in 1966 this incredible rate will only decline to 23.2 per cent. What this figure tells us is that the rise in Negro employment has largely resulted from the calling of men with previous experience back to work. This is an ominous trend, for it is estimated that in the coming year, 20 per cent of the new entrants into the labor force will be Negro (almost twice as high as the Negro percentage of the population). Approximately half of these young Negroes will not have the equivalent of a high-school education and they will be competing in an economy in which the demand for skill and training is increasing sharply.

Thus there is bound to be a further deterioration of the Negro's economic—and hence social—position, despite the important political victories being achieved by the civil-rights movement. For many young Negroes, who are learning that economic servitude can be as effective an instrument of discrimination as racist laws, the new "freedom" has already become a bitter thing indeed. No wonder that the men of Watts were incensed by reports that the poverty program was being obstructed in Los Angeles by administrative wrangling. (As I write this, the New York *Times* reports that political rivalries and ambitions have now virtually paralyzed the program in that area.)

How does the McCone Report propose to halt this "dull, devastating spiral of failure"? First, through education—"our fundamental resource." The commission's analysis begins with a comparison of class size in white and Negro areas (the latter are referred to throughout as "disadvantaged areas" and Negro schools, as "disadvantaged schools"). It immediately notes that classes in the disadvantaged schools are slightly smaller; on the other hand, the more experienced teachers are likely to be found in the *non*-disadvantaged areas, and there is tremendous overcrowding in the disadvantaged schools because of double sessions. The buildings in the "disadvantaged areas are in better repair"; on the other hand, there are "cafeterias in the advantaged schools" but not in the disadvantaged schools, which also have no libraries. This random balance sheet of "resources" shows no sense of priorities; moreover, despite the alarming deficiencies it uncovers in the "disadvantaged schools," the McCone Report, in consistent fashion, places its emphasis on the Negro child's "deficiency in environmental experiences" and on "his homelife [which] all too often fails to give him incentive. . . ."

The two major recommendations of the commission in this area will hardly serve to correct the imbalances revealed. The first is that elementary and junior high schools in the "disadvantaged areas" which have achievement levels substantially below the city average should be designated "Emergency Schools." In each of these schools an emergency literacy program is to be established with a maximum of 22 students in each class and an enlarged and supportive corps of teachers. The second recommendation is to establish a permanent pre-school program to help prepare three- and four-year-old children to read and write.

W. T. Bassett, executive secretary of the Los Angeles AFL-CIO, has criticized the report for its failure to deal with education and training for adolescents and adults who are no longer in school. Another glaring omission is of a specific plan to decrease school segregation. While most of us now agree that the major goal of American education must be that of quality integrated schools, we cannot, as even the report suggests, achieve the quality without at the same time moving toward integration. The stated goal of the McCone Commission, however, is to "reverse the trend of defacto segregation" by improving the quality of the Negro schools; in short, separate but equal schools that do not disturb the existing social patterns which isolate the Negro child in his "disadvantaged areas."

That the commission's explicit concern for Negro problems falls short of its implicit concern for the status quo is also evident in its proposals for housing. It calls for the liberalization of credit and FHA-insured loans in "disadvantaged areas," the implementation of rehabilitation measures and other urban-renewal programs and, as its particular innovation, the creation of a "wide area data bank." Meanwhile it refuses to discuss, much less to criticize, the effect of Proposition 14 or to recommend a new fair-housing code. To protect the Negro against discrimination, the McCone Report supports the creation of a Commission on Human Relations, but does not present any proposals that would enable it to do more than collect information and conduct public-relations campaigns.

The most crucial section of the report is the one on employment and, not unexpectedly, it is also the most ignorant, unimaginative, and conservative—despite its dramatic recommendation that 50,000 new jobs be created. On the matter of youth unemployment, the report suggests that the existing federal projects initiate a series of "attitudinal training" programs to help young Negroes develop the necessary motivation to hold on to these new jobs which are to come from somewhere that the commission keeps secret. This is just another example of the commission's continued reliance on public relations, and of its preoccupation with the "dull, devastating spiral" of Negro failure. The truth of the matter is that Negro youths cannot change their attitudes until they see that they can get jobs. When what they see is unemployment and their Economic Opportunity programs being manipulated in behalf of politicians, their attitudes will remain realistically cynical.

Once again, let me try to cut through the obscurantism which has increasingly come to cloud this issue of Negro attitudes. I am on a committee which administers the Apprenticeship Training Program of the Workers Defense League. For many years the League had heard that there were not enough Negro applicants to fill the various openings for apprenticeship training and had also repeatedly been told by vocational-school counselors that Negro students could not pay attention to key subjects such as English and mathematics. The League began its own recruitment and placement program two years ago and now has more than 500 apprentice applicants on file. When, last fall, Local 28 of the Sheetmetal Workers Union—to take one example—announced that a new admission test for apprentices was to be given soon, the League contacted those applicants who had indicated an interest in sheetmetal work. The young men came to the office, filled out a 10-page application form, filed a ten-dollar fee, and returned it to the Local 28 office. Then, five nights a week for three weeks, they came to Harlem, in many cases from

Brooklyn and Queens, to be tutored. Most of the young men showed up for all fifteen sessions, and scored well on the test. At their interviews they were poised and confident. Eleven of these men finally were admitted to a class of 33. The WDL doesn't attribute this success to a miraculous program; it merely knows that when young people are told that at the end of a given period of study those who perform well will obtain decent work, then their attitudes will be markedly different from those who are sent off to a work camp with vague promises.

To cut the cost of job training programs, the McCone Commission avers that compensation "should not be necessary for those trainees who are receiving welfare support." Earlier in the report the authors point out that welfare services tend to destroy family life by giving more money to a woman who lives alone; yet they have the audacity to ask that the practice of not allowing men who are on family relief to earn an additional income be maintained for young men who are working and being trained. How is a young man to be adequately motivated if he cannot feel that his work is meaningful and necessary? The McCone Report would have us say to him, "There, there, young man, we're going to keep you off the streets—just putter around doing this make-work." But the young man knows that he can collect welfare checks and also hustle on street corners to increase his earnings. A man's share of a welfare allotment is pitifully small, but more than that, he should be paid for his work; and if one is interested in his morale, he should not be treated as a charity case.

Continuing with the problem of employment, the report recommends that "there should immediately be developed in the affected area a job training and placement center through the combined efforts of Negroes, employers, labor unions and government." In the absence of actual jobs, this would mean merely setting up a new division, albeit voluntary, of the unemployment insurance program. "Federal and state governments should seek to insure through development of new facilities and additional means of communication that advantage is taken of government and private training programs and employment opportunities in our disadvantaged communities." Perhaps the only thing the Job Corps program doesn't lack is publicity: last summer it received ten times as many applications as it could handle. Nor can new types of information centers and questionnaires provide 50,000 new jobs. They may provide positions for social workers and vocational counselors, but very few of them will be unemployed Negroes.

The report goes on: "Legislation should be enacted requiring employers with more than 250 employees and all labor unions to report annually to the state Fair Employment Practices Commission, the racial composition of the work force and membership." But an FEP Commission that merely collects information and propaganda is powerless. And even with the fullest cooperation of labor and management to promote equality of opportunity, the fact remains that there are not enough jobs in the Los Angeles area to go around, even for those who are fortunate enough to be included in the retraining programs. As long as unions cannot find work for many of their own members, there is not much they can do to help unemployed Negroes. And the McCone Report places much of its hope in private enterprise, whose response so far has been meager. The highest estimate of the number of jobs given to Los Angeles Negroes since the Watts crisis is less than 1,000.

The Negro slums today are ghettoes of despair. In Watts, as elsewhere, there are the unemployable poor: the children, the aging, the permanently handicapped. No measure of employment or of economic growth will put an end to their misery, and only government programs can provide them with a decent way of life. The care of these people could be made a major area of job growth. Los Angeles officials could immediately train and put to work women and unemployed youths as school attendants, recreation counselors, practical nurses, and community workers. The federal government and the state of California could aid the people of Watts by beginning a massive public-works program to build needed housing, schools, hospitals, neighborhood centers, and transportation facilities: this, too, would create new jobs. In short, they could begin to develop the $100-billion freedom budget advocated by A. Philip Randolph.

Such proposals may seem impractical and even incredible. But what is truly impractical and incredible is that America, with its enormous wealth, has allowed Watts to become what it is and that a commission empowered to study this explosive situation should come up with answers that boil down to voluntary actions by business and labor, new public-relations campaigns for municipal agencies, and information-gathering for housing, fair-employment, and welfare departments. The Watts manifesto is a response to realities that the McCone Report is barely beginning to grasp. Like the liberal consensus which it embodies and reflects, the commission's imagination and political intelligence appear paralyzed by the hard facts of Negro deprivation it has unearthed, and it lacks the political will to demand that the vast resources of contemporary America be used to build a genuinely great society that will finally put an end to these deprivations. And what is most impractical and incredible of all is that we may very well continue to teach impoverished, segregated, and ignored Negroes that the only way they can get the ear of America is to rise up in violence.

Note: This article was written previous to the March, 1966 disturbances in Watts.

30

Segregation Blights Our Schools

JOHN W. CAUGHEY

> *One of the shocks of the post-1954 racial scene for many liberals has been the truly massive resistance of the supposedly non-prejudiced North and West to any significant integration in cities with large numbers of ghetto residents. The author of this exposé is the doyen of California historians and a noted civil libertarian who placed his own academic career on the line during the famous "loyalty oath" controversy in the University of California. Until his recent retirement, he taught and made California history at UCLA.*

LOS Angeles never intended to segregate its schools. At least, it never put up apartheid signs: "This School for Whites," "This School for Colored." Nor has it experienced the disgrace of federal marshals or troops sent to escort Negro pupils to their rightful place in integrated schools. But today the appalling reality is that Los Angeles has segregated schools.

Approximately half its Mexican-American pupils are assigned to schools that are predominantly Mexican-American. And the great majority of its Negro pupils, five sixths or more, are in schools that are black, ghetto black, with no more than a token number of students of the white majority.

These assertions are not guesswork. They are based on official figures, released last December 20 by the office of the Los Angeles Superintendent of Schools in a 104-page report, *Racial and Ethnic Survey: Los Angeles, 1966*, at one dollar a bargain. It is based on a visual census taken simply by looking at faces and surnames. Wordless though it is, this tabulation is compelling reading, a revelation on the separateness that exists in our schools.

The minorities noted are not the ones that would have been chosen in earlier Los Angeles. There are no figures on Irish-Americans, Italian-Americans, or immigrant-born. Once upon a time the first concern would have been to count the Chinese, and a bit later to count the Japanese. Today's categories, in ascending order of magnitude, are: American

SOURCE: John W. Caughey, *Segregation Blights Our Schools* (Los Angeles: Quail Books, 1967), pp. 5-20. Reprinted by permission of author.

Indians, Orientals, Mexican Americans (here registered as Spanish-surname), and Negroes. Another column reporting on the majority has the curious heading "Other Whites," meaning other than Spanish-surname whites. In most discussions it will be far simpler to refer to this classification as the white majority or the whites.

Reporting on teachers, administrators, and school employees as well as pupils, this census spells it out to the first decimal point that all minorities are less than proportionately represented in teaching and administration, the Oriental Americans slightly, the Negroes badly, and the Mexican Americans outrageously.

Indians in the Los Angeles school system number only about one in a thousand and are broadly distributed. The census does not suggest a

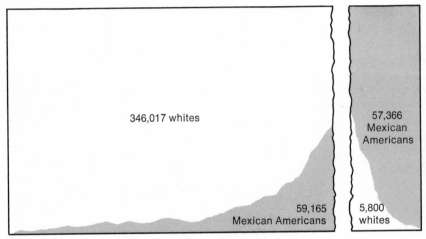

486 Schools with more whites than Mexican Americans   66 Schools with
                                                                    more than 50%
                                                                    Mexican Americans

FIGURE 30–1. Ratio of Pupils, White and Mexican-American
Los Angeles Schools, Elementary through High School

segregation problem. Although three schools are predominantly Oriental, by far the greater number of this 3.5 per cent of the district enrollment is spread out in many schools. In the light of earlier race prejudice, it is a sign of progress that this census found one column sufficient for tabulating Japanese, Chinese, and Koreans.

Se Habla Español

The census makes clear that the Spanish-surname contingent, 19.2 per cent of the total, has phenomenal dispersal in the system, exceeding even that of the "other whites." One reason is that they have been here since the Year One—1781—when Spain established the Pueblo of Nuestra Señora La Reina de Los Angeles de Porciúncula. The "other whites" did not show up until forty years later and not until the time of the Civil War did they become the majority. The wide distribution demonstrates that members of the Spanish-surname classification are penetrating Greater Los Angeles and the majority. Nevertheless, approximately half of the Mexican-American pupils are concentrated in 5 high schools, 6 junior high schools, and 55 elementary schools, in which they account for more than 50 per cent of the enrollment.

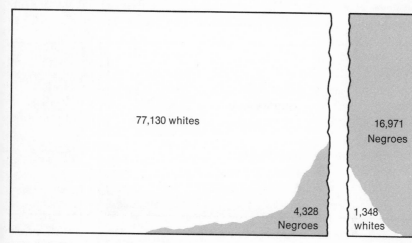

77,130 whites

16,971
Negroes

4,328
Negroes

1,348
whites

45 Schools with more whites than Negroes

8 Schools with
more Negroes
than whites

FIGURE 30–2. Ratio of Pupils, White and Negro
Los Angeles Senior High Schools

That means that for any Mexican-American youngster in Los Angeles the chances are about one in two that he will find himself in a school that has the built-in handicap of being a minority school, predominantly Mexican-American. The likelihood is considerably greater that a youngster who starts in such an elementary school goes on to a Mexican-American junior high school and from there to a Mexican-American high school.

Figure 30-1 shows the ratio of white-majority pupils to Mexican-American (Spanish-surname) pupils in the elementary, junior high, and senior high schools of the Los Angeles Unified District. Reading from left to right across this chart, one moves from school to school, meeting more and more Mexican-American pupils. The break in the graph sets off 66 schools in which more than half of the enrollment is Mexican-American.

In these schools Mexican-Americans outnumber whites on the average about 9 to 1 and ranging up to 35 to 1, a ratio which would work out to not quite one "white" to a classroom.

This graph treats only the relative numbers of white pupils and Mexican American pupils school by school. It should not be read as indicating that all 59,165 Mexican-Americans shown to the left of the divider are in white schools. In point of fact, in some 93 of these schools, the white enrollment in turn is exceeded by Negroes in sufficient numbers to con-

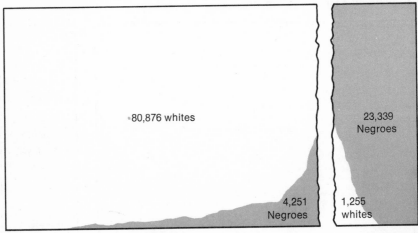

58 Schools with more whites than Negroes   13 Schools with
                                                           more Negroes
                                                           than whites

FIGURE 30–3 Ratio of Pupils, White and Negro
Los Angeles Junior High Schools

stitute a majority. These 93 Negro schools do not stand as one block along the scale of white/Mexican-American ratios. A few would be far to the left, claiming very few Mexican Americans. Others would be well to the right, claiming many Mexican Americans. A conservative estimate would be that another quarter of the grand total of Mexican-American pupils have this experience and, though not in a Mexican-American school, are under the handicap of being in a predominantly minority school.

Ninety-Three Negro Schools

The impact of segregation on Los Angeles' 149,563 Negro pupils is much more severe. The 1966 survey makes it official that 130 of the district schools are lily-white; they have not a single Negro enrolled. It shows many more with only a token presence of Negroes, one per cent or less.

At the other end of the scale are 93 Negro schools, so identified because Negroes are an outright majority in them. Of high school Negroes 4 out of 5 are in such schools; of junior high school Negroes 5 out of 6;

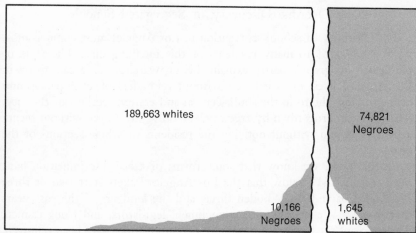

189,663 whites

74,821 Negroes

10,166 Negroes

1,645 whites

356 Schools with more whites than Negroes

72 Schools with more Negroes than whites

FIGURE 30–4. Ratio of Pupils, White and Negro
Los Angeles Elementary Schools

of elementary school Negroes 6 out of 7. And in these schools the Negro-to-white ratios run exceedingly high. In the Negro high schools Negroes outnumber whites 13 to 1, in junior highs 18 to 1, and in elementary schools 44 to 1. The tokenism of "integration" is on that order.

Again that does not mean that all the rest of the Negro students, approximately one sixth, are in predominantly white schools. Many, in fact, are in schools in which another minority accounts for more than half the enrollment.

Figures 30-2, 30-3, and 30-4, based on the official data in the 1966 survey, are similarly constructed to show the ratio of white to Negro pupils in high schools, junior highs, and elementary schools. Here too the torn-off right hand part of each chart shows the ratio in schools which have an actual Negro majority of pupils, not just a preponderance of Negroes over whites.

Reading each of these charts from left to right, one passes through a number of schools without encountering a single Negro pupil. Then come others with a token presence of Negroes, and by the time a school is reached with what would be the evened-out average, 20.8 per cent of the total student body, it is almost time to jump the divider and visit the schools in which Negroes outnumber whites and all other pupils enrolled.

The Long Overdue Discovery of Segregated Schools

The enormity of school segregation in Los Angeles must come as most unexpected news to many residents of this far-flung city. The facts of our urban geography partly explain this unawareness. Life can go on in Los Angeles West or Northwest without reminders of an impacted and ever-growing ghetto in the south-central and eastern sections of the city. Also, one can cross town by freeway, the only way to go, without seeing a pedestrian and without noticing the residents of whole sections of the city.

Furthermore, we know that some forms of racial discrimination have been reduced. We know that the Los Angeles Lakers start two or three Negroes, Coach John Wooden three, and the Dodgers of the past years three to six. We have Negro councilmen, legislators, and Congressmen. The worst of the barriers as to public accommodations have been removed. Doors have opened in the professions, in business, and at most job levels.

Great strides have also been made toward open housing. Culminating a drive spearheaded by Los Angeles attorney (now judge) Loren Miller, the Supreme Court struck down restrictive covenants. State and local actions forbid outright discrimination in sales and leases. The posture of the law thus is favorable.

The actuality is less favorable, because property ownership is mostly private, neighborhood pressures often are adverse, and few real estate men have seen it to their advantage to act aggressively. Some Negroes have moved into new neighborhoods. Statistically they are overshadowed by the Negro population that has piled up in Watts and vicinity.

On several occasions, the issue of equal access to housing has had the full glare of publicity. It was not as much in the open as it should have been, some fifteen years ago, when Los Angeles had its referendum on cancelling its application for federal aid in building a dozen or more slum-clearing or slum-avoiding housing projects. With the loudest arguments directed against the alleged iniquity of federal aid, the voters turned down these developments. In consequence, public housing did not rise at nine or ten of the proposed sites—one of them Chavez Ravine—housing that would have been open without racial discrimination. The state's Rumford Act clearly intends non-discriminatory housing. The real-estate-agent-supported initiative of a couple of years ago was recognized by the voters as having the contrary purpose, and on exactly that ground was set aside by the State Supreme Court.

The question of segregated public schools has not had similar airing before the voters of Los Angeles. That is all the more odd since the schools, unlike most housing, are not private but public. The "my home is my castle" argument does not enter in. The issue is merely how to carry on a function already accepted as a responsibility of state and local government.

Thirteen years ago the Supreme Court sounded an alert in its landmark decision condemning the racially segregated school. Such a school, it said, is inevitably inferior and in violation of guarantees to every American set forth in the Fourteenth Amendment.

The people of Los Angeles, along with those of most of the West and North, saw this decision as purely a rebuke to the Jim Crow practices of the Old South. The cluster of cases on which the court was ruling came from states where separate schools for whites and Negroes were specified by law. The findings of the Court were not so limited, but the impression was possible that the applicability was only to segregation imposed by law.

Unfortunately, the Court tempered its order to desegregate by adding the phrase "with all deliberate speed." Much of the South seized on this loophole and has dragged along at snail's pace or slower in bringing about actual desegregation. As of this writing, the Supreme Court, by upholding an order for immediate action in Louisiana, seems to have discarded the option to delay. Southern California, it is true, has had its share of the Impeach-Earl-Warren fringe, but most local residents, along with most Americans, have looked on the southern recalcitrance against school integration as a national disgrace.

Perhaps equally important, the fact of local school segregation was obscured by a policy of the local schools. The Board operated by rule of color-blindness. It is indeed a proper goal that we reach the plane where a pupil is a pupil, a teacher a teacher, and never shall intrude an adjective such as white or Negro or Mexican-American. But the Board policy also amounted to a see-no-segregation, hear-no-segregation, speak-no-segregation routine which hid the existence of this defect and shut off most efforts to get rid of it. The stance of color-blindness even kept the Board from having full realization of the problem.

Thus as recently as 1962, eight years after *Brown v. Board of Education*, when ACLU, NAACP, and CORE called on the school authorities to face up to school segregation, Board members took the position that the segregated school was news to them. They maintained that they were presiding over a system which accepted students as they came, by neighborhood, attendance area by area throughout the district.

Color-blindness also meant no official records alluding to race or ethnic backgrounds. For another five years every complaint against segregation was dulled by the lack of figures that the Board would accept as reliable on its existence or location. Time and again the Board refused to permit any such stock taking. Only when required to do so by mandate of the State Board of Education did it gather, compile school by school, and release these vital statistics.

In June, 1962, under pressure from concerned groups, the Board set up a special committee to study, as they phrased it, "equal educational opportunity." Throughout the next school year this committee deliberated. At open meetings interested citizens had opportunity to make suggestions. The next May, though one Board member declaimed against "social engineering," the Board affirmed that "equal educational opportunity is best achieved in schools which provide pupils an opportunity for interaction with persons of different cultures and ethnic backgrounds." That was as close as the Board came to endorsing integration. Toward achieving that goal, the Board did acknowledge a responsibility to act positively.

For the better part of another year the Board debated recommendations rising out of this committee study. The specific steps proposed were hardly more than palliative and led to little effective implementing of the announced policy.

Meanwhile, atrocities in Alabama and Mississippi and an eloquent appeal by Martin Luther King galvanized the Negroes of Los Angeles. Under the banner of the United Civil Rights Council, they demanded fair employment, fair housing, and fair police treatment, and they called on the city schools for rapid action on several points. To make these demands register, the UCRC and some of its associated organizations staged marches, sit-ins, study-ins, sleep-ins, and a hunger strike, besides stepping up the pressure through appearances before the Board.

The story of this two-phase drive for integrating the Los Angeles schools is told in a small book, *School Segregation on Our Doorstep*, by John and LaRee Caughey, published last October by Quail Books.

Discussion was handicapped by the Board's ability to push aside any allegation of segregation as not reliably authenticated statistically.

How To Integrate

School Segregation on Our Doorstep recites a long array of specific actions urged on the Board as tested methods of moving from segregated to integrated schools. Among them is the Princeton plan of pairing a Negro school and a white school. With one graded K-3 and the other 4-6, instant integration is achieved. Another is to build a school park, a community campus for everything from kindergarten through high school. Such a combine offers economies and a bonus in usefulness to the community. It also can be as integrated as the total population it serves. Many school systems have closed certain ghetto schools and diverted the pupils elsewhere. Transporting pupils outward from the ghetto is usually an initial necessity. Often it has been possible to make transportation for the relief of over-enrollment serve the added purpose of relieving segregation.

In the use of these and other tested methods, Berkeley, Sacramento, Riverside, and some other California cities have set excellent examples. Repeatedly, these and other instances of school systems making ingenious and determined onslaughts on segregation have been called to the attention of the Los Angeles school authorities.

Although the Board had committed itself to work for "equal educational opportunity," a majority could seldom be mustered for action to produce classroom integration. A couple of attendance area boundaries were moved. One small appropriation was made for transporting pupils from overcrowded Negro schools to underpopulated white schools. This appropriation was not renewed. The Board never paired any schools on the Princeton plan. It developed no educational park. It closed no ghetto school in order to induct its pupils into a multiracial America. Until compelled by the mandate of the State Board of Education, the Los Angeles Board adamantly refused to make a racial census. Furthermore, no general program of integrating was ever proposed by the Superintendent or considered by the Board. Mrs. Mary Tinglof Smith and her successor as Board member, Rev. James E. Jones, urged steps that would have been far reaching, but the Board majority again and again showed itself at peace with the status quo as to distribution of racial and ethnic components in the school enrollments.

The Board, in contrast, showed great generosity in providing remedial programs and compensatory education in the underprivileged areas. Board members were mindful that the "disadvantaged" and the "low achievers" who would be touched by these programs were mostly Negroes and Mexican Americans. With the exception of one member, Mr. Charles Smoot, who as a matter of conviction objects to federal aid in any shape, the Board majority showed itself especially enthusiastic about remedial programs when federally funded. An accountant might find that these programs yielded a financial profit to the Los Angeles schools. Under efficient management, the overhead on contract research often provides a useful surplus to a university. But that is not to impugn the genuineness of the Board's approval of extra education support to disadvantaged youngsters. For these programs it appropriated from local revenues as well as federal.

The essence of remedial programs, however, is to operate in the segregated schools. The intent is to take the schools that are separate and therefore less than equal and try to make them equal but still separate, an intent that goes contrary to the Supreme Court finding of 1954. Such remedial programs operate on the fallacy that with better bootstraps the segregated schools can pull themselves up.

Some excuse might be made for the Board's eight-year disregard of the landmark decision outlawing the segregated school. Since 1962, however, local clamor and nationwide comment have made it clearly and generally known that there is a northern and western counterpart to the school segregation practiced in the Old South. The jargon for it is "de facto segregation," which in translation means actual segregation or segregation in fact. To a child in Watts, trapped in the black ghetto of Los Angeles and consigned to a Negro school, the segregation is just as real, just as tragic, as was Linda Brown's, whose plea was heard by the Supreme Court in 1954.

Separate but Unequal

School Segregation on Our Doorstep reports five years of earnest but almost completely frustrated efforts to stir action toward desegregating the Los Angeles Schools.

Racial and Ethnic Survey: Los Angeles, 1966 nails down the fact that Los Angeles has segregated schools. The information there tabulated identifies the Negro schools, the Mexican-American schools, the Oriental-American schools, and the others in which combined minority enrollments add up to more than half of the total.

With that quantitative information in hand it should be easy for the school staff with its access to other school records to check out the relationship to qualitative factors such as these:

Do the Negro or other minority schools have more than their relative share of half-day sessions? Prima facie evidence indicates that they do operate under this handicap.

Do the minority schools have less than their relative share of cafeterias in operation? Prima facie evidence indicates that they do.

Do the minority schools have more or less than their relative share of bus transportation provided?

Do the minority schools have less than the relative fraction of fully accredited and experienced teachers? Here again prima facie evidence indicates that they have this handicap.

Do they have more than the relative number of dropouts? That is the universal testimony.

Do they have less than the average number of their graduates making good in college? Unquestionably that is the case.

Common knowledge suggests that the segregated schools of the ghetto are disadvantaged in many other such particulars.

Findings of the Civil Rights Commission

A still more recent official publication, released on February 20, 1967, demolishes any lingering rationalized justification of the segregated school. It is a two-volume report, *Racial Isolation in the Public Schools,* issued by the United States Civil Rights Commission and based on a recent formidable research study headed by Professor James Coleman of Johns Hopkins University. This report is available from the Government Printing Office in Washington at a dollar a volume.

Racial Isolation in the Public Schools confirms that the segregated school is a nationwide problem at its most impacted worse in the largest cities. With 20.8 per cent Negro enrollment, Los Angeles is much lower on the scale than Washington, New York, Chicago, Detroit, and many others. But from that start, its degree of confining Negro pupils in Negro schools is startlingly high.

The Civil Rights Commission report endorses as tested and validated the definition of a segregated school as one in which more than 50 per cent of the pupils are of a minority.

The report brings proof that compensatory programs in segregated schools are not likely to yield more than temporary and illusory benefit.

It reveals that supplementary centers, such as Los Angeles proposes in its Mid-City project, draw students only on an intermittent basis and provide little experience in a desegregated setting.

It finds that magnet schools leave the other schools relatively unaffected.

It substantiates the Supreme Court finding of 1954 that the racially separate school is "inherently less than equal." "Negro children," the 1967 report concludes, "suffer serious harm when their education takes place in public schools which are racially segregated, *whatever the source of such segregation may be.*" (Emphasis on the last clause of that sentence is added.)

Laying the old bogey that education deteriorates when minority students enter an all-white school, the report affirms that "in most cases . . . advantaged children have not suffered from educational exposure to others not as well off, and that the results have been of benefit to all children, white and Negro alike."

The Commission sees a role for the federal government to encourage and support school integration along with the constitutional obligation to require it. The Commission recognizes opportunity for local school districts to proceed with integration. It points to the states as best positioned for effective action. Significantly, California is one of the states mentioned as benefiting already from state leadership.

In conclusion the Commission calls for stepped-up action to remove present racial imbalances in our public schools, thereby eliminating the dire effects of racial isolation and providing real equality of educational opportunity. The summons to California and Los Angeles to take action to integrate comes as an imperative. In the words of the Commission, let integration be less "deliberate" and with more "speed."

Superintendent Neil Sullivan of the Berkeley schools is emphatic that education "cannot long flourish in 'separate but equal' schools." Of the Coleman researches and the Civil Rights Commission report he says, "they document with hard evidence from across the country the fact that the needed unique excellence in education cannot be attained short of racial integration of the public schools." And he continues, "if this means educational parks or centers, district reorganization across city-suburb lines as well as intra-district, or temporary busing on a grand scale, so be it. If this sounds the deathknell of the 'neighborhood school,' so be it."

The Case for Busing

However many other methods are used to bring about integration—school pairing, school clusters, school parks, magnet schools, non-graded schools, and so on—transportation of pupils is certain to be at least an initial necessity. In that transportation the emphasis clearly should be on transportation of minority pupils outward from the crowded ghetto. Since the objective is schools each having whites in the majority, arithmetic points to this kind of busing as the simpler logistics.

Los Angeles has features that favor such a program. Its residents are mobile by habit. Their business, social, and other attachments are to something larger than the tiny attendance area of the neighborhood school. The school district owns more busses than the city's bus lines. And, greatest of good fortune, our freeway architects rayed the freeways out in all directions from the ghetto. The pattern of traffic flow also is so ordered that our freeways can carry a reverse flow at the rush hours. That is exactly what the transporting of pupils from the ghetto would be, outbound in the morning and inbound in the afternoon.

One heroic step would be to relieve the eight segregated Negro high schools and the thirteen segregated junior highs of some 8,000 and 12,000 pupils. School pairings and park development might take care of some of these shifts. Even if all are to go by bus, that is a matter of moving less than 3 per cent of the 719,325 pupils in the district. On other missions unrelated to integration, it appears that more than that many school children are being bussed now.

Similar attack on the seventy-two segregated Negro elementary schools may be even more advisable educationally. The numbers are larger and the children are smaller. The problem is more difficult, but not impossible of progressive solution.

The Los Angeles schools do not lack much of being token integrated. With its lily-white schools down to 130 and its 100 per cent Negro schools down to 6 or 8, Los Angeles could go the rest of the way to completing token integration by transporting 130 Negro pupils outward and 6 or 8 white pupils into the ghetto. But the system lacks a great deal of being truly integrated.

To test that proposition, perhaps we should ask a hypothetical question. Suppose California were to elect a reactionary governor. Suppose the Birch Society were to carry through on that promise to impeach Earl Warren. Suppose the courts were to reverse the federal and state school desegregation decisions, *Brown v. Board of Education* and *Jackson v. Pasadena*. What would have to be done to make Los Angeles' schools completely segregated?

A single bus could haul away all the white students in Fremont, Jefferson, Jordan, Manual, and Riis high schools. One shuttle on the soon-to-be constructed Century City underground would just about clear the white students from the other three ghetto high schools. From the Negro junior highs there would be fewer white pupils to send away and from the Negro elementary schools only 1,645.

Gathering in the Negroes from the outer four hundred-odd white schools would be a task of somewhat larger dimensions, but for all thirteen grades it would involve about 3 per cent of the district enrollment. That, it will be recalled, was about the number of pupil moves needed to integrate just the senior and junior high schools. Based on the official figures released by the Los Angeles school authorities, it thus appears that our schools stand much closer to the wish of the segregationists than to the hopes of the integrationists.

Racial and Ethnic Survey, 1966, I hasten to add, does not advocate the atrocity of resegregation. It does not advocate anything. Its intricate columns merely make clear where the schools are. Next year's *Racial and Ethnic Survey* will show whether we are moving ahead into the Twentieth Century or further back into Jim Crow.

31

Prejudice Toward Mexican and Negro Americans: A Comparison

ALPHONSO PINKNEY

Segregation and racism have, in California at least, many faces. Not nearly enough investigation has yet been made of the comparative aspects of segregation as they affect different ethnic groups. One of the few who has done so is Alphonso Pinkney, a black sociologist who teaches at Hunter College of the City University of New York.

THE presence of numerous racial and cultural minorities in the United States has stimulated much empirical research, which has subsequently led to many well-established generalizations in sociology. However, the presence of one minority—Mexican Americans—has led to little or no quantitative research, either in terms of its attitudes toward the dominant group or the attitudes of members of the dominant group toward it. Carey McWilliams has said:

No effort whatever has been made, on a national scale, to assist these immigrants in their adjustment to a radically different environment. Culturally, racially, linguistically, Mexican immigrants are sharply set apart from the general population. Instead of assisting in a process of gradual acculturation, we have abandoned the people to chance and circumstance.

In terms of research, sociologists, like others, have virtually forgotten about the Mexican Americans in our midst.

The largest of America's racial minorities—the Negro—on the other hand, frequently has been the subject of investigation, both in terms of his attitudes and of the attitudes of others toward him. The aim of this paper is to compare the attitudes of native white Americans, in one city, toward Mexican and Negro Americans, in an attempt to determine if there are differences in extent and nature of prejudice expressed toward the members of these two social categories.

The city in which these data were collected had an approximate popu-

SOURCE: Alphonso Pinkney, "Prejudice Toward Mexican and Negro Americans: A Comparison," *PHYLON*, 24 (Winter 1963), pp. 253–259. Reprinted by permission of *Phylon*.

lation of 100,000 in 1952, the year the survey was made. Located in the West, it had a wide diversity of racial and cultural minorities; present in the population were Chinese, Filipino, Japanese, Jewish, Mexican, and Negro Americans. The two largest minorities were Mexican and Negro Americans, both of which accounted for roughly 8 percent of the population during the greater part of the year. The Mexican Americans were employed mainly as unskilled laborers in agriculture and the oil industry, usually working only with other Mexican Americans. Few of them held either skilled or professional jobs, and as a community they lived in segregated areas, either by themselves or in areas which they shared with Negroes. In education, while they attended schools with non-Mexicans, one school was reserved for Mexican American grade school pupils.

The Negro residents of this community were mainly recent arrivals from the South, and their general situation was similar to that of the Mexican Americans, with minor exceptions. They were mainly working class, and employment in this category was relegated mainly to the cotton industry and other low-status occupations. While Negro skilled and professional workers were rare, there were more Negro Americans in these types of jobs than Mexican Americans. Like the Mexican Americans, most of the Negro grade school pupils attended one all-Negro school.

Both Negro and Mexican Americans were relegated to the lowest possible status in the community. But the status of Mexican Americans was somewhat more rigid, since, because of the language barrier, they were relegated to a caste-like position in the occupational structure. This study was accomplished before the advent of state laws barring discrimination in places of public accommodation and employment, and such practices were widespread in the city.

These data were collected by means of interview schedules with a random sample of 319 native white American adults. A wide range of data was collected, but in this paper concern will be focused mainly on (1) the responses of members of the dominant group to what may be called attitudes toward local policy in regard to the rights of both Negro and Mexican Americans, and (2) attitudes toward rights in general for individuals in these two social categories. Judging from the responses, these sets of questions appear to be valid indicators of prejudice. This is further indicated by a comparison of these replies to other indicators of this attitude.

The items concerned with local policy regard attitudes toward both Negro and Mexican Americans: (1) living in integrated neighborhoods, (2) joining integrated social clubs, (3) using unsegregated barber and beauty shops, (4) staying in local hotels, (5) being served in local restaurants, and (6) being hired as clerks in local department stores. The questions were asked in regard to the local situation, *i.e.*, the community in which they lived.

In the category of general rights, each of the 319 respondents was asked four questions about the approval of rights for individuals in these two minorities with regard to: (1) integrated neighborhoods, (2) social mixing, (3) membership in integrated organizations, and (4) equality in employment. In both cases the respondent was simply asked a straightforward question which required a "yes" or "no" answer, or given a statement to which he was to express either agreement or disagreement.

When the respondents were asked to express opinions in regard to what local policy they approved of insofar as the relations between members of the dominant group and Mexican and Negro Americans were concerned, on the whole they approved of greater integration of Mexican Americans than of Negroes into the life of the community. The order in which they were willing to approve of the policy items for the two social categories of individuals is the same: greatest disapproval of integrated housing, and greatest approval of integration in employment in department stores. However, the difference in proportion approving in each case is striking. For example, twice as many people indicated that they would not object to living in neighborhoods with Mexican Americans as those who said they would consider integrated neighborhoods with Negro Americans acceptable (see Table 31–1). For each of the items the differences in response are significantly more in favor of integration with Mexican than with Negro Americans. The range of difference is from 22 percent on the question of integrated neighborhoods to 28 percent on the question of service in local restaurants.

These differences in attitudes may be attributed, in part, to the general feeling among Americans that race is a function of skin color and that the closer a minority approaches the dominant group on this trait, the more acceptable its members. That is, these attitudes may be part of a feeling of racism. That is not to say that Mexican Americans are in any way exempted from this feeling. They are not, but there is greater tolerance of them than of Negro Americans. In his early study of race attitudes, Bogardus found that in terms of social distance, both Negro and Mexican Americans were ranked toward the bottom of the list of the forty different social categories used. Mexicans, placing thirty-second, ranked higher than Negroes, who ranked thirty-fifth. Between these two were Japanese and Filipinos, and following them were Turks, Chinese, mulattoes, Koreans, and Hindus, in that order. It is not surprising, then, that in the present study, attitudes toward Mexican Americans are more favorable than attitudes toward Negro Americans. That is to say, this community mirrors the larger society.

TABLE 31-1. PERCENTAGE OF RESPONDENTS EXPRESSING TOLERANCE IN
LOCAL POLICY TOWARD MEXICAN AND NEGRO AMERICANS

	Percentage Approving *		Range of Difference
	Mexicans	Negroes	
I wonder if you would tell me whether you approve of the following for Mexicans and Negroes:			
living in mixed neighborhoods with other Americans (*i.e.*, whites)	45	23	22
joining social clubs with other Americans	48	25	23
using integrated barber and beauty shops	61	34	27
staying in integrated hotels	61	38	23
being served in integrated restaurants	74	46	28
being hired as department store sales clerks	76	52	24

* Those who expressed disapproval and those who refused to answer are omitted. However, in no case did more than 3 percent of the respondents in the sample fail to respond.

The ranking of these items forms a definite hierarchy, *i.e.*, the items form a scale pattern; but there does not seem to be any single principle running through the ordering of the practices as to acceptability. There appears to be no direct relation between acceptability and impersonality, or public character, of the type of activity characterizing the various situations. While it is true that being a member of the same social club may involve a greater possibility of interpersonal relations than being served by a Negro or Mexican American sales clerk in a department store, to have a member of one of these minorities as a neighbor does not necessarily imply interpersonal association.

One possible explanation for the ordering of the items is that they imply to the respondent certain degrees of social equality. That is, it is possible that an individual perceives of residence in the same neighborhood as indicative of greater social equality than being served in the same restaurant, and so on. This may be the case regardless of the degree of physical proximity involved. It is also likely that these situations indicate the degrees of association which members of the dominant group have come to regard as "appropriate" or "normal" for members of minorities. For example, it is entirely possible that if serving members of a minority in restaurants has been taken for granted over the years in a particular location, and staying in hotels has not, the residents would be more likely to approve of the former than the latter. Field observations in this community indicate that there is greater acceptance of Mexican Americans in places of public accommodation than Negro Americans;

hence, greater approval of integration with Mexican Americans as a matter of local policy.

It is true that in the South Negro Americans have been preparing food and serving as nursemaids for families in the dominant group for centuries. Both of these activities involve intimate (although not equal-status) association, yet the same people who permit or even expect this type of association are unwilling to patronize a drive-in restaurant where Negroes are served in the privacy of their automobiles where no association is likely. In the one case the behavior is "appropriate"; in the other it is not.

These two explanations, of course, are not necessarily separate; they may be part of the same pattern. An individual may perceive of the existing local situation as one which has become "appropriate" or "normal" because it protects his position of social superiority.

Many of the residents of this city felt that minorities should be deprived of the rights they themselves enjoy. In each case, as was the situation with the local policy items, the members of the dominant group were willing to accord greater rights to Mexican than to Negro Americans. The range of difference varies from 11 percent on the item concerning social mixing to 22 percent on the item pertaining to membership in the same organizations. That is, in the first case, 11 percent more of the respondents were willing to grant this as a right to Mexican than to Negro Americans, and in the latter case, 22 percent more were willing to grant Mexican Americans this right than Negro Americans.

The order in which members of the dominant group were willing to accord these as rights to individuals in these two social categories is not unlike the ordering of the social policy items. A majority of the respondents felt that both should have the right to equal employment, while few felt that they should have the right to equality in housing (see Table 31–2). Again, in the case of these items, if one knows how many of these rights are acceptable, one can predict with reasonable assurance which they are. A respondent who is willing to grant individuals in these two social categories the right to live in an integrated neighborhood is also likely to approve of social mixing, integration in organizations and integrated employment.

There is a slight difference in the attitudes of individuals in the dominant group toward minority rights in general as against what rights should be granted to minorities as a matter of local policy. There appears to be a greater willingness to grant rights as a matter of local policy than to accept them as something to which minorities might be entitled on a national scale. To take the case of integrated neighborhoods, 45 percent of the respondents said they would approve of this as local policy for Mexican Americans, but only 36 percent felt they should have this

TABLE 31-2. PERCENTAGE OF RESPONDENTS EXPRESSING APPROVAL OF
EQUAL RIGHTS FOR MEXICAN AND NEGRO AMERICANS

	Percentage Approving *		Range of Difference
	Mexicans	Negroes	
Should Mexicans and Negroes have the right to:			
live with other Americans	36	22	14
mix socially with other Americans	46	52	21
join the same organizations as other Americans	53	31	22
work side-by-side on the same jobs as other Americans	83	66	17

* Negative responses and instances where individuals refused to respond are not included. In no case did the latter exceed 4 percent.

as a general right. There are slight differences on other comparable items, but these are not as great. Apparently these people feel that to put these questions in terms of rights is to accord to these minorities more than they are entitled to expect and that social and economic equality for minorities is more a privilege than a right.

The difference in degree of prejudice expressed toward Negro and Mexican Americans is, in part, a function of the nature of the two communities. In this city Mexican Americans as a community were less well-organized than the Negro Americans, and there was less pressure from the former for equal rights than from the latter. For example, the respondents were asked: "As you see it, are Negro Americans today demanding more than they have a right to or not?" One-third of them thought they were, while only 9 percent responded similarly regarding Mexican Americans when asked the same question about them. Greater pressure for equality on the part of Negro Americans, then, may have resulted in greater antipathy toward them. The greater prejudice toward Negro Americans is also probably partially a result of economic competition. In this community both Negro and Mexican Americans are engaged principally in unskilled occupations; however, Mexican Americans generally are limited to occupations with other Mexican Americans, while Negro Americans tend to compete with unskilled members of the dominant group for work. Hence the latter may be more likely to perceive of Negro Americans as greater economic threats than Mexican Americans. The caste-like occupational status of Mexican Americans in the labor force in this community is characteristic of the status of Mexican Americans in other cities in the United States.

In the United States as a whole the Mexican American community has been without leadership and without organized political action groups. This is due partially to their lack of intergenerational social mobility. First and second generation Mexican Americans alike engage in the same low-status occupations. In general, they have been relegated to the lowest paid jobs in agriculture and industry. Many of them are seasonal agricultural workers. In this city alone, an additional 2,000 appear during the peak crop season. The long-time residents of Mexican descent are often resentful of their migratory fellow-countrymen and endeavor to have the members of the dominant community perceive of them as "different." Finally, the Mexican American community is made up to a large extent of people who speak only Spanish. Rarely does the highly literate, English-speaking Mexican immigrate to the United States.

The pattern of prejudice toward Negro and Mexican Americans in this community is essentially the same. The differences which exist are in the degree to which the respondents expressed prejudice toward these two minorities. In this regard the differences are often great. Insofar as attitudes are concerned then, there is considerably less prejudice expressed toward Mexican than toward Negro Americans. In addition to the series of responses discussed above, the respondents were asked the rather direct question: "On the whole would you say you like or dislike Mexican people?" They were then asked the same question about Negroes. The first question elicited a "dislike" reply from only 6 percent of the respondents while the latter drew this response from 21 percent. These responses are not unlike those to the two sets of questions concerning local policy and rights insofar as the differences in attitudes toward these two minorities are concerned. Nevertheless, the status of the two minorities in practice is not significantly different. While it must be admitted that attitudes and behavior are not always correlated, it seems likely that in this community the possibility for improving the status of Mexican Americans is greater than for Negro Americans. While the former have language as an additional major barrier, they have potentially fewer handicaps than the latter.

PART V
The Future of California:
Progress or Repression?

> The deepening racial division is not inevitable. The
> movement apart can be reversed. Choice is still
> possible. Our principal task is to define that choice
> and to press for a national resolution.
>
> *Report of the National Advisory Commission
> on Civil Disorders* (Kerner Commission, 1968)

> I am not a very nice person, I confess. . . . I don't
> believe in mercy or forgiveness or restraint. . . .
> They've created in me one irate, resentful nigger—
> and it's building—to what climax?
>
> George Jackson, in a letter to Angela Davis
> (1970)

As we have seen, racial conflict has played an important role in
California's past and is a major element in California's present. National developments—the civil rights movement of the 1950s and
early-1960s, the Supreme Court's epoch-making 1954 decision in
Brown v. Board of Education, the urban violence of the middle and
late 1960s, the well-intentioned but largely impotent antipoverty
crusade of the Kennedy-Johnson administrations, the war in Southeast Asia and the campus reactions to that war—have all had their
effect on the racial conflict in California. And in many ways this
conflict has affected national patterns. In times past, California racism
with its special targets has been a local or regional manifestation of
a national phenomenon; today the problems of California are the
problems of the nation, with regional phenomena taking a secondary
role. It is not mere chance, we believe, that three of the most significant manifestations of the new mood of America's oppressed minorities in the decade of the 1960s—the Watts riot, the rise of the Black
Panther Party, and the occupation of Alcatraz—all occurred or began
in the Golden State. And, as the 1970s began, the ethnic struggle
seemed to be moving into a new and unprecedented arena—the nation's prisons. In more and more prisons—often situated in and staffed

from white rural areas—white guards confront largely urban black prison populations, as the ethnic tensions of society become even more exacerbated in close confinement. Struggles that first came to prominence in California's prisons—Soledad and San Quentin—soon spread to the penal institutions in other states, most notably Attica in upstate New York, where a prison revolt in September, 1971, resulted in a blood bath when National Guard and state police bullets killed more than 40 prisoners and their guard hostages. California, just a century ago a frontier backwater, has become the pacesetter for the nation, not merely in size but in politics and cultural styles as well.

This being so, any analysis of California's racial and ethnic problems in the immediate future becomes, in essence, a national analysis. There are, of course, intrinsic differences between Harlem and Watts, between Columbia and Berkeley, between Attica and San Quentin, between Governor Rockefeller and Governor Reagan. But the similarities, in these instances and elsewhere, are surely more important than the differences.

32

Conclusion: The Ethnic Crisis of Our Time

ROGER DANIELS and HARRY KITANO

> *Our final selection, written as the decade of the 1960's closed, is the joint effort of a historian and a social psychologist based on their study of the California past. If their conclusions are essentially pessimistic—and, in the final analysis, pessimism about the future is the ultimate form of subversion in liberal America —that pessimism is more firmly rooted in the past practices of America (and California) than are the traditional platitudes about "life, liberty, and the pursuit of happiness" and the "melting pot."*

ACCORDING to Ambrose Bierce's *Devil's Dictionary*, "only God can fortell the future, but only an Historian can distort the past." Recognizing the inevitability of Bierce's definition, we hope that our distortion has been minimal. At the same time, without any claim to clairvoyance, we do think that our examination of the past does provide some clues about the shape of the future, some indication of the general direction of events.

Although contemporary observers are notoriously inaccurate in their assessment of events, it is worth noting that in the late 1960s many, if not most, of the wisest commentators on race relations in the United States saw new dangers: for many of these the greatest danger seemed to be that America was drifting or splitting into two societies. Our analysis—and our perhaps too optimistic preconceptions—leads to opposite conclusions. There have been two societies in the past. No one who thinks for even a moment about the California Indians, the Chinese, the Japanese, the Mexican Americans, and the Negroes can really believe that any of these minorities were truly integrated into our society. They were, each in their own way, separate and unequal groups, existing below and apart from the general cultural level, and only tangentially coming into contact with the majority society.

If this has been true throughout our past, what then is the nature of

SOURCE: Roger Daniels and Harry Kitano, *American Racism: Exploration of the Nature of Prejudice* (Englewood Cliffs, N.J.: Prentice-Hall, Inc., 1970), pp. 117–130. Copyright © 1970. Reprinted by permission of Prentice-Hall, Inc., Englewood Cliffs, New Jersey.

what we call the ethnic crisis of our time? That crisis consists, we think, of simply this: for the first time in our history almost all of the submerged groups in our country—groups that Gunnar Myrdal styles the "underclass"—are demanding entrance into the major institutions of our society. And, in addition, they are demanding admission on their own terms. They come often not as humble petitioners seeking boons, but as free Americans demanding what they regard as their stolen birthright. Sometimes they even ask for compound interest to cover past injustices.

It is this new militance, this rejection of the gradual Americanization process that seemed to work so well for earlier ethnic minorities—the Germans and the Irish of the mid-nineteenth century, the Italians, Greeks, Slavs, and East European Jews of the "new immigration" of the late nineteenth and early twentieth centuries—that has provoked the current crisis. And although the long range causes of the current crisis are many, the conclusion is almost inescapable that the root cause was the pervasive nature of American racism—a racism which, although it grew less and less oppressive as the twentieth century wore on, consistently refused admission into full membership in society to the vast majority of colored Americans.

We feel then that the commentators—for example the National Advisory Commission on Civil Disorders—mistake the true nature of the crisis. Since we have never had one society in this country, the danger of social mitosis does not really exist. The visible and often violent and ugly racial and ethnic clashes do not represent new fracture lines in a previously unitary society, but represent rather the friction resulting from the attempts of these groups to enter into full membership in American society. We will later attempt to assess the chances for success of this massive breakthrough attempt, but first it will be in order to note briefly the critical areas of struggle and see how the form that these struggles take differs from that waged by earlier ethnic groups.

The three areas of conflict are education, jobs, and housing, and it is clear that, by the standards of the past, significant progress is being made in each of them, particularly the first two. But it is one of the landmarks of the present crisis that gradual progress, however significant, is no longer acceptable to the militant spokesmen for minority groups, and the mere existence of these militants tends to force even the most accommodating minority spokesman into more radical postures. The causes of this new radicalism, this ever-increasing militance, are various, but surely the following must be included among the major factors:

1. The increasing openness of American society to all white persons and to some members of nonwhite communities.
2. The "revolution of rising expectations" among nonwhites.

3. The communications revolution, particularly television, which perhaps more in its commercials than in its program content, makes clear to the poor of the ghettoes just how little they participate in our commodity-oriented society. If this is an accurate observation, it is a wonderfully ironic one. The very aspect of television so despised by radical intellectuals may well have a more profoundly revolutionary effect than a century of agitation!

Having identified the present crisis, it might be well, in the first instance, to examine some of the changes in the ethnic scene in the last quarter century. For no group have these changes been more dramatic than for the Japanese Americans. No sane observer, writing in 1942, the year of the evacuation, would have dared to predict the current high status of the group. Hailed by a leading sociologist as "our model minority," their success story can be symbolized by Senator Daniel Inouye of Hawaii, who was the keynote speaker at the Democratic National Convention in 1968. The same society that raised no significant protest when Japanese Americans were herded behind barbed wire, was willing, just twenty-six years later, to have a member of that community play a key ceremonial role within a basic political institution. The success of Senator Inouye cannot be written off as an isolated example. As previously noted, statistical examination of the socioeconomic position of both Japanese and Chinese in America shows truly remarkable achievement.

But perhaps even more symbolic of the new role of the Oriental Americans was the sudden emergence of the semanticist, S. I. Hayakawa, as a popular culture hero late in 1968. Taking over as Acting President of San Francisco State College during a period of ethnically based student unrest that had brought the school to a standstill, Hayakawa "got tough" with the protesters—largely members of the Black Students' Union—and restored at least a semblance of order with the assistance of large numbers of San Francisco police. No more popular or, at first glance unlikely, exponent of "law and order" could be imagined. Hayakawa, an authentic intellectual (one of the few real scholars to head a California state college as well as the first nonwhite to do so) nevertheless seemed to speak for the WASP middle-class. Without attempting to judge the merits of either the dispute or the disputants at San Francisco State, the alignment of the Oriental college president against the young blacks and the radical students, probably accurately reflects the direction and identification that most Oriental Americans wished to take and establish—with the middle-class white majority and against the disruptive elements beneath.

Many Mexican Americans would like to consider themselves, like many Oriental Americans, as essentially allies of the majority community and, like them, opposed to the disruptive Negro community. But the objective conditions of Mexican-American life—they are distinctly not middle class in terms of either income or education—seriously inhibit such an identification. Although an outside observer like Gunnar Myrdal sees a logical alliance between blacks and Mexican Americans—the two most numerous ethnic minorities in California—there are long-standing animosities between the two groups. Many Mexican Americans resent bitterly what they consider the favored treatment of the Negro poor and their attitudes toward Negroes are often quite similar to those of the economically disadvantaged "Anglo" community. Yet it is also apparent that there is much institutional mimesis of the black community among militant Mexican Americans. They too are pressing for community control of schools and other institutions. But, opposed to the militants, are very strong passive and conservative elements and traditions quite different from those of the blacks. There is thus a decided ambiguity within the community, although the militants seem to be gaining strength. With young and dynamic leadership—one thinks of Caesar Chavez of the Farm Workers and Julian Nava of the Los Angeles School Board—the community may be stirred to consistent mass action; however, the old passive, conservative tradition may continue to hold sway.

To imagine that either the course taken by so many Orientals—identification with the power structure and against disruptive protest—or the passivity of the Mexican Americans could in any way serve as a "model" for the Negro, is to indulge in fantasy. Equally fantastic, and much more prevalent, is what we may call the "immigrant analogy." The analogy runs something like this:

> The Germans, the Irish, the Jews, the Poles, the Orientals, etc. have "made it," why can't the Negroes? These groups came to this country poor, they were discriminated against, and look at them now. The Negroes want everything given to them. Negroes aren't willing to work for success like others have.

The fatuity of this analogy will be obvious to some, but not so obvious to many. Although it is often advanced by those who know better, many who use it do so in ignorant confidence that it is true. The defects in this false analogy are many but the essential flaw is this: the white immigrant can, in a generation or so, fairly successfully merge with the general population if he wishes. In addition, the overt tension between white and nonwhite has tended to blur differences between white ethnic groups, to "promote" all white persons.

But what of the Orientals? Certainly they are nonwhite. Has the two-category system broken down as far as Orientals are concerned? Not really. It has changed, in many ways it has weakened, but it still remains essentially intact. The Orientals are clearly an achieving minority and have, as a group, even surpassed the white majority in terms of educational attainment. But they remain nonwhite, and are still largely segregated in terms of housing, social life, and of course, marriage. Even for the Oriental American—the "whitest" of the nonwhite—a total merging with the majority seems, at the very least, highly improbable in the foreseeable future, although we must here reiterate that no sane observer, writing in 1942, could have predicted the truly amazing increase in social acceptance that has occurred since then.

If this is true for the Orientals, how much more true must it be for other groups and particularly for the Negro, who is, by American criteria, the most nonwhite of all. The increasing recognition by more and more members of the black community of at least the relative permanence of the two-category system (although, of course, they do not call it that) is yet another factor contributing to the current ethnic crisis. The progress made by the Negro in the last quarter century is not as spectacular, on a mass basis, as that of the Oriental group. The educational achievement is still well below that of the general level of the population. Again, using the 1960 census data for California, Negroes are only half as likely to gain admittance to an institution of higher education as a white; Negro income is similarly depressed. Yet, for some individuals, the group that W. E. B. Du Bois once identified as the "talented tenth," there have been truly spectacular advances.

First and foremost, of course, despite the many disappointments inherent in it, was the United States Supreme Court's 9–0 decision in *Brown v. Board of Education* (1954) which outlawed segregation. Whatever failings there have been in its enforcement, and despite its almost total lack of relevance in the urban ghetto situation, it was truly a turning point. Despite local practices, it was important that federal policy, at least, was no longer *officially* racist. The Constitution had finally been brought into line with the Declaration of Independence. One should also note the ending of segregation in the armed forces and in many lines of endeavor—for example, UCLA's Jackie Robinson broke the color barrier in professional baseball, which now seems, like most sports, to be dominated by Negroes.

On the political scene the breakthrough for the Negro elite was almost equally sensational. At the end of 1968 there was a Negro, Thurgood Marshall, on the Supreme Court, and another, Robert C. Weaver, in the cabinet. (Perhaps an even more telling demonstration of this breakthrough came when Richard M. Nixon announced his first cabinet—the initial reaction was that there was not a Negro in it, although only the preceding cabinet had had a Negro.) Impressive electoral victories were scored, North and South. Most impressive, perhaps, was Edward Brooke's capture of a U.S. Senate seat in Massachusetts, specifically because he had no statistically significant Negro vote base, as did almost all the other Negroes who had ever been elected. Of more consequence was the election of Negro mayors in Cleveland, Ohio and Gary, Indiana, and the 385 state and local Negro office holders in the South. In California the contingent of Negro office holders—the first had been state assemblyman Frederic M. Roberts elected from Los Angeles in 1918!—grew with every election. Augustus Hawkins of Los Angeles was one of the state's senior congressmen and state legislators like Willie Brown of San Francisco and Mervyn Dymally of Los Angeles were important figures. In Los Angeles there were three Negro city councilmen, slightly more than the numerical incidence of Negroes in the city population would indicate. In terms of local elective office, in California at least, it can be argued that Negroes have achieved almost their "fair" share of representation. But the illusory nature of that "fairness" was spelled out in no uncertain terms in the Los Angeles mayoralty elections in the spring of 1969.

In the April primary Thomas R. Bradley, one of the city's three black councilmen, led all candidates with some 42 percent of the vote. Since Negroes make up less than 20 percent of the electorate, Bradley had won more white votes than black. The incumbent mayor, Samuel W. Yorty, polled only 26 percent of the vote. By the normal rules of California politics an incumbent rejected by almost three-quarters of the electorate has almost no chance in the runoff, but any election that pits black against white is not normal. As the May 27 runoff approached, incumbent Yorty, who had run on his rather poor eight-year record in the primary, switched to a blatantly racist campaign. Bumper stickers appeared calling for "A Majority Mayor for the Majority of the People" and Yorty himself constantly spoke of Los Angeles as a "city under siege by militants" and referred repeatedly to real and imaginary problems in Gary and Cleveland, cities which had elected black mayors. Although Bradley was far from being a militant and was clearly well-qualified for the office— he possessed a law degree, had been an outstanding councilman for six years and before that a police lieutenant with 21 years on the force— Yorty's fear campaign was successful. In the runoff election he received some 53 percent of the vote to Bradley's 46 percent. The election demonstrated clearly the racist nature of the electorate. Despite disillusionment with Yorty, the real choice of only a quarter of the voters, a majority was willing to continue him (or probably any white man) in office rather than try a black man. Although it is possible to emphasize the positive aspects of Bradley's performance—after all most of his votes did not come from the black community—the election could only serve to heighten the already prevalent mood of disenchantment in the Negro community.

Disenchantment was derived from that part of the American Dream which emphasized total integration. Black Americans were vocally denying that the melting pot—that archtypical American myth—would ever merge black and white. Actually, as ethnic historians like Will Herberg pointed out some time ago, there has been no real melting pot, even for whites. Herberg called attention to what he called a "triple melting pot" in which Catholics, Protestants, and Jews, largely maintained their own identities but tended, after a couple of generations, to pay less attention to ethnic differences within the religion. If the melting pot has actually dissolved so few of the differences between whites, was it reasonable to expect it to blend black into white? Most Negro leaders today, and particularly those of the younger generation, would give a resounding "No" to that question, and we, however reluctantly, are forced to conclude that they are right. The two-category system, in some form or other, is likely to be with us for some time. Negroes, Mexican Americans, and Orientals are probably going to continue to exist as at least partially self-contained and self-conscious communities within our society for generations. Social scientists and others, then, would probably do well to concentrate their efforts on making the two-category system work as well as possible.

When we say this we are neither advocating nor predicting an American version of apartheid, although that remains a distinct, if somewhat remote, possibility. We are not endorsing this as an optimum social system. What we are saying is that our observation and analysis of American ethnic history and practice lead unambiguously to this conclusion.

This being the case, our analysis of certain trends in the black community—a trend toward black nationalism, ethnic pride and, in extreme cases, a black separatism and black racism that is a curious mirror image of white racism—leads us to argue that they are almost inevitable, and that these trends are, in their major emphasis, a manifestation of a keener awareness of social reality than is shown by the more socially acceptable positions of such organizations as the National Association for the Advancement of Colored People. In saying this we are not endorsing such chimeras as an independent Negro republic carved out of U.S. territory, or, on the academic level, some of the more extreme demands of the various Black Student Unions. One author (Daniels) recently participated in an angry meeting with a BSU spokesman who vainly tried to convince a faculty committee that only blacks should teach and lecture on subjects concerning blacks. This kind of racism is neither rational nor viable, but in condemning and rejecting it we should remember that, historically speaking, there is a distinct difference between the origins of white and black racism. The first is an instrument of oppression; the second a response to oppression.

But short of the extreme position—and the electoral performance of Negroes in the 1968 elections suggests that more than 90 percent of voting Negro Americans are well short of it—there remains a decided trend among blacks, in and out of the ghetto, towards community control of those things which most directly affect the community: schools, jobs, and housing.

In no area is the selective nature of black nationalism more clearly demonstrated than in education. In terms of the public school system, kindergarten through high school, black communities throughout the nation are struggling, with various degrees of success, to gain control of the schools in their areas. The tactics will vary from school district to school district depending on the militancy of the blacks and the degree of intransigence of the groups that usually oppose them: the school boards, the teachers and the white community. But from New York to Los Angeles the basic tenor of the demands is essentially the same. Throughout the nation the schools that the majority of urban Negroes attend are all black or predominantly black because they are located in all black or predominantly black neighborhoods. The years since the Supreme Court's decision in 1954 have actually witnessed an intensification of this de facto segregation. As a general rule these segregated schools—for a variety of reasons, not all of them explicitly racist—are distinctly inferior in physical plant, equipment, and in teaching personnel.

Black communities, from coast to coast, are tending to give up the struggle for ethnic balance in the schools and are instead beginning to accept what seems to them the inevitable and at least semi-permanent fact of de facto segregation. Their new demands focus on black control of schools for blacks—black school boards, black principals, more black teachers, and a curriculum more oriented to the realities of ghetto life. This struggle, just beginning, has already involved violence, an interruption of the educational process, and the alienation of some of the white liberal support which the black community has enjoyed in recent years.

On the college and university level, however, the same struggle has taken an entirely different form. Although there have been isolated demands for more Negro colleges and universities in the North, the real thrust of the new militance at the college level has been for the recognition of a black identity within the existing college and university structure. The typical instruments for these demands are the Black Student Unions, almost always self-segregating organizations with alliances connecting them to radical student groups, with the latter becoming more and more white in the process. The typical demands of the BSUs and their allies are for more black students, black professors, and a black or Afro-American studies are within the curriculum. Of these demands, the second seems the hardest to satisfy, simply because, as in other "trade union" situations, few Negroes have the requisite union card, in this case the doctoral degree. The university community is adjusting to these demands with varying degrees of success. Several California universities have set up at least rudimentary courses and programs in black history and culture. In late 1968, in a move almost sure to be emulated elsewhere, Yale University lent its enormous prestige to one aspect of BSU demands by announcing the establishment of an interdisciplinary major in Afro-American studies.

More than any other institution in American society, the higher educational establishment has shown itself willing to adapt at least partially to the new black demands. Crucial to this goal have been a variety of public and private programs aimed at upgrading the educational opportunities for the poor in general, and the disadvantaged ethnic poor in particular. These programs, like the federally financed Head Start for pre-schoolers, Upward Bound for high school students, and such private activities as the Danforth Foundation's Masters Opportunity Program which subsidizes Negro and Mexican-American college graduates in search of an M.A., are all initial steps toward eradicating the educational disadvantage of the ethnic poor which is one of the hallmarks of American racism. These programs so far have involved only a very minor fraction of those who need them and if they are to be more than another token movement, their scope and funding will have to be increased enormously.

In terms of jobs, the same kind of selective black nationalism has asserted itself. There is a growing emphasis on black entrepreneurship in the ghettoes. While no one should underestimate the importance of developing a stronger black entrepreneurial class or what is sometimes called "black capitalism," the basic facts of American economic life severely inhibit the role that can be played by small businessmen, regardless of their color or ethnicity. The business of America, to paraphrase Calvin Coolidge, is corporate business, and the trend toward giantism, toward the conglomerate super corporation is growing more pronounced every year. A major part of the new economic thrust of the blacks, therefore, has been a concentrated attack on the barriers erected by the white-controlled power structures, the corporations and the trade unions. Their weapons have been the anti-discrimination edicts of various branches of government, largely the federal government, and to a lesser degree, economic boycotts (and sometimes physical destruction) of the ghetto branches of white corporations—supermarkets, service stations, and the like.

There is obviously an increased willingness on the part of corporations to hire *qualified* members of disadvantaged ethnic communities at all levels, and, in some cases, to lower or alter certain of their requirements, like the intelligence tests for factory workers, which, by accident or design, are oriented to favor those with a majority cultural background. By the late 1960s, corporate recruiters were actually seeking more Negro college graduates than they could find. Some corporations were beginning to locate plants in or adjacent to the ghettoes. Even in television commercials—not exactly the most enlightened area of American culture —the Negro consumer has suddenly become visible, although there are still such probably unintentional slurs as advertisements for flesh-colored bandages. For the educated ethnic minority, decent jobs are no longer a problem, although the matter of promotion, particularly to positions in which a minority group member could hire and fire whites, is often something else again. On the other hand, according to the *Wall Street Journal*, Negro engineering graduates in 1968 got higher starting salaries than did whites. This was the result of federal insistence that firms with government contracts, particularly defense contracts, show evidence of nondiscriminatory employment at all levels, coupled with a very small crop of Negro engineers. (Demand exceeded supply, so the price went up.)

But for vast numbers of the ethnic unemployed—the drop-outs, the functional illiterates, the unskilled—little real possibility of private employment exists. In an earlier era our industrial labor force could absorb —in good times—almost unlimited numbers of immigrants who often had nothing but brawn to offer. Today our increasingly sophisticated economy needs less "muscle" every year. Thus there are literally millions of healthy Americans for whom no real economic opportunity exists, regardless of their willingness to work. The much heralded training and retraining programs—public and private—have reached an even smaller portion of their potential constituency than have the programs for the educationally disadvantaged. This problem, too, has its roots in the cultural deprivation of past American racist policy. The programs and phenomena described in the preceding sentences will at least inhibit the production of future generations of "unemployables," but even if every youngster of school age in America's ethnic ghettos were assured of an education adequate for today's complex society (a state of affairs not likely to come about soon) unemployables of adult years would be with us for decades. The fact of the matter is that the number, if not the percentage, of such persons is growing with every passing year. There will be no real peace in the ghettoes until every able-bodied person who wants to work is furnished with a job or meaningful access to a training program that will provide him with the means of getting one.

In the field of housing there has been less progress than in the areas of education and employment, partially because no significant sector of the economy is so "privatized," so atomistic, so archaic. Despite a number of government housing programs, dating back to the New Deal, there is in the central city ghettoes more deterioration than construction every year. These central city ghettoes are growing constantly, as a result of migration from the South and Puerto Rico. The militants of the black communities are much more interested now in controlling the ghetto communities and making them better places in which to live than in trying to "break out" into white or partially integrated suburbs. Apart from desire, most ghetto residents lack the means to move. We may assume then, that the ghetto is here to stay. It is also safe to assume that as part of their attempt to gain more control over their own lives, blacks and other ghetto residents will move increasingly towards community organizations, organizations that will stress self-help and attempt to attract public and private financial and technical assistance. In Los Angeles, the Watts' Labor Council, headed by Ted Watkins, is perhaps a prototype of this kind of organization.

But crucial to the future of the ghettos is the one institution of the majority society that has proved to be the least responsive to the plight of the ethnically disadvantaged—the police. No major institution of American life is less amenable to outside control, more contemptuous of "civilian" criticism. No institution of the majority society is more resented by the ghetto dweller. It is clear that if the black community is truly to control its own inner life, it must have some control or influence over the forces that police it. As yet this goal has not been achieved anywhere. Even the election of a Negro mayor in Cleveland has not noticeably lessened—and may possibly have intensified—tensions between the black community and those whom society has deputized to preserve and protect it. The one method for outside control of the police that has been attempted—the civilian review board—has been either blocked or scuttled by vigorous and astute pressure on the part of militant police groups and their allies in the white community. No one who followed the 1968 campaign can doubt the political impact of the linguistically innocuous slogan of "law and order," which became, from some rostrums, a kind of code phrase which really meant keeping the Negro in his place.

This matter of community control—of schools, of jobs, of the police, and all the other institutions which bear directly on the ghetto dweller— is likely to be the crucial issue between black and white America in the foreseeable future. It seems to us that, even within the two-category system which we find in the American past, present, and future, there are distinct possibilities for progress, for amelioration, for social peace. We suspect that this progress, if it comes at all, will come within a modified system rather than by a fracturing of the one which exists. The traditional liberal solutions and slogans—the melting pot and total integration—do not seem to us to be particularly relevant.

It is all too possible, however, that the communal clashes and conflicts which are sure to continue will harden rather than soften the mechanics of the system. It is at least within the realm of the conceivable that the cities of America will be wracked by real communal warfare. Should this occur, it would undoubtedly be accompanied by an intensification of the so-called white backlash in the majority community. It would be foolish to attempt to predict in detail the forms that oppression might take in such an eventuality, but certainly the concentration camps provided for in the McCarran Act of 1950 are a distinct possibility.

It is not likely, however, that a total or nearly total incarceration, like the wartime evacuation of the Japanese Americans, would even be seriously contemplated. On mere logistical grounds alone the site of the black community in the United States—some 25 million people—precludes that. Nor, given the American experience, is a "final solution" likely, although the charge of genocide or attempted genocide falls lightly and often from some black militant lips. One would expect, at the very least, repression, incarceration of militant groups, and perhaps a reinstitution of legal segregation with modifications designed to meet problems arising from the Northern urban environment. There would certainly be those who would look to South Africa for institutional solutions.

This gloomy prospect, we would like to emphasize, does not seem to us to represent the probable course of events. We think that, within limits, there are solutions for the ethnic crisis of our time. But societies do not always resolve their pressing problems in a rational way. A totalitarian, racist solution could happen here.

Suggestions for Further Reading

Racism: The phenomenon of intolerance in American life has not been studied nearly enough. For the national scene, the two most useful books by historians are Ray A. Billington, *The Protestant Crusade*, New York, 1938, which treats the pre-civil war era and John Higham, *Strangers in the Land*, New Brunswick, N.J., 1955, which examines later developments. For general treatments of the California scene, see Roger Daniels and Harry H. L. Kitano, *American Racism: Exploration of the Nature of Prejudice*, Englewood Cliffs, N.J., 1970, and Robert F. Heizer and Alan J. Almquist, *The Other Californians: Prejudice and Discrimination under Spain, Mexico and the United States to 1920*, Berkeley and Los Angeles, 1971. Two important works on prejudice by psychologists are T. W. Adorno *et al.*, *The Authoritarian Personality*, New York, 1950, and Gordon W. Allport, *The Nature of Prejudice*, Cambridge, Mass., 1954. Milton Gordon, *Assimilation in American Life*, New York, 1964, is a perceptive treatment by a sociologist. A provocative and controversial interpretation of the origins of American racism may be found in Winthrop D. Jordan, *White over Black: American Attitudes toward the Negro, 1550–1812*, Chapel Hill, N.C., 1968.

Indians: For a general treatment of the American Indian, the brief William T. Hagan, *American Indians*, Chicago, 1961, and the longer Angie Debo, *A History of the Indians of the United States*, Norman, Oklahoma, 1971, provide good introductions to a highly complex subject. On the California Indian, Robert F. Heizer and M. A. Whipple, eds., *The California Indians, A Source Book*, Berkeley and Los Angeles, 1951, is an invaluable introduction to the anthropological literature, while A. L. Kroeber, *Handbook of the Indians of California*, Berkeley, 1925 is a major work of perhaps the greatest American anthropologist. For an attack on the anthropological point of view, the writings of Vine Deloria, especially *Custer Died for Your Sins*, New York, 1969, are illustrative of the "new" Indian viewpoint, as is the periodical, *The Indian Historian*, San Francisco, 1968+.

Asians: There is no general work surveying the Asian American experience, but Daniels and Kitano, *American Racism*, cited previously, contains a sketch of their experience treated comparatively. On the Chinese, the standard but sadly outdated work is Mary Roberts Coolidge, *Chinese Immigration*, New York, 1909, and Rose Hum Lee, *The Chinese in the United States of America*, Hong Kong, 1960, is often factually unreliable. Gunther Barth, *Bitter Strength: A History of the Chinese in the United States, 1850–1870*, Cambridge, Mass., 1964, is a sophisticated treatment of a narrow period. Elmer Sandmeyer, *The Anti-Chinese Movement in California*, Urbana, 1939, is standard, but see also Alexander Saxton, *The Indispensable Enemy*, Berkeley and Los Angeles, 1971, and Stuart Creighton Miller, *The Unwelcome Immigrant: The American Image of the Chinese, 1785–1882*, Berkeley and Los Angeles, 1969. Of the books written about Chinese life in America, Jade Snow Wong, *Fifth Chinese Daughter*, New York, 1954, is a charming memoir of a Chinese girlhood and Calvin Lee, *Chinatown, U.S.A.*, New York, 1963, contains many valuable insights into the special communal nature of Chinese life in America. On the Japanese, much more has been written. The best general survey is Harry H. L. Kitano, *Japanese Americans: The Evolution of a Subculture*, Englewood Cliffs, N.J., 1969. On the treatment of the Japanese in California, see Roger Daniels, *The Politics of Prejudice: The Anti-Japanese Movement in California and the Struggle for Japanese Exclusion*, Berkeley and Los Angeles, 1962, and *Concentration Camps, U.S.A.: Japanese Americans and World War II*, New York, 1971. Also useful are Carey McWilliams, *Prejudice: Japanese-Americans: Symbols of Racial Intolerance*, Boston, 1944; Morton Grodzins, *Americans Betrayed: Politics and the Japanese Evacuation*, Chicago, 1949; Dorothy Swaine Thomas *et al.*, *The Spoilage*, Berkeley and Los Angeles, 1946, and *The Salvage*, Berkeley and Los Angeles, 1952; Jacobus ten Broek, *et al.*, *Prejudice, War and the Constitution*, Berkeley and Los Angeles, 1958; Allen R. Bosworth, *America's Concentration Camps*, New York, 1967; Bill Hosokawa, *Nisei: The Quiet Americans*, New York, 1970; and Audrie Girdner and Anne Loftis, *The Great Betrayal: The Evacuation of the Japanese Americans in World War II*, New York, 1971.

Mexican Americans: Although they are California's most numerous minority, the literature about Mexican Americans is still quite sparse. Leo Grebler *et al.*, *The Mexican-American People*, Glencoe, Ill., 1970, a production of a UCLA-based research project, should serve as a basic building block and contains an exhaustive bibliography. The best single narrative work remains Carey McWilliams, *North from Mexico*, Boston, 1948. For the earlier period, Leonard Pitt, *The Decline of the Californios*, Berkeley and Los Angeles, 1966, is the best treatment. Joan Moore, *The Mexican American*, Englewood Cliffs, N.J., 1970, is a sensitive account by a sociologist. Two books of readings, Julian Samora, ed., *La Raza: Forgotten Americans*, South Bend, Ind., 1966, and John H. Burma, ed., *Mexican-Americans in the United States: A reader*, New York, 1969, contain much of interest. Three recent popular accounts reflect the growing Mexican American militancy and the beginnings of what one writer has called "Bronze consciousness": John Gregory Dunne, *Delano: The Story of the California Grape Strike*, New York, 1967; Peter Matthiesen, *Sal si Puedes: Caesar Chavez and the New American Revolution*, New York, 1969; and Stan Steiner, *La Raza: The Mexican-Americans*, New York, 1970. Much concise statistical data may be found in two publications by the California Fair Employment Practices Commission, *Californians of Spanish Surname*, San Francisco, 1964, and *Negroes and Mexican Americans in South and East Los Angeles*, San Francisco, 1966.

Blacks: Despite the vast flood of black studies in recent years, virtually nothing has been done from the historical point of view on the black experience in the Golden State: that this is still true is a major indictment of California historiography. One important recent article is Lawrence B. De Graaf, "The City of Black Angels. Emergence of the Los Angeles Ghetto, 1890–1930," *Pacific Historical Review* (Aug., 1970). For treatments of the black experience on the national scene, John Hope Franklin, *From Slavery to Freedom*, 3rd ed., New York, 1968, is encyclopedic whereas August Meier and Elliot Rudwick, *From Plantation to Ghetto*, New York, 1966, is the best brief account. Some of the chapters in the classic Gunnar Myrdal, *et al.*, *An American Dilemma*, New York, 1944, give insights into the California experience. Although slavery was not particularly important in California, no estimate of the black experience is possible without an understanding of it; Kenneth Stampp, *The Peculiar Institution*, New York, 1956, remains the best single treatment. Jack D. Forbes, *Afro-Americans in the Far West: A Handbook for Educators*, U.S. Government Printing Office, Washington, D.C., n.d., contains a good guide to contemporary materials about black Californians.